锦天城法律实务丛书

美国联邦破产程序规则

U.S. FEDERAL RULES OF BANKRUPTCY PROCEDURE

（中英对照译本）

申林平 / 译

法律出版社 LAW PRESS·CHINA
北京

图书在版编目(CIP)数据

美国联邦破产程序规则：中英对照译本 ／ 申林平译．-- 北京：法律出版社，2023
（锦天城法律实务丛书）
ISBN 978-7-5197-7521-6

Ⅰ.①美… Ⅱ.①申… Ⅲ.①破产法-研究-美国-汉、英 Ⅳ.①D971.239.91

中国国家版本馆 CIP 数据核字（2023）第 015399 号

| 锦天城法律实务丛书 | 美国联邦破产程序规则（中英对照译本）
MEIGUO LIANBANG POCHAN CHENGXU GUIZE
（ZHONG YING DUIZHAO YIBEN） | 申林平 译 | 策划编辑 薛　晗　田　浩
责任编辑 薛　晗　田　浩
装帧设计 汪奇峰 |

出版发行	法律出版社	开本	787 毫米×1092 毫米 1/16
编辑统筹	法商出版分社	印张	30.5　　字数　465 千
责任校对	王　丰	版本	2023 年 4 月第 1 版
责任印制	胡晓雅	印次	2023 年 4 月第 1 次印刷
经　　销	新华书店	印刷	北京金康利印刷有限公司

地址：北京市丰台区莲花池西里 7 号（100073）
网址：www.lawpress.com.cn　　　　　　　　销售电话：010-83938349
投稿邮箱：info@lawpress.com.cn　　　　　　客服电话：010-83938350
举报盗版邮箱：jbwq@lawpress.com.cn　　　　咨询电话：010-63939796
版权所有·侵权必究

书号：ISBN 978-7-5197-7521-6　　　　　　　定价：128.00 元

凡购买本社图书，如有印装错误，我社负责退换。电话：010-83938349

前　言

2022年年初，我在恩师李曙光教授、众多学者、实务人士、翻译团队成员以及法律出版社的大力支持下出版了《美国破产法典》（中英文对照本），近来收到了一些读者的积极反馈，我也很高兴能够为同在破产法领域耕耘的理论界和实务界人士提供一本还比较专业的基础工具书。其实早在2020年初步完成《美国破产法典》的翻译工作后，我便开展了《美国联邦破产程序规则》（*U.S. Federal Rules of Bankruptcy Procedure*）的翻译工作，有了《美国破产法典》出版的基础，作为姊妹篇《美国联邦破产程序规则》也终于有机会和大家见面了。

一、《美国联邦破产程序规则》是什么？

1787年美国《宪法》第1条第8款列举了联邦国会的立法权，其中有一项就是制定统一的破产法。基于宪法的授权，美国国会于1978年颁布了破产法典作为《美国联邦法典》的第11篇，因此，《美国破产法典》是一部适用于所有破产案件的联邦法律。破产案件的具体程序则规定于《美国联邦破产程序规则》以及各破产法院的地方规则（"local rules"）之中。一直为众人所知的是《美国破产法典》是《美国联邦法典》的第11篇，但鲜为人知的是《美国联邦法典》第11篇后便有一附录（appendix），该附录即为《美国联邦破产程序规则》，其与《美国破产法典》共同组成了《美国联邦法典》的第11篇，也在美国破产案件中各自又协同地发挥着重要作用。

以债务人意图进入破产程序为例，《美国破产法典》主要规定了不同破产程序中谁可以申请破产、谁可以担任托管人、哪些财产属于破产财产、哪些债务可以被豁免、债务人与托管人的权利与义务等实体内容，债务人可以通过《美国破产法典》衡量破产程序的利弊，决定是否进入破产程序并了解其在破产程序中将发生什么；而债务人一旦决定申请破产后，就必须了解并遵守《美国联邦破产程

U.S. Federal Rules of Bankruptcy Procedure
（Chinese-English bilingual version）

序规则》的规定，知道破产申请应当在何时何地向何人提交、破产申请资料的形式及应当包含的内容、如何缴纳申请费、债务人与其关联人的破产程序如何进行实质合并或程序合并等。总之，《美国破产法典》主要规定了破产案件的实体内容，而《美国联邦破产程序规则》主要规定了破产案件的司法程序，两者相辅相成，协力推动破产案件的顺利进行。因此，《美国联邦破产程序规则》与《美国破产法典》具有同等的重要性，并且是一体的、不可分割的。

二、《美国联邦破产程序规则》的翻译缘起

我认为本次《美国联邦破产程序规则》的翻译及出版可以说是恰逢其时。

第一，美国破产法作为域外破产法的经典代表之一，一直都对国内破产法的修订、破产领域的实务操作以及破产理论的研究产生着重要影响。《美国联邦破产程序规则》作为美国破产法不可分割的一部分，也必然要进入我们的视野中来。

第二，国内学界和实务界对美国破产法的实体制度研究较为丰富，因此对《美国破产法典》的引述并不少见。不同于《美国破产法典》所主要规定的实体制度的高关注度，《美国联邦破产程序规则》作为程序法此前在国内并未得到系统研究。但是，随着近年来我国破产法实务中大型集团、跨国企业破产案件频发，以破产案件实质合并、程序合并为典型的破产程序问题逐步成为破产领域讨论的热点问题之一，中国律师也逐步参与到跨境破产案件中，如向美国法院申请美国债务人破产或申报债权等，相信美国破产案件的程序细节也将逐步得到学界和实务界的重视。

第三，《美国破产法典》的出版前期工作以及最终出版确实为《美国联邦破产程序规则》奠定了良好的基础。《美国破产法典》的翻译工作是2020年年初启动的，由于这是我们首次尝试翻译完整体例的外国法典，所以翻译工作就耗时较长。初步翻译完成后，2020年下半年到2021年上半年，李曙光教授抽出宝贵时间和法律出版社法商分社薛晗社长、编辑田浩老师一起举行了多次审定会议，在这期间李曙光教授对此译本逐条提出了诸多指导和修改意见，这些宝贵的意见我们也沿用到本次《美国联邦破产程序规则》的翻译中。2021年下半年，由于《美国破产法典》体量庞大，法律出版社编辑团队又为其出版做了大量校对工作。总之，基于前期的大量工作，《美国破产法典》才最终得以于2022年年初面世，而

美国联邦破产程序规则
（中英对照译本）

这些前期工作及经验完全可以应用到《美国联邦破产程序规则》的翻译及出版工作中来，事实证明我们此次的翻译与出版工作确实更为成熟与高效率。

三、美国联邦破产程序规则的体例与内容

（一）《美国联邦破产程序规则》的九个部分

本书的翻译基于 2021 年 12 月 1 日最新修订且现行有效的《美国联邦破产程序规则》，版本号（Release Point）为 117-168not167，共有九个部分（第 X 部分已于 1991 年被依法废除）。第 I 部分共有 24 条，主要规定破产案件启动阶段的相关程序；第 II 部分共有 25 条，主要规定破产案件的管理事宜以及相关参与人员；第 III 部分共有 25 条，主要规定了与债权人、股本证券持有人权益相关的程序及事宜；第 IV 部分共有 8 条，主要规定了债务人的义务与利益相关事宜；第 V 部分共有 9 条，主要规定了法院内部事宜；第 VI 部分共有 11 条，主要规定了破产财产的归集与处置；第 VII 部分共有 90 条，主要规定了对抗制诉讼程序，其中包含对《联邦民事诉讼规则》的大量引用；第 VIII 部分共有 19 条，主要规定了就破产法院所作的判决、裁定、法令所提起的上诉程序；第 IX 部分共有 38 条，为"一般规定"（General Provision）。

（二）官方模板（Official Forms）

《美国联邦破产程序规则》第 1001 条规定，破产规则以及官方模板适用于《美国联邦法典》第 11 篇即《美国破产法典》规定的所有案件，同时，《美国联邦破产程序规则》中也有三十余次提及官方模板。因此，虽然官方模板并未编入《美国联邦破产程序规则》而是公布于美国法院官方网站，但其与破产规则相互配合、共同规制了美国联邦破产程序，事实上构成了《美国联邦破产程序规则》的"隐形"附录。

我们可以试想一下，如果破产申请书、债权申报文件、债权人清单、财务事项声明、豁免财产申请书、重整计划书等破产程序中必须的文件均有统一的制式模板以供参考，破产程序会呈现怎样的特点？我认为，首先，破产程序可能将具有更高的可及性（accessibility），尤其对于中小企业与自然人的简单破产案件而言，

U.S. Federal Rules of Bankruptcy Procedure
（Chinese-English bilingual version）

将降低其聘请律师的经济成本以及搜寻、摸索文书的时间成本，从而提高其申请破产的意愿；其次，破产程序将可能更具效率，统一的制式模板将可能降低法官、书记员审查无关信息的工作量，提高其审查效率。美国破产程序的官方模板可以在美国法院官方网站任意下载，各类问题设置简单明了、解释详尽，使用者只需要通过电脑根据问题在对应框内输入内容或勾选即可。我觉得这是信息化时代下我们在未来破产法实践中可以学习和借鉴的地方，对于个人破产或债务调整的实践将可能发挥重要作用。

（三）《美国联邦破产程序规则》的后续修订

为了解决美国破产重整制度对大多数小企业而言负担过重的问题，美国国会早于 2019 年通过《小企业重整法》（*The Small Business Reorganization Act of 2019*）因而我们在 2022 年年初出版的《美国破产法典》（中英文对照本）也涵盖了《小企业重整法》的内容，即《美国破产法典》第 11 章第五附章的内容。由于在《小企业破产法》出台前，第 11 章下已经存在针对小企业的特殊规则，所以在《小企业破产法》生效后，小企业根据《美国破产法典》可以在三种程序路径中择一：第一，采用一般的重整规则，不适用针对小企业的特殊规则以及第五附章；第二，采用一般的程序规则并适用针对小企业的特殊规则，不适用第五附章；第三，适用第五附章的小企业重整程序。而小企业重整的程序路径的选择无疑需要破产程序规则的配合，因而程序规则也需进行调整。

基于此，美国破产规则咨询委员会编制了临时破产规则（Interim Amendments to the Federal Rules of Bankruptcy Procedure）并经美国司法会议批准由破产法院作为地方规则采用，从而实施《小企业破产法》对《美国破产法典》所作的程序性和实质性修改，临时破产规则将在《联邦破产程序规则》依合法程序予以相应修订后失效。2022 年 4 月 11 日，美国最高法院根据《美国联邦法典》第 28 篇第 2075 条裁定对《联邦破产程序规则》进行修订并将修正案递交国会，该修正案主要吸收了临时破产规则的内容，对第 1007 条、1020 条、2009 条、2012 条、2015 条、3002 条、3010 条、3011 条、3014 条、3016 条、3017.1 条、3018 条、3019 条、5005 条、7004 条、8023 条予以修订，并增加了第 3017.2 条。

根据美国最高法院的说明，该修正案将于 2022 年 12 月 1 日正式生效并适用

美国联邦破产程序规则
（中英对照译本）

于 2022 年 12 月 1 日启动的破产案件或在公正可行的情况下适用于所有正在进行的破产案件。因此，截至我们完成《美国联邦破产程序规则》的相关翻译、校对工作时，这部法律尚未生效且无法预计本书出版发行之际是否得以生效，同时现行有效的《美国联邦破产程序规则》针对 2022 年 12 月 1 日前启动的破产案件仍有适用的空间和可能性，所以我们选择将本次修正案的内容附于全文最后，这样既能保证时效性也能保证可适用性。

四、美国破产法及程序规则的演进

从我们启动《美国破产法典》的翻译工作以来，我们一直关注着美国破产法及程序规则在近几年的演进以及引起的讨论。从成文的《美国破产法典》、配套的《联邦破产程序规则》以及作以辅助的官方模板；从 2019 年的《小企业重整法》到我们团队此前也翻译并分享过的《2020 年消费者破产改革议案》（"沃伦议案"），我最直观的感受就是近几年美国破产法及程序规则演进的重点之一就是提高破产程序的可及性、易得性，包括降低破产程序的时间成本以及经济成本。

我国《企业破产法》于 2007 年 6 月 1 日施行至今有十五年多了，《深圳经济特区个人破产条例》于 2021 年 3 月 1 日施行也有一年半多了，破产制度是否在破产从业人员外的世界里为人所熟知了呢？中小民营企业是否能在面临资不抵债困境时首先想到破产制度呢？债权人包括大、中、小型企业以及我们身边普普通通的市民能否在债务人无力清偿且不作为的情况下想到申请债务人破产呢？债务人或者债权人申请破产以后法院是否就能依法受理呢？大家的权益通过破产程序是否能得到有效的保护呢？这些是我办理一些破产案件的所思、所想、所感，而通过对美国破产法及程序规则的翻译与学习，我觉得或许解决不愿"破"、不敢"破"、不能"破"的问题就是要回归到提高破产制度的可及性上来，当"破"人皆可"破"且想"破"就"破"，我有何不愿"破"、不敢"破"、不能"破"？

《美国破产法典》出版发行以来，我收到了很多读者的反馈，其中不乏破产学界、实务界的资深人士。他们对《美国破产法典》中个别术语的翻译以及美国破产制度本身都有独到的见解，通过与他们的深入交流及讨论，我很有收获并应用于本次《美国联邦破产程序规则》的翻译中。尽管有此前的翻译基础，但"一千个读者就有一千个哈姆雷特"，虽然不同于文学著作，法律条文的翻译有其相当

U.S. Federal Rules of Bankruptcy Procedure
(Chinese-English bilingual version)

的确定性，但语言的表达不可避免地有其局限性并使读者产生不同的理解，因此，译者还是希望与诸多读者进行更加深入的讨论，也欢迎各位再次不吝赐教。

五、致谢

我们以《美国联邦破产程序规则》（中英对照译本）申报了《锦天城法律文库》并成功入选从而得以与大家见面，因此要感谢我所律师学院、企业破产与清算专业委员会的支持，也衷心感谢本所顾耕耘老师对法律理论研究和案例实务总结的高度重视。在《美国破产法典》的翻译和出版过程中，译者也受到了师友、团队成员以及编辑老师等人的支持。十分感谢恩师李曙光教授对我的教诲和对本译本的指导意见，帮助我们把握住英美法系的特点以求翻译出"原汁原味"的《美国联邦破产程序规则》。要感谢团队成员胡玉斐律师对本译本和《美国破产法典》一书出版做出的重大贡献，她本科毕业于国内著名法学院，法学基本功非常扎实，海外法学硕士学成归来加入我的团队投入到本次翻译工作来，就其中的核心词汇和段落的翻译方法与我展开热烈讨论，经常因为一个单词或一个词组需要我们查阅大量资料并请教业界权威学者，最终促使我们对此译本的效果和质量更加有信心。

感谢破产法著名学者韩长印教授、齐明教授平时对我的指导，感谢有关破产法庭、破产法学研究会、破产管理人协会、律师协会的朋友对本翻译稿的关注，感谢法律出版社法商分社薛晗社长、田浩编辑等各位老师的热忱支持！

译者 2023 年 3 月于北京东方广场

Key Words

核心词汇

U.S. Federal Rules of Bankruptcy Procedure
(Chinese-English bilingual version)

adequate protection

adjournment

administrative expense

adversary proceeding

affidavit

affiliate

allowance of a claim

Amicus Curiae

ancillary

appeal

appraiser

apprehension

assign

attorney of record

auctioneer

automatic stay

bankruptcy petition preparer

bankruptcy appellate panel, BAP

bona fide

burden of proof

cash collateral

cause

center of main interests

change of venue

class proceedings

classification of claims

clerk

confirmation of plan

美国联邦破产程序规则
（中英对照译本）

充分保护

休会

管理费用

对抗制诉讼

宣誓书

关联方

债权确认

法庭之友

辅助程序

上诉

评估师

羁押

转让

备案律师

拍卖师

自动冻结

破产申请准备人

破产上诉合议庭

善意

证明责任

现金担保物

事由

主要利益中心

审理法院的变更

集体诉讼

债权分组

书记员

计划的批准

U.S. Federal Rules of Bankruptcy Procedure
(Chinese-English bilingual version)

conversion

counterclaim

creditor

creditors' committee

custodian

debtor in possession

default

defendant

defense

derivative actions

discharge

discretion

dismissal

distribution

docket

entity

equity security holders

estate

examination

examiner

executory contract

exemption

expiration of the period

general partner

good faith

hearing

impound

indenture

injunction

interim trustee

美国联邦破产程序规则
（中英对照译本）

（程序的）转换

反诉

债权人

债权人委员会

保管人

经管债务人

违约

被告

抗辩

股东代表诉讼

免除（债务）

自由裁量权

驳回

分配

作为动词使用时，受理；作为名词使用时，案卷

实体

股本证券持有人

破产实体

质询

监督人

待履行合同

豁免

期间届满

普通合伙人

善意

听证

没收

契约

禁令

临时托管人

U.S. Federal Rules of Bankruptcy Procedure
(Chinese-English bilingual version)

labor union

lien

liquidation

litigation

motion

order

order for relief

party in interest

patient care ombudsman

pay in installments

petition

plaintiff

postponement

presumption of abuse

proof of claim

prosecution

provisional relief

proxy

reaffirmation agreement

rebut

recognition

redemption

reimbursement

reorganization

service

service by publication

small business debtor

subdivision

subordination

summons

美国联邦破产程序规则
（中英对照译本）

工会

财产上担保权

清算

诉讼

动议

裁定

破产救济令

利益相关方

患者护理监察人

分期付款

申请

原告

延期

滥用推定

债权证明

起诉

临时救济

代理权

再认协议

推翻

承认

赎回

报销

重整

送达

公告送达

小企业债务人

附条

居次

传票

U.S. Federal Rules of Bankruptcy Procedure
(Chinese-English bilingual version)

suspension

sustain

tax return

the United States trustee

transcript

transfer

turnover

unexpired lease

validity

waiver

withdrawal

美国联邦破产程序规则
（中英对照译本）

中止

支持

报税表

联邦托管人

书面记录

转让

移交

未完成租约

合法性

豁免

撤回

CONTENTS

目　录

U.S. Federal Rules of Bankruptcy Procedure
(Chinese-English bilingual version)

TITLE 11—APPENDIX FEDERAL RULES OF BANKRUPTCY PROCEDURE

PART I COMMENCEMENT OF CASE; PROCEEDINGS RELATING TO PETITION AND ORDER FOR RELIEF | 026

PART II OFFICERS AND ADMINISTRATION; NOTICES; MEETINGS; EXAMINATIONS; ELECTIONS; ATTORNEYS AND ACCOUNTANTS | 072

PART III CLAIMS AND DISTRIBUTION TO CREDITORS AND EQUITY INTEREST HOLDERS; PLANS | 142

PART IV THE DEBTOR: DUTIES AND BENEFITS | 194

PART V COURTS AND CLERKS | 220

PART VI COLLECTION AND LIQUIDATION OF THE ESTATE | 238

PART VII ADVERSARY PROCEEDINGS | 254

PART VIII APPEALS TO DISTRICT COURT OR BANKRUPTCY APPELLATE PANEL | 284

PART IX GENERAL PROVISIONS | 368

PART X UNITED STATES TRUSTEES (Abrogated Apr. 30, 1991, eff. Aug. 1, 1991) | 418

PROPOSED AMENDMENTS TO THE FEDERAL RULES OF BANKRUPTCY PROCEDURE | 420

第十一篇——附录　联邦破产程序规则

第 I 部分　　　案件的启动；与破产申请和破产救济令有关的程序 | 027

第 II 部分　　破产从业人员和案件的管理；通知；会议；质询；选任；律师和会计师 | 073

第 III 部分　　债权以及向债权人和股本证券持有人的分配；计划 | 143

第 IV 部分　　债务人：义务和利益 | 195

第 V 部分　　　法院和书记员 | 221

第 VI 部分　　破产实体的收集和清算 | 239

第 VII 部分　　对抗制诉讼程序 | 255

第 VIII 部分　向地区法院或破产上诉合议庭提起上诉 | 285

第 IX 部分　　一般规定 | 369

第 X 部分　　　联邦托管人（经 Apr. 30, 1991, eff. Aug. 1, 1991 而被废除） | 419

对《联邦破产程序规则》的拟议修正案 | 421

U.S. Federal Rules of Bankruptcy Procedure
(Chinese-English bilingual version)

Rule 1001　Scope of Rules and Forms; Short Title

PART I　COMMENCEMENT OF CASE; PROCEEDINGS RELATING TO PETITION AND ORDER FOR RELIEF

Rule 1002. Commencement of Case ｜ 026

Rule 1003. Involuntary Petition ｜ 028

Rule 1004. Involuntary Petition Against a Partnership ｜ 028

Rule 1004.1. Petition for an Infant or Incompetent Person ｜ 028

Rule 1004.2. Petition in Chapter 15 Cases ｜ 030

Rule 1005. Caption of Petition ｜ 030

Rule 1006. Filing Fee ｜ 032

Rule 1007. Lists, Schedules, Statements, and Other Documents; Time Limits ｜ 034

Rule 1008. Verification of Petitions and Accompanying Papers ｜ 046

Rule 1009. Amendments of Voluntary Petitions, Lists, Schedules and Statements ｜ 046

Rule 1010. Service of Involuntary Petition and Summons ｜ 048

Rule 1011. Responsive Pleading or Motion in Involuntary Cases ｜ 048

Rule 1012. Responsive Pleading in Cross-Border Cases ｜ 050

Rule 1013. Hearing and Disposition of a Petition in an Involuntary Case ｜ 052

Rule 1014. Dismissal and Change of Venue ｜ 052

Rule 1015. Consolidation or Joint Administration of Cases Pending in Same Court ｜ 054

Rule 1016. Death or Incompetency of Debtor ｜ 056

Rule 1017. Dismissal or Conversion of Case; Suspension ｜ 056

Rule 1018. Contested Involuntary Petitions; Contested Petitions Commencing Chapter 15 Cases; Proceedings to Vacate Order for Relief; Applicability of Rules in Part VII Governing Adversary Proceedings ｜ 060

Rule 1019. Conversion of a Chapter 11 Reorganization Case, Chapter 12 Family Farmer's Debt Adjustment Case, or Chapter 13 Individual's Debt Adjustment Case to a Chapter 7 Liquidation Case ｜ 060

美国联邦破产程序规则
（中英对照译本）

第 1001 条　规则和模板的适用范围；简称

第 I 部分　案件的启动；与破产申请和破产救济令有关的程序

第 1002 条　案件的启动　｜　027

第 1003 条　强制破产申请　｜　029

第 1004 条　对合伙组织提起的强制破产申请　｜　029

第 1004.1 条　婴儿或无行为能力人的申请　｜　029

第 1004.2 条　第 15 章案件中的申请　｜　031

第 1005 条　破产申请的标题　｜　031

第 1006 条　申请费　｜　033

第 1007 条　清单、报表、声明和其他文件；时间限制　｜　035

第 1008 条　申请和附随文件的核实　｜　047

第 1009 条　自愿破产申请、清单、报表和声明的修改　｜　047

第 1010 条　强制破产申请和传票的送达　｜　049

第 1011 条　强制破产案件中的应答文状或动议　｜　049

第 1012 条　跨境案件中的应答文状　｜　051

第 1013 条　在强制破产案件中对申请的听证和处理　｜　053

第 1014 条　驳回和审理法院的变更　｜　053

第 1015 条　同一法院审理的多个案件的合并或共同管理　｜　055

第 1016 条　债务人的死亡或行为能力的丧失　｜　057

第 1017 条　案件的驳回或转换；中止　｜　057

第 1018 条　对其提出异议的强制破产申请；对其提出异议的启动第 15 章程序的申请；撤销破产救济令的程序；第 VII 部分规制诉讼程序的规则的适用　｜　061

第 1019 条　第 11 章重整案件、第 12 章家庭农场主债务调整案件或第 13 章个人债务调整案件至第 7 章清算案件的转换　｜　061

U.S. Federal Rules of Bankruptcy Procedure
(Chinese-English bilingual version)

Rule 1020. Small Business Chapter 11 Reorganization Case | 066

Rule 1021. Health Care Business Case | 068

PART II OFFICERS AND ADMINISTRATION; NOTICES; MEETINGS; EXAMINATIONS; ELECTIONS; ATTORNEYS AND ACCOUNTANTS

Rule 2001. Appointment of Interim Trustee Before Order for Relief in a Chapter 7 Liquidation Case | 072

Rule 2002. Notices to Creditors, Equity Security Holders, Administrators in Foreign Proceedings, Persons Against Whom Provisional Relief is Sought in Ancillary and Other Cross-Border Cases, United States, and United States Trustee | 074

Rule 2003. Meeting of Creditors or Equity Security Holders | 090

Rule 2004. Examination | 094

Rule 2005. Apprehension and Removal of Debtor to Compel Attendance for Examination | 096

Rule 2006. Solicitation and Voting of Proxies in Chapter 7 Liquidation Cases | 100

Rule 2007. Review of Appointment of Creditors' Committee Organized Before Commencement of the Case | 104

Rule 2007.1. Appointment of Trustee or Examiner in a Chapter 11 Reorganization Case | 106

Rule 2007.2. Appointment of Patient Care Ombudsman in a Health Care Business Case | 110

Rule 2008. Notice to Trustee of Selection | 112

Rule 2009. Trustees for Estates When Joint Administration Ordered | 114

Rule 2010. Qualification by Trustee; Proceeding on Bond | 116

Rule 2011. Evidence of Debtor in Possession or Qualification of Trustee | 116

Rule 2012. Substitution of Trustee or Successor Trustee; Accounting | 116

Rule 2013. Public Record of Compensation Awarded to Trustees, Examiners, and Professionals | 118

Rule 2014. Employment of Professional Persons | 118

第 1020 条　第 11 章小企业重整案件 | 067
第 1021 条　医疗护理机构破产案件 | 069

第 II 部分　破产从业人员和案件的管理；通知；会议；质询；选任；律师和会计师

第 2001 条　第 7 章清算案件中破产救济令被作出前临时托管人的任命 | 073

第 2002 条　向债权人、股本证券持有人、外国程序中的管理人、在辅助程序和其他跨境案件中寻求的临时救济所针对的人、美国政府机构和联邦托管人发出通知 | 075

第 2003 条　债权人或股本证券持有人会议 | 091
第 2004 条　质询 | 095
第 2005 条　羁押并转移债务人以强制其出席接受质询 | 097

第 2006 条　第 7 章清算案件中表决代理权的征集 | 101
第 2007 条　就案件启动前组建的债权人委员会的任命的审查 | 105

第 2007.1 条　第 11 章重整案件中托管人或监督人的任命 | 107

第 2007.2 条　医疗护理机构中患者护理监察员的任命 | 111

第 2008 条　向被选任的托管人发出的通知 | 113
第 2009 条　被裁定合并管理时多个破产实体的托管人 | 115
第 2010 条　托管人的资格；就保证保险提起的诉讼 | 117
第 2011 条　经管债务人的证明或托管人的资格 | 117
第 2012 条　托管人的取代或继任托管人；账目 | 117
第 2013 条　向托管人、监督人和专业人员给付的报酬的公共记录 | 119

第 2014 条　雇佣专业人员 | 119

U.S. Federal Rules of Bankruptcy Procedure
(Chinese-English bilingual version)

Rule 2015. Duty to Keep Records, Make Reports, and Give Notice of Case or Change of Status | 120

Rule 2015.1. Patient Care Ombudsman | 124

Rule 2015.2. Transfer of Patient in Health Care Business Case | 126

Rule 2015.3. Reports of Financial Information on Entities in Which a Chapter 11 Estate Holds a Controlling or Substantial Interest | 126

Rule 2016. Compensation for Services Rendered and Reimbursement of Expenses | 130

Rule 2017. Examination of Debtor's Transactions with Debtor's Attorney | 132

Rule 2018. Intervention; Right to Be Heard | 134

Rule 2019. Disclosure Regarding Creditors and Equity Security Holders in Chapter 9 and Chapter 11 Cases | 136

Rule 2020. Review of Acts by United States Trustee | 140

PART III CLAIMS AND DISTRIBUTION TO CREDITORS AND EQUITY INTEREST HOLDERS; PLANS

Rule 3001. Proof of Claim | 142

Rule 3002. Filing Proof of Claim or Interest | 148

Rule 3002.1. Notice Relating to Claims Secured by Security Interest in the Debtor's Principal Residence | 152

Rule 3003. Filing Proof of Claim or Equity Security Interest in Chapter 9 Municipality or Chapter 11 Reorganization Cases | 156

Rule 3004. Filing of Claims by Debtor or Trustee | 160

Rule 3005. Filing of Claim, Acceptance, or Rejection by Guarantor, Surety, Indorser, or Other Codebtor | 160

Rule 3006. Withdrawal of Claim; Effect on Acceptance or Rejection of Plan | 162

Rule 3007. Objections to Claims | 162

Rule 3008. Reconsideration of Claims | 166

第 2015 条　保存档案、制作档案以及就案件或状态的变化发出通知的义务 | 121

第 2015.1 条　患者护理监察员 | 125

第 2015.2 条　医疗护理机构破产案件中患者的转移 | 127

第 2015.3 条　第 11 章破产实体对其享有控制权或重大利益的实体的财务信息报告 | 127

第 2016 条　就被提供的服务而支付的报酬以及费用的报销 | 131

第 2017 条　审查债务人与其律师间的交易 | 133

第 2018 条　介入；发表意见的权利 | 135

第 2019 条　针对第 9 章和第 11 章案件中的债权人和股本证券持有人所作的披露 | 137

第 2020 条　对联邦托管人行为的审查 | 141

第 III 部分　债权以及向债权人和股本证券持有人的分配；计划

第 3001 条　债权证明 | 143

第 3002 条　提交债权或权益证明 | 149

第 3002.1 条　与由债务人主要住所所担保的债权有关的通知 | 153

第 3003 条　在第 9 章市政机构破产案件或第 11 章重整案件中提交债权或股本权益证明 | 157

第 3004 条　由债务人或托管人提交债权 | 161

第 3005 条　由连带保证人、一般保证人、背书人或其他共同债务人提交债权、接受或拒绝计划 | 161

第 3006 条　撤回债权主张；接受或拒绝计划的效力 | 163

第 3007 条　对债权的异议 | 163

第 3008 条　债权的复议 | 167

U.S. Federal Rules of Bankruptcy Procedure
(Chinese-English bilingual version)

Rule 3009. Declaration and Payment of Dividends in a Chapter 7 Liquidation Case | 166

Rule 3010. Small Dividends and Payments in Chapter 7 Liquidation, Chapter 12 Family Farmer's Debt Adjustment, and Chapter 13 Individual's Debt Adjustment Cases | 166

Rule 3011. Unclaimed Funds in Chapter 7 Liquidation, Chapter 12 Family Farmer's Debt Adjustment, and Chapter 13 Individual's Debt Adjustment Cases | 168

Rule 3012. Determining the Amount of Secured and Priority Claims | 168

Rule 3013. Classification of Claims and Interests | 170

Rule 3014. Election Under §1111 (b) by Secured Creditor in Chapter 9 Municipality or Chapter 11 Reorganization Case | 170

Rule 3015. Filing, Objection to Confirmation, Effect of Confirmation, and Modification of a Plan in a Chapter 12 or a Chapter 13 Case | 172

Rule 3015.1. Requirements for a Local Form for Plans Filed in a Chapter 13 Case | 176

Rule 3016. Filing of Plan and Disclosure Statement in a Chapter 9 Municipality or Chapter 11 Reorganization Case | 178

Rule 3017. Court Consideration of Disclosure Statement in a Chapter 9 Municipality or Chapter 11 Reorganization Case | 178

Rule 3017.1. Court Consideration of Disclosure Statement in a Small Business Case | 184

Rule 3018. Acceptance or Rejection of Plan in a Chapter 9 Municipality or a Chapter 11 Reorganization Case | 186

Rule 3019. Modification of Accepted Plan in a Chapter 9 Municipality or a Chapter 11 Reorganization Case | 188

Rule 3020. Deposit; Confirmation of Plan in a Chapter 9 Municipality or Chapter 11 Reorganization Case | 190

Rule 3021. Distribution under Plan | 192

Rule 3022. Final Decree in Chapter 11 Reorganization Case | 192

美国联邦破产程序规则
（中英对照译本）

第 3009 条　在第 7 章清算案件中的还款宣告和支付 ｜ 167

第 3010 条　在第 7 章清算案件、第 12 章家庭农场主债务调整案件和第 13 章个人债务调整案件中的小额还款 ｜ 167

第 3011 条　第 7 章清算案件、第 12 章家庭农场主债务调整案件和第 13 章个人债务调整案件中无人主张的资金 ｜ 169

第 3012 条　就担保和优先债权的金额认定 ｜ 169

第 3013 条　债权和权益分组 ｜ 171

第 3014 条　在第 9 章市政机构破产案件或第 11 章重整案件中担保债权人根据第 1111 条（b）所作的选择 ｜ 171

第 3015 条　在第 12 章或第 13 章案件中提交计划、对计划的批准提出异议、批准的效力以及计划的修改 ｜ 173

第 3015.1 条　第 13 章计划适用地方模板的条件 ｜ 177

第 3016 条　在第 9 章市政机构破产案件或第 11 章重整案件中计划和披露声明的提交 ｜ 179

第 3017 条　在第 9 章市政机构破产案件或第 11 章重整案件中法院对披露声明的审议 ｜ 179

第 3017.1 条　在小企业案件中法院就披露声明的审议 ｜ 185

第 3018 条　第 9 章市政机构破产案件或第 11 章重整案件中对计划的接受或拒绝 ｜ 187

第 3019 条　第 9 章市政机构破产案件或第 11 章重整案件中已被接受的计划的修改 ｜ 189

第 3020 条　交存；第 9 章市政机构破产案件或第 11 章重整案件中计划的批准 ｜ 191

第 3021 条　根据计划进行的分配 ｜ 193

第 3022 条　第 11 章重整案件中的终局裁定 ｜ 193

U.S. Federal Rules of Bankruptcy Procedure
(Chinese-English bilingual version)

PART IV   THE DEBTOR: DUTIES AND BENEFITS

Rule 4001. Relief from Automatic Stay; Prohibiting or Conditioning the Use, Sale, or Lease of Property; Use of Cash Collateral; Obtaining Credit; Agreements | 194

Rule 4002. Duties of Debtor | 204

Rule 4003. Exemptions | 208

Rule 4004. Grant or Denial of Discharge | 210

Rule 4005. Burden of Proof in Objecting to Discharge | 214

Rule 4006. Notice of No Discharge | 216

Rule 4007. Determination of Dischargeability of a Debt | 216

Rule 4008. Filing of Reaffirmation Agreement; Statement in Support of Reaffirmation Agreement | 218

PART V   COURTS AND CLERKS

Rule 5001. Courts and Clerks' Offices | 220

Rule 5002. Restrictions on Approval of Appointments | 220

Rule 5003. Records Kept by the Clerk | 222

Rule 5004. Disqualification | 226

Rule 5005. Filing and Transmittal of Papers | 226

Rule 5006. Certification of Copies of Papers | 230

Rule 5007. Record of Proceedings and Transcripts | 230

Rule 5008. Notice Regarding Presumption of Abuse in Chapter 7 Cases of Individual Debtors | 230

Rule 5009. Closing Chapter 7, Chapter 12, Chapter 13, and Chapter 15 Cases;Order Declaring Lien Satisfied | 232

Rule 5010. Reopening Cases | 234

Rule 5011. Withdrawal and Abstention from Hearing a Proceeding | 234

第 IV 部分　债务人：义务和利益

第 4001 条　自动冻结的解除；禁止或附条件使用、出售或出租财产；现金担保物的使用；获取信贷；协议 | 195

第 4002 条　债务人的义务 | 205

第 4003 条　豁免 | 209

第 4004 条　免责的授予或拒绝 | 211

第 4005 条　就免责提出异议的举证责任 | 215

第 4006 条　不予免责的通知 | 217

第 4007 条　就债务不可免责所作的认定 | 217

第 4008 条　再认协议的提交；支持再认协议的声明 | 219

第 V 部分　法院和书记员

第 5001 条　法院和书记员办公室 | 221

第 5002 条　就任命批准的限制 | 221

第 5003 条　由书记员所保存的档案 | 223

第 5004 条　丧失资格 | 227

第 5005 条　材料的提交和移送 | 227

第 5006 条　材料副本的证明 | 231

第 5007 条　程序记录和报告单 | 231

第 5008 条　在第 7 章个人债务人案件中就滥用推定而发出的通知 | 231

第 5009 条　第 7 章、第 12 章、第 13 章及第 15 章案件结案；宣告解除优先权 | 233

第 5010 条　案件的重启 | 235

第 5011 条　撤回及放弃就程序举行听证 | 235

U.S. Federal Rules of Bankruptcy Procedure
(Chinese-English bilingual version)

Rule 5012. Agreements Concerning Coordination of Proceedings in Chapter 15 Cases | 236

PART VI COLLECTION AND LIQUIDATION OF THE ESTATE

Rule 6001. Burden of Proof As to Validity of Postpetition Transfer | 238

Rule 6002. Accounting by Prior Custodian of Property of the Estate | 238

Rule 6003. Interim and Final Relief Immediately Following the Commencement of the Case—Applications for Employment; Motions for Use, Sale, or Lease of Property; and Motions for Assumption or Assignment of Executory Contracts | 238

Rule 6004. Use, Sale, or Lease of Property | 240

Rule 6005. Appraisers and Auctioneers | 244

Rule 6006. Assumption, Rejection or Assignment of an Executory Contract or Unexpired Lease | 244

Rule 6007. Abandonment or Disposition of Property | 248

Rule 6008. Redemption of Property from Lien or Sale | 250

Rule 6009. Prosecution and Defense of Proceedings by Trustee or Debtor in Possession | 250

Rule 6010. Proceeding to Avoid Indemnifying Lien or Transfer to Surety | 250

Rule 6011. Disposal of Patient Records in Health Care Business Case | 250

PART VII ADVERSARY PROCEEDINGS

Rule 7001. Scope of Rules of Part VII | 254

Rule 7002. References to Federal Rules of Civil Procedure | 256

Rule 7003. Commencement of Adversary Proceeding | 256

Rule 7004. Process; Service of Summons, Complaint | 256

Rule 7005. Service and Filing of Pleadings and Other Papers | 264

Rule 7007. Pleadings Allowed | 264

第 5012 条　在第 15 章案件中有关程序间协调的协议 ｜ 237

第 VI 部分　　破产实体的收集和清算

第 6001 条　申请后转让的合法性的举证责任 ｜ 239

第 6002 条　破产财产先前保管人所作的核算 ｜ 239

第 6003 条　案件启动后即进行的临时及最终救济——申请雇佣；申请使用、出售或出租财产的动议；以及申请确认或拒绝确认待履行合同的动议 ｜ 239

第 6004 条　财产的使用、出售或出租 ｜ 241

第 6005 条　评估师和拍卖师 ｜ 245

第 6006 条　待履行合同或未完成租约的确认、拒绝确认或转让 ｜ 245

第 6007 条　财产的放弃或处置 ｜ 249

第 6008 条　从财产上担保权或出售中赎回财产 ｜ 251

第 6009 条　托管人或经管债务人的起诉和抗辩 ｜ 251

第 6010 条　撤销为补偿保证人而设的财产上担保权或所作转让的程序 ｜ 251

第 6011 条　在医疗护理机构破产案件中就患者档案的处置 ｜ 251

第 VII 部分　　对抗制诉讼程序

第 7001 条　第 VII 部分规则的适用范围 ｜ 255

第 7002 条　《联邦民事诉讼规则》的引用 ｜ 257

第 7003 条　对抗制诉讼程序的启动 ｜ 257

第 7004 条　司法文书；传票、诉状的送达 ｜ 257

第 7005 条　诉状及其他文书的送达与提交 ｜ 265

第 7007 条　诉状的受理 ｜ 265

U.S. Federal Rules of Bankruptcy Procedure
(Chinese-English bilingual version)

Rule 7007.1. Corporate Ownership Statement | 264

Rule 7008. General Rules of Pleading | 266

Rule 7009. Pleading Special Matters | 266

Rule 7010. Form of Pleadings | 266

Rule 7012. Defenses and Objections—When and How Presented—by Pleading or Motion—Motion for Judgment on the Pleadings | 266

Rule 7013. Counterclaim and Cross-Claim | 268

Rule 7014. Third-Party Practice | 268

Rule 7015. Amended and Supplemental Pleadings | 268

Rule 7016. Pretrial Procedures | 270

Rule 7017. Parties Plaintiff and Defendant; Capacity | 270

Rule 7018. Joinder of Claims and Remedies | 270

Rule 7019. Joinder of Persons Needed for Just Determination | 270

Rule 7020. Permissive Joinder of Parties | 272

Rule 7021. Misjoinder and Non-Joinder of Parties | 272

Rule 7022. Interpleader | 272

Rule 7023. Class Proceedings | 272

Rule 7023.1. Derivative Actions | 272

Rule 7023.2. Adversary Proceedings Relating to Unincorporated Associations | 272

Rule 7024. Intervention | 272

Rule 7025. Substitution of Parties | 272

Rule 7026. General Provisions Governing Discovery | 274

Rule 7027. Depositions Before Adversary Proceedings or Pending Appeal | 274

Rule 7028. Persons Before Whom Depositions May Be Taken | 274

Rule 7029. Stipulations Regarding Discovery Procedure | 274

Rule 7030. Depositions Upon Oral Examination | 274

Rule 7031. Deposition Upon Written Questions | 274

Rule 7032. Use of Depositions in Adversary Proceedings | 274

Rule 7033. Interrogatories to Parties | 274

美国联邦破产程序规则
（中英对照译本）

第 7007.1 条　公司所有权声明 ｜ 265

第 7008 条　诉状的一般规定 ｜ 267

第 7009 条　有关诉状的特殊事项 ｜ 267

第 7010 条　诉状的形式 ｜ 267

第 7012 条　抗辩及异议—何时及如何提出—通过诉状或动议—申请就诉状作出判决的动议 ｜ 267

第 7013 条　反诉及交叉请求 ｜ 269

第 7014 条　第三方当事人程序 ｜ 269

第 7015 条　修正及补充起诉状 ｜ 269

第 7016 条　审前程序 ｜ 271

第 7017 条　原告及被告；诉讼能力 ｜ 271

第 7018 条　权利主张和救济的合并 ｜ 271

第 7019 条　为获得公正裁决而有必要参加的人 ｜ 271

第 7020 条　被准予参加的当事人 ｜ 273

第 7021 条　当事人的错误参加及不参加 ｜ 273

第 7022 条　竞合权利诉讼 ｜ 273

第 7023 条　集体诉讼 ｜ 273

第 7023.1 条　股东代表诉讼 ｜ 273

第 7023.2 条　涉及非法人组织的对抗制诉讼程序 ｜ 273

第 7024 条　参加诉讼 ｜ 273

第 7025 条　当事人的更换 ｜ 273

第 7026 条　有关证据开示的一般规定 ｜ 275

第 7027 条　对抗制诉讼程序前或上诉期间的书面证词 ｜ 275

第 7028 条　收集书面证词时的见证人 ｜ 275

第 7029 条　有关证据开示程序的约定 ｜ 275

第 7030 条　口头质询时的宣誓作证 ｜ 275

第 7031 条　书面质询时的宣誓作证 ｜ 275

第 7032 条　对抗制诉讼程序中书面证词的使用 ｜ 275

第 7033 条　向当事人所作的书面质询 ｜ 275

U.S. Federal Rules of Bankruptcy Procedure
(Chinese-English bilingual version)

Rule 7034. Production of Documents and Things and Entry Upon Land for Inspection and Other Purposes | 274

Rule 7035. Physical and Mental Examination of Persons | 276

Rule 7036. Requests for Admission | 276

Rule 7037. Failure to Make Discovery: Sanctions | 276

Rule 7040. Assignment of Cases for Trial | 276

Rule 7041. Dismissal of Adversary Proceedings | 276

Rule 7042. Consolidation of Adversary Proceedings; Separate Trials | 276

Rule 7052. Findings by the Court | 276

Rule 7054. Judgments; Costs | 278

Rule 7055. Default | 278

Rule 7056. Summary Judgment | 278

Rule 7058. Entering Judgment in Adversary Proceeding | 278

Rule 7062. Stay of Proceedings to Enforce a Judgment | 280

Rule 7064. Seizure of Person or Property | 280

Rule 7065. Injunctions | 280

Rule 7067. Deposit in Court | 280

Rule 7068. Offer of Judgment | 280

Rule 7069. Execution | 280

Rule 7070. Judgment for Specific Acts; Vesting Title | 280

Rule 7071. Process in Behalf of and Against Persons Not Parties | 282

Rule 7087. Transfer of Adversary Proceeding | 282

PART VIII APPEALS TO DISTRICT COURT OR BANKRUPTCY APPELLATE PANEL

Rule 8001. Scope of Part VIII Rules; Definition of "BAP"; Method of Transmission | 284

Rule 8002. Time for Filing Notice of Appeal | 284

第 7034 条　材料和物品的制作以及出于调查及其他目的进入某地 | 275

第 7035 条　对人的身体及精神检查 | 277

第 7036 条　申请采信 | 277

第 7037 条　未能提供书面证词；处罚 | 277

第 7040 条　案件审理的安排 | 277

第 7041 条　对抗制诉讼程序的驳回 | 277

第 7042 条　对抗制诉讼程序的合并；分别审理 | 277

第 7052 条　法院的事实认定 | 277

第 7054 条　判决；诉讼费用 | 279

第 7055 条　缺席 | 279

第 7056 条　简易判决 | 279

第 7058 条　在对抗制诉讼程序中作出判决 | 279

第 7062 条　执行判决的程序的冻结 | 281

第 7064 条　对人或财产的强制措施 | 281

第 7065 条　禁令 | 281

第 7067 条　向法院缴纳的押金 | 281

第 7068 条　判决要约 | 281

第 7069 条　执行 | 281

第 7070 条　就特定行为所作的判决；所有权的授予 | 281

第 7071 条　代表非当事人或对非当事人所进行的程序 | 283

第 7087 条　对抗制诉讼程序的移送 | 283

第 VIII 部分　向地区法院或破产上诉合议庭提起上诉

第 8001 条　第 VIII 部分规则的适用范围；"破产上诉合议庭"的定义；递交材料的方式 | 285

第 8002 条　提交上诉通知书的时间 | 285

U.S. Federal Rules of Bankruptcy Procedure
(Chinese-English bilingual version)

Rule 8003. Appeal as of Right—How Taken; Docketing the Appeal | 290

Rule 8004. Appeal by Leave—How Taken; Docketing the Appeal | 294

Rule 8005. Election to Have an Appeal Heard by the District Court Instead of the BAP | 296

Rule 8006. Certifying a Direct Appeal to the Court of Appeals | 298

Rule 8007. Stay Pending Appeal; Bonds; Suspension of Proceedings | 302

Rule 8008. Indicative Rulings | 306

Rule 8009. Record on Appeal; Sealed Documents | 306

Rule 8010. Completing and Transmitting the Record | 314

Rule 8011. Filing and Service; Signature | 318

Rule 8012. Corporate Disclosure Statement | 324

Rule 8013. Motions; Intervention | 324

Rule 8014. Briefs | 330

Rule 8015. Form and Length of Briefs; Form of Appendices and Other Papers | 334

Rule 8016. Cross-Appeals | 340

Rule 8017. Brief of an Amicus Curiae | 344

Rule 8018. Serving and Filing Briefs; Appendices | 348

Rule 8018.1. District-Court Review of a Judgment that the Bankruptcy Court Lacked the Constitutional Authority to Enter | 352

Rule 8019. Oral Argument | 352

Rule 8020. Frivolous Appeal and Other Misconduct | 356

Rule 8021. Costs | 356

Rule 8022. Motion for Rehearing | 358

Rule 8023. Voluntary Dismissal | 360

Rule 8024. Clerk's Duties on Disposition of the Appeal | 360

Rule 8025. Stay of a District Court or BAP Judgment | 362

Rule 8026. Rules by Circuit Councils and District Courts; Procedure When There Is No Controlling Law | 364

美国联邦破产程序规则
（中英对照译本）

第 8003 条　作为权利的上诉——如何提起上诉；上诉案件的立案 | 291

第 8004 条　须经许可的上诉——如何提起上诉；上诉案件的立案 | 295

第 8005 条　选择由地区法院代替破产上诉合议庭审理上诉案件 | 297

第 8006 条　向上诉法院证明直接上诉 | 299

第 8007 条　正在进行中的上诉的冻结；保证金；程序的中止 | 303

第 8008 条　指示性裁决 | 307

第 8009 条　上诉档案；封存材料 | 307

第 8010 条　完成并移交档案 | 315

第 8011 条　提交及送达；签名 | 319

第 8012 条　公司披露声明 | 325

第 8013 条　动议；介入 | 325

第 8014 条　摘要 | 331

第 8015 条　摘要的格式及篇幅；附录及其他文件的格式 | 335

第 8016 条　交叉上诉 | 341

第 8017 条　法庭之友的摘要 | 345

第 8018 条　送达并提交摘要；附录 | 349

第 8018.1 条　地区法院对破产法院未经宪法授权而作出的判决的审查 | 353

第 8019 条　口头辩论 | 353

第 8020 条　无正当依据的上诉以及其他错误行为 | 357

第 8021 条　成本费用 | 357

第 8022 条　申请重审的动议 | 359

第 8023 条　自愿撤诉 | 361

第 8024 条　书记员就上诉案件的处理所承担的义务 | 361

第 8025 条　地区法院或破产上诉合议庭的判决的冻结 | 363

第 8026 条　巡回理事会及地区法院的规则；没有约束法时采用的程序 | 365

U.S. Federal Rules of Bankruptcy Procedure
(Chinese-English bilingual version)

Rule 8027. Notice of a Mediation Procedure | 364

Rule 8028. Suspension of Rules in Part VIII | 366

PART IX GENERAL PROVISIONS

Rule 9001. General Definitions | 368

Rule 9002. Meanings of Words in the Federal Rules of Civil Procedure When Applicable to Cases Under the Code | 370

Rule 9003. Prohibition of Ex Parte Contacts | 370

Rule 9004. General Requirements of Form | 372

Rule 9005. Harmless Error | 372

Rule 9005.1. Constitutional Challenge to a Statute—Notice, Certification, and Intervention | 372

Rule 9006. Computing and Extending Time; Time for Motion Papers | 374

Rule 9007. General Authority to Regulate Notices | 380

Rule 9008. Service or Notice by Publication | 380

Rule 9009. Forms | 380

Rule 9010. Representation and Appearances; Powers of Attorney | 382

Rule 9011. Signing of Papers; Representations to the Court; Sanctions; Verification and Copies of Papers | 382

Rule 9012. Oaths and Affirmations | 388

Rule 9013. Motions: Form and Service | 388

Rule 9014. Contested Matters | 388

Rule 9015. Jury Trials | 392

Rule 9016. Subpoena | 392

Rule 9017. Evidence | 392

Rule 9018. Secret, Confidential, Scandalous, or Defamatory Matter | 392

Rule 9019. Compromise and Arbitration | 394

Rule 9020. Contempt Proceedings | 394

第 8027 条　调解程序的通知　|　365

第 8028 条　第 VIII 部分中规则的中止　|　367

第 IX 部分　一般规定

第 9001 条　通用定义　|　369

第 9002 条　《联邦民事诉讼规则》中的词汇适用于根据法典所提起的案件中的含义　|　371

第 9003 条　禁止单方接触　|　371

第 9004 条　对格式的一般性要求　|　373

第 9005 条　无害的错误　|　373

第 9005.1 条　对法律的宪法挑战——通知、证明以及介入　|　373

第 9006 条　期间的计算与延长；与动议书相关的期间规定　|　375

第 9007 条　规制通知的一般权力　|　381

第 9008 条　以公告方式送达或通知　|　381

第 9009 条　模板　|　381

第 9010 条　代表及出席；律师的权力　|　383

第 9011 条　文件的签署；向法院证明；处罚；文件的核证与副本　|　383

第 9012 条　宣誓及发誓　|　389

第 9013 条　动议：格式及送达　|　389

第 9014 条　争议事项　|　389

第 9015 条　陪审团庭审　|　393

第 9016 条　传票　|　393

第 9017 条　证据　|　393

第 9018 条　秘密、机密、绯闻或诽谤事项　|　393

第 9019 条　和解及仲裁　|　395

第 9020 条　藐视法庭程序　|　395

U.S. Federal Rules of Bankruptcy Procedure
(Chinese-English bilingual version)

Rule 9021. Entry of Judgment | 394

Rule 9022. Notice of Judgment or Order | 396

Rule 9023. New Trials; Amendment of Judgments | 396

Rule 9024. Relief from Judgment or Order | 396

Rule 9025. Security: Proceedings Against Security Providers | 398

Rule 9026. Exceptions Unnecessary | 398

Rule 9027. Removal | 398

Rule 9028. Disability of a Judge | 404

Rule 9029. Local Bankruptcy Rules; Procedure When There Is No Controlling Law | 404

Rule 9030. Jurisdiction and Venue Unaffected | 406

Rule 9031. Masters Not Authorized | 406

Rule 9032. Effect of Amendment of Federal Rules of Civil Procedure | 406

Rule 9033. Proposed Findings of Fact and Conclusions of Law | 406

Rule 9034. Transmittal of Pleadings, Motion Papers, Objections, and Other Papers to the United States Trustee | 408

Rule 9035. Applicability of Rules in Judicial Districts in Alabama and North Carolina | 410

Rule 9036. Notice and Service by Electronic Transmission | 410

Rule 9037. Privacy Protection for Filings Made with the Court | 412

PART X　UNITED STATES TRUSTEES (Abrogated Apr. 30, 1991, eff. Aug. 1, 1991)

OFFICIAL FORMS | 418

APPENDIX | 418

LENGTH LIMITS STATED IN PART VIII OF THE FEDERAL RULES OF BANKRUPTCY PROCEDURE | 418

第 9021 条　判决的载入 | 395

第 9022 条　判决或裁定的通知 | 397

第 9023 条　新的庭审；判决的修正 | 397

第 9024 条　就判决或裁定获得救济 | 397

第 9025 条　担保：针对担保人所提起的程序 | 399

第 9026 条　没有必要的例外 | 399

第 9027 条　移案 | 399

第 9028 条　法官无法履职 | 405

第 9029 条　地方破产规则；没有约束法时采用的程序 | 405

第 9030 条　管辖权及管辖区域不受影响 | 407

第 9031 条　未被准予的事项 | 407

第 9032 条　《联邦民事诉讼规则》的修正案的影响 | 407

第 9033 条　拟定的事实认定及法律结论 | 407

第 9034 条　将诉状、动议书、异议以及其他文件移交给联邦托管人 | 409

第 9035 条　本法在阿拉巴马州和北卡罗来纳州内的司法辖区内的适用 | 411

第 9036 条　电子通知与送达 | 411

第 9037 条　向法院提交材料的情形下的隐私保护 | 413

第 X 部分　联邦托管人（经 Apr. 30, 1991, eff. Aug. 1, 1991 而被废除）

官方模板 | 419

附录 | 419

《联邦破产程序规则》第 VIII 部分所述的篇幅限制 | 419

U.S. Federal Rules of Bankruptcy Procedure
(Chinese-English bilingual version)

PROPOSED AMENDMENTS TO THE FEDERAL RULES OF BANKRUPTCY PROCEDURE
Court Order

Rule 1007.Lists, Schedules, Statements, and Other Documents; Time Limits | 422

Rule 1020.Chapter 11 Reorganization Case for Small Business Debtors | 424

Rule 2009. Trustees for Estates When Joint Administration Ordered | 424

Rule 2012.Substitution of Trustee or Successor Trustee; Accounting | 426

Rule 2015.Duty to Keep Records, Make Reports, and Give Notice of Case or Change of Status | 426

Rule 3002.Filing Proof of Claim or Interest | 432

Rule 3010.Small Dividends and Payments in Cases Under Chapter 7, Subchapter V of Chapter 11, Chapter 12, and Chapter 13 | 432

Rule 3011.Unclaimed Funds in Cases Under Chapter 7, Subchapter V of Chapter 11, Chapter 12, and Chapter 13 | 434

Rule 3014.Election Under § 1111 (b) by Secured Creditor in Chapter 9 Municipality or Chapter 11 Reorganization Case | 434

Rule 3016.Filing of Plan and Disclosure Statement in a Chapter 9 Municipality or Chapter 11 Reorganization Case | 434

Rule 3017.1. Court Consideration of Disclosure Statement in a Small Business Case or in a Case Under Subchapter V of Chapter 11 | 436

Rule 3017.2. Fixing of Dates by the Court in Subchapter V Cases in Which There Is No Disclosure Statement | 436

Rule 3018. Acceptance or Rejection of Plan in a Chapter 9 Municipality or a Chapter 11 Reorganization Case | 438

Rule 3019. Modification of Accepted Plan in a Chapter 9 Municipality or a Chapter 11 Reorganization Case | 438

Rule 5005. Filing and Transmittal of Papers | 440

Rule 7004.Process; Service of Summons, Complaint | 442

Rule 8023.Voluntary Dismissal | 442

对《联邦破产程序规则》的拟议修正案

法院裁定

第 1007 条　清单、报表、声明和其他文件；时间限制 | 423

第 1020 条　第 11 章小企业重整案件 | 425

第 2009 条　被裁定合并管理时多个破产实体的托管人 | 425

第 2012 条　托管人的取代或继任托管人；账目 | 427

第 2015 条　保存档案、制作档案以及就案件或状态的变化发出通知的义务 | 427

第 3002 条　提交债权或权益证明 | 433

第 3010 条　在第 7 章、第 11 章第五附章、第 12 章、第 13 章案件中的小额还款 | 433

第 3011 条　第 7 章、第 11 章第五附章、第 12 章和第 13 章案件中无人主张的资金 | 435

第 3014 条　在第 9 章市政机构破产案件或第 11 章重整案件中担保债权人根据第 1111 条（b）所作的选择 | 435

第 3016 条　在第 9 章市政机构破产案件或第 11 章重整案件中计划和披露声明的提交 | 435

第 3017.1 条　在小企业案件或第 11 章第五附章案件中法院就披露声明的审议 | 437

第 3017.2 条　法院在不涉及披露声明的第五附章案件中对时间的确定 | 437

第 3018 条　第 9 章市政机构破产案件或第 11 章重整案件中对计划的接受或拒绝 | 439

第 3019 条　第 9 章市政机构破产案件或第 11 章重整案件中已被接受的计划的修改 | 439

第 5005 条　材料的提交和移送 | 441

第 7004 条　司法文书；传票、诉状的送达 | 443

第 8023 条　自愿撤诉 | 443

U.S. Federal Rules of Bankruptcy Procedure

美国联邦破产程序规则

TITLE 11—APPENDIX

FEDERAL RULES OF BANKRUPTCY PROCEDURE

(*Effective August 1, 1983, as amended to December 1, 2021*)

Rule

1001. Scope of Rules and Forms; Short Title

PART I
COMMENCEMENT OF CASE; PROCEEDINGS RELATING TO PETITION AND ORDER FOR RELIEF

1002. Commencement of Case

1003. Involuntary Petition

1004. Involuntary Petition Against a Partnership

1004.1. Petition for an Infant or Incompetent Person

1004.2. Petition in Chapter 15 Cases

1005. Caption of Petition

1006. Filing Fee

1007. Lists, Schedules, Statements, and Other Documents; Time Limits

1008. Verification of Petitions and Accompanying Papers

1009. Amendments of Voluntary Petitions, Lists, Schedules and Statements

1010. Service of Involuntary Petition and Summons

第十一篇——附录
联邦破产程序规则

（1983 年 8 月 1 日生效，2021 年 12 月 1 日修正）

条
1001. 规则和模板的适用范围；简称

第 I 部分
案件的启动；与破产申请和破产救济令有关的程序

1002. 案件的启动
1003. 强制破产申请
1004. 对合伙组织提起的强制破产申请
1004.1. 婴儿或无行为能力人的申请
1004.2. 第 15 章案件中的申请
1005. 破产申请的标题
1006. 申请费
1007. 清单、报表、声明和其他文件；时间限制
1008. 申请和附随文件的核实
1009. 自愿破产申请、清单、报表和声明的修改
1010. 强制破产申请和传票的送达

U.S. Federal Rules of Bankruptcy Procedure
(Chinese-English bilingual version)

1011. Responsive Pleading or Motion in Involuntary Cases

1012. Responsive Pleading in Cross-Border Cases

1013. Hearing and Disposition of a Petition in an Involuntary Case

1014. Dismissal and Change of Venue

1015. Consolidation or Joint Administration of Cases Pending in Same Court

1016. Death or Incompetency of Debtor

1017. Dismissal or Conversion of Case; Suspension

1018. Contested Involuntary Petitions; Contested Petitions Commencing Chapter 15 Cases; Proceedings to Vacate Order for Relief; Applicability of Rules in Part VII Governing Adversary Proceedings

1019. Conversion of a Chapter 11 Reorganization Case, Chapter 12 Family Farmer's Debt Adjustment Case, or Chapter 13 Individual's Debt Adjustment Case to a Chapter 7 Liquidation Case

1020. Small Business Chapter 11 Reorganization Case

1021. Health Care Business Case

PART II

OFFICERS AND ADMINISTRATION; NOTICES; MEETINGS; EXAMINATIONS; ELECTIONS; ATTORNEYS AND ACCOUNTANTS

2001. Appointment of Interim Trustee Before Order for Relief in a Chapter 7 Liquidation Case

2002. Notices to Creditors, Equity Security Holders, Administrators in Foreign Proceedings, Persons Against Whom Provisional Relief is Sought in Ancillary and Other Cross-Border Cases, United States, and United States Trustee

1011. 强制破产案件中的应答文状或动议

1012. 跨境案件中的应答文状

1013. 在强制破产案件中对申请的听证和处理

1014. 驳回和审理法院的变更

1015. 同一法院审理的多个案件的合并或共同管理

1016. 债务人的死亡或行为能力的丧失

1017. 案件的驳回或转换；中止

1018. 对其提出异议的强制破产申请；对其提出异议的启动第 15 章程序的申请；撤销破产救济令的程序；第 VII 部分规制诉讼程序的规则的适用

1019. 第 11 章重整案件、第 12 章家庭农场主债务调整案件或第 13 章个人债务调整案件至第 7 章清算案件的转换

1020. 第 11 章小企业重整案件

1021. 医疗护理机构破产案件

第 II 部分

破产从业人员和案件的管理；通知；会议；质询；选任；律师和会计师

2001. 第 7 章清算案件中破产救济令被作出前临时托管人的任命

2002. 向债权人、股本证券持有人、外国程序中的管理人、在辅助程序和其他跨境案件中寻求的临时救济所针对的人、美国政府机构和联邦托管人发出通知

U.S. Federal Rules of Bankruptcy Procedure
(Chinese-English bilingual version)

2003.	Meeting of Creditors or Equity Security Holders
2004.	Examination
2005.	Apprehension and Removal of Debtor to Compel Attendance for Examination
2006.	Solicitation and Voting of Proxies in Chapter 7 Liquidation Cases
2007.	Review of Appointment of Creditors' Committee Organized Before Commencement of the Case
2007.1.	Appointment of Trustee or Examiner in a Chapter 11 Reorganization Case
2007.2.	Appointment of Patient Care Ombudsman in a Health Care Business Case
2008.	Notice to Trustee of Selection
2009.	Trustees for Estates When Joint Administration Ordered
2010.	Qualification by Trustee; Proceeding on Bond
2011.	Evidence of Debtor in Possession or Qualification of Trustee
2012.	Substitution of Trustee or Successor Trustee; Accounting
2013.	Public Record of Compensation Awarded to Trustees, Examiners, and Professionals
2014.	Employment of Professional Persons
2015.	Duty to Keep Records, Make Reports, and Give Notice of Case or Change of Status
2015.1.	Patient Care Ombudsman
2015.2.	Transfer of Patient in Health Care Business Case
2015.3.	Reports of Financial Information on Entities in Which a Chapter 11 Estate Holds a Controlling or Substantial Interest
2016.	Compensation for Services Rendered and Reimbursement of Expenses
2017.	Examination of Debtor's Transactions with Debtor's Attorney
2018.	Intervention; Right to Be Heard
2019.	Disclosure Regarding Creditors and Equity Security Holders in Chapter 9 and Chapter 11 Cases

美国联邦破产程序规则
（中英对照译本）

2003. 债权人或股本证券持有人会议
2004. 质询
2005. 羁押并转移债务人以强制其出席接受质询

2006. 第 7 章清算案件中表决代理权的征集
2007. 就案件启动前组建的债权人委员会的任命的审查

2007.1. 第 11 章重整案件中托管人或监督人的任命

2007.2. 医疗护理机构中患者护理监察员的任命

2008. 向被选任的托管人发出的通知
2009. 被裁定合并管理时多个破产实体的托管人
2010. 托管人的资格；就保证保险提起的诉讼
2011. 经管债务人的证明或托管人的资格
2012. 托管人的取代或继任托管人；账目
2013. 向托管人、监督人和专业人员给付的报酬的公共记录

2014. 雇佣专业人员
2015. 保存档案、制作档案以及就案件或状态的变化发出通知的义务

2015.1. 患者护理监察员
2015.2. 医疗护理机构破产案件中患者的转移
2015.3. 第 11 章破产实体对其享有控制权或重大利益的实体的财务信息报告
2016. 就被提供的服务而支付的报酬以及费用的报销
2017. 审查债务人与其律师间的交易
2018. 介入；发表意见的权利
2019. 针对第 9 章和第 11 章案件中的债权人和股本证券持有人所作的披露

U.S. Federal Rules of Bankruptcy Procedure
(Chinese-English bilingual version)

2020. Review of Acts by United States Trustee

PART III
CLAIMS AND DISTRIBUTION TO CREDITORS AND EQUITY INTEREST HOLDERS; PLANS

3001.	Proof of Claim
3002.	Filing Proof of Claim or Interest
3002.1.	Notice Relating to Claims Secured by Security Interest in the Debtor's Principal Residence
3003.	Filing Proof of Claim or Equity Security Interest in Chapter 9 Municipality or Chapter 11 Reorganization Cases
3004.	Filing of Claims by Debtor or Trustee
3005.	Filing of Claim, Acceptance, or Rejection by Guarantor, Surety, Indorser, or Other Codebtor
3006.	Withdrawal of Claim; Effect on Acceptance or Rejection of Plan
3007.	Objections to Claims
3008.	Reconsideration of Claims.
3009.	Declaration and Payment of Dividends in a Chapter 7 Liquidation Case
3010.	Small Dividends and Payments in Chapter 7 Liquidation, Chapter 12 Family Farmer's Debt Adjustment, and Chapter 13 Individual's Debt Adjustment Cases
3011.	Unclaimed Funds in Chapter 7 Liquidation, Chapter 12 Family Farmer's Debt Adjustment, and Chapter 13 Individual's Debt Adjustment Cases
3012.	Determining the Amount of Secured and Priority Claims
3013.	Classification of Claims and Interests

2020. 对联邦托管人行为的审查

第 III 部分
债权以及向债权人和股本证券持有人的分配；计划

3001. 债权证明

3002. 提交债权或权益证明

3002.1. 与由债务人主要住所所担保的债权有关的通知

3003. 在第 9 章市政机构破产案件或第 11 章重整案件中提交债权或股本权益证明

3004. 由债务人或托管人提交债权

3005. 由连带保证人、一般保证人、背书人或其他共同债务人提交债权、接受或拒绝计划

3006. 撤回债权主张；接受或拒绝计划的效力

3007. 对债权的异议

3008. 债权的复议

3009. 在第 7 章清算案件中的还款宣告和支付

3010. 在第 7 章清算案件、第 12 章家庭农场主债务调整案件和第 13 章个人债务调整案件中的小额还款

3011. 第 7 章清算案件、第 12 章家庭农场主债务调整案件和第 13 章个人债务调整案件中无人主张的资金

3012. 就担保和优先债权的金额认定

3013. 债权和权益分组

3014.	Election Under §1111（b）by Secured Creditor in Chapter 9 Municipality or Chapter 11 Reorganization Case
3015.	Filing, Objection to Confirmation, Effect of Confirmation, and Modification of a Plan in a Chapter 12 or a Chapter 13 Case
3015.1.	Requirements for a Local Form for Plans Filed in a Chapter 13 Case
3016.	Filing of Plan and Disclosure Statement in a Chapter 9 Municipality or Chapter 11 Reorganization Case
3017.	Court Consideration of Disclosure Statement in a Chapter 9 Municipality or Chapter 11 Reorganization Case
3017.1.	Court Consideration of Disclosure Statement in a Small Business Case
3018.	Acceptance or Rejection of Plan in a Chapter 9 Municipality or a Chapter 11 Reorganization Case
3019.	Modification of Accepted Plan in a Chapter 9 Municipality or a Chapter 11 Reorganization Case
3020.	Deposit; Confirmation of Plan in a Chapter 9 Municipality or Chapter 11 Reorganization Case
3021.	Distribution under Plan
3022.	Final Decree in Chapter 11 Reorganization Case

PART IV

THE DEBTOR: DUTIES AND BENEFITS

4001.	Relief from Automatic Stay; Prohibiting or Conditioning the Use, Sale, or Lease of Property; Use of Cash Collateral; Obtaining Credit; Agreements
4002.	Duties of Debtor
4003.	Exemptions

3014.	在第 9 章市政机构破产案件或第 11 章重整案件中担保债权人根据第 1111 条（b）所作的选择
3015.	在第 12 章或第 13 章案件中提交计划、对计划的批准提出异议、批准的效力以及计划的修改
3015.1.	第 13 章计划适用地方模板的条件
3016.	在第 9 章市政机构破产案件或第 11 章重整案件中计划和披露声明的提交
3017.	在第 9 章市政机构破产案件或第 11 章重整案件中法院对披露声明的审议
3017.1.	在小企业案件中法院就披露声明的审议
3018.	第 9 章市政机构破产案件或第 11 章重整案件中对计划的接受或拒绝
3019.	第 9 章市政机构破产案件或第 11 章重整案件中已被接受的计划的修改
3020.	交存；第 9 章市政机构破产案件或第 11 章重整案件中计划的批准
3021.	根据计划进行的分配
3022.	第 11 章重整案件中的终局裁定

第 IV 部分

债务人：义务和利益

4001.	自动冻结的解除；禁止或附条件使用、出售或出租财产；现金担保物的使用；获取信贷；协议
4002.	债务人的义务
4003.	豁免

U.S. Federal Rules of Bankruptcy Procedure
(Chinese-English bilingual version)

4004.	Grant or Denial of Discharge
4005.	Burden of Proof in Objecting to Discharge
4006.	Notice of No Discharge
4007.	Determination of Dischargeability of a Debt
4008.	Filing of Reaffirmation Agreement; Statement in Support of Reaffirmation Agreement.

PART V
COURTS AND CLERKS

5001.	Courts and Clerks' Offices
5002.	Restrictions on Approval of Appointments
5003.	Records Kept by the Clerk
5004.	Disqualification
5005.	Filing and Transmittal of Papers
5006.	Certification of Copies of Papers
5007.	Record of Proceedings and Transcripts
5008.	Notice Regarding Presumption of Abuse in Chapter 7 Cases of Individual Debtors.
5009.	Closing Chapter 7, Chapter 12, Chapter 13, and Chapter 15 Cases; Order Declaring Lien Satisfied
5010.	Reopening Cases
5011.	Withdrawal and Abstention from Hearing a Proceeding
5012.	Agreements Concerning Coordination of Proceedings in Chapter 15 Cases.

4004.	免责的授予或拒绝
4005.	就免责提出异议的举证责任
4006.	不予免责的通知
4007.	就债务不可免责所作的认定
4008.	再认协议的提交；支持再认协议的声明

第 V 部分
法院和书记员

5001.	法院和书记员办公室
5002.	就任命批准的限制
5003.	由书记员所保存的档案
5004.	丧失资格
5005.	材料的提交和移送
5006.	材料副本的证明
5007.	程序记录和报告单
5008.	在第 7 章个人债务人案件中就滥用推定而发出的通知
5009.	第 7 章、第 12 章、第 13 章及第 15 章案件结案；宣告解除优先权
5010.	案件的重启
5011.	撤回及放弃就程序举行听证
5012.	在第 15 章案件中有关程序间协调的协议

U.S. Federal Rules of Bankruptcy Procedure
(Chinese-English bilingual version)

PART VI
COLLECTION AND LIQUIDATION OF THE ESTATE

6001.　　Burden of Proof As to Validity of Postpetition Transfer

6002.　　Accounting by Prior Custodian of Property of the Estate

6003.　　Interim and Final Relief Immediately Following the Commencement of the Case—Applications for Employment; Motions for Use, Sale, or Lease of Property; and Motions for Assumption or Assignment of Executory Contracts

6004.　　Use, Sale, or Lease of Property

6005.　　Appraisers and Auctioneers

6006.　　Assumption, Rejection or Assignment of an Executory Contract or Unexpired Lease

6007.　　Abandonment or Disposition of Property

6008.　　Redemption of Property from Lien or Sale

6009.　　Prosecution and Defense of Proceedings by Trustee or Debtor in Possession

6010.　　Proceeding to Avoid Indemnifying Lien or Transfer to Surety

6011.　　Disposal of Patient Records in Health Care Business Case

PART VII
ADVERSARY PROCEEDINGS

7001.　　Scope of Rules of Part VII

第VI部分
破产实体的收集和清算

6001. 申请后转让的合法性的举证责任
6002. 破产财产先前保管人所作的核算
6003. 案件启动后即进行的临时及最终救济——申请雇佣；申请使用、出售或出租财产的动议；以及申请确认或拒绝确认待履行合同的动议

6004. 财产的使用、出售或出租
6005. 评估师和拍卖师
6006. 待履行合同或未完成租约的确认、拒绝确认或转让

6007. 财产的放弃或处置
6008. 从财产上担保权或出售中赎回财产
6009. 托管人或经管债务人的起诉和抗辩

6010. 撤销为补偿保证人而设的财产上担保权或所作转让的程序
6011. 在医疗护理机构破产案件中就患者档案的处置

第VII部分
对抗制诉讼程序

7001. 第VII部分规则的适用范围

U.S. Federal Rules of Bankruptcy Procedure
(Chinese-English bilingual version)

7002.	References to Federal Rules of Civil Procedure
7003.	Commencement of Adversary Proceeding
7004.	Process; Service of Summons, Complaint
7005.	Service and Filing of Pleadings and Other Papers
7007.	Pleadings Allowed
7007.1.	Corporate Ownership Statement
7008.	General Rules of Pleading
7009.	Pleading Special Matters
7010.	Form of Pleadings
7012.	Defenses and Objections—When and How Presented—by Pleading or Motion—Motion for Judgment on the Pleadings
7013.	Counterclaim and Cross-Claim
7014.	Third-Party Practice
7015.	Amended and Supplemental Pleadings
7016.	Pretrial Procedures
7017.	Parties Plaintiff and Defendant; Capacity
7018.	Joinder of Claims and Remedies
7019.	Joinder of Persons Needed for Just Determination
7020.	Permissive Joinder of Parties
7021.	Misjoinder and Non-Joinder of Parties
7022.	Interpleader
7023.	Class Proceedings
7023.1.	Derivative Actions
7023.2.	Adversary Proceedings Relating to Unincorporated Associations
7024.	Intervention
7025.	Substitution of Parties
7026.	General Provisions Governing Discovery
7027.	Depositions Before Adversary Proceedings or Pending Appeal
7028.	Persons Before Whom Depositions May Be Taken
7029.	Stipulations Regarding Discovery Procedure

美国联邦破产程序规则
（中英对照译本）

7002. 《联邦民事诉讼规则》的引用

7003. 对抗制诉讼程序的启动

7004. 司法文书；传票、诉状的送达

7005. 诉状及其他文书的送达与提交

7007. 诉状的受理

7007.1. 公司所有权声明

7008. 诉状的一般规定

7009. 有关诉状的特殊事项

7010. 诉状的形式

7012. 抗辩及异议—何时及如何提出—通过诉状或动议—申请就诉状作出判决的动议

7013. 反诉及交叉请求

7014. 第三方当事人程序

7015. 修正及补充起诉状

7016. 审前程序

7017. 原告及被告；诉讼能力

7018. 权利主张和救济的合并

7019. 为获得公正裁决而有必要参加的人

7020. 被准予参加的当事人

7021. 当事人的错误参加及不参加

7022. 竞合权利诉讼

7023. 集体诉讼

7023.1. 股东代表诉讼

7023.2. 涉及非法人组织的对抗制诉讼程序

7024. 参加诉讼

7025. 当事人的更换

7026. 有关证据开示的一般规定

7027. 对抗制诉讼程序前或上诉期间的书面证词

7028. 收集书面证词时的见证人

7029. 有关证据开示程序的约定

U.S. Federal Rules of Bankruptcy Procedure
(Chinese-English bilingual version)

7030.	Depositions Upon Oral Examination
7031.	Deposition Upon Written Questions
7032.	Use of Depositions in Adversary Proceedings
7033.	Interrogatories to Parties
7034.	Production of Documents and Things and Entry Upon Land for Inspection and Other Purposes
7035.	Physical and Mental Examination of Persons
7036.	Requests for Admission
7037.	Failure to Make Discovery: Sanctions
7040.	Assignment of Cases for Trial
7041.	Dismissal of Adversary Proceedings
7042.	Consolidation of Adversary Proceedings; Separate Trials
7052.	Findings by the Court
7054.	Judgments; Costs
7055.	Default
7056.	Summary Judgment
7058.	Entering Judgment in Adversary Proceeding
7062.	Stay of Proceedings to Enforce a Judgment
7064.	Seizure of Person or Property
7065.	Injunctions
7067.	Deposit in Court
7068.	Offer of Judgment
7069.	Execution
7070.	Judgment for Specific Acts; Vesting Title
7071.	Process in Behalf of and Against Persons Not Parties
7087.	Transfer of Adversary Proceeding

7030.	口头质询时的宣誓作证
7031.	书面质询时的宣誓作证
7032.	对抗制诉讼程序中书面证词的使用
7033.	向当事人所作的书面质询
7034.	材料和物品的制作以及出于调查及其他目的进入某地
7035.	对人的身体及精神检查
7036.	申请采信
7037.	未能提供书面证词；处罚
7040.	案件审理的安排
7041.	对抗制诉讼程序的驳回
7042.	对抗制诉讼程序的合并；分别审理
7052.	法院的事实认定
7054.	判决；诉讼费用
7055.	缺席
7056.	简易判决
7058.	在对抗制诉讼程序中作出判决
7062.	执行判决的程序的冻结
7064.	对人或财产的强制措施
7065.	禁令
7067.	向法院缴纳的押金
7068.	判决要约
7069.	执行
7070.	就特定行为所作的判决；所有权的授予
7071.	代表非当事人或对非当事人所进行的程序
7087.	对抗制诉讼程序的移送

U.S. Federal Rules of Bankruptcy Procedure
(Chinese-English bilingual version)

PART VIII

APPEALS TO DISTRICT COURT OR BANKRUPTCY APPELLATE PANEL

8001.	Scope of Part VIII Rules; Definition of "BAP" ; Method of Transmission
8002.	Time for Filing Notice of Appeal
8003.	Appeal as of Right—How Taken; Docketing the Appeal
8004.	Appeal by Leave—How Taken; Docketing the Appeal
8005.	Election to Have an Appeal Heard by the District Court Instead of the BAP
8006.	Certifying a Direct Appeal to the Court of Appeals
8007.	Stay Pending Appeal; Bonds; Suspension of Proceedings
8008.	Indicative Rulings
8009.	Record on Appeal; Sealed Documents
8010.	Completing and Transmitting the Record
8011.	Filing and Service; Signature
8012.	Disclosure Statement
8013.	Motions; Intervention
8014.	Briefs
8015.	Form and Length of Briefs; Form of Appendices and Other Papers
8016.	Cross-Appeals
8017.	Brief of an Amicus Curiae
8018.	Serving and Filing Briefs; Appendices
8018.1.	District-Court Review of a Judgment that the Bankruptcy Court Lacked the Constitutional Authority to Enter
8019.	Oral Argument
8020.	Frivolous Appeal and Other Misconduct

第 VIII 部分
向地区法院或破产上诉合议庭提起上诉

8001. 第 VIII 部分规则的适用范围；"破产上诉合议庭"的定义；递交材料的方式

8002. 提交上诉通知书的时间

8003. 作为权利的上诉——如何提起上诉；上诉案件的立案

8004. 须经许可的上诉——如何提起上诉；上诉案件的立案

8005. 选择由地区法院代替破产上诉合议庭审理上诉案件

8006. 向上诉法院证明直接上诉

8007. 正在进行中的上诉的冻结；保证金；程序的中止

8008. 指示性裁决

8009. 上诉档案；封存材料

8010. 完成并移交档案

8011. 提交及送达；签名

8012. 公司披露声明

8013. 动议；介入

8014. 摘要

8015. 摘要的格式及篇幅；附录及其他文件的格式

8016. 交叉上诉

8017. 法庭之友的摘要

8018. 送达并提交摘要；附录

8018.1. 地区法院对破产法院未经宪法授权而作出的判决的审查

8019. 口头辩论

8020. 无正当依据的上诉以及其他错误行为

U.S. Federal Rules of Bankruptcy Procedure
(Chinese-English bilingual version)

8021.	Costs
8022.	Motion for Rehearing
8023.	Voluntary Dismissal
8024.	Clerk's Duties on Disposition of the Appeal
8025.	Stay of a District Court or BAP Judgment
8026.	Rules by Circuit Councils and District Courts; Procedure When There Is No Controlling Law
8027.	Notice of a Mediation Procedure
8028.	Suspension of Rules in Part VIII

PART IX
GENERAL PROVISIONS

9001.	General Definitions
9002.	Meanings of Words in the Federal Rules of Civil Procedure When Applicable to Cases Under the Code
9003.	Prohibition of Ex Parte Contacts
9004.	General Requirements of Form
9005.	Harmless Error
9005.1.	Constitutional Challenge to a Statute—Notice, Certification, and Intervention
9006.	Computing and Extending Time; Time for Motion Papers
9007.	General Authority to Regulate Notices
9008.	Service or Notice by Publication
9009.	Forms
9010.	Representation and Appearances; Powers of Attorney
9011.	Signing of Papers; Representations to the Court; Sanctions; Verification and Copies of Papers

8021.	成本费用
8022.	申请重审的动议
8023.	自愿撤回
8024.	书记员就上诉案件的处理所承担的义务
8025.	地区法院或破产上诉合议庭的判决的冻结
8026.	巡回理事会及地区法院的规则；没有约束法时采用的程序
8027.	调解程序的通知
8028.	第 VIII 部分中规则的中止

第 IX 部分
一般规定

9001.	通用定义
9002.	《联邦民事诉讼规则》中的词汇适用于根据法典所提起的案件中的含义
9003.	禁止单方接触
9004.	对格式的一般性要求
9005.	无害的错误
9005.1.	对法律的宪法挑战——通知、证明以及介入
9006.	期间的计算与延长；与动议书相关的期间规定
9007.	规制通知的一般权力
9008.	以公告方式送达或通知
9009.	模板
9010.	代表及出席；律师的权力
9011.	文件的签署；向法院证明；处罚；文件的核证与副本

U.S. Federal Rules of Bankruptcy Procedure
(Chinese-English bilingual version)

9012.	Oaths and Affirmations
9013.	Motions: Form and Service
9014.	Contested Matters
9015.	Jury Trials
9016.	Subpoena
9017.	Evidence
9018.	Secret, Confidential, Scandalous, or Defamatory Matter
9019.	Compromise and Arbitration
9020.	Contempt Proceedings
9021.	Entry of Judgment
9022.	Notice of Judgment or Order
9023.	New Trials; Amendment of Judgments
9024.	Relief from Judgment or Order
9025.	Security: Proceedings Against Security Providers
9026.	Exceptions Unnecessary
9027.	Removal
9028.	Disability of a Judge
9029.	Local Bankruptcy Rules; Procedure When There is No Controlling Law
9030.	Jurisdiction and Venue Unaffected
9031.	Masters Not Authorized
9032.	Effect of Amendment of Federal Rules of Civil Procedure
9033.	Proposed Findings of Fact and Conclusions of Law
9034.	Transmittal of Pleadings, Motion Papers, Objections, and Other Papers to the United States Trustee
9035.	Applicability of Rules in Judicial Districts in Alabama and North Carolina.
9036.	Notice and Service by Electronic Transmission
9037.	Privacy Protection for Filings Made with the Court

美国联邦破产程序规则
（中英对照译本）

9012.　宣誓及发誓

9013.　动议：格式及送达

9014.　争议事项

9015.　陪审团庭审

9016.　传票

9017.　证据

9018.　秘密、机密、绯闻或诽谤事项

9019.　和解及仲裁

9020.　藐视法庭程序

9021.　判决的载入

9022.　判决或裁定的通知

9023.　新的庭审；判决的修正

9024.　就判决或裁定获得救济

9025.　担保：针对担保人所提起的程序

9026.　没有必要的例外

9027.　移案

9028.　法官无法履职

9029.　地方破产规则；没有约束法时采用的程序

9030.　管辖权及管辖区域不受影响

9031.　未被准予的事项

9032.　《联邦民事诉讼规则》的修正案的影响

9033.　拟定的事实认定及法律结论

9034.　将诉状、动议书、异议以及其他文件移交给联邦托管人

9035.　本法在阿拉巴马州和北卡罗来纳州内的司法辖区内的适用

9036.　有关通知及送达的一般规定

9037.　向法院提交材料的情形下的隐私保护

Rule 1001. Scope of Rules and Forms; Short Title

The Bankruptcy Rules and Forms govern procedure in cases under title 11 of the United States Code. The rules shall be cited as the Federal Rules of Bankruptcy Procedure and the forms as the Official Bankruptcy Forms. These rules shall be construed, administered, and employed by the court and the parties to secure the just, speedy, and inexpensive determination of every case and proceeding.

(As amended Mar. 30, 1987, eff. Aug. 1, 1987; Apr. 30, 1991, eff. Aug. 1, 1991; Apr. 27, 2017, eff.Dec. 1, 2017.)

PART I

COMMENCEMENT OF CASE; PROCEEDINGS RELATING TO PETITION AND ORDER FOR RELIEF

Rule 1002. Commencement of Case

(a) PETITION. A petition commencing a case under the Code shall be filed with the clerk.

(b)TRANSMISSION TO UNITED STATES TRUSTEE. The clerk shall forthwith transmit to the United States trustee a copy of the petition filed pursuant to subdivision (a) of this rule.

(As amended Mar. 30, 1987, eff. Aug. 1, 1987; Apr. 30, 1991, eff. Aug. 1, 1991.)

第1001条 规则和模板的适用范围；简称

破产规则和模板规制着《美国联邦法典》第11篇案件中的程序。该类规则应为引用为"联邦破产程序规则"，该类模板应被引用为"官方破产模板"。该类规则应由法院和当事人进行解释、实施和适用从而保证每个案件和程序都能得到公正、快速和低成本的解决。

（经 Mar. 30, 1987, eff. Aug. 1, 1987; Apr. 30, 1991, eff. Aug. 1, 1991; Apr. 27, 2017, eff.Dec. 1, 2017. 修正）

第 I 部分
案件的启动；与破产申请和破产救济令有关的程序

第1002条 案件的启动

（a）**破产申请**。根据法典[①]启动破产案件的申请应向书记员提交。

（b）**向联邦托管人移交**。书记员应立刻将根据本条的（a）附条提交的破产申请的副本移交联邦托管人。

（经 Mar. 30, 1987, eff. Aug. 1, 1987; Apr. 30, 1991, eff. Aug. 1, 1991. 修正）

---

① 本法所称"Code"（法典）即指《美国破产法典》(《美国联邦法典》第11篇)，此外，英文原文中出现"§"符号，中文翻译中对应出现"条"时，也均指《美国破产法典》中的条文。——译者注

U.S. Federal Rules of Bankruptcy Procedure
(Chinese-English bilingual version)

Rule 1003. Involuntary Petition

(a) TRANSFEROR OR TRANSFEREE OF CLAIM. A transferor or transferee of a claim shall annex to the original and each copy of the petition a copy of all documents evidencing the transfer, whether transferred unconditionally, for security, or otherwise, and a signed statement that the claim was not transferred for the purpose of commencing the case and setting forth the consideration for and terms of the transfer. An entity that has transferred or acquired a claim for the purpose of commencing a case for liquidation under chapter 7 or for reorganization under chapter 11 shall not be a qualified petitioner.

(b) JOINDER OF PETITIONERS AFTER FILING. If the answer to an involuntary petition filed by fewer than three creditors avers the existence of 12 or more creditors, the debtor shall file with the answer a list of all creditors with their addresses, a brief statement of the nature of their claims, and the amounts thereof. If it appears that there are 12 or more creditors as provided in §303 (b) of the Code, the court shall afford a reasonable opportunity for other creditors to join in the petition before a hearing is held thereon.

(As amended Mar. 30, 1987, eff. Aug. 1, 1987.)

Rule 1004. Involuntary Petition Against a Partnership

After filing of an involuntary petition under §303 (b) (3) of the Code, (1) the petitioning partners or other petitioners shall promptly send to or serve on each general partner who is not a petitioner a copy of the petition; and (2) the clerk shall promptly issue a summons for service on each general partner who is not a petitioner. Rule 1010 applies to the form and service of the summons.

(As amended Apr. 29, 2002, eff. Dec. 1, 2002.)

Rule 1004.1. Petition for an Infant or Incompetent Person

If an infant or incompetent person has a representative, including a general guardian, committee, conservator, or similar fiduciary, the representative may file a voluntary petition on behalf of the infant or incompetent person. An infant or incompetent

美国联邦破产程序规则
（中英对照译本）

第1003条　强制破产申请

（a）债权的转让人或受让人。债权的转让人或受让人应将证明该转让的所有文件的副本附于破产申请原件和各份副本后，无论该转让是否附有条件，是否设有担保或存在其他情况；并且也应附有说明该债权的转让不是以启动破产案件为目的的签字声明，并在该声明上载明转让的对价和条件。以启动第7章清算案件或第11章重整案件为目的而转让或取得债权的实体不得被认定为合格的申请人。

（b）提交（申请）后申请人的加入。若针对由少于3名的债权人提交的强制破产申请的答辩状中，主张存在12名或12名以上的债权人，则债务人应在提交该答辩状的同时，一并提交一份列有所有债权人及其地址的名单，有关其债权性质的简述以及各债权的金额。若根据法典第303条（b）的规定，认定存在12名或12名以上的债权人，则法院应为其他债权人提供合理的机会以在举行听证前加入破产申请。

（经 Mar. 30, 1987, eff. Aug. 1, 1987. 修正）

第1004条　对合伙组织提起的强制破产申请

在根据法典第303条（b）(3)提交强制破产申请后，(1)提交申请的合伙人或其他申请人应及时向并未提交申请的各普通合伙人寄送或送达破产申请的副本；并且(2)书记员应及时签发传票并向并未提交申请的各普通合伙人送达。第1010条适用于传票的程序和送达。

（经 Apr. 29, 2002, eff. Dec. 1, 2002. 修正）

第1004.1条　婴儿或无行为能力人的申请

若婴儿或无行为能力人有代表人，包括监护人、委员会、管理人或类似的受托人，则代表人可代表婴儿或无行为能力人提交自愿破产申请。针对并无通过正当程序而被任命的代表人的婴儿或无行为能力人，其可由亲近的朋友或诉

person who does not have a duly appointed representative may file a voluntary petition by next friend or guardian ad litem. The court shall appoint a guardian ad litem for an infant or incompetent person who is a debtor and is not otherwise represented or shall make any other order to protect the infant or incompetent debtor.

（Added Apr. 29, 2002, eff. Dec. 1, 2002.）

Rule 1004.2. Petition in Chapter 15 Cases

（a）DESIGNATING CENTER OF MAIN INTERESTS. A petition for recognition of a foreign proceeding under chapter 15 of the Code shall state the country where the debtor has its center of main interests. The petition shall also identify each country in which a foreign proceeding by, regarding, or against the debtor is pending.

（b）CHALLENGING DESIGNATION. The United States trustee or a party in interest may file a motion for a determination that the debtor's center of main interests is other than as stated in the petition for recognition commencing the chapter 15 case. Unless the court orders otherwise, the motion shall be filed no later than seven days before the date set for the hearing on the petition. The motion shall be transmitted to the United States trustee and served on the debtor, all persons or bodies authorized to administer foreign proceedings of the debtor, all entities against whom provisional relief is being sought under §1519 of the Code, all parties to litigation pending in the United States in which the debtor was a party as of the time the petition was filed, and such other entities as the court may direct.

（Added Apr. 26, 2011, eff. Dec. 1, 2011.）

Rule 1005. Caption of Petition

The caption of a petition commencing a case under the Code shall contain the name of the court, the title of the case, and the docket number. The title of the case shall include the following information about the debtor: name, employer identification number, last four digits of the social-security number or individual debtor's taxpayer-identification number, any other federal taxpayer-identification number, and all other names used within eight years before filing the petition. If the petition is not filed by the debtor, it shall include all names used by the debtor which are known to the petitioners.

讼监护人提交自愿破产申请。针对作为债务人，但并无任何代表人的婴儿或无行为能力人，法院应为其指定诉讼监护人或作出任何其他裁定以保护该婴儿或无行为能力人。

（经 Apr. 29, 2002, eff. Dec. 1, 2002. 修正）

第 1004.2 条　第 15 章案件中的申请

（a）**认定主要利益中心**。根据法典第 15 章为申请承认外国程序而提交的申请中应注明债务人的主要利益中心所在的国家。该申请也应注明由债务人提起、涉及债务人或针对债务人提起的，正在进行中的外国程序所在的各个国家。

（b）**对该认定的异议**。联邦托管人或利益相关方可提交动议以申请认定为启动第 15 章案件而提交的承认申请中载明的国家并非债务人的主要利益中心。除非法院作出其他裁定，否则其应在确定的破产申请听证日前 7 日内提交该动议。该动议应被移交给联邦托管人并送达债务人、被授权处理债务人外国程序的所有人或机构、根据法典第 1519 条而寻求的临时救济所针对的所有实体、该申请被提交时债务人作为当事人而在美国正在进行的诉讼的所有其他当事人，以及法院可指定的该类其他实体。

（经 Apr. 26, 2011, eff. Dec. 1, 2011. 增补）

第 1005 条　破产申请的标题

根据法典启动破产案件的破产申请的标题应载有法院的名称、案件的标题以及案件的编号。案件的标题应包含有关债务人的以下信息：姓名、雇主身份号码、社保账号或个人纳税人识别号码的后四位数字，任何其他联邦纳税人识别号码以及在提交破产申请前 8 年内使用过的所有其他姓名。若破产申请并非由债务人所提交，则应载有申请人所知的债务人的所有曾用名。

U.S. Federal Rules of Bankruptcy Procedure
(Chinese-English bilingual version)

(As amended Mar. 30, 1987, eff. Aug. 1, 1987; Mar. 27, 2003, eff. Dec. 1, 2003; Apr. 23, 2008, eff.Dec. 1, 2008.)

Rule 1006. Filing Fee

(a) GENERAL REQUIREMENT. Every petition shall be accompanied by the filing fee except as provided in subdivisions (b) and (c) of this rule. For the purpose of this rule, "filing fee" means the filing fee prescribed by 28 U.S.C. §1930 (a)(1) - (a)(5) and any other fee prescribed by the Judicial Conference of the United States under 28 U.S.C. §1930 (b) that is payable to the clerk upon the commencement of a case under the Code.

(b) PAYMENT OF FILING FEE IN INSTALLMENTS.

(1) *Application to Pay Filing Fee in Installments*. A voluntary petition by an individual shall be accepted for filing, regardless of whether any portion of the filing fee is paid, if accompanied by the debtor's signed application, prepared as prescribed by the appropriate Official Form, stating that the debtor is unable to pay the filing fee except in installments.

(2) *Action on Application*. Prior to the meeting of creditors, the court may order the filing fee paid to the clerk or grant leave to pay in installments and fix the number, amount and dates of payment. The number of installments shall not exceed four, and the final installment shall be payable not later than 120 days after filing the petition. For cause shown, the court may extend the time of any installment, provided the last installment is paid not later than 180 days after filing the petition.

(3) *Postponement of Attorney's Fees*. All installments of the filing fee must be paid in full before the debtor or chapter 13 trustee may make further payments to an attorney or any otherperson who renders services to the debtor in connection with the case.

(c) WAIVER OF FILING FEE. A voluntary chapter 7 petition filed by an individual shall be accepted for filing if accompanied by the debtor's application requesting a waiver under 28 U.S.C.§1930 (f), prepared as prescribed by the appropriate Official Form.

(As amended Mar. 30, 1987, eff. Aug. 1, 1987; Apr. 23, 1996, eff. Dec. 1, 1996;

（经 Mar. 30, 1987, eff. Aug. 1, 1987; Mar. 27, 2003, eff. Dec. 1, 2003; Apr. 23, 2008, eff.Dec. 1, 2008. 修正）

第1006条　申请费

（a）**一般要求**。除本条的（b）和（c）附条中另有规定外，针对各破产申请，均应支付申请费。就本条而言，"申请费"指在根据法典启动破产案件时应向书记员支付的，《美国联邦法典》第28篇第1930条（a）(1)至（a）(5)中的申请费和美国司法会议根据《美国联邦法典》第28篇第1930条（b）而规定的任何其他费用。

（b）**申请费的分期支付**。

（1）申请分期支付申请费。针对由自然人提起的自愿破产申请，若其附有根据相应的官方模板的规定而准备的，载明债务人除分期付款外没有能力支付申请费，且经过债务人签名的申请，则无论是否已经支付申请费，均应受理其破产申请。

（2）针对该申请的措施。债权人会议前，法院可裁定向书记员支付申请费或准予其分期付款并确定付款的期数、金额和日期。期数不得超过4，并且最后一期应在破产申请被提交后120日内支付。出于被主张的特定事由，法院可延长任意一期的期间，但最后一期仍应在破产申请被提交后180日内支付。

（3）律师费的延期支付。应在债务人或第13章案件中的托管人向律师或任何其他人就其在本案中提供的服务而支付费用前，首先全额支付申请费的所有分期金额。

（c）**申请费的豁免**。针对由自然人提交的第7章自愿破产案件的破产申请，若附有根据相应官方模板的规定而准备的，请求根据《美国联邦法典》第28篇第1930条（f）豁免申请费的申请，则应受理该破产申请。

（经 Mar. 30, 1987, eff. Aug. 1, 1987; Apr. 23, 1996, eff. Dec. 1, 1996; Apr. 23,

U.S. Federal Rules of Bankruptcy Procedure
(Chinese-English bilingual version)

Apr. 23, 2008, eff.Dec. 1, 2008; Apr. 27, 2017, eff. Dec. 1, 2017.)

Rule 1007. Lists, Schedules, Statements, and Other Documents; Time Limits

(a) CORPORATE OWNERSHIP STATEMENT, LIST OF CREDITORS AND EQUITY SECURITY HOLDERS, AND OTHER LISTS.

(1) *Voluntary Case*. In a voluntary case, the debtor shall file with the petition a list containing the name and address of each entity included or to be included on Schedules D, E/F, G, and H as prescribed by the Official Forms. If the debtor is a corporation, other than a governmental unit, the debtor shall file with the petition a corporate ownership statement containing the information described in Rule 7007.1. The debtor shall file a supplemental statement promptly upon any change in circumstances that renders the corporate ownership statement inaccurate.

(2) *Involuntary Case*. In an involuntary case, the debtor shall file, within seven days after entry of the order for relief, a list containing the name and address of each entity included or to be included on Schedules D, E/F, G, and H as prescribed by the Official Forms.

(3) *Equity Security Holders*. In a chapter 11 reorganization case, unless the court orders otherwise, the debtor shall file within 14 days after entry of the order for relief a list of the debtor's equity security holders of each class showing the number and kind of interests registered in the name of each holder, and the last known address or place of business of each holder.

(4) *Chapter 15 Case*. In addition to the documents required under §1515 of the Code, a foreign representative filing a petition for recognition under chapter 15 shall file with the petition: (A) a corporate ownership statement containing the information described in Rule 7007.1; and (B) unless the court orders otherwise, a list containing the names and addresses of all persons or bodies authorized to administer foreign proceedings of the debtor, all parties to litigation pending in the United States in which the debtor is a party at the time of the filing of the petition, and all entities against whom provisional relief is being sought under §1519 of the Code.

(5) *Extension of Time*. Any extension of time for the filing of the lists required

美国联邦破产程序规则
（中英对照译本）

2008, eff.Dec. 1, 2008; Apr. 27, 2017, eff. Dec. 1, 2017. 修正）

第1007条 清单、报表、声明和其他文件；时间限制

（a）法人所有权声明、债权人和股本证券持有人名单以及其他清单。

（1）自愿破产案件。在自愿破产案件中，债务人应提交一份官方模板规定的报表D、E/F、G以及H中填写的或将填写的各实体的姓名和住址的清单。若债务人为除政府机构外的法人，则债务人还应与破产申请一同提交一份载有第7007.1条所述信息的法人所有权声明。当因任何情形的变化而使法人所有权声明有误时，债务人应及时提交补充声明。

（2）强制破产案件。在强制破产案件中，债务人应在破产救济令被正式作出后7日内提交一份官方模板规定的报表D、E/F、G以及H中填写的或将填写的各实体的姓名和住址的清单。

（3）股本证券持有人。在第11章重整案件中，除非法院作出其他裁定，否则债务人应在破产救济令被正式作出后14日内提交一份所有小组的债务人的股本证券持有人的名单，并载明以各持有人的姓名登记的权益的数量及种类，以及各持有人最后为人所知的住所或经营场所。

（4）第15章案件。除法典第1515条要求的文件外，根据第15章提交承认申请的外国代表还应一并提交：(A)载有第7007.1条所述信息的法人所有权声明；以及（B）除非法院作出其他裁定，否则应提交一份载有被授权处理债务人外国程序的所有人或机构、破产申请被提交时债务人作为当事人在美国正在进行的诉讼的所有其他当事人、根据法典第1519条而寻求的临时救济所针对的所有实体的姓名和住址的清单。

（5）期间的延长。仅当有人就特定事由提出动议，并向联邦托管人和任何托

U.S. Federal Rules of Bankruptcy Procedure
(Chinese-English bilingual version)

by this subdivision may be granted only on motion for cause shown and on notice to the United States trustee and to any trustee, committee elected under §705 or appointed under §1102 of the Code, or other party as the court may direct.

(b) SCHEDULES, STATEMENTS, AND OTHER DOCUMENTS REQUIRED.

(1) Except in a chapter 9 municipality case, the debtor, unless the court orders otherwise, shall file the following schedules, statements, and other documents, prepared as prescribed by the appropriate Official Forms, if any:

(A) schedules of assets and liabilities;

(B) a schedule of current income and expenditures;

(C) a schedule of executory contracts and unexpired leases;

(D) a statement of financial affairs;

(E) copies of all payment advices or other evidence of payment, if any, received by the debtor from an employer within 60 days before the filing of the petition, with redaction of all but the last four digits of the debtor's social-security number or individual taxpayer-identification number; and

(F) a record of any interest that the debtor has in an account or program of the type specified in §521 (c) of the Code.

(2) An individual debtor in a chapter 7 case shall file a statement of intention as required by §521 (a) of the Code, prepared as prescribed by the appropriate Official Form. A copy of the statement of intention shall be served on the trustee and the creditors named in the statement on or before the filing of the statement.

(3) Unless the United States trustee has determined that the credit counseling requirement of §109 (h) does not apply in the district, an individual debtor must file a statement of compliance with the credit counseling requirement, prepared as prescribed by the appropriate Official Form which must include one of the following:

(A) an attached certificate and debt repayment plan, if any, required by §521 (b);

(B) a statement that the debtor has received the credit counseling briefing required by §109 (h) (1) but does not have the certificate required by §521 (b);

(C) a certification under §109 (h) (3); or

(D) a request for a determination by the court under §109 (h) (4).

美国联邦破产程序规则
（中英对照译本）

管人、根据法典第 705 条被选任或根据第 1102 条被任命的委员会或者法院可指定的其他主体发出通知时，才可准予延期提交本附条所要求的清单。

（b）报表、声明和其他被要求的文件。

（1）除第 9 章市政机构的破产案件外，除非法院作出其他裁定，否则债务人应提供以下报表、声明以及根据相应的官方模板的规定准备的其他文件（如有）：

（A）资产负债表；

（B）当前收入支出表；

（C）待履行合同和未完成租约的清单；

（D）财务状况的说明；

（E）债务人在破产申请被提交前 60 日内从雇主处收到的所有付款通知书或其他付款证明（如有）的副本，该文件应对其进行隐私化处理，但仍须保留债务人社保账号或个人纳税人号码的后四位；以及

（F）载有债务人在法典第 521 条（c）所述的账户或计划中享有的任何权益的记录。

（2）第 7 章案件中的个人债务人应提交按照相应官方模板的规定而准备的，法典第 521 条（a）所要求的意向声明。该意向声明的副本应在提交该声明时或之前向托管人及该声明中涉及的债权人送达。

（3）除非联邦托管人已经认定第 109 条（h）中的信用咨询要求不适用于该地区，否则个人债务人应提交按照相应官方模板的规定准备的，表明其遵守信用咨询要求的声明，并且该声明中必须包含以下任意一项：

（A）第 521 条（b）所要求的附加证明文件以及债务清偿计划（如有）；

（B）载明债务人已经收到第 109 条（h）（1）要求的信用咨询简报但没有第 521 条（b）要求的证明文件的声明；

（C）第 109 条（h）（3）中的证明；或

（D）根据第 109 条（h）（4）请求法院作出认定的申请。

(4) Unless §707(b)(2)(D) applies, an individual debtor in a chapter 7 case shall file a statement of current monthly income prepared as prescribed by the appropriate Official Form, and, if the current monthly income exceeds the median family income for the applicable state and household size, the information, including calculations, required by §707(b), prepared as prescribed by the appropriate Official Form.

(5) An individual debtor in a chapter 11 case shall file a statement of current monthly income, prepared as prescribed by the appropriate Official Form.

(6) A debtor in a chapter 13 case shall file a statement of current monthly income, prepared as prescribed by the appropriate Official Form, and, if the current monthly income exceeds the median family income for the applicable state and household size, a calculation of disposable income made in accordance with §1325(b)(3), prepared as prescribed by the appropriate Official Form.

(7) Unless an approved provider of an instructional course concerning personal financial management has notified the court that a debtor has completed the course after filing the petition:

(A) An individual debtor in a chapter 7 or chapter 13 case shall file a statement of completion of the course, prepared as prescribed by the appropriate Official Form; and

(B) An individual debtor in a chapter 11 case shall file the statement if §1141(d)(3) applies.

(8) If an individual debtor in a chapter 11, 12, or 13 case has claimed an exemption under §522(b)(3)(A) in property of the kind described in §522(p)(1) with a value in excess of the amount set out in §522(q)(1), the debtor shall file a statement as to whether there is any proceeding pending in which the debtor may be found guilty of a felony of a kind described in §522(q)(1)(A) or found liable for a debt of the kind described in §522(q)(1)(B).

(c) TIME LIMITS. In a voluntary case, the schedules, statements, and other documents required by subdivision (b)(1), (4), (5), and (6) shall be filed with the petition or within 14 days thereafter, except as otherwise provided in subdivisions (d), (e), (f), and (h) of this rule. In an involuntary case, the

（4）除了适用第707条（b）(2)（D）的情况外，第7章案件中的个人债务人应提交按照相应官方模板的规定准备的当前月收入的说明，并且，若其当前月收入超过适用于其所在州和其家庭规模的家庭收入中位数，则应载有第707条（b）要求的，按照相应官方模板的规定准备的计算过程等信息。

（5）第11章案件中的个人债务人应提交按照相应官方模板的规定准备的当前月收入的说明。

（6）第13章案件中的债务人应提交按照相应官方模板的规定准备的当前月收入的说明，并且，若其当前月收入超过适用于其所在州和其家庭规模的家庭收入中位数，则应载有按照相应官方模板的规定准备的，根据第1325条（b）(3)计算可支配收入的过程。

（7）除非有关个人财务管理的指导课程的获批提供者已经通知法院债务人已经在破产申请被提交后完成了该课程，否则：

（A）第7章或第13章案件中的个人债务人应提交按照相应官方模板的规定准备的，表明已完成该课程的声明；以及

（B）在适用第1141条（d）(3)规定的情况下，第11章案件中的个人债务人应提交该声明。

（8）若第11、12或13章案件中的个人债务人主张根据第522条（b）(3)（A），就第522条（p）(1)所述的，价值超过第522条（q）(1)设定金额的财产获得豁免，则债务人应提交有关是否存在正在进行中的，债务人可能被认定为犯有第522条（q）(1)（A）所述重罪或因第522条（q）(1)（B）所述债务而承担责任的任何程序的声明。

（c）**时间限制**。在自愿破产案件中，申请人应在提交破产申请时或提交破产申请后14日内提交（b）附条的（1）、（4）、（5）和（6）要求的报表、声明以及其他文件，除非本条的（d）、（e）、（f）和（h）附条作出其他规定。在强制破产案件中，债务人应在破产救济令被正式作出后14日内提交（b）附条的（1）要

schedules, statements, and other documents required by subdivision (b) (1) shall be filed by the debtor within 14 days after the entry of the order for relief. In a voluntary case, the documents required by paragraphs (A) , (C) , and (D) of subdivision (b) (3) shall be filed with the petition. Unless the court orders otherwise, a debtor who has filed a statement under subdivision (b) (3) (B) , shall file the documents required by subdivision (b) (3) (A) within 14 days of the order for relief. In a chapter 7 case, the debtor shall file the statement required by subdivision (b) (7) within 60 days after the first date set for the meeting of creditors under §341 of the Code, and in a chapter 11 or 13 case no later than the date when the last payment was made by the debtor as required by the plan or the filing of a motion for a discharge under §1141 (d) (5) (B) or §1328 (b) of the Code. The court may, at any time and in its discretion, enlarge the time to file the statement required by subdivision (b)(7). The debtor shall file the statement required by subdivision (b) (8) no earlier than the date of the last payment made under the plan or the date of the filing of a motion for a discharge under §1141 (d) (5) (B) [①], 1228 (b) , or 1328 (b) of the Code. Lists, schedules, statements, and other documents filed prior to the conversion of a case to another chapter shall be deemed filed in the converted case unless the court directs otherwise. Except as provided in §1116 (3) , any extension of time to file schedules, statements, and other documents required under this rule may be granted only on motion for cause shown and on notice to the United States trustee, any committee elected under §705 or appointed under §1102 of the Code, trustee, examiner, or other party as the court may direct. Notice of an extension shall be given to the United States trustee and to any committee, trustee, or other party as the court may direct.

　　(d) LIST OF 20 LARGEST CREDITORS IN CHAPTER 9 MUNICIPALITY CASE OR CHAPTER 11 REORGANIZATION CASE. In addition to the list required by subdivision (a) of this rule, a debtor in a chapter 9 municipality case or a debtor in a voluntary chapter 11 reorganization case shall file with the petition a list containing the name, address and claim of the creditors that hold the 20 largest unsecured claims,

---

[①] So in original. Probably should be only one section symbol.

求报表、声明以及其他文件。在自愿破产案件中，申请人应在提交破产申请时提交（b）附条（3）的（A）、（C）和（D）要求的文件。除非法院作出其他裁定，否则根据（b）附条（3）（B）提交声明的债务人，应在破产救济令被作出后14日内提交（b）附条（3）（A）要求的文件。在第7章案件中，债务人应在法典第341条中确定的首次债权人会议举行后60日内；在第11章或第13章案件中，债务人应在根据计划支付最后一笔还款或提交动议以根据法典第1141条（d）（5）（B）或第1328条（b）获得免责前，提交（b）附条（7）所要求的声明。法院可在任意时间内，依其自由裁量权，延长用以提交（b）附条（7）所要求的声明的时限。债务人应在根据计划支付最后一笔还款或提交动议以根据法典第1141条（d）（5）（B）①、第1228条（b）或第1328条（b）获得免责前，提交（b）附条（8）所要求的声明。在案件被转换至其他章节规定的程序前已被提交的清单、报表、声明以及其他文件，除非法院作出其他指示，否则均应被视为在转换后的案件中被提交的材料。除第1116条（3）另有规定外，仅当有人就特定事由提出动议，并向联邦托管人、任何根据法典第705条被选任或根据第1102条被任命的委员会、托管人、监督人或者法院可指定的其他主体发出通知时，才可准予延期提交本条所要求的报表、声明和其他文件。就期间的延长应向联邦托管人和任何委员会、托管人或法院可指定的其他主体发出通知。

（d）第9章市政机构破产案件或第11章重整案件中前20名债权人的清单。除本条的（a）附条所要求的清单外，第9章市政机构破产案件或第11章自愿重整案件中的债务人应在提交破产申请时，一同提交根据相应官方模板的规定而准备的，载有其所持无担保债权的金额位列前20名的债权人（除内部人员外）的姓名、住址和债权的清单。在第11章的强制破产重整案件中，债务人应在法典

---

① 原文于此有误。应当仅有一个符号。

excluding insiders, as prescribed by the appropriate Official Form. In an involuntary chapter 11 reorganization case, such list shall be filed by the debtor within 2 days after entry of the order for relief under §303 (h) of the Code.

(e) LIST IN CHAPTER 9 MUNICIPALITY CASES. The list required by subdivision (a) of this rule shall be filed by the debtor in a chapter 9 municipality case within such time as the court shall fix. If a proposed plan requires a revision of assessments so that the proportion of special assessments or special taxes to be assessed against some real property will be different from the proportion in effect at the date the petition is filed, the debtor shall also file a list showing the name and address of each known holder of title, legal or equitable, to real property adversely affected. On motion for cause shown, the court may modify the requirements of this subdivision and subdivision (a) ofthis rule.

(f) STATEMENT OF SOCIAL SECURITY NUMBER. An individual debtor shall submit a verified statement that sets out the debtor's social security number, or states that the debtor does not have a social security number. In a voluntary case, the debtor shall submit the statement with the petition. In an involuntary case, the debtor shall submit the statement within 14 days after the entry of the order for relief.

(g) PARTNERSHIP AND PARTNERS. The general partners of a debtor partnership shall prepare and file the list required under subdivision (a) , schedules of the assets and liabilities, schedule of current income and expenditures, schedule of executory contracts and unexpired leases, and statement of financial affairs of the partnership. The court may order any general partner to file a statement of personal assets and liabilities within such time as the court may fix.

(h) INTERESTS ACQUIRED OR ARISING AFTER PETITION. If, as provided by §541 (a) (5) of the Code, the debtor acquires or becomes entitled to acquire any interest in property, the debtor shall within 14 days after the information comes to the debtor's knowledge or within such further time the court may allow, file a supplemental schedule in the chapter 7 liquidation case, chapter 11 reorganization case, chapter 12 family farmer's debt adjustment case, or chapter 13 individual debt adjustment case. If any of the property required to be reported

第 303 条（h）所述的破产救济令被正式作出后 2 日内提交。

（e）**第 9 章市政机构破产案件中的清单**。本条（a）附条所要求的清单应由第 9 章市政机构的破产案件中的债务人在法院应确定的时间内提交。若拟议的计划要求对评估额进行修正从而使针对不动产核定的特定估价或特殊税的比例与破产申请被提交之日的生效比例有所区别，则债务人也应提交一份清单以列明其不动产受到不利影响的各法定或衡平所有权人的姓名和住址。若有人主张存在特定事由并提出动议，则法院可修改本附条和本条（a）附条中的要求。

（f）**社保账号的说明**。个人债务人应提交经核实的，载有债务人的社保账号或表明其并无社保账号的说明。在自愿破产案件中，债务人应在提交破产申请时，一并提交该声明。在强制破产案件中，债务人应在破产救济令被正式作出后 14 日内提交该声明。

（g）**合伙组织和合伙人**。债务人合伙的普通合伙人应准备并提交（a）附条要求的清单、资产负债表、当前收入支出表、待履行合同和未完成租约的清单以及合伙组织的财务状况的说明。法院可要求任意普通合伙人在法院可确定的时间内提交个人资产和负债的说明。

（h）**申请后取得或产生的权益**。若按照法典第 541 条（a）(5) 的规定，债务人取得或有权取得任何财产权益，则债务人应在其获知该信息后的 14 日内或法院可准予的更长的期间内，在第 7 章清算案件、第 11 章重整案件、第 12 章家庭农场主债务调整案件或第 13 章个人债务调整案件中提交补充清单。若债务人主张豁免本附条中被要求进行报告的财产，则债务人应在该补充清单中主张进行豁免。即使本案结案，债务人仍然承担根据本附条提交补充报表的责任，但若该财产系在批准第 11 章计划的裁定被正式作出后取得或在第 12 章案件或第 13 章

under this subdivision is claimed by the debtor as exempt, the debtor shall claim the exemptions in the supplemental schedule. The duty to file a supplemental schedule in accordance with this subdivision continues notwithstanding the closing of the case, except that the schedule need not be filed in a chapter 11, chapter 12, or chapter 13 case with respect to property acquired after entry of the order confirming a chapter 11 plan or discharging the debtor in a chapter 12 or chapter 13 case.

(i) DISCLOSURE OF LIST OF SECURITY HOLDERS. After notice and hearing and for cause shown, the court may direct an entity other than the debtor or trustee to disclose any list of security holders of the debtor in its possession or under its control, indicating the name, address and security held by any of them. The entity possessing this list may be required either to produce the list or a true copy thereof, or permit inspection or copying, or otherwise disclose the information contained on the list.

(j) IMPOUNDING OF LISTS. On motion of a party in interest and for cause shown the court may direct the impounding of the lists filed under this rule, and may refuse to permit inspection by any entity. The court may permit inspection or use of the lists, however, by any party in interest on terms prescribed by the court.

(k) PREPARATION OF LIST, SCHEDULES, OR STATEMENTS ON DEFAULT OF DEBTOR. If a list, schedule, or statement, other than a statement of intention, is not prepared and filed as required by this rule, the court may order the trustee, a petitioning creditor, committee, or other party to prepare and file any of these papers within a time fixed by the court. The court may approve reimbursement of the cost incurred in complying with such an order as an administrative expense.

(l) TRANSMISSION TO UNITED STATES TRUSTEE. The clerk shall forthwith transmit to the United States trustee a copy of every list, schedule, and statement filed pursuant to subdivision (a)(1), (a)(2), (b), (d), or (h) of this rule.

(m) INFANTS AND INCOMPETENT PERSONS. If the debtor knows that a person on the list of creditors or schedules is an infant or incompetent person, the debtor also shall include the name, address, and legal relationship of any person upon whom

美国联邦破产程序规则
（中英对照译本）

案件中债务人已被免责，则债务人在该情况下无须在第 11 章、第 12 章或第 13 章案件中提交该报表。

（i）**证券持有人清单的披露**。经过通知和听证，出于被主张的特定事由，法院可裁定除债务人或托管人外的实体披露其掌握或控制的债务人的证券持有人的清单，并注明持有人的姓名、住址和持有的证券。掌握该名单的实体可被要求制作该清单或提供真实副本，或准予他人审查或复印，或通过其他方式披露该清单载明的信息。

（j）**清单的没收**。应利益相关方的动议，出于被主张的特定事由，法院可裁定没收根据本条被提交的清单，并可拒绝任何实体进行审查。但法院可准予任何利益相关方按照法院规定的要求审查或使用该清单。

（k）**债务人未能准备清单、报表或声明**。若债务人未能按照本条的要求准备并提交清单、报表或除意向声明外的声明，则法院可裁定托管人、提交破产申请的债权人、委员会或其他主体在法院确定的时间内准备并提交前述任何文件。法院可准予将因遵守该裁定而产生的费用作为管理费用进行报销。

（l）**向联邦托管人移交**。书记员应立刻向联邦托管人移交根据本条的（a）(1)、(a)(2)、(b)、(d) 或 (h) 附条提交的各清单、报表和声明的副本。

（m）**婴儿和无行为能力人**。若债务人已知债权人清单或其他列表上的人为婴儿或无行为能力人，则债务人也应载明若针对婴儿或无行为能力人提起诉讼时，本将根据第 7004 条（b）(2) 的规定向其送达司法文书[①]的任何人的姓名、住址

---

① 法院的传票（summons）和原告的起诉状（complaint）统称为 process，故在此将其译为"司法文书"。——译者注

process would be served in an adversary proceeding against the infant or incompetent person in accordance with Rule 7004 (b) (2) .

(As amended Mar. 30, 1987, eff. Aug. 1, 1987; Apr. 30, 1991, eff. Aug. 1, 1991; Apr. 23, 1996, eff.Dec. 1, 1996; Apr. 23, 2001, eff. Dec. 1, 2001; Mar. 27, 2003, eff. Dec. 1, 2003; Apr. 25, 2005, eff.Dec. 1, 2005; Apr. 23, 2008, eff. Dec. 1, 2008; Mar. 26, 2009, eff. Dec. 1, 2009; Apr. 28, 2010, eff.Dec. 1, 2010; Apr. 23, 2012, eff. Dec. 1, 2012; Apr. 16, 2013, eff. Dec. 1, 2013; Apr. 29, 2015, eff.Dec. 1, 2015.)

Rule 1008. Verification of Petitions and Accompanying Papers

All petitions, lists, schedules, statements and amendments thereto shall be verified or contain an unsworn declaration as provided in 28 U.S.C. §1746.

(As amended Apr. 30, 1991, eff. Aug. 1, 1991.)

Rule 1009. Amendments of Voluntary Petitions, Lists, Schedules and Statements

(a) GENERAL RIGHT TO AMEND. A voluntary petition, list, schedule, or statement may be amended by the debtor as a matter of course at any time before the case is closed. The debtor shall give notice of the amendment to the trustee and to any entity affected thereby. On motion of a party in interest, after notice and a hearing, the court may order any voluntary petition, list, schedule, or statement to be amended and the clerk shall give notice of the amendment to entities designated by the court.

(b) STATEMENT OF INTENTION. The statement of intention may be amended by the debtor at any time before the expiration of the period provided in §521 (a) of the Code. The debtor shall give notice of the amendment to the trustee and to any entity affected thereby.

(c) STATEMENT OF SOCIAL SECURITY NUMBER. If a debtor becomes aware that the statement of social security number submitted under Rule 1007 (f) is incorrect, the debtor shall promptly submit an amended verified statement setting forth the correct social security number. The debtor shall give notice of the amendment to all of the entities required to be included on the list filed under Rule 1007 (a) (1) or (a) (2) .

以及与婴儿或无行为能力人间的法律关系。

（经 Mar. 30, 1987, eff. Aug. 1, 1987; Apr. 30, 1991, eff. Aug. 1, 1991; Apr. 23, 1996, eff.Dec. 1, 1996; Apr. 23, 2001, eff. Dec. 1, 2001; Mar. 27, 2003, eff. Dec. 1, 2003; Apr. 25, 2005, eff.Dec. 1, 2005; Apr. 23, 2008, eff. Dec. 1, 2008; Mar. 26, 2009, eff. Dec. 1, 2009; Apr. 28, 2010, eff.Dec. 1, 2010; Apr. 23, 2012, eff. Dec. 1, 2012; Apr. 16, 2013, eff. Dec. 1, 2013; Apr. 29, 2015, eff.Dec. 1, 2015. 修正）

第1008条　申请和附随文件的核实

所有申请、清单、报表、声明和前述各项的修改均应经过核实或载有美国联邦法典第28篇第1746条规定的声明。①

（经 Apr. 30, 1991, eff. Aug. 1, 1991. 修正）

第1009条　自愿破产申请、清单、报表和声明的修改

（a）**修改的一般权利**。自愿破产申请、清单、报表或声明均可当然由债务人在案件结案前的任意时间内进行修改。债务人应就该修改向托管人或受该修改影响的任何实体发出通知。应利益相关方的动议，经过通知和听证后，法院可裁定对任何自愿破产申请、清单、报表或声明进行修改，并且书记员应就该修改向法院指定的实体发出通知。

（b）**意向声明**。意向声明可由债务人在法典第521条（a）规定的期间届满前的任意时间内进行修改。债务人应就该修改向托管人或受该修改影响的任何实体发出通知。

（c）**社保账号的声明**。若债务人意识到根据第1007条（f）提交的社保账号有误，则债务人应及时提交经过修改和核实的，载明其正确社保账号的声明。债务人应就该修改向所有被要求载入根据第1007条（a）(1)或（a）(2)被提交的清单中的实体。

---

① 根据《美国联邦法典》第28篇第1746条的规定，系指伪证罚则下的声明。——译者注

(d) TRANSMISSION TO UNITED STATES TRUSTEE. The clerk shall promptly transmit to the United States trustee a copy of every amendment filed or submitted under subdivision (a), (b), or (c) of this rule.

(As amended Mar. 30, 1987, eff. Aug. 1, 1987; Apr. 30, 1991, eff. Aug. 1, 1991; Apr. 12, 2006, eff.Dec. 1, 2006; Apr. 23, 2008, eff. Dec. 1, 2008.)

Rule 1010. Service of Involuntary Petition and Summons

(a) SERVICE OF INVOLUNTARY PETITION AND SUMMONS. On the filing of an involuntary petition, the clerk shall forthwith issue a summons for service. When an involuntary petition is filed, service shall be made on the debtor. The summons shall be served with a copy of the petition in the manner provided for service of a summons and complaint by Rule 7004 (a) or (b). If service cannot be so made, the court may order that the summons and petition be served by mailing copies to the party's last known address, and by at least one publication in a manner and form directed by the court. The summons and petition may be served on the party anywhere. Rule 7004 (e) and Rule 4 (1) F.R.Civ.P. apply when service is made or attempted under this rule.

(b) CORPORATE OWNERSHIP STATEMENT. Each petitioner that is a corporation shall file with the involuntary petition a corporate ownership statement containing the information described in Rule 7007.1.

(As amended Mar. 30, 1987, eff. Aug. 1, 1987; Apr. 30, 1991, eff. Aug. 1, 1991; Apr. 22, 1993, eff.Aug. 1, 1993; Apr. 11, 1997, eff. Dec. 1, 1997; Apr. 23, 2008, eff. Dec. 1, 2008; Apr. 28, 2016, eff.Dec. 1, 2016.)

Rule 1011. Responsive Pleading or Motion in Involuntary Cases

(a) WHO MAY CONTEST PETITION. The debtor named in an involuntary petition may contest the petition. In the case of a petition against a partnership under Rule 1004, a nonpetitioning general partner, or a person who is alleged to be a general partner but denies the allegation, may contest the petition.

(b) DEFENSES AND OBJECTIONS; WHEN PRESENTED. Defenses and

（d）**向联邦托管人移交**。书记员应立刻向联邦托管人移交根据本条（a）、（b）或（c）附条被提交的各项修改。

（经 Mar. 30, 1987, eff. Aug. 1, 1987; Apr. 30, 1991, eff. Aug. 1, 1991; Apr. 12, 2006, eff.Dec. 1, 2006; Apr. 23, 2008, eff. Dec. 1, 2008. 修正）

第 1010 条　强制破产申请和传票的送达

（a）**强制破产申请和传票的送达**。在有人提交强制破产申请时，书记员应立刻签发传票并送达。当强制破产申请被提交时，送达的对象为债务人。传票应与申请书的副本一同被按第 7004 条（a）或（b）规定的传票和起诉状的送达方式送达。若不能按照前述方式送达传票，则法院可裁定通过向当事人最后为人所知的住址邮寄传票和申请书的副本的方式来送达，并且至少应按照法院要求的方式和程序进行一次公告送达。传票和通知书可向任何地方的当事人送达。当系根据本条或意图根据本条送达时，适用第 7004 条（e）和《联邦民事诉讼规则》[①]第 4 条（1）的规定。

（b）**法人所有权声明**。各法人申请人应在提交强制破产申请时一并提交载有第 7007.1 所述信息的法人所有权声明。

（经 Mar. 30, 1987, eff. Aug. 1, 1987; Apr. 30, 1991, eff. Aug. 1, 1991; Apr. 22, 1993, eff.Aug. 1, 1993; Apr. 11, 1997, eff. Dec. 1, 1997; Apr. 23, 2008, eff. Dec. 1, 2008; Apr. 28, 2016, eff.Dec. 1, 2016. 修正）

第 1011 条　强制破产案件中的应答文状或动议

（a）**可对破产申请进行答辩的主体**。强制破产申请中列明的债务人可就该申请进行答辩。当破产申请系根据第 1004 条对合伙组织提起，则未参与申请的普通合伙人，或被主张其为普通合伙人但其拒绝该主张的人，可就该申请进行答辩。

（b）**抗辩和异议；当被提出时**。应按照《联邦民事诉讼规则》第 12 条规定

---

① F.R.Civ.P. 的全称为 "Federal Rule of Civil Procedure"，即美国《联邦民事诉讼规则》。——译者注

objections to the petition shall be presented in the manner prescribed by Rule 12 F.R.Civ. P. and shall be filed and served within 21 days after service of the summons, except that if service is made by publication on a party or partner not residing or found within the state in which the court sits, the court shall prescribe the time for filing and serving the response.

(c) EFFECT OF MOTION. Service of a motion under Rule 12 (b) F.R.Civ.P. shall extend the time for filing and serving a responsive pleading as permitted by Rule 12 (a) F.R.Civ.P.

(d) CLAIMS AGAINST PETITIONERS. A claim against a petitioning creditor may not be asserted in the answer except for the purpose of defeating the petition.

(e) OTHER PLEADINGS. No other pleadings shall be permitted, except that the court may order a reply to an answer and prescribe the time for filing and service.

(f) CORPORATE OWNERSHIP STATEMENT. If the entity responding to the involuntary petition is a corporation, the entity shall file with its first appearance, pleading, motion, response, or other request addressed to the court a corporate ownership statement containing the information described in Rule 7007.1.

(As amended Mar. 30, 1987, eff. Aug. 1, 1987; Apr. 26, 2004, eff. Dec. 1, 2004; Apr. 23, 2008, eff.Dec. 1, 2008; Mar. 26, 2009, eff. Dec. 1, 2009; Apr. 28, 2016, eff. Dec. 1, 2016.)

Rule 1012. Responsive Pleading in Cross-Border Cases

(a) WHO MAY CONTEST PETITION. The debtor or any party in interest may contest a petition for recognition of a foreign proceeding.

(b) OBJECTIONS AND RESPONSES; WHEN PRESENTED. Objections and other responses to the petition shall be presented no later than seven days before the date set for the hearing on the petition, unless the court prescribes some other time or manner for responses.

(c) CORPORATE OWNERSHIP STATEMENT. If the entity responding to the petition is a corporation, then the entity shall file a corporate ownership statement containing the information described in Rule 7007.1 with its first appearance, pleading, motion, response, or other request addressed to the court.

的方式提出抗辩和异议,并且应在传票被送达后 21 日内提交并送达,但若系通过公告的方式而向并未居住于法院所在州或在该州并未找到其踪迹的当事人或合伙人送达,则法院应就提交并送达该抗辩的期间作出规定。

(c)**动议的效力**。根据《联邦民事诉讼规则》第 12 条(b)而进行的动议的送达,应按照《联邦民事诉讼规则》第 12 条(a)的规定延长提交并送达抗辩文书的期间。

(d)**对申请人享有的权利主张**。除了出于反驳破产申请的目的,否则不得在答辩状中主张对提交申请的债权人享有的权利主张。

(e)**其他诉状**。除非法院可裁定对答辩状进行回复并规定了提交和送达的时间,否则不得提交其他诉状。

(f)**法人所有权声明**。若就强制破产申请作出答辩的实体为法人,则该实体应在其首次出庭或提交诉状、动议、答辩或其他请求时一并向法院提交载有第 7007.1 条所述信息的法人所有权声明。

(经 Mar. 30, 1987, eff. Aug. 1, 1987; Apr. 26, 2004, eff. Dec. 1, 2004; Apr. 23, 2008, eff.Dec. 1, 2008; Mar. 26, 2009, eff. Dec. 1, 2009; Apr. 28, 2016, eff. Dec. 1, 2016. 修正)

第 1012 条 跨境案件中的应答文状

(a)**可对申请进行答辩的主体**。债务人或任何利益相关方均可就承认外国程序的申请进行答辩。

(b)**抗辩和异议;当被提出时**。除非法院规定了抗辩的其他时间或方式,否则应在确定的就申请举行听证之日前 7 日内提出对申请的异议和其他抗辩。

(c)**法人所有权声明**。若就该申请作出答辩的实体为法人,则该实体应在其首次出庭或提交诉状、动议、答辩或其他请求时一并向法院提交载有第 7007.1 条所述信息的法人所有权声明。

(Added Apr. 28, 2016, eff. Dec. 1, 2016.)

Rule 1013. Hearing and Disposition of a Petition in an Involuntary Case

(a) CONTESTED PETITION. The court shall determine the issues of a contested petition at the earliest practicable time and forthwith enter an order for relief, dismiss the petition, or enter any other appropriate order.

(b) DEFAULT. If no pleading or other defense to a petition is filed within the time provided by Rule 1011, the court, on the next day, or as soon thereafter as practicable, shall enter an order for the relief requested in the petition.

[(c) ORDER FOR RELIEF] (Abrogated Apr. 22, 1993, eff. Aug. 1, 1993)

(As amended Apr. 30, 1991, eff. Aug. 1, 1991; Apr. 22, 1993, eff. Aug. 1, 1993.)

Rule 1014. Dismissal and Change of Venue

(a) DISMISSAL AND TRANSFER OF CASES.

(1) *Cases Filed in Proper District.* If a petition is filed in the proper district, the court, on the timely motion of a party in interest or on its own motion, and after hearing on notice to the petitioners, the United States trustee, and other entities as directed by the court, may transfer the case to any other district if the court determines that the transfer is in the interest of justice or for the convenience of the parties.

(2) *Cases Filed in Improper District.* If a petition is filed in an improper district, the court, on the timely motion of a party in interest or on its own motion, and after hearing on notice to the petitioners, the United States trustee, and other entities as directed by the court, may dismiss the case or transfer it to any other district if the court determines that transfer is in the interest of justice or for the convenience of the parties.

(b) PROCEDURE WHEN PETITIONS INVOLVING THE SAME DEBTOR OR RELATED DEBTORS ARE FILED IN DIFFERENT COURTS. If petitions commencing cases under the Code or seeking recognition under chapter 15 are filed in different districts by, regarding, or against (1) the same debtor, (2) a partnership and one or more of its general partners, (3) two or more general partners, or (4) a debtor

美国联邦破产程序规则
（中英对照译本）

（经 Apr. 28, 2016, eff. Dec. 1, 2016. 增补）

第1013条　在强制破产案件中对申请的听证和处理

（a）**对其提出异议的申请**。法院应在切实可行的情况下，尽快就存在异议的申请中的问题作出决定，并立刻作出破产救济令、驳回破产申请或作出任何其他合适的裁定。

（b）**不存在异议的情况**。若在第1011条规定的时间内无人就申请提交诉状或其他抗辩，则法院应在隔天，或在其后切实可行的情况下尽快，正式就该申请作出破产救济令。

［（c）**破产救济令**］（经 Apr. 22, 1993, eff. Aug. 1, 1993 废除）

（经 Apr. 30, 1991, eff. Aug. 1, 1991; Apr. 22, 1993, eff. Aug. 1, 1993. 修正）

第1014条　驳回和审理法院的变更

（a）**案件的驳回和移送**。

（1）在正确辖区被提交的案件。若破产申请系在正确辖区而被提交，则法院在利益相关方及时提出的动议或其自身的动议下，向申请人、联邦托管人和法院指定的其他实体发出通知并经过听证后，若法院认为将本案移送到其他辖区更符合司法正义和当事人的便利，则法院可将本案移送到其他辖区。

（2）在错误辖区被提交的案件。若破产申请系在错误辖区而被提交，则法院在利益相关方及时提出的动议或其自身的动议下，向申请人、联邦托管人和法院指定的其他实体发出通知并经过听证后，若法院认为将该案驳回或移送到其他辖区更符合司法正义和当事人的便利，则法院可驳回该案或将其移送到任何其他辖区。

（b）**涉及同一债务人或关联债务人的破产申请被提交给不同法院适用的程序**。若根据法典启动破产案件或根据第15章寻求承认的多项申请系在不同辖区而由（1）同一债务人，（2）合伙组织以及其一名或多名普通合伙人，（3）两名或两名以上的普通合伙人，或（4）债务人及其关联方，或者涉及或针对前述主体提交，则最先向其提交申请的辖区内的法院在考虑司法正义和当事人

and an affiliate, the court in the district in which the first-filed petition is pending may determine, in the interest of justice or for the convenience of the parties, the district or districts in which any of the cases should proceed. The court may so determine on motion and after a hearing, with notice to the following entities in the affected cases: the United States trustee, entities entitled to notice under Rule 2002 (a) , and other entities as the court directs. The court may order the parties to the later-filed cases not to proceed further until it makes the determination.

(As amended Mar. 30, 1987, eff. Aug. 1, 1987; Apr. 30, 1991, eff. Aug. 1, 1991; Apr. 30, 2007, eff.Dec. 1, 2007; Apr. 28, 2010, eff. Dec. 1, 2010; Apr. 25, 2014, eff. Dec. 1, 2014.)

Rule 1015. Consolidation or Joint Administration of Cases Pending in Same Court

(a) CASES INVOLVING SAME DEBTOR. If two or more petitions by, regarding, or against the same debtor are pending in the same court, the court may order consolidation of the cases.

(b) CASES INVOLVING TWO OR MORE RELATED DEBTORS. If a joint petition or two or more petitions are pending in the same court by or against (1) spouses, or (2) a partnership and one or more of its general partners, or (3) two or more general partners, or (4) a debtor and an affiliate, the court may order a joint administration of the estates. Prior to entering an order the court shall give consideration to protecting creditors of different estates against potential conflicts of interest. An order directing joint administration of individual cases of spouses shall, if one spouse has elected the exemptions under §522 (b) (2) of the Code and the other has elected the exemptions under §522 (b) (3) , fix a reasonable time within which either may amend the election so that both shall have elected the same exemptions. The order shall notify the debtors that unless they elect the same exemptions within the time fixed by the court, they will be deemed to have elected the exemptions provided by §522 (b) (2) .

(c) EXPEDITING AND PROTECTIVE ORDERS. When an order for consolidation or joint administration of a joint case or two or more cases is entered

的便利的情况下，可决定应当由哪个或哪些辖区审理该些案件。法院应动议，在向受影响的案件中的后述实体：联邦托管人、根据第2002条（a）有权接到通知的实体以及法院指定的其他实体发出通知并举行听证后，可以作出前述决定。法院可裁定后被提交的案件中的当事人在法院作出该决定前不得继续该案件。

（经 Mar. 30, 1987, eff. Aug. 1, 1987; Apr. 30, 1991, eff. Aug. 1, 1991; Apr. 30, 2007, eff.Dec. 1, 2007; Apr. 28, 2010, eff. Dec. 1, 2010; Apr. 25, 2014, eff. Dec. 1, 2014. 修正）

第1015条　同一法院审理的多个案件的合并或共同管理

（a）**涉及同一债务人的多个案件**。若有两项或两项以上的破产申请系由同一债务人，或者涉及或针对同一债务人提交至同一法院，则法院可裁定合并多个案件。

（b）**涉及两名或两名以上关联债务人的多个案件**。若共同破产申请或者两项或两项以上的破产申请系由（1）夫妻双方，（2）合伙组织和其一名或多名普通合伙人，（3）两名或两名以上的普通合伙人或（4）债务人及其关联方，或针对前述主体而提交至同一法院，则法院可裁定对其破产实体进行共同管理。在作出正式裁定前，法院应考虑保护不同破产实体的债权人，避免潜在的利益冲突。在裁定共同管理夫妻双方各自的破产案件的情况下，若一方已经根据法典第522条（b）（2）选择豁免，而另一方已经根据法典第522条（b）（3）选择豁免，则该裁定也应确定任意一方均可修改其选择以便双方就豁免达成共识的合理期间。该裁定应告知债务人除非其在法院确定的期间内就豁免达成共识，否则其将被视为已经选择第522条（b）（2）规定的豁免。

（c）**加速和保护令**。当法院根据本条正式作出合并或共同管理夫妻共同破产案件或者两个或两个以上的案件的裁定，在根据法典保护当事人的权利的同时，

pursuant to this rule, while protecting the rights of the parties under the Code, the court may enter orders as may tend to avoid unnecessary costs and delay.

(As amended Mar. 30, 1987, eff. Aug. 1, 1987; Apr. 23, 2008, eff. Dec. 1, 2008; Apr. 28, 2010, eff.Dec. 1, 2010; Apr. 27, 2017, eff. Dec. 1, 2017.)

Rule 1016. Death or Incompetency of Debtor

Death or incompetency of the debtor shall not abate a liquidation case under chapter 7 of the Code. In such event the estate shall be administered and the case concluded in the same manner, so far as possible, as though the death or incompetency had not occurred. If a reorganization, family farmer's debt adjustment, or individual's debt adjustment case is pending under chapter 11, chapter 12, or chapter 13, the case may be dismissed; or if further administration is possible and in the best interest of the parties, the case may proceed and be concluded in the same manner, so far as possible, as though the death or incompetency had not occurred.

(As amended Apr. 30, 1991, eff. Aug. 1, 1991.)

Rule 1017. Dismissal or Conversion of Case; Suspension

(a) VOLUNTARY DISMISSAL; DISMISSAL FOR WANT OF PROSECUTION OR OTHER CAUSE. Except as provided in §§707 (a)(3), 707 (b), 1208 (b), and 1307 (b) of the Code, and in Rule 1017 (b), (c), and (e), a case shall not be dismissed on motion of the petitioner, for want of prosecution or other cause, or by consent of the parties, before a hearing on notice as provided in Rule 2002. For the purpose of the notice, the debtor shall file a list of creditors with their addresses within the time fixed by the court unless the list was previously filed. If the debtor fails to file the list, the court may order the debtor or another entity to prepare and file it.

(b) DISMISSAL FOR FAILURE TO PAY FILING FEE.

(1) If any installment of the filing fee has not been paid, the court may, after a hearing on notice to the debtor and the trustee, dismiss the case.

(2) If the case is dismissed or closed without full payment of the filing fee, the

法院可作出其他裁定从而避免产生不必要的费用和延迟。

（经 Mar. 30, 1987, eff. Aug. 1, 1987; Apr. 23, 2008, eff. Dec. 1, 2008; Apr. 28, 2010, eff.Dec. 1, 2010; Apr. 27, 2017, eff. Dec. 1, 2017. 修正）

第1016条　债务人的死亡或行为能力的丧失

债务人的死亡或行为能力的丧失不应影响法典第7章清算案件的实施。在这种情况下，应尽可能按照该死亡或丧失行为能力的事件未曾发生的情况下采取的方式来管理破产实体并以相同的方式结案。但在第11章、第12章或第13章中的重整案件、家庭农场主的债务调整或个人债务人的债务调整案件中，该案可被驳回，但若有可能继续实施该案并且这样符合当事人的最大利益，则应尽可能当作该死亡或丧失行为能力的事件未曾发生，继续本案的实施并以相同的方式结案。

（经 Apr. 30, 1991, eff. Aug. 1, 1991. 修正）

第1017条　案件的驳回或转换；中止

（a）**自愿被驳回；因不应诉或其他事由**。除非法典第707（a）（3）、707（b）、1208（b）和1307（b）条以及本法第1017条（b）、（c）和（e）附条中另有规定外，在根据第2002条发出通知并举行听证前，案件不得因申请人的动议、不应诉或其他事由或者多方当事人的同意而被驳回。就该通知而言，债务人应在法院确定的时间内提交债权人名单并载明各债权人的住址，除非该名单先前已被提交。若债务人未能提交该名单，则法院可裁定债务人或其他实体准备并提交该名单。

（b）**因未能支付申请费而被驳回**。

（1）若申请费有任何一期未被支付，则在向债务人和托管人发出通知并举行听证后，法院可驳回该案。

（2）若在未能全额支付申请费的情况下案件被驳回或结案，则已收取的各期

U.S. Federal Rules of Bankruptcy Procedure
(Chinese-English bilingual version)

installments collected shall be distributed in the same manner and proportions as if the filing fee had been paid in full.

(c) DISMISSAL OF VOLUNTARY CHAPTER 7 OR CHAPTER 13 CASE FOR FAILURE TO TIMELY FILE LIST OF CREDITORS, SCHEDULES, AND STATEMENT OF FINANCIAL AFFAIRS. The court may dismiss a voluntary chapter 7 or chapter 13 case under §707 (a) (3) or §1307 (c) (9) after a hearing on notice served by the United States trustee on the debtor, the trustee, and any other entities as the court directs.

(d) SUSPENSION. The court shall not dismiss a case or suspend proceedings under §305 before a hearing on notice as provided in Rule 2002 (a).

(e) DISMISSAL OF AN INDIVIDUAL DEBTOR'S CHAPTER 7 CASE, OR CONVERSION TO A CASE UNDER CHAPTER 11 OR 13, FOR ABUSE. The court may dismiss or, with the debtor's consent, convert an individual debtor's case for abuse under §707 (b) only on motion and after a hearing on notice to the debtor, the trustee, the United States trustee, and any other entity as the court directs.

(1) Except as otherwise provided in §704 (b) (2), a motion to dismiss a case for abuse under §707 (b) or (c) may be filed only within 60 days after the first date set for the meeting of creditors under §341 (a), unless, on request filed before the time has expired, the court for cause extends the time for filing the motion to dismiss. The party filing the motion shall set forth in the motion all matters to be considered at the hearing. In addition, a motion to dismiss under §707 (b) (1) and (3) shall state with particularity the circumstances alleged to constitute abuse.

(2) If the hearing is set on the court's own motion, notice of the hearing shall be served on the debtor no later than 60 days after the first date set for the meeting of creditors under §341 (a). The notice shall set forth all matters to be considered by the court at the hearing.

(f) PROCEDURE FOR DISMISSAL, CONVERSION, OR SUSPENSION.

(1) Rule 9014 governs a proceeding to dismiss or suspend a case, or to convert a case to another chapter, except under §§706 (a), 1112 (a), 1208 (a) or (b), or 1307 (a) or (b).

(2) Conversion or dismissal under §§706 (a), 1112 (a), 1208 (b), or 1307 (b)

美国联邦破产程序规则
（中英对照译本）

费用应按照申请费已被全额支付时本将采用的方式和比例进行分配。

（c）**因未能及时提交债权人名单、报表以及财务状况说明而导致第 7 章或第 13 章自愿破产案件的驳回**。在联邦托管人向债务人、托管人以及法院指定的任何其他实体送达通知并举行听证后，法院可根据法典第 707 条（a）（3）或第 1307 条（c）（9）驳回第 7 章或第 13 章中的自愿破产案件。

（d）**中止**。法院在根据第 2002 条（a）发出通知并举行听证前，不得根据第 305 条驳回案件或中止程序。

（e）**因滥用而导致个人债务人的第 7 章破产案件的驳回或被转换至第 11 章或第 13 章**。仅当有人提出动议，并向债务人、托管人、联邦托管人以及法院指定的任何其他实体发出通知并举行听证后，法院才可因法典第 707 条（b）规定的滥用而驳回个人债务人的破产案件，或在债务人同意的情况下转换案件。

（1）除法典第 704 条（b）（2）中另有规定外，因法典第 707 条（b）或（c）规定的滥用而申请驳回案件的动议仅可在第 341 条（a）中被确定的首次债权人会议之日后 60 日内被提交，除非在该期间届满前有人提交延期申请，并且法院出于特定事由延长了提交驳回案件的动议的期间。提交动议的当事人应在该动议中列明所有需要在听证会上被讨论的事项。除此之外，根据第 707 条（b）（1）和（3）驳回案件的动议应详细载明被主张构成滥用的情形。

（2）若法院应自身动议决定举行听证，则就该听证发出的通知应在第 341 条（a）中被确定的首次债权人会议之日后 60 日内向债务人送达。该通知应列明所有需要在听证上被讨论的事项。

（f）**驳回、转换或中止的程序**。
（1）除法典第 706（a）、1112（a）、1208（a）或（b）、1307（a）或（b）条另有规定外，驳回或中止案件的程序，或将案件转换至另一章节的程序须按照第 9014 条的规定进行。

（2）若要根据法典第 706（a）、1112（a）、1208（b）或 1307（b）条转换或

shall be on motion filed and served as required by Rule 9013.

（3）A chapter 12 or chapter 13 case shall be converted without court order when the debtor files a notice of conversion under §§1208（a）or 1307（a）. The filing date of the notice becomes the date of the conversion order for the purposes of applying §348（c）and Rule 1019. The clerk shall promptly transmit a copy of the notice to the United States trustee.

（As amended Mar. 30, 1987, eff. Aug. 1, 1987; Apr. 30, 1991, eff. Aug. 1, 1991; Apr. 22, 1993, eff.Aug. 1, 1993; Apr. 26, 1999, eff. Dec. 1, 1999; Apr. 17, 2000, eff. Dec. 1, 2000; Apr. 23, 2008, eff.Dec. 1, 2008.）

Rule 1018. Contested Involuntary Petitions; Contested Petitions Commencing Chapter 15 Cases; Proceedings to Vacate Order for Relief; Applicability of Rules in Part VII Governing Adversary Proceedings

Unless the court otherwise directs and except as otherwise prescribed in Part I of these rules, the following rules in Part VII apply to all proceedings contesting an involuntary petition or a chapter 15 petition for recognition, and to all proceedings to vacate an order for relief: Rules 7005, 7008-7010, 7015, 7016, 7024-7026, 7028-7037, 7052, 7054, 7056, and 7062. The court may direct that other rules in Part VII shall also apply. For the purposes of this rule a reference in the Part VII rules to adversary proceedings shall be read as a reference to proceedings contesting an involuntary petition or a chapter 15 petition for recognition, or proceedings to vacate an order for relief. Reference in the Federal Rules of Civil Procedure to the complaint shall be read as a reference to the petition.

（As amended Mar. 30, 1987, eff. Aug. 1, 1987; Apr. 28, 2010, eff. Dec. 1, 2010.）

Rule 1019. Conversion of a Chapter 11 Reorganization Case, Chapter 12 Family Farmer's Debt Adjustment Case, or Chapter 13 Individual's Debt Adjustment Case to a Chapter 7 Liquidation Case

When a chapter 11, chapter 12, or chapter 13 case has been converted or reconverted to a chapter 7 case:

驳回案件，则应按照第 9013 条的要求提交并送达动议。

（3）若债务人根据法典第 1208 条（a）或第 1307 条（a）提交转换通知，则第 12 章或第 13 章案件应直接被转换而无须法院的裁定。就法典第 348 条（c）和本法第 1019 条的适用而言，通知的提交日即为转换裁定被作出之日。书记员应立刻将该通知的副本移交联邦托管人。

（经 Mar. 30, 1987, eff. Aug. 1, 1987; Apr. 30, 1991, eff. Aug. 1, 1991; Apr. 22, 1993, eff.Aug. 1, 1993; Apr. 26, 1999, eff. Dec. 1, 1999; Apr. 17, 2000, eff. Dec. 1, 2000; Apr. 23, 2008, eff.Dec. 1, 2008. 修正）

第 1018 条　对其提出异议的强制破产申请；对其提出异议的启动第 15 章程序的申请；撤销破产救济令的程序；第 VII 部分规制诉讼程序的规则的适用

除非法院作出其他指示或第 I 部分中的条文作出其他规定，否则第 VII 部分的后述条文将适用于所有就强制破产申请或第 15 章承认申请提出异议的程序或撤销破产救济令的程序：第 7005、7008 至 7010、7015、7016、7024 至 7026、7028 至 7037、7052、7054、7056 及 7062 条。法院可指定适用第 VII 部分中的其他条文。就本条而言，第 VII 部分条文中提到的诉讼程序应被理解为就强制破产申请或第 15 章承认申请提出异议的程序或撤销破产救济令的程序。在《联邦民事诉讼规则》中提到的起诉状应被视为前述申请。

（经 Mar. 30, 1987, eff. Aug. 1, 1987; Apr. 28, 2010, eff. Dec. 1, 2010. 修正）

第 1019 条　第 11 章重整案件、第 12 章家庭农场主债务调整案件或第 13 章个人债务调整案件至第 7 章清算案件的转换

当第 11 章、第 12 章或第 13 章案件已经被转换或再次被转换至第 7 章案件时：

(1) *Filing of Lists, Inventories, Schedules, Statements.*

(A) Lists, inventories, schedules, and statements of financial affairs theretofore filed shall be deemed to be filed in the chapter 7 case, unless the court directs otherwise. If they have not been previously filed, the debtor shall comply with Rule 1007 as if an order for relief had been entered on an involuntary petition on the date of the entry of the order directing that the case continue under chapter 7.

(B) If a statement of intention is required, it shall be filed within 30 days after entry of the order of conversion or before the first date set for the meeting of creditors, whichever is earlier.

The court may grant an extension of time for cause only on written motion filed, or oral request made during a hearing, before the time has expired. Notice of an extension shall be given to the United States trustee and to any committee, trustee, or other party as the court may direct.

(2) *New Filing Periods.*

(A) A new time period for filing a motion under §707 (b) or (c), a claim, a complaint objecting to discharge, or a complaint to obtain a determination of dischargeability of any debt shall commence under Rules[①] 1017, 3002, 4004, or 4007, but a new time period shall not commence if a chapter 7 case had been converted to a chapter 11, 12, or 13 case and thereafter reconverted to a chapter 7 case and the time for filing a motion under §707 (b) or (c), a claim, a complaint objecting to discharge, or a complaint to obtain a determination of the dischargeability of any debt, or any extension thereof, expired in the original chapter 7 case.

(B) A new time period for filing an objection to a claim of exemptions shall commence under Rule 4003 (b) after conversion of a case to chapter 7 unless:

(i) the case was converted to chapter 7 more than one year after the entry of the first order confirming a plan under chapter 11, 12, or 13; or

(ii) the case was previously pending in chapter 7 and the time to object to a claimed exemption had expired in the original chapter 7 case.

[①] So in original. Probably should be "Rule".

美国联邦破产程序规则
（中英对照译本）

（1）名单、财产清单、报表、声明的提交。

（A）除非法院作出其他指示，否则先前已提交的名单、财产清单、报表和财务状况说明应被视为在第7章案件中被提交。若先前无人提交前述文件，则债务人应将正式裁定按照第7章程序继续进行该案之日视为就强制破产申请作出破产救济令之日，并遵守第1007的规定。

（B）若要求提交意向声明，则其应在转换裁定被正式作出之日后30日内，或在确定的首次债权人会议之日前，以二者中较早者为准，而被提交。

仅当在前述期间届满前，有人提交书面动议或在听证中作出口头请求的情况下，法院才可出于特定事由准予延期。就期间的延长应向联邦托管人以及任何委员会、托管人或法院可指定的其他主体发出通知。

（2）新的提交期间。

（A）用于根据第707条（b）或（c）提交动议，或提交债权、反对免责的控告或为了获得任何债务的免责认定而提出的异议的新的期间，应根据第1017、3002、4004或4007条的规定启动，但若案件曾被从第7章程序转换至第11、12或13章程序，后又被重新转换至第7章程序，并且用于根据第707条（b）或（c）提交动议，或提交债权、反对免责的控告或为了获得任何债务的免责认定而提出的异议的期间或延长的期间在原第7章案件中已经届满，则不得启用新的期间。

（B）除下列情形外，用于提交对豁免主张的异议的新的期间应在案件被转换至第7章程序后根据第4003条（b）的规定启用：

（i）在首次根据第11、12或13章正式作出批准计划的裁定1年以后，案件才被转换至第7章；或

（ii）案件先前曾根据第7章进行，并且在原第7章案件中就被主张的豁免提出异议的期间已经届满。

(3) *Claims Filed Before Conversion.* All claims actually filed by a creditor before conversion of the case are deemed filed in the chapter 7 case.

(4) *Turnover of Records and Property.* After qualification of, or assumption of duties by the chapter 7 trustee, any debtor in possession or trustee previously acting in the chapter 11, 12, or 13 case shall, forthwith, unless otherwise ordered, turn over to the chapter 7 trustee all records and property of the estate in the possession or control of the debtor in possession or trustee.

(5) *Filing Final Report and Schedule of Postpetition Debts.*

(A) *Conversion of Chapter 11 or Chapter 12 Case.* Unless the court directs otherwise, if a chapter 11 or chapter 12 case is converted to chapter 7, the debtor in possession or, if the debtor is not a debtor in possession, the trustee serving at the time of conversion, shall:

(i) not later than 14 days after conversion of the case, file a schedule of unpaid debts incurred after the filing of the petition and before conversion of the case, including the name and address of each holder of a claim; and

(ii) not later than 30 days after conversion of the case, file and transmit to the United States trustee a final report and account;

(B) *Conversion of Chapter 13 Case.* Unless the court directs otherwise, if a chapter 13 case is converted to chapter 7,

(i) the debtor, not later than 14 days after conversion of the case, shall file a schedule of unpaid debts incurred after the filing of the petition and before conversion of the case, including the name and address of each holder of a claim; and

(ii) the trustee, not later than 30 days after conversion of the case, shall file and transmit to the United States trustee a final report and account;

(C) *Conversion After Confirmation of a Plan.* Unless the court orders otherwise, if a chapter 11, chapter 12, or chapter 13 case is converted to chapter 7 after confirmation of a plan, the debtor shall file:

(i) a schedule of property not listed in the final report and account acquired after the filing of the petition but before conversion, except if the case is converted from chapter 13 to chapter 7 and §348 (f) (2) does not apply;

美国联邦破产程序规则
（中英对照译本）

（3）转换前提交的债权。实际在案件被转换前由债权人提交的所有债权均被视为在第7章案件中被提交的债权。

（4）移交资料和财产。当第7章托管人符合资格并且承继职责后，除非法院作出其他裁定，否则原第11、12或13章案件中的任何经管债务人或托管人均应立刻向第7章托管人移交其占有或控制的破产实体的所有材料和财产。

（5）提交最终报告和申请破产后产生的债务的报表。

（A）第11章或第12章案件的转换。除非法院作出其他指示，否则若第11章或第12章案件被转换至第7章案件，则经管债务人，或当债务人不是经管债务人的情况下，在案件被转换时履职的托管人应履行以下各项：

（i）在案件被转换后14日内，提交在破产申请被提交后，但在案件被转换前成立的任何尚未清偿的债务的清单，包括各债权人的姓名和住址；以及

（ii）在案件被转换后30日内，提交并向联邦托管人移送最终报告和账目；

（B）第13章案件的转换。除非法院作出其他指示，否则若第13章案件被转换至第7章案件，则

（i）在案件被转换后14日内，债务人应提交在破产申请被提交后，但在案件被转换前成立的任何尚未清偿的债务的清单，包括各债权人的姓名和住址；以及

（ii）在案件被转换后30日内，托管人应提交并向联邦托管人移送最终报告和账目；

（C）计划得到批准后的转换。除非法院作出其他裁定，否则若第11章、第12章或第13章案件系在计划得到批准后被转换至第7章案件，则债务人应提交以下各项：

（i）在破产申请被提交后，但在转换前取得的，未被列入最终报告和账目的财产的清单，除非案件系由第13章转换至第7章并且不适用法典第348条（f）（2）；

(ⅱ) a schedule of unpaid debts not listed in the final report and account incurred after confirmation but before the conversion; and

(ⅲ) a schedule of executory contracts and unexpired leases entered into or assumed after the filing of the petition but before conversion.

(D) *Transmission to United States Trustee.* The clerk shall forthwith transmit to the United States trustee a copy of every schedule filed pursuant to Rule 1019 (5).

(6) *Postpetition Claims; Preconversion Administrative Expenses; Notice.* A request for payment of an administrative expense incurred before conversion of the case is timely filed under §503 (a) of the Code if it is filed before conversion or a time fixed by the court. If the request is filed by a governmental unit, it is timely if it is filed before conversion or within the later of a time fixed by the court or 180 days after the date of the conversion. A claim of a kind specified in §348 (d) may be filed in accordance with Rules 3001 (a) - (d) and 3002. Upon the filing of the schedule of unpaid debts incurred after commencement of the case and before conversion, the clerk, or some other person as the court may direct, shall give notice to those entities listed on the schedule of the time for filing a request for payment of an administrative expense and, unless a notice of insufficient assets to pay a dividend is mailed in accordance with Rule 2002 (e), the time for filing a claim of a kind specified in §348 (d).

(As amended Mar. 30, 1987, eff. Aug. 1, 1987; Apr. 30, 1991, eff. Aug. 1, 1991; Apr. 23, 1996, eff.Dec. 1, 1996; Apr. 11, 1997, eff. Dec. 1, 1997; Apr. 26, 1999, eff. Dec. 1, 1999; Apr. 23, 2008, eff.Dec. 1, 2008; Mar. 26, 2009, eff. Dec. 1, 2009; Apr. 28, 2010, eff. Dec. 1, 2010.)

Rule 1020. Small Business Chapter 11 Reorganization Case

(a) SMALL BUSINESS DEBTOR DESIGNATION. In a voluntary chapter 11 case, the debtor shall state in the petition whether the debtor is a small business debtor. In an involuntary chapter 11 case, the debtor shall file within 14 days after entry of the order for relief a statement as to whether the debtor is a small business debtor. Except as

（ii）在计划得到批准后，但在转换前成立的未被列入最终报告和账目中的尚未清偿的债务的清单；以及

（iii）破产申请被提交后，但在转换前签订或承继的待履行合同和未完成租约的清单。

（D）向联邦托管人移送。书记员应立刻将根据第1019条（5）被提交的各清单的副本移送联邦托管人。

（6）提交破产申请后成立的债权；案件转换前的管理费用；通知。针对就支付案件被转换前发生的管理费用的请求，若其在案件被转换前或法院确定的期间内被提交，则被视为根据法典第503条（a）已被按时提交。若该请求系由政府机构所提交，则若其在案件被转换前，或法院确定的期间或案件被转换后180日内（二者中较晚者）被提交，则被视为已被按时提交。第348条（d）所述的债权可根据本法第3001条（a）至（d）以及第3002条被提交。针对在案件启动后，但在案件被转换前成立的债务，在提交尚未清偿的前述债务的清单时，书记员或法院可指定的其他人应向清单上所列的实体通知提交管理费付费申请的时间，并且除非根据第2002条（e）邮寄了没有资产用于还款的通知，否则也应向其通知提交法典第348条（d）规定的债权的时间。

（经 Mar. 30, 1987, eff. Aug. 1, 1987; Apr. 30, 1991, eff. Aug. 1, 1991; Apr. 23, 1996, eff. Dec. 1, 1996; Apr. 11, 1997, eff. Dec. 1, 1997; Apr. 26, 1999, eff. Dec. 1, 1999; Apr. 23, 2008, eff. Dec. 1, 2008; Mar. 26, 2009, eff. Dec. 1, 2009; Apr. 28, 2010, eff. Dec. 1, 2010. 修正）

第1020条　第11章小企业重整案件

（a）小企业债务人的认定。在第11章中的自愿破产案件里，债务人应在破产申请中注明其是否为小企业债务人。在第11章中的强制破产案件里，在破产救济令被正式作出后14日内，债务人应提交一份声明以表明其是否为小企业债务人。除（c）附条另有规定外，应按照债务人根据本附条所作的声明确定案件是否为小企业破产案件，除非并且直至法院正式作出裁定认定债务

provided in subdivision (c), the status of the case as a small business case shall be in accordance with the debtor's statement under this subdivision, unless and until the court enters an order finding that the debtor's statement is incorrect.

(b) OBJECTING TO DESIGNATION. Except as provided in subdivision (c), the United States trustee or a party in interest may file an objection to the debtor's statement under subdivision (a) no later than 30 days after the conclusion of the meeting of creditors held under §341 (a) of the Code, or within 30 days after any amendment to the statement, whichever is later.

(c) APPOINTMENT OF COMMITTEE OF UNSECURED CREDITORS. If a committee of unsecured creditors has been appointed under §1102 (a)(1), the case shall proceed as a small business case only if, and from the time when, the court enters an order determining that the committee has not been sufficiently active and representative to provide effective oversight of the debtor and that the debtor satisfies all the other requirements for being a small business. A request for a determination under this subdivision may be filed by the United States trustee or a party in interest only within a reasonable time after the failure of the committee to be sufficiently active and representative. The debtor may file a request for a determination at any time as to whether the committee has been sufficiently active and representative.

(d) PROCEDURE FOR OBJECTION OR DETERMINATION. Any objection or request for a determination under this rule shall be governed by Rule 9014 and served on: the debtor; the debtor's attorney; the United States trustee; the trustee; any committee appointed under §1102 or its authorized agent, or, if no committee of unsecured creditors has been appointed under §1102, the creditors included on the list filed under Rule 1007 (d); and any other entity as the court directs.

(Added Apr. 11, 1997, eff. Dec. 1, 1997; amended Apr. 23, 2008, eff. Dec. 1, 2008; Mar. 26, 2009,eff. Dec. 1, 2009.)

Rule 1021. Health Care Business Case

(a) HEALTH CARE BUSINESS DESIGNATION. Unless the court orders

人的声明有误。

（b）**对该认定的异议**。除（c）附条另有规定外，联邦托管人或利益相关方可在根据法典第341条（a）举行的债权人会议结束后30日内或在就（a）附条中债务人的声明作出任何修改后30日内，以二者中较晚者为准，就该声明提交异议。

（c）**无担保债权人委员会的任命**。若无担保债权人委员会已被根据第1102条（a）（1）任命，则仅当且仅从法院正式裁定认定该委员会没有足够的积极性和代表性来对债务人进行有效的监督，并且该债务人满足小企业的所有其他要求时，该案才应作为小企业破产案件继续进行。联邦托管人或利益相关方可在委员会丧失足够的积极性和代表性后的合理时间内根据本附条申请法院作出认定。债务人可随时请求法院作出认定，无论该委员会是否有足够的积极性和代表性。

（d）**异议或认定的程序**。本条中就该认定的任何异议或请求均应按照第9014条的规定进行并送达给：债务人、债务人的律师、联邦托管人、托管人；根据法典第1102条任命的任何委员或其授权的代理机构，或者若尚未根据第1102条任命无担保债权人委员会，则为根据本法第1007条（d）提交的名单上所列的债权人以及法院指定的任何其他实体。

（经 Apr. 11, 1997, eff. Dec. 1, 1997; amended Apr. 23, 2008, eff. Dec. 1, 2008; Mar. 26, 2009, eff. Dec. 1, 2009. 增补）

第1021条　医疗护理机构破产案件

（a）**医疗护理机构的认定**。除非法院作出其他裁定，否则若第7章、第9章

otherwise, if a petition in a case under chapter 7, chapter 9, or chapter 11 states that the debtor is a health care business, the case shall proceed as a case in which the debtor is a health care business.

(b) MOTION. The United States trustee or a party in interest may file a motion to determine whether the debtor is a health care business. The motion shall be transmitted to the United States trustee and served on: the debtor; the trustee; any committee elected under §705 or appointed under §1102 of the Code or its authorized agent, or, if the case is a chapter 9 municipality case or a chapter 11 reorganization case and no committee of unsecured creditors has been appointed under §1102, the creditors included on the list filed under Rule 1007 (d); and any other entity as the court directs. The motion shall be governed by Rule 9014.

(Added Apr. 23, 2008, eff. Dec. 1, 2008.)

或第 11 章案件中的破产申请中注明债务人为医疗护理机构，则该案应按医疗护理机构破产案件进行。

（b）**动议**。联邦托管人或利益相关方可提交动议以申请就债务人是否为医疗护理机构作出认定。该动议应被移送至联邦托管人并送达给：债务人、托管人；根据法典第 705 条选任或根据第 1102 条任命的任何委员会或其授权的代理机构，或者，若该案为第 9 章市政机构破产案件或第 11 章重整案件，并且尚未根据第 1102 条任命无担保债权人委员会，则为根据本法第 1007 条（d）提交的名单中所列的债权人；以及法院指定的任何其他实体。该动议应按照第 9014 条的规定进行。

（经 Apr. 23, 2008, eff. Dec. 1, 2008. 增补）

PART II

OFFICERS AND ADMINISTRATION; NOTICES; MEETINGS; EXAMINATIONS; ELECTIONS; ATTORNEYS AND ACCOUNTANTS

Rule 2001. Appointment of Interim Trustee Before Order for Relief in a Chapter 7 Liquidation Case

(a) APPOINTMENT. At any time following the commencement of an involuntary liquidation case and before an order for relief, the court on written motion of a party in interest may order the appointment of an interim trustee under §303 (g) of the Code. The motion shall set forth the necessity for the appointment and may be granted only after hearing on notice to the debtor, the petitioning creditors, the United States trustee, and other parties in interest as the court may designate.

(b) BOND OF MOVANT. An interim trustee may not be appointed under this rule unless the movant furnishes a bond in an amount approved by the court, conditioned to indemnify the debtor for costs, attorney's fee, expenses, and damages allowable under §303 (i) of the Code.

(c) ORDER OF APPOINTMENT. The order directing the appointment of an interim trustee shall state the reason the appointment is necessary and shall specify the trustee's duties.

(d) TURNOVER AND REPORT. Following qualification of the trustee selected under §702 of the Code, the interim trustee, unless otherwise ordered, shall (1) forthwith deliver to the trustee all the records and property of the estate in possession or subject to control of the interim trustee and, (2) within 30 days thereafter file a final report and account.

(As amended Mar. 30, 1987, eff. Aug. 1, 1987; Apr. 30, 1991, eff. Aug. 1, 1991.)

第 II 部分
破产从业人员和案件的管理；
通知；会议；质询；选任；律师和会计师

第 2001 条　第 7 章清算案件中破产救济令被作出前临时托管人的任命

（a）**任命**。在强制清算案件启动后，但在破产救济令被作出前的任意时间内，法院应利益相关方的书面动议，可裁定根据法典第 303 条（g）任命临时托管人。该动议应载明该任命的必要性并且仅当向债务人、提交申请的债权人、联邦托管人以及法院可指定的其他利益相关方发出通知并举行听证后，该动议才可被准予。

（b）**动议人的保证金**。除非动议人提交法院确定的数额的保证金，用于补偿债务人根据法典第 303 条（i）而确定的成本、律师费、支出和损害，否则不得根据本条任命临时托管人。

（c）**任命的裁定**。裁定任命临时托管人的裁定应写明进行该任命的必要性并应列明托管人的职责。

（d）**移交和报告**。在根据法典第 702 条选任的托管人符合资格后，除非法院作出其他裁定，否则临时托管人应（1）立刻向托管人移交其占有或控制的破产实体的所有资料和财产，并且（2）在此后 30 日内提交最终报告和账目。

（经 Mar. 30, 1987, eff. Aug. 1, 1987; Apr. 30, 1991, eff. Aug. 1, 1991. 修正）

U.S. Federal Rules of Bankruptcy Procedure
(Chinese-English bilingual version)

Rule 2002. Notices to Creditors, Equity Security Holders, Administrators in Foreign Proceedings, Persons Against Whom Provisional Relief is Sought in Ancillary and Other Cross-Border Cases, United States, and United States Trustee

(a) TWENTY-ONE-DAY NOTICES TO PARTIES IN INTEREST. Except as provided in subdivisions (h), (i), (l), (p), and (q) of this rule, the clerk, or some other person as the court may direct, shall give the debtor, the trustee, all creditors and indenture trustees at least 21 days' notice by mail of:

(1) the meeting of creditors under §341 or §1104 (b) of the Code, which notice, unless the court orders otherwise, shall include the debtor's employer identification number, social security number, and any other federal taxpayer identification number;

(2) a proposed use, sale, or lease of property of the estate other than in the ordinary course of business, unless the court for cause shown shortens the time or directs another method of giving notice;

(3) the hearing on approval of a compromise or settlement of a controversy other than approval of an agreement pursuant to Rule 4001 (d), unless the court for cause shown directs that notice not be sent;

(4) in a chapter 7 liquidation, a chapter 11 reorganization case, or a chapter 12 family farmer debt adjustment case, the hearing on the dismissal of the case or the conversion of the case to another chapter, unless the hearing is under §707 (a) (3) or §707 (b) or is on dismissal of the case for failure to pay the filing fee;

(5) the time fixed to accept or reject a proposed modification of a plan;

(6) a hearing on any entity's request for compensation or reimbursement of expenses if the request exceeds $1,000;

(7) the time fixed for filing proofs of claims pursuant to Rule 3003 (c);

(8) the time fixed for filing objections and the hearing to consider confirmation of a chapter 12 plan; and

(9) the time fixed for filing objections to confirmation of a chapter 13 plan.

(b) TWENTY-EIGHT-DAY NOTICES TO PARTIES IN INTEREST. Except as

美国联邦破产程序规则
(中英对照译本)

第 2002 条　向债权人、股本证券持有人、外国程序中的管理人、在辅助程序和其他跨境案件中寻求的临时救济所针对的人、美国政府机构和联邦托管人发出通知

（a）**提前 21 日向利益相关方发出通知**。除本条的（h）、（i）、（l）、（p）和（q）另有规定外，书记员或法院可指定的其他人应至少提前 21 日通过邮寄的方式向债务人、托管人、所有债权人和契约受托人就以下事项发出通知：

（1）法典第 341 条或第 1104 条（b）中的债权人会议，并且除非法院作出其他裁定，否则该通知应载有债务人的雇主身份号码、社保账号和任何其他联邦纳税人身份号码；

（2）在常规营业范围外对破产财产的计划使用、出售或出租，除非法院出于被主张的特定事由而缩短发出通知的时间或就发出通知的方式作出其他指示；

（3）除了根据第 4001 条（d）达成的协议的批准外，就争议事项的和解的批准而举行的听证，除非法院出于被主张的特定事由决定不发出该通知；

（4）在第 7 章清算案件、第 11 章重整案件或第 12 章家庭农场主债务调整案件中，就案件的驳回或案件被转换至其他章节而举行的听证，除非该听证系根据法典第 707 条（a）（3）或第 707 条（b）而举行的听证或该案系因未能支付申请费而被驳回；

（5）确定的用于接受或拒绝计划的拟议修改的时间；
（6）当某实体请求的报酬或报销的费用的金额超过 1000 美元时，就该实体的请求而举行的听证；
（7）确定的用于根据第 3003 条（c）提交债权证明的时间；
（8）确定的用于就第 12 章计划的批准提出异议和举行听证的时间；以及
（9）确定的用于就第 13 章计划的批准提出异议的时间。
（b）**提前 28 日向利益相关方发出通知**。除本条（1）附条另有规定外，书记

provided in subdivision (1) of this rule, the clerk, or some other person as the court may direct, shall give the debtor, the trustee, all creditors and indenture trustees not less than 28 days' notice by mail of the time fixed (1) for filing objections and the hearing to consider approval of a disclosure statement or, under §1125 (f), to make a final determination whether the plan provides adequate information so that a separate disclosure statement is not necessary; (2) for filing objections and the hearing to consider confirmation of a chapter 9 or chapter 11 plan; and (3) for the hearing to consider confirmation of a chapter 13 plan.

(c) CONTENT OF NOTICE.

(1) *Proposed Use, Sale, or Lease of Property*. Subject to Rule 6004, the notice of a proposed use, sale, or lease of property required by subdivision (a)(2) of this rule shall include the time and place of any public sale, the terms and conditions of any private sale and the time fixed for filing objections. The notice of a proposed use, sale, or lease of property, including real estate, is sufficient if it generally describes the property. The notice of a proposed sale or lease of personally identifiable information under §363 (b)(1) of the Code shall state whether the sale is consistent with any policy prohibiting the transfer of the information.

(2) *Notice of Hearing on Compensation*. The notice of a hearing on an application for compensation or reimbursement of expenses required by subdivision (a)(6) of this rule shall identify the applicant and the amounts requested.

(3) *Notice of Hearing on Confirmation When Plan Provides for an Injunction*. If a plan provides for an injunction against conduct not otherwise enjoined under the Code, the notice required under Rule 2002 (b)(2) shall:

(A) include in conspicuous language (bold, italic, or underlined text) a statement that the plan proposes an injunction;

(B) describe briefly the nature of the injunction; and

(C) identify the entities that would be subject to the injunction.

(d) NOTICE TO EQUITY SECURITY HOLDERS. In a chapter 11 reorganization case, unless otherwise ordered by the court, the clerk, or some other person as the court may direct, shall in the manner and form directed by the court give

美国联邦破产程序规则
（中英对照译本）

员或法院可指定的其他人应至少提前 28 日通过邮寄的方式向债务人、托管人、所有债权人和契约受托人就确定的用于以下事项的时间发出通知：（1）就披露声明的批准提出异议和举行听证，或根据第 1125 条（f），为了判断是否有必要提供单独的披露声明而就计划是否提供有充分信息作出最终认定而提出异议和举行听证；（2）就第 9 章和第 11 章计划的批准提出异议和举行听证；以及（3）就第 13 章计划的批准而举行的听证。

（c）通知的内容。

（1）财产的计划使用、出售或出租。在符合第 6004 条规定的情况下，本条（a）附条（2）要求的就财产的计划使用、出售或出租的通知应载明任何公开出售的时间和地点、任何私人出售的条款和条件以及确定的用于提交异议的时间。就财产（包括不动产）的计划使用、出售或出租的通知只需大致描述该财产。就法典第 363 条（b）（1）中的个人身份信息的计划出售或出租的通知应注明该出售是否符合任何禁止转让信息的政策。

（2）就报酬举行听证的通知。本条（a）（6）要求就报酬或报销费用的申请举行听证的通知应载明申请人的身份和其请求的金额。

（3）就规定有禁令的计划的批准举行听证的通知。若计划规定的禁令并不属于法典所禁止的行为，则第 2002 条（b）（2）所要求的通知应符合以下条件：

（A）以醒目的方式（粗体、斜体或下画线）载明该计划规定有禁令；

（B）简述该禁令的性质；以及

（C）列明该禁令所将针对的实体。

（d）向股本证券持有人发出的通知。 在第 11 章重整案件中，除非法院作出其他裁定，否则书记员或法院可指定的其他人应按照法院指定的方式和形式向所有股本证券持有人就以下各项发出通知：（1）破产救济令；（2）根据法典第 341

notice to all equity security holders of (1) the order for relief; (2) any meeting of equity security holders held pursuant to §341 of the Code; (3) the hearing on the proposed sale of all or substantially all of the debtor's assets; (4) the hearing on the dismissal or conversion of a case to another chapter; (5) the time fixed for filing objections to and the hearing to consider approval of a disclosure statement; (6) the time fixed for filing objections to and the hearing to consider confirmation of a plan; and (7) the time fixed to accept or reject a proposed modification of a plan.

(e) NOTICE OF NO DIVIDEND. In a chapter 7 liquidation case, if it appears from the schedules that there are no assets from which a dividend can be paid, the notice of the meeting of creditors may include a statement to that effect; that it is unnecessary to file claims; and that if sufficient assets become available for the payment of a dividend, further notice will be given for the filing of claims.

(f) OTHER NOTICES. Except as provided in subdivision (1) of this rule, the clerk, or some other person as the court may direct, shall give the debtor, all creditors, and indenture trustees notice by mail of:

(1) the order for relief;

(2) the dismissal or the conversion of the case to another chapter, or the suspension of proceedings under §305;

(3) the time allowed for filing claims pursuant to Rule 3002;

(4) the time fixed for filing a complaint objecting to the debtor's discharge pursuant to §727 of the Code as provided in Rule 4004;

(5) the time fixed for filing a complaint to determine the dischargeability of a debt pursuant to §523 of the Code as provided in Rule 4007;

(6) the waiver, denial, or revocation of a discharge as provided in Rule 4006;

(7) entry of an order confirming a chapter 9, 11, 12 or 13 plan;

(8) a summary of the trustee's final report in a chapter 7 case if the net proceeds realized exceed $1,500;

(9) a notice under Rule 5008 regarding the presumption of abuse;

(10) a statement under §704 (b) (1) as to whether the debtor's case would be presumed to be an abuse under §707 (b); and

美国联邦破产程序规则
（中英对照译本）

条举行的任何股本证券持有人会议；（3）就债务人全部或几乎全部资产的计划出售举行的听证；（4）就案件的驳回或被转换至其他章节举行的听证；（5）确定的用于就披露声明的批准提出异议和举行听证的时间；（6）确定的用于就计划的批准提出异议和举行听证的时间；以及（7）确定的用于接受或拒绝计划的拟议修改的时间。

（e）**就无法还款而发出的通知**。在第 7 章清算案件中，若从报表中显示，没有可以用于还款的资产，则就债权人会议而发出的通知中可载明其后果；并说明无提交债权的必要；以及若其后有充足的资产用于还款，则之后将就提交债权而向其发出通知。

（f）**其他通知**。除本条（1）附条另有规定外，书记员或法院可指定的其他人应通过邮寄的方式向债务人、所有债权人和契约受托人就以下事项发出通知：

（1）破产救济令；

（2）案件被驳回或被转换至其他章节规定的程序，或第 305 条中程序的中止；

（3）根据第 3002 条确定的用于提交债权的时间；

（4）根据第 4004 条确定的，用于根据法典第 727 条就债务人的免责提交异议的时间；

（5）根据第 4007 条确定的，用于根据法典第 523 条就债务是否可被予以免责的认定提交申诉的时间；

（6）第 4006 条中免责的放弃、拒绝或撤销；

（7）正式作出批准第 9、11、12 或 13 章计划的裁定；

（8）当实现的净收益超过 1500 美元时，第 7 章案件中托管人的最终报告的摘要；

（9）第 5008 条中滥用推定的通知；

（10）法典第 704 条（b）（1）中涉及债务人的破产案件根据第 707 条（b）是否会被推定为滥用（破产）的声明；以及

U.S. Federal Rules of Bankruptcy Procedure
(Chinese-English bilingual version)

(11) the time to request a delay in the entry of the discharge under §§1141(d)(5)(C), 1228(f), and 1328(h). Notice of the time fixed for accepting or rejecting a plan pursuant to Rule 3017(c) shall be given in accordance with Rule 3017(d).

(g) ADDRESSING NOTICES.

(1) Notices required to be mailed under Rule 2002 to a creditor, indenture trustee, or equity security holder shall be addressed as such entity or an authorized agent has directed in its last request filed in the particular case. For the purposes of this subdivision—

(A) a proof of claim filed by a creditor or indenture trustee that designates a mailing address constitutes a filed request to mail notices to that address, unless a notice of no dividend has been given under Rule 2002(e) and a later notice of possible dividend under Rule 3002(c)(5) has not been given; and

(B) a proof of interest filed by an equity security holder that designates a mailing address constitutes a filed request to mail notices to that address.

(2) Except as provided in §342(f) of the Code, if a creditor or indenture trustee has not filed a request designating a mailing address under Rule 2002(g)(1) or Rule 5003(e), the notices shall be mailed to the address shown on the list of creditors or schedule of liabilities, whichever is filed later. If an equity security holder has not filed a request designating a mailing address under Rule 2002(g)(1) or Rule 5003(e), the notices shall be mailed to the address shown on the list of equity security holders.

(3) If a list or schedule filed under Rule 1007 includes the name and address of a legal representative of an infant or incompetent person, and a person other than that representative files a request or proof of claim designating a name and mailing address that differs from the name and address of the representative included in the list or schedule, unless the court orders otherwise, notices under Rule 2002 shall be mailed to the representative included in the list or schedules and to the name and address designated in the request or proof of claim.

(4) Notwithstanding Rule 2002(g)(1)-(3), an entity and a notice provider may agree that whenthe notice provider is directed by the court to give a notice, the notice provider shall give the notice to the entity in the manner agreed to

美国联邦破产程序规则
（中英对照译本）

（11）用于请求推迟根据法典第 1141（d）(5)(C)、1228（f）和 1328（h）条授予免责的时间。就根据第 3017 条（c）确定的用于接受或拒绝计划的时间的通知，应按照第 3017 条（d）的规定发出。

（g）**通知的地址。**

（1）根据第 2002 条被要求向债权人、契约受托人或股本证券持有人邮寄的通知，邮寄地址应以该实体或其授权代理人在某一程序中最近提交的请求中指定的地址为准。就本附条而言：

（A）由债权人或契约受托人提交的，指定有邮寄地址的债权证明即构成已提交的将通知邮寄至该地址的请求，除非曾根据第 2002 条（e）发出无法还款的通知，但其后尚未根据第 3002 条（c）(5) 发出可能还款的通知；并且

（B）由股本证券持有人提交的，指定有邮寄地址的权益证明即构成已提交的将通知邮寄至该地址的请求。

（2）除法典第 342 条（f）另有规定外，若债权人或契约受托人未曾根据第 2002 条（g）(1) 或第 5003 条（e）提交指定邮寄地址的请求，则该通知应被邮寄至债权人名单或债务清单（以二者中较晚被提交者为准）上载有的地址。若股本证券持有人未曾根据第 2002 条（g）(1) 或第 5003 条（e）提交指定邮寄地址的请求，则该通知应被邮寄至股本证券持有人名单上载有的地址。

（3）若根据第 1007 条提交的名单或清单载有婴儿或无行为能力人的法定代表的姓名和住址，并且除该代表外，有人在提交请求或在提交债权证明时一并指定了与前述名单或清单上载明的代表的姓名与住址不同的姓名与邮寄地址，则除非法院作出其他裁定，否则第 2002 条中的通知应被邮寄给前述名单或报表上载明的代表以及在前述请求或债权证明中被指定的人和住址。

（4）即使存在第 2002 条（g）(1) 至（3）的规定，某实体可以与送达人达成合意，当法院指定送达人发出通知时，送达人应以该实体同意的方式向其提供给送达人的地址发出通知。该地址将被完全推定为寄送该通知的合适地址。送达

and at the address or addresses the entity supplies to the notice provider. That address is conclusively presumed to be a proper address for the notice. The notice provider's failure to use the supplied address does not invalidate any notice that is otherwise effective under applicable law.

(5) A creditor may treat a notice as not having been brought to the creditor's attention under §342 (g)(1) only if, prior to issuance of the notice, the creditor has filed a statement that designates the name and address of the person or organizational subdivision of the creditor responsible for receiving notices under the Code, and that describes the procedures established by the creditor to cause such notices to be delivered to the designated person or subdivision.

(h) NOTICES TO CREDITORS WHOSE CLAIMS ARE FILED.

(1) *Voluntary Case.* In a voluntary chapter 7 case, chapter 12 case, or chapter 13 case, after 70 days following the order for relief under that chapter or the date of the order converting the case to chapter 12 or chapter 13, the court may direct that all notices required by subdivision (a) of this rule be mailed only to:

- the debtor;
- the trustee;
- all indenture trustees;
- creditors that hold claims for which proofs of claim have been filed; and
- creditors, if any, that are still permitted to file claims because an extension was granted under Rule 3002 (c)(1) or (c)(2).

(2) *Involuntary Case.* In an involuntary chapter 7 case, after 90 days following the order for relief under that chapter, the court may direct that all notices required by subdivision (a) of this rule be mailed only to:

- the debtor;
- the trustee;
- all indenture trustees;
- creditors that hold claims for which proofs of claim have been filed; and
- creditors, if any, that are still permitted to file claims because an extension was granted under Rule 3002 (c)(1) or (c)(2).

(3) *Insufficient Assets.* In a case where notice of insufficient assets to pay a

人未能使用被提供的地址并不会使任何根据相应法律而有效的通知因此无效。

（5）当且仅当通知被签发前，债权人已经提交声明以指定根据法典负责接收其通知的人或组织部门的姓名和地址，并且载明由该债权人制定的用于向被指定的人或部门送达该通知的程序，债权人才可将该通知视为法典第 342 条（g）（1）中未能引起债权人注意的通知。

（h）**向提交债权的债权人发出的通知**。

（1）自愿破产案件。在第 7 章、第 12 章或第 13 章规定的自愿破产案件中，下发破产救济令或裁定将案件转换至第 12 章或第 13 章案件后 70 日以后，法院可指示本条（a）附条规定的所有通知均仅向下列人员邮寄：

- 债务人；
- 托管人；
- 所有契约受托人；
- 针对其享有的债权已提交债权证明的债权人；以及
- 根据第 3002 条（c）（1）or（c）（2）就延期（申报债权）的规定，仍被允许申报债权的债权人（如有）。

（2）强制破产案件。在第 7 章强制破产案件中，在根据该章下发破产救济令 90 日后，法院可指示本条（a）附条规定的所有通知均仅向下列人员邮寄：

- 债务人；
- 托管人；
- 所有契约受托人；
- 针对其享有的债权已提交债权证明的债权人；以及
- 根据第 3002 条（c）（1）or（c）（2）就延期（申报债权）的规定，仍被允许申报债权的债权人（如有）。

（3）资产不足。在已经根据本条的（e）附条就没有用以还款的资产而向债

U.S. Federal Rules of Bankruptcy Procedure
(Chinese-English bilingual version)

dividend has been given to creditors under subdivision (e) of this rule, after 90 days following the mailing of a notice of the time for filing claims under Rule 3002 (c) (5), the court may direct that notices be mailed only to the entities specified in the preceding sentence.

(i) NOTICES TO COMMITTEES. Copies of all notices required to be mailed pursuant to this rule shall be mailed to the committees elected under §705 or appointed under §1102 of the Code or to their authorized agents. Notwithstanding the foregoing subdivisions, the court may order that notices required by subdivision (a)(2), (3) and (6) of this rule be transmitted to the United States trustee and be mailed only to the committees elected under §705 or appointed under §1102 of the Code or to their authorized agents and to the creditors and equity security holders who serve on the trustee or debtor in possession and file a request that all notices be mailed to them. A committee appointed under §1114 of the code shall receive copies of all notices required by subdivisions (a)(1), (a)(5), (b), (f)(2), and (f)(7), and such other notices as the court may direct.

(j) NOTICES TO THE UNITED STATES. Copies of notices required to be mailed to all creditors under this rule shall be mailed (1) in a chapter 11 reorganization case, to the Securities and Exchange Commission at any place the Commission designates, if the Commission has filed either a notice of appearance in the case or a written request to receive notices; (2) in a commodity broker case, to the Commodity Futures Trading Commission at Washington, D.C.; (3) in a chapter 11 case, to the Internal Revenue Service at its address set out in the register maintained under Rule 5003 (e) for the district in which the case is pending; (4) if the papers in the case disclose a debt to the United States other than for taxes, to the United States attorney for the district in which the case is pending and to the department, agency, or instrumentality of the United States through which the debtor became indebted; or (5) if the filed papers disclose a stock interest of the United States, to the Secretary of the Treasury at Washington, D.C.

(k) NOTICES TO UNITED STATES TRUSTEE. Unless the case is a chapter 9 municipality case or unless the United States trustee requests otherwise, the clerk, or some other person as the court may direct, shall transmit to the United States trustee

权人发出通知的案件中，在就第3002条（c）（5）中用以申报债权的时间发出通知后90日以后，法院可指示仅将该通知邮寄给前述主体。

（i）**向委员会发出的通知**。本条所要求邮寄的所有通知的副本均应邮寄给根据法典第705条选任或根据第1102条任命的委员会或其授权代理机关。即使存在后续附条的规定，法院仍可裁定将本条（a）附条的（2）、（3）、（6）所要求的通知移交给联邦托管人并仅邮寄给根据法典第705条选任或根据第1102条任命的委员会或其授权代理机关以及提交要求向其寄送所有通知的请求并送达至托管人或经管债务人的债权人和股本证券持有人。根据法典第1114条被任命的委员会应接收（a）（1）、（a）（5）、（b）、（f）（2）和（f）（7）附条所要求的所有通知的副本，以及法院可指定的该类其他通知。

（j）**向美国政府机构发出的通知**。本条中被要求向所有债权人邮寄的通知的副本应被邮寄给（1）在第11章重整案件中，若美国证券交易委员会已经提交了出席本案的通知或接收通知的书面请求，则应被邮寄给该委员会并送至该委员会指定的任何地点；（2）在商品经纪商破产案件中，应被邮寄给华盛顿特区的商品期货交易委员会；（3）在第11章案件中，应被邮寄给国税局并送达至国税局在第5003条（e）规定的被保存的登记簿中就案件所在辖区而指定的地址；（4）若案件中的材料表明债务人对美国政府负有除税款外的其他债务，则应被邮寄给案件所在辖区的美国联邦检察官以及债务人因其而负有债务的部门、机构或机关；或（5）若被提交的材料披露了美国政府的股票权益，则应被邮寄给华盛顿特区的财政部长。

（k）**向联邦托管人发出的通知**。除非本案为第9章市政机构破产案件或联邦托管人作出其他请求，否则书记员或法院可指定的其他人应向联邦托管人移交就本条（a）（2）、（a）（3）、（a）（4）、（a）（8）、（a）（9）、（b）、（f）（1）、（f）（2）、（f）（4）、

U.S. Federal Rules of Bankruptcy Procedure
(Chinese-English bilingual version)

notice of the matters described in subdivisions (a)(2), (a)(3), (a)(4), (a)(8), (a)(9), (b),(f)(1),(f)(2),(f)(4),(f)(6),(f)(7),(f)(8), and (q) of this rule and notice of hearings on all applications for compensation or reimbursement of expenses. Notices to the United States trustee shall be transmitted within the time prescribed in subdivision (a) or (b) of this rule. The United States trustee shall also receive notice of any other matter if such notice is requested by the United States trustee or ordered by the court. Nothing in these rules requires the clerk or any other person to transmit to the United States trustee any notice, schedule, report, application or other document in a case under the Securities Investor Protection Act, 15 U.S.C. §78aaa et.[①] seq.

(1) NOTICE BY PUBLICATION. The court may order notice by publication if it finds that notice by mail is impracticable or that it is desirable to supplement the notice.

(m) ORDERS DESIGNATING MATTER OF NOTICES. The court may from time to time enterorders designating the matters in respect to which, the entity to whom, and the form and manner in which notices shall be sent except as otherwise provided by these rules.

(n) CAPTION. The caption of every notice given under this rule shall comply with Rule 1005. The caption of every notice required to be given by the debtor to a creditor shall include the information required to be in the notice by §342 (c) of the Code.

(o) NOTICE OF ORDER FOR RELIEF IN CONSUMER CASE. In a voluntary case commenced by an individual debtor whose debts are primarily consumer debts, the clerk or some other person as the court may direct shall give the trustee and all creditors notice by mail of the order for relief within 21 days from the date thereof.

(p) NOTICE TO A CREDITOR WITH A FOREIGN ADDRESS.

(1) If, at the request of the United States trustee or a party in interest, or on its own initiative, the court finds that a notice mailed within the time prescribed by these rules would not be sufficient to give a creditor with a foreign address to which notices under these rules are mailed reasonable notice under the circumstances, the court may order that the notice be supplemented with notice by other means or that the time prescribed for the notice by mail be enlarged.

---

① So in original. Period probably should not appear.

（f）（6）、（f）（7）、（f）（8）以及（q）所述事项发出的通知以及就报酬或报销费用的所有申请而举行听证的通知。前述通知应在本条（a）或（b）附条规定的期间内被移交给联邦托管人。若联邦托管人作此请求或法院作此裁定，则联邦托管人也应接收就任何其他事项而被发出的通知。本条并未要求书记员或任何其他人向联邦托管人移交任何《证券投资者保护法》(《美国联邦法典》第15篇第78aaa条）下案件中的任何通知、报表、报告、申请或其他文件。

（1）**公告送达的通知**。若法院认为邮寄通知并不可行或者需要补充通知，则可裁定公告送达该通知。

（m）**裁定就有关通知的事项作出指示**。除本法另有规定外，法院可随时裁定就与通知有关的事项、向其发出通知的实体以及发出通知的形式和方式作出指示。

（n）**标题**。所有根据本条被发出的各通知的标题均应符合第1005条的规定。被要求由债务人向债权人发出的各通知的标题均应载明法典第342条（c）中的通知所要求含有的信息。

（o）**在消费者破产案件中就破产救济令发出的通知**。在由其债务主要为消费债务的个人债务人启动的自愿破产案件中，书记员或法院可指定的其他人应在破产救济令被作出后21日内，通过邮寄的方式向托管人和所有债权人就破产救济令发出通知。

（p）**向其地址在国外的债权人发出的通知**。

（1）若法院应联邦托管人或利益相关方的请求或主动裁定，认为在本法规定的期间内向其地址在国外的债权人邮寄的通知不足以构成本法中在该情形下被以合理方式邮寄的通知，则法院可裁定通过其他方式发出该通知或延长规定用以邮寄通知的期间，从而对该通知进行补充。

though the court for cause orders otherwise, a creditor with a foreign address to which notices under this rule are mailed shall be given at least 30 days' notice of the time fixed for filing a proof of claim under Rule 3002 (c) or Rule 3003 (c).

(3) Unless the court for cause orders otherwise, the mailing address of a creditor with a foreign address shall be determined under Rule 2002 (g).

(q) NOTICE OF PETITION FOR RECOGNITION OF FOREIGN PROCEEDING AND OF COURT'S INTENTION TO COMMUNICATE WITH FOREIGN COURTS AND FOREIGN REPRESENTATIVES.

(1) *Notice of Petition for Recognition.* After the filing of a petition for recognition of a foreign proceeding, the court shall promptly schedule and hold a hearing on the petition. The clerk, or some other person as the court may direct, shall forthwith give the debtor, all persons or bodies authorized to administer foreign proceedings of the debtor, all entities against whom provisional relief is being sought under §1519 of the Code, all parties to litigation pending in the United States in which the debtor is a party at the time of the filing of the petition, and such other entities as the court may direct, at least 21 days' notice by mail of the hearing. The notice shall state whether the petition seeks recognition as a foreign main proceeding or foreign nonmain proceeding and shall include the petition and any other document the court may require. If the court consolidates the hearing on the petition with the hearing on a request for provisional relief, the court may set a shorter notice period, with notice to the entities listed in this subdivision.

(2) *Notice of Court's Intention to Communicate with Foreign Courts and Foreign Representatives.* The clerk, or some other person as the court may direct, shall give the debtor, all persons or bodies authorized to administer foreign proceedings of the debtor, all entities against whom provisional relief is being sought under §1519 of the Code, all parties to litigation pending in the United States in which the debtor is a party at the time of the filing of the petition, and such other entities as the court may direct, notice by mail of the court's intention to communicate with a foreign court or foreign representative.

(As amended Pub. L. 98-91, §2 (a), Aug. 30, 1983, 97 Stat. 607; Pub. L. 98-353, title III, §321, July10, 1984, 98 Stat. 357; Mar. 30, 1987, eff. Aug. 1, 1987; Apr. 30, 1991, eff. Aug. 1, 1991; Apr. 22,1993, eff. Aug. 1, 1993; Apr. 23, 1996, eff. Dec. 1,

（2）除非法院出于特定事由作出其他裁定，否则针对本条中向其邮寄通知的其地址在国外的债权人，应至少提前 30 日就根据第 3002 条（c）或第 3003 条（c）确定的用于提交债权的时间向该债权人发出通知。

（3）除非法院出于特定事由作出其他裁定，否则应根据第 2002 条（g）确定其地址在国外的债权人的邮寄地址。

（q）就承认外国程序的申请以及本国法院与外国法院和外国代表沟通的意向而发出的通知。

（1）就承认申请发出的通知。在承认外国程序的申请被提交后，法院应及时安排并就该申请举行听证。书记员或法院可指定的其他人应至少提前 21 日通过邮寄的方式向债务人、所有被授权处理债务人的外国程序的人或机构、所有根据法典第 1519 条寻求的临时救济所针对的实体、债务人在该申请被提交时在美国进行中的诉讼的所有当事人，以及法院可指定的其他人就该听证及时发出通知。该通知应载明该申请是否寻求将外国程序承认为外国主要程序或外国非主要程序，并且应包含申请书和法院可要求的任何其他文件。若法院将就该申请而举行的听证与就申请临时救济而举行的听证合并，则法院可确定一个更短的通知期间以向本附条所列明的实体发出通知。

（2）就本国法院与外国法院和外国代表沟通的意向而发出的通知。书记员或法院可指定的其他人，应通过邮寄的方式向债务人、所有被授权处理债务人的外国程序的人或机构、所有根据法典第 1519 条寻求的临时救济所针对的实体、债务人在该申请被提交时在美国进行中的诉讼的所有当事人，以及向法院可指定的其他人就本国法院与外国法院或外国代表进行沟通的发出通知。

［经 Pub. L. 98-91, §2（a）, Aug. 30, 1983, 97 Stat. 607; Pub. L. 98-353, title III, §321, July10, 1984, 98 Stat. 357; Mar. 30, 1987, eff. Aug. 1, 1987; Apr. 30, 1991, eff. Aug. 1, 1991; Apr. 22,1993, eff. Aug. 1, 1993; Apr. 23, 1996, eff. Dec. 1, 1996; Apr.

U.S. Federal Rules of Bankruptcy Procedure
(Chinese-English bilingual version)

1996; Apr. 11, 1997, eff. Dec. 1, 1997; Apr. 26,1999, eff. Dec. 1, 1999; Apr. 17, 2000, eff. Dec. 1, 2000; Apr. 23, 2001, eff. Dec. 1, 2001; Mar. 27,2003, eff. Dec. 1, 2003; Apr. 26, 2004, eff. Dec. 1, 2004; Apr. 25, 2005, eff. Dec. 1, 2005; Apr. 23,2008, eff. Dec. 1, 2008; Mar. 26, 2009, eff. Dec. 1, 2009; Apr. 28, 2016, eff. Dec. 1, 2016; Apr. 27,2017, eff. Dec. 1, 2017; Apr. 27, 2020, eff. Dec. 1, 2020.)

Rule 2003. Meeting of Creditors or Equity Security Holders

(a) DATE AND PLACE. Except as otherwise provided in §341 (e) of the Code, in a chapter 7 liquidation or a chapter 11 reorganization case, the United States trustee shall call a meeting of creditors to be held no fewer than 21 and no more than 40 days after the order for relief. In a chapter 12 family farmer debt adjustment case, the United States trustee shall call a meeting of creditors to be held no fewer than 21 and no more than 35 days after the order for relief. In a chapter 13 individual's debt adjustment case, the United States trustee shall call a meeting of creditors to be held no fewer than 21 and no more than 50 days after the order for relief. If there is an appeal from or a motion to vacate the order for relief, or if there is a motion to dismiss the case, the United States trustee may set a later date for the meeting. The meeting may be held at a regular place for holding court or at any other place designated by the United States trustee within the district convenient for the parties in interest. If the United States trustee designates a place for the meeting which is not regularly staffed by the United States trustee or an assistant who may preside at the meeting, the meeting may be held not more than 60 days after the order for relief.

(b) ORDER OF MEETING.

(1) *Meeting of Creditors*. The United States trustee shall preside at the meeting of creditors. The business of the meeting shall include the examination of the debtor under oath and, in a chapter 7 liquidation case, may include the election of a creditors' committee and, if the case is not under subchapter V of chapter 7, the election of a trustee. The presiding officer shall have the authority to administer oaths.

(2) *Meeting of Equity Security Holders*. If the United States trustee convenes a meeting of equity security holders pursuant to §341 (b) of the Code, the United States trustee shall fix a date for the meeting and shall preside.

11, 1997, eff. Dec. 1, 1997; Apr. 26,1999, eff. Dec. 1, 1999; Apr. 17, 2000, eff. Dec. 1, 2000; Apr. 23, 2001, eff. Dec. 1, 2001; Mar. 27,2003, eff. Dec. 1, 2003; Apr. 26, 2004, eff. Dec. 1, 2004; Apr. 25, 2005, eff. Dec. 1, 2005; Apr. 23,2008, eff. Dec. 1, 2008; Mar. 26, 2009, eff. Dec. 1, 2009; Apr. 28, 2016, eff. Dec. 1, 2016; Apr. 27,2017, eff. Dec. 1, 2017; Apr. 27, 2020, eff. Dec. 1, 2020. 修正］

第 2003 条　债权人或股本证券持有人会议

（a）日期和地点。除法典第 341 条（e）另有规定外，在第 7 章清算案件或第 11 章重整案件中，联邦托管人应在破产救济令被作出后第 21 日至第 40 日内召集举行债权人会议。在第 12 章家庭农场主债务调整案件中，联邦托管人应在破产救济令被作出后第 21 日至第 35 日内召集举行债权人会议。在第 13 章个人债务调整案件中，联邦托管人应在破产救济令被作出后第 21 日至第 50 日内召集举行债权人会议。若有人提出上诉或动议以撤销破产救济令，或有人提出动议驳回该案，则联邦托管人可推迟该会议的举行。该会议可在开庭的常规地点举行，也可在联邦托管人在该辖区内指定的方便利益相关方的任何其他地点举行。若在联邦托管人指定的会议地点没有常规任职的联邦托管人或可主持会议的助手，则该会议可在破产救济令被作出后 60 日内举行。

（b）会议流程。

（1）债权人会议。联邦托管人应主持债权人会议。会议的内容应包括在宣誓下对债务人的质询；在第 7 章清算案件中可包括对债权人委员会的选任，若该案不是第 7 章第五附章中的案件，则可包括对托管人的选任。主持会议的工作人员应有权组织宣誓。

（2）股本证券持有人会议。若联邦托管人根据法典第 341 条（b）召集举行股本证券持有人会议，则联邦托管人应确定举行该会议的时间并主持该会议。

(3) *Right To Vote*. In a chapter 7 liquidation case, a creditor is entitled to vote at a meeting if, at or before the meeting, the creditor has filed a proof of claim or a writing setting forth facts evidencing a right to vote pursuant to §702 (a) of the Code unless objection is made to the claim or the proof of claim is insufficient on its face. A creditor of a partnership may file a proof of claim or writing evidencing a right to vote for the trustee for the estate of the general partner notwithstanding that a trustee for the estate of the partnership has previously qualified. In the event of an objection to the amount or allowability of a claim for the purpose of voting, unless the court orders otherwise, the United States trustee shall tabulate the votes for each alternative presented by the dispute and, if resolution of such dispute is necessary to determine the result of the election, the tabulations for each alternative shall be reported to the court.

(c) RECORD OF MEETING. Any examination under oath at the meeting of creditors held pursuant to §341 (a) of the Code shall be recorded verbatim by the United States trustee using electronic sound recording equipment or other means of recording, and such record shall be preserved by the United States trustee and available for public access until two years after the conclusion of the meeting of creditors. Upon request of any entity, the United States trustee shall certify and provide a copy or transcript of such recording at the entity's expense.

(d) REPORT OF ELECTION AND RESOLUTION OF DISPUTES IN A CHAPTER 7 CASE.

(1) *Report of Undisputed Election*. In a chapter 7 case, if the election of a trustee or a member of a creditors' committee is not disputed, the United States trustee shall promptly file a report of the election, including the name and address of the person or entity elected and a statement that the election is undisputed.

(2) Disputed Election. If the election is disputed, the United States trustee shall promptly file a report stating that the election is disputed, informing the court of the nature of the dispute, and listing the name and address of any candidate elected under any alternative presented by the dispute. No later than the date on which the report is filed, the United States trustee shall mail a copy of the report to any party in interest that has made a request to receive a copy of the report. Pending disposition

（3）表决权。在第 7 章清算案件中，若在举行会议时或之前，债权人已经提交债权证明或列明其根据法典第 702 条（a）有权参与表决的事实的书面证明，则除非有人就该债权提出异议或证明该债权的证据明显不足，否则该债权人有权在会议上参与表决。合伙组织的债权人可提交债权证明或证明其享有选举管理普通合伙人的破产实体的托管人的权利的书面证据，即使已经存在管理合伙组织的破产实体的合格托管人。当有人因该表决事项而就债权的金额或确认提出异议，则除非法院作出其他裁定，否则联邦托管人应将因该争议而产生的各个备选方案的选票汇总成表格，并且若必须通过解决该争议来确定选举结果，则应将各个备选方案的汇总表报告法院。

（c）**会议记录**。在根据法典第 341 条（a）举行的债权人会议中，宣誓下所作的任何质询均应由联邦托管人通过电子录音设备或其他记录方式逐字记录，并且该记录应由联邦托管人保存并在债权人会议结束 2 年内供公众访问。应任何实体的请求，联邦托管人应提供该记录的核证副本或报告单，该费用由该实体承担。

（d）**选任报告和第 7 章案件中争议的解决**。

（1）无争议选任的报告。在第 7 章案件中，若托管人或债权人委员会成员的选任不存在争议，则联邦托管人应立刻提交选任报告，并载明被选任的人或实体的姓名和住址以及说明该选任并不存在争议的声明。

（2）有争议的选任。若该选任存在争议，则联邦托管人应立刻提交报告并注明该选任存在争议，还要告知法院该争议的性质并列明因该争议而产生的任何备选方案下被选任的任何候选人的姓名和住址。在不晚于提交报告之日，联邦托管人应向曾请求获得该报告副本的任何利益相关人邮寄该副本。在法院处理托管人的争议选任的期间内，临时托管人应继续履行其职责。除非在联邦托管人就托管人的争议选任提交报告后 14 日内，有人提出动议申请解决该争议，否则临时托

by the court of a disputed election for trustee, the interim trustee shall continue in office. Unless a motion for the resolution of the dispute is filed no later than 14 days after the United States trustee files a report of a disputed election for trustee, the interim trustee shall serve as trustee in the case.

(e) ADJOURNMENT. The meeting may be adjourned from time to time by announcement at the meeting of the adjourned date and time. The presiding official shall promptly file a statement specifying the date and time to which the meeting is adjourned.

(f) SPECIAL MEETINGS. The United States trustee may call a special meeting of creditors on request of a party in interest or on the United States trustee's own initiative.

(g) FINAL MEETING. If the United States trustee calls a final meeting of creditors in a case in which the net proceeds realized exceed $1,500, the clerk shall mail a summary of the trustee's final account to the creditors with a notice of the meeting, together with a statement of the amount of the claims allowed. The trustee shall attend the final meeting and shall, if requested, report on the administration of the estate.

(As amended Mar. 30, 1987, eff. Aug. 1, 1987; Apr. 30, 1991, eff. Aug. 1, 1991; Apr. 22, 1993, eff.Aug. 1, 1993; Apr. 26, 1999, eff. Dec. 1, 1999; Mar. 27, 2003, eff. Dec. 1, 2003; Apr. 23, 2008, eff.Dec. 1, 2008; Mar. 26, 2009, eff. Dec. 1, 2009; Apr. 26, 2011, eff. Dec. 1, 2011.)

Rule 2004. Examination

(a) EXAMINATION ON MOTION. On motion of any party in interest, the court may order the examination of any entity.

(b) SCOPE OF EXAMINATION. The examination of an entity under this rule or of the debtor under §343 of the Code may relate only to the acts, conduct, or property or to the liabilities and financial condition of the debtor, or to any matter which may affect the administration of the debtor's estate, or to the debtor's right to a discharge. In a family farmer's debt adjustment case under chapter 12, an individual's debt adjustment case under chapter 13, or a reorganization case under chapter 11 of the Code, other than for the reorganization of a railroad, the examination may also relate to the operation

管人应在该案中担任托管人。

（e）**休会**。该会议可随时通过在会议上宣布休会日期和期间而休会。主持会议的工作人员应立刻提交声明以说明休会的日期及期间。

（f）**特别会议**。联邦托管人可应利益相关方的请求或主动召集举行债权人特别会议。

（g）**最终会议**。若联邦托管人在实现的净收益超过 1500 美元的情况下召集举行债权人最终会议，则书记员应将托管人的最终账目的摘要和会议的通知邮寄给债权人，并载明经确认的债权金额。托管人应参加最终会议，并在有人提出请求的情况下，就破产实体的管理进行报告。

（经 Mar. 30, 1987, eff. Aug. 1, 1987; Apr. 30, 1991, eff. Aug. 1, 1991; Apr. 22, 1993, eff.Aug. 1, 1993; Apr. 26, 1999, eff. Dec. 1, 1999; Mar. 27, 2003, eff. Dec. 1, 2003; Apr. 23, 2008, eff.Dec. 1, 2008; Mar. 26, 2009, eff. Dec. 1, 2009; Apr. 26, 2011, eff. Dec. 1, 2011. 修正）

第 2004 条　质询

（a）**应动议质询**。应利益相关方的动议，法院可裁定质询任何实体。

（b）**质询的范围**。根据本条向某实体或根据法典第 343 条向债务人质询的范围仅限于债务人的作为、行为或财产，或者其负债和财务状况，或者任何可能影响债务人破产实体管理的事项或债务人获得免责的权利。在法典第 12 章中的家庭农场主的债务调整案件、第 13 章中的个人债务调整案件或第 11 章重整案件（不包括铁路公司重整案件）中，该质询也可涉及其任何商事业务的运营以及继续该商事业务的意愿，用于完成计划而由债务人取得或将取得的任何金钱或财产的来源和为此而提供或支付的对价，以及与破产案件或计划的制订有

of any business and the desirability of its continuance, the source of any money or property acquired or to be acquired by the debtor for purposes of consummating a plan and the consideration given or offered therefor, and any other matter relevant to the case or to the formulation of a plan.

(c) COMPELLING ATTENDANCE AND PRODUCTION OF DOCUMENTS OR ELECTRONICALLY STORED INFORMATION. The attendance of an entity for examination and for the production of documents or electronically stored information, whether the examination is to be conducted within or without the district in which the case is pending, may be compelled as provided in Rule 9016 for the attendance of a witness at a hearing or trial. As an officer of the court, an attorney may issue and sign a subpoena on behalf of the court where the case is pending if the attorney is admitted to practice in that court.

(d) TIME AND PLACE OF EXAMINATION OF DEBTOR. The court may for cause shown and on terms as it may impose order the debtor to be examined under this rule at any time or place it designates, whether within or without the district wherein the case is pending.

(e) MILEAGE. An entity other than a debtor shall not be required to attend as a witness unless lawful mileage and witness fee for one day's attendance shall be first tendered. If the debtor resides more than 100 miles from the place of examination when required to appear for an examination under this rule, the mileage allowed by law to a witness shall be tendered for any distance more than 100 miles from the debtor's residence at the date of the filing of the first petition commencing a case under the Code or the residence at the time the debtor is required to appear for the examination, whichever is the lesser.

(As amended Mar. 30, 1987, eff. Aug. 1, 1987; Apr. 30, 1991, eff. Aug. 1, 1991; Apr. 29, 2002, eff.Dec. 1, 2002; Apr. 27, 2020, eff. Dec. 1, 2020.)

Rule 2005. Apprehension and Removal of Debtor to Compel Attendance for Examination

(a) ORDER TO COMPEL ATTENDANCE FOR EXAMINATION. On motion of any party in interest supported by an affidavit alleging (1) that the

关的任何其他事项。

（c）**强制出席和提供文件或电子存储信息**。可根据第 9016 条对证人在听证或庭审中出席的规定，强制某实体出庭进行质询和提供文件或电子存储信息，无论该质询是否将在案件所在辖区内进行。作为法院的工作人员，若某律师被准予在将举行质询的辖区内法院或破产案件所在法院执业，则该律师可代表将举行质询的辖区内法院签发并签署传票。

（d）**债务人接受质询的时间和地点**。法院可出于特定事由并施以特定条件，裁定债务人根据本条规定在法院指定的任何时间或地点接受质询，无论该地点是否在案件所在的辖区内。

（e）**交通补贴**。除非首先为其提供一日出庭的合法交通补贴和证人费用，否则除债务人外的实体均不得被要求作为证人出庭。若债务人在被要求出席接受质询时位居质询地 100 英里以外，则应针对债务人在根据法典启动案件的首次破产申请被提交时的居住地或债务人被要求出席接受质询时的居住地与质询地间超过 100 英里的距离（以较短者为准），为其提供法院准予证人获得的交通补贴。

（经 Mar. 30, 1987, eff. Aug. 1, 1987; Apr. 30, 1991, eff. Aug. 1, 1991; Apr. 29, 2002, eff.Dec. 1, 2002; Apr. 27, 2020, eff. Dec. 1, 2020. 修正）

第 2005 条　羁押并转移债务人以强制其出席接受质询

（a）**裁定强制出席接受质询**。当有任何利益相关方提出动议并提供宣誓书主张（1）为破产实体的适当管理，有必要对债权人进行质询，并且有合理理由相

examination of the debtor is necessary for the proper administration of the estate and that there is reasonable cause to believe that the debtor is about to leave or has left the debtor's residence or principal place of business to avoid examination, or (2) that the debtor has evaded service of a subpoena or of an order to attend for examination, or (3) that the debtor has willfully disobeyed a subpoena or order to attend for examination, duly served, the court may issue to the marshal, or some other officer authorized by law, an order directing the officer to bring the debtor before the court without unnecessary delay. If, after hearing, the court finds the allegations to be true, the court shall thereupon cause the debtor to be examined forthwith. If necessary, the court shall fix conditions for further examination and for the debtor's obedience to all orders made in reference thereto.

(b) REMOVAL. Whenever any order to bring the debtor before the court is issued under this rule and the debtor is found in a district other than that of the court issuing the order, the debtor may be taken into custody under the order and removed in accordance with the following rules:

(1) If the debtor is taken into custody under the order at a place less than 100 miles from the place of issue of the order, the debtor shall be brought forthwith before the court that issued the order.

(2) If the debtor is taken into custody under the order at a place 100 miles or more from the place of issue of the order, the debtor shall be brought without unnecessary delay before the nearest available United States magistrate judge, bankruptcy judge, or district judge. If, afterhearing, the magistrate judge, bankruptcy judge, or district judge finds that an order has issued under this rule and that the person in custody is the debtor, or if the person in custody waives a hearing, the magistrate judge, bankruptcy judge, or district judge shall order removal, and the person in custody shall be released on conditions ensuring prompt appearance before the court that issued the order to compel the attendance.

(c) CONDITIONS OF RELEASE. In determining what conditions will reasonably assure attendance or obedience under subdivision (a) of this rule or appearance under subdivision (b) of this rule, the court shall be governed by the relevant provisions and policies of title 18 U.S.C. §3142.

美国联邦破产程序规则
（中英对照译本）

信债务人为逃避接受质询将离开或已经离开其居住地或主要营业场所；或（2）债务人逃避传票的送达或出席接受质询的裁定，或（3）债务人有意不遵守正当送达的传票的规定或出席接受质询的裁定，则法院可向法警或法律授权的其他官员签发裁定，指示该官员立刻将债务人带至庭前。若经过听证后，法院认为该主张属实，则法院应立刻要求对债务人进行质询。在必要的情况下，法院应施加条件以使得债务人接受进一步的质询并服从相应作出的所有裁定。

（b）**转移**。每当根据本条规定法院签发将债务人带至庭前的裁定时，若债务人被发现位于签发该裁定的法院所在辖区外的辖区时，该债务人可被根据该裁定而拘留并根据以下规定对其进行转移：

（1）若债务人在被根据该裁定拘留时，位于裁定被签发地100英里以内，则债务人应被立刻带至签发该裁定的法院。

（2）若债务人在被根据该裁定拘留时，位于裁定被签发地100英里处或以外，则债务人应被立刻带至最近的美国治安法官、破产法官或地方法官面前。若在经过听证后，治安法官、破产法官或地方法官认定确实存在根据本条而被签发的裁定并且被羁押人为债务人，或者被羁押人放弃听证，则治安法官、破产法官或地方法官应裁定其离开，并且在确保被羁押人能及时出现在签发裁定以强制其出席的法院面前的情况下，被羁押人应被解除羁押。

（c）**解除羁押的条件**。在决定能合理确保债务人将根据本条的（a）附条出席或遵守该规定或者根据本条的（b）附条出席的条件时，法院应遵守《美国联邦法典》第18篇第3142条的有关条文和政策。

099

U.S. Federal Rules of Bankruptcy Procedure
(Chinese-English bilingual version)

(As amended Mar. 30, 1987, eff. Aug. 1, 1987; Apr. 22, 1993, eff. Aug. 1, 1993; Apr. 14, 2021, eff.Dec. 1, 2021.)

Rule 2006. Solicitation and Voting of Proxies in Chapter 7 Liquidation Cases

(a) APPLICABILITY. This rule applies only in a liquidation case pending under chapter 7 of the Code.

(b) DEFINITIONS.

(1) Proxy. A proxy is a written power of attorney authorizing any entity to vote the claim or otherwise act as the owner's attorney in fact in connection with the administration of the estate.

(2) Solicitation of Proxy. The solicitation of a proxy is any communication, other than one from an attorney to a regular client who owns a claim or from an attorney to the owner of a claim who has requested the attorney to represent the owner, by which a creditor is asked, directly or indirectly, to give a proxy after or in contemplation of the filing of a petition by or against the debtor.

(c) AUTHORIZED SOLICITATION.

(1) A proxy may be solicited only by (A) a creditor owning an allowable unsecured claim against the estate on the date of the filing of the petition; (B) a committee elected pursuant to §705 of the Code; (C) a committee of creditors selected by a majority in number and amount of claims of creditors (i) whose claims are not contingent or unliquidated, (ii) who are not disqualified from voting under §702 (a) of the Code and (iii) who were present or represented at a meeting of which all creditors having claims of over $500 or the 100 creditors having the largest claims had at least seven days' notice in writing and of which meeting written minutes were kept and are available reporting the names of the creditors present or represented and voting and the amounts of their claims; or (D) a bona fide trade or credit association, but such association may solicit only creditors who were its members or subscribers in good standing and had allowable unsecured claims on the date of the filing of the petition.

(2) A proxy may be solicited only in writing.

（经 Mar. 30, 1987, eff. Aug. 1, 1987; Apr. 22, 1993, eff. Aug. 1, 1993; Apr. 14, 2021, eff.Dec. 1, 2021. 修正）

第 2006 条　第 7 章清算案件中表决代理权的征集

（a）**适用范围**。本条仅适用于法典第 7 章中的破产清算案件。

（b）**定义**。
（1）**授权代理书**。授权代理书系授权任何实体代表自己就与管理破产实体有关的事项参与表决或采取其他行动的书面授权书。

（2）**征集代理权**。征集代理权系除了发生在代理人与持有债权的固定客户间或代理人与要求该代理人代表自己的债权人间以外的沟通，该沟通的目的系以直接或间接的方式在债务人主动提交或他人针对债务人提交破产申请时或之后向债权人征集代理权。

（c）**被准予的征集**。
（1）代理权仅可由后述主体征集：（A）在破产申请被提交当日就破产实体享有可予以确认的无担保债权的债权人；（B）根据法典第 705 条被选任的委员会；（C）由持多数债权金额的多数债权人选任的债权人委员会，并且前述债权人（i）其债权是实然的且数额是确定的，（ii）有资格根据法典第 702 条（a）参与表决，并且（iii）其亲自或由他人代表出席的债权人会议中，所有债权人持有的债权的金额均超过 500 美元或者所有债权人均为债权金额位列前 100 名的债权人，并且该些债权人系至少提前 7 日接到书面通知后出席或被代表出席，并且该会议记录已被保存并可用于报告亲自出席或被代表出席并参与表决的债权人的姓名及其债权金额；或（D）善意的贸易或信贷协会，但该协会只能向在破产申请被提交当日持有无担保债权的优秀会员征集表决权。

（2）仅可以书面方式征集代理权。

(d) SOLICITATION NOT AUTHORIZED. This rule does not permit solicitation (1) in any interest other than that of general creditors; (2) by or on behalf of any custodian; (3) by the interim trustee or by or on behalf of any entity not qualified to vote under §702 (a) of the Code; (4) by or on behalf of an attorney at law; or (5) by or on behalf of a transferee of a claim for collection only.

(e) DATA REQUIRED FROM HOLDERS OF MULTIPLE PROXIES. At any time before the voting commences at any meeting of creditors pursuant to §341 (a) of the Code, or at any other time as the court may direct, a holder of two or more proxies shall file and transmit to the United States trustee a verified list of the proxies to be voted and a verified statement of the pertinent facts and circumstances in connection with the execution and delivery of each proxy, including:

(1) a copy of the solicitation;

(2) identification of the solicitor, the forwarder, if the forwarder is neither the solicitor nor the owner of the claim, and the proxyholder, including their connections with the debtor and with each other. If the solicitor, forwarder, or proxyholder is an association, there shall also be included a statement that the creditors whose claims have been solicited and the creditors whose claims are to be voted were members or subscribers in good standing and had allowable unsecured claims on the date of the filing of the petition. If the solicitor, forwarder, or proxyholder is a committee of creditors, the statement shall also set forth the date and place the committee was organized, that the committee was organized in accordance with clause (B) or (C) of paragraph (c)(1) of this rule, the members of the committee, the amounts of their claims, when the claims were acquired, the amounts paid therefor, and the extent to which the claims of the committee members are secured or entitled to priority;

(3) a statement that no consideration has been paid or promised by the proxyholder for the proxy;

(4) a statement as to whether there is any agreement and, if so, the particulars thereof, between the proxyholder and any other entity for the payment of any consideration in connection with voting the proxy, or for the sharing of compensation with any entity, other than a member or regular associate of the proxyholder's law firm, which may be allowed the trustee or any entity for services rendered in the case, or for the employment of any

美国联邦破产程序规则
（中英对照译本）

（d）**未被准予的征集**。本条不允许后述征集：（1）不是为全体债权人的利益而征集；（2）由任何保管人或代表任何保管人征集；（3）由临时托管人，或由任何根据法典第702条（a）并无资格参与表决的任何实体或代表该实体而征集；（4）由律师或代表律师征集；或（5）由以追债为目的而受让债权的受让人或代表该受让人征集。

（e）**多项代理权的持有人被要求提供的信息**。在根据法典第341条（a）举行债权人会议上开始表决前的任何时间内，或在法院可指定的任何其他时间内，持有两项或两项以上代理权的主体应提交并向联邦托管人移交一份宣誓清单，该清单上应列明将就其参与表决的代理权，以及一份宣誓声明，该声明上应载有与各份授权代理书的制作和交付有关的事实和情形，包括以下各项：

（1）征集书的副本；

（2）征集人、运输代理人（若其既不是征集人也不是债权人）和代理权持有人的身份信息，包括其与债务人间的关系以及彼此间的关系。若征集人、运输代理人或代理权持有人是协会，则还应载有一份声明以说明向其征集代理权并就其债权代表其参与表决的债权人均为该协会的优秀会员，并且前述债权人在破产申请被提交当日享有可予以确认的无担保债权。若征集人、运输代理人或代理权持有人为债权人委员会，则该声明也应列明该委员会组建的日期和地点，说明该委员会系根据本条的（c）（1）的（B）或（C）组建，列明该委员会的成员，其债权金额，其取得债权的时间，此后已被偿还的金额以及该委员会成员的债权上的担保和优先顺位的情况；

（3）说明代理权持有人并未就代理权支付或承诺支付对价的声明；

（4）一份声明，以说明在代理权持有人和任何其他实体间是否存在任何就支付与代理参与表决相关的任何对价而达成的协议，或者与任何实体（不包括代理权持有人的律师事务所的成员或长期员工）间就共享托管人或任何实体可被准予其就在本案中所提供的服务为破产实体雇佣任何律师、会计师、评估师、拍卖师或其他员工获得的报酬而达成的协议，并且若存在该协议，还应说明该协议

person as attorney, accountant, appraiser, auctioneer, or other employee for the estate;

(5) if the proxy was solicited by an entity other than the proxyholder, or forwarded to the holder by an entity who is neither a solicitor of the proxy nor the owner of the claim, a statement signed and verified by the solicitor or forwarder that no consideration has been paid or promised for the proxy, and whether there is any agreement, and, if so, the particulars thereof, between the solicitor or forwarder and any other entity for the payment of any consideration in connection with voting the proxy, or for sharing compensation with any entity other than a member or regular associate of the solicitor's or forwarder's law firm which may be allowed the trustee or any entity for services rendered in the case, or for the employment of any person as attorney, accountant, appraiser, auctioneer, or other employee for the estate;

(6) if the solicitor, forwarder, or proxyholder is a committee, a statement signed and verified by each member as to the amount and source of any consideration paid or to be paid to such member in connection with the case other than by way of dividend on the member's claim.

(f) ENFORCEMENT OF RESTRICTIONS ON SOLICITATION. On motion of any party in interest or on its own initiative, the court may determine whether there has been a failure to comply with the provisions of this rule or any other impropriety in connection with the solicitation or voting of a proxy. After notice and a hearing the court may reject any proxy for cause, vacate any order entered in consequence of the voting of any proxy which should have been rejected, or take any other appropriate action.

(As amended Mar. 30, 1987, eff. Aug. 1, 1987; Apr. 30, 1991, eff. Aug. 1, 1991; Mar. 26, 2009, eff.Dec. 1, 2009.)

Rule 2007. Review of Appointment of Creditors' Committee Organized Before Commencement of the Case

(a) MOTION TO REVIEW APPOINTMENT. If a committee appointed by the United States trustee pursuant to §1102 (a) of the Code consists of the members of a committee organized by creditors before the commencement of a chapter 9 or chapter 11 case, on motion of a party in interest and after a hearing on notice to the United

的细节；

（5）若该代理权的征集人不是代理权持有人，或者运输代理人不是该代理权的征集人或债权人，则应附有一份声明，该声明应由征集人或运输代理人签名并宣誓说明代理权持有人并未就代理权支付或承诺支付对价，以及在征集人或运输代理人和任何其他实体间是否存在任何就支付与代理参与表决相关的任何对价而达成的协议，或者与任何实体（不包括征集人或运输代理人的律师事务所的成员或长期员工）间就共享托管人或任何实体可被准予其就在本案中所提供的服务或者为破产实体雇佣任何律师、会计师、评估师、拍卖师或其他员工获得的报酬而达成的协议，并且若存在该协议，还应说明该协议的细节；

（6）若征集人、运输代理人或代理权持有人为委员会，则各成员均应签署一份声明以核实向该成员支付或将要支付的与本案相关的任何对价的金额和来源，但不包括因其债权而被分配所得的款项。

（f）**征集限制的执行**。应任何利益相关方的动议或者法院也可主动就是否存在违反本条规定的情况或与代理表决权的征集有关的任何其他不当行为作出认定。经过通知和听证后，法院可出于特定事由拒绝任何授权代理书，撤销基于本应被拒绝的任何表决权的代理而被正式作出的任何裁定，或采取其他适当的行动。

（经 Mar. 30, 1987, eff. Aug. 1, 1987; Apr. 30, 1991, eff. Aug. 1, 1991; Mar. 26, 2009, eff.Dec. 1, 2009. 修正）

第 2007 条　就案件启动前组建的债权人委员会的任命的审查

（a）**审查该任命的动议**。若在第 9 章或第 11 章案件中，联邦托管人根据法典第 1102 条（a）任命的委员会系由案件启动前债权人组建的委员会的成员组成，则应利益相关方的动议，在向联邦托管人以及法院可指定的其他实体发出通知并举行听证后，法院可就该委员会的任命是否符合法典第 1102 条（b）（1）的要求

States trustee and other entities as the court may direct, the court may determine whether the appointment of the committee satisfies the requirements of §1102 (b) (1) of the Code.

(b) SELECTION OF MEMBERS OF COMMITTEE. The court may find that a committee organized by unsecured creditors before the commencement of a chapter 9 or chapter 11 case was fairly chosen if:

(1) it was selected by a majority in number and amount of claims of unsecured creditors who may vote under §702 (a) of the Code and were present in person or represented at a meeting of which all creditors having unsecured claims of over $1,000 or the 100 unsecured creditors having the largest claims had at least seven days' notice in writing, and of which meeting written minutes reporting the names of the creditors present or represented and voting and the amounts of their claims were kept and are available for inspection;

(2) all proxies voted at the meeting for the elected committee were solicited pursuant to Rule 2006 and the lists and statements required by subdivision (e) thereof have been transmitted to the United States trustee; and

(3) the organization of the committee was in all other respects fair and proper.

(c) FAILURE TO COMPLY WITH REQUIREMENTS FOR APPOINTMENT. After a hearing on notice pursuant to subdivision (a) of this rule, the court shall direct the United States trustee to vacate the appointment of the committee and may order other appropriate action if the court finds that such appointment failed to satisfy the requirements of §1102 (b) (1) of the Code.

(As amended Mar. 30, 1987, eff. Aug. 1, 1987; Apr. 30, 1991, eff. Aug. 1, 1991; Mar. 26, 2009, eff.Dec. 1, 2009.)

Rule 2007.1. Appointment of Trustee or Examiner in a Chapter 11 Reorganization Case

(a) ORDER TO APPOINT TRUSTEE OR EXAMINER. In a chapter 11 reorganization case, a motion for an order to appoint a trustee or an examiner under §1104 (a) or §1104 (c) of the Code shall be made in accordance with Rule 9014.

作出认定。

（b）**委员会成员的选任**。在下列情形中，该法院可认定在第 9 章或第 11 章案件中，案件启动前由无担保债权人组建的委员会系经公平选任而产生：

（1）该委员会系由根据法典第 702 条（a）有权参与表决的无担保债权人在会议上经持多数债权金额的多数债权人选任，并且该会议可由债权人亲自出席或由他人代表出席，但其持有的无担保债权的金额均需超过 1000 美元或者该会议系由债权金额位列前 100 名的无担保债权人提前 7 日接到通知后出席或被代表出席，并且应记录出席或被代表出席并参与表决的债权人的姓名及其债权金额，并保留该会议记录以供检查；

（2）在就选任委员会而举行的会议上，所有参与表决的代理权的征集均符合第 2006 条的规定，并且该条（e）附条所要求的清单和声明均已被移交给联邦托管人；并且

（3）该委员会的组建在所有其他方面均公平合理。

（c）**不符合要求的任命**。在根据本条的（a）附条发出通知并举行听证后，若法院认为该任命不符合法典第 1102 条（b）（1）中的要求，则法院应指示联邦托管人免去委员会的任命，法院也可作出其他相应裁定。

（经 Mar. 30, 1987, eff. Aug. 1, 1987; Apr. 30, 1991, eff. Aug. 1, 1991; Mar. 26, 2009, eff.Dec. 1, 2009. 修正）

第 2007.1 条　第 11 章重整案件中托管人或监督人的任命

（a）**裁定任命托管人或监督人**。在第 11 章重整案件中，在提出动议申请裁定根据法典第 1104 条（a）或第 1104 条（c）任命托管人或监督人时，应遵守本法第 9014 条的规定。

(b) ELECTION OF TRUSTEE.

(1) *Request for an Election*. A request to convene a meeting of creditors for the purpose of electing a trustee in a chapter 11 reorganization case shall be filed and transmitted to the United States trustee in accordance with Rule 5005 within the time prescribed by §1104 (b) of the Code. Pending court approval of the person elected, anyperson appointed by the United States trustee under §1104 (d) and approved in accordance with subdivision (c) of this rule shall serve as trustee.

(2) *Manner of Election and Notice*. An election of a trustee under §1104 (b) of the Code shall be conducted in the manner provided in Rules 2003 (b)(3) and 2006. Notice of the meeting of creditors convened under §1104 (b) shall be given as provided in Rule 2002. The United States trustee shall preside at the meeting. A proxy for the purpose of voting in the election may be solicited only by a committee of creditors appointed under §1102 of the Code or by any other party entitled to solicit a proxy pursuant to Rule 2006.

(3) *Report of Election and Resolution of Disputes*.

(A) *Report of Undisputed Election*. If no dispute arises out of the election, the United States trustee shall promptly file a report certifying the election, including the name and address of the person elected and a statement that the election is undisputed. The report shall be accompanied by a verified statement of the person elected setting forth that person's connections with the debtor, creditors, any other party in interest, their respective attorneys and accountants, the United States trustee, or any person employed in the office of the United States trustee.

(B) *Dispute Arising out of an Election*. If a dispute arises out of an election, the United States trustee shall promptly file a report stating that the election is disputed, informing the court of the nature of the dispute, and listing the name and address of any candidate elected under any alternative presented by the dispute. The report shall be accompanied by a verified statement by each candidate elected under each alternative presented by the dispute, setting forth the person's connections with the debtor, creditors, any other party in interest, their respective attorneys and accountants, the United States trustee, or any person employed in the office of the United States trustee. Not later than

美国联邦破产程序规则
（中英对照译本）

（b）托管人的选任。

（1）请求选任托管人。申请召集债权人会议以选任第11章重整案件中的托管人的请求应按照本法第5005条的规定，在法典第1104条（b）规定的时间内被提交法院并被移交给联邦托管人。在法院尚未就被选任的人作出批准的期间内，被联邦托管人根据第1104条（d）任命并根据本条的（c）附条批准的人应继续担任托管人。

（2）选任和通知的方式。应按照本法第2003条（b）（3）和第2006条规定的方式，根据法典第1104条（b）选任托管人。应按照本法第2002条规定的方式就根据法典第1104条（b）召集举行的债权人会议发出通知。联邦托管人应出席该会议。仅有根据法典第1102条而被任命的债权人委员会或根据本法第2006条有权征集代理权的任何其他主体才可以就该选任参与表决为目的征集代理权。

（3）选任报告和争议解决。

（A）无争议选任的报告。若就该选任不存在任何争议，则联邦托管人应及时提交报告以确认该选任，并载明被选任的人的姓名和住址以及说明该选任并不存在争议的声明。该报告应附有被选任的人所出具的宣誓声明以列明其与债务人、债权人、任何其他利益相关方、前述主体的代理律师和会计师、联邦托管人或联邦托管人办公室内的任何工作人员间的关系。

（B）因选任而产生的争议。若就该选任存在争议，则联邦托管人应及时提交报告并注明该选任存在争议，还要告知法院该争议的性质并列明因该争议而产生的任何备选方案下被选任的任何候选人的姓名和住址。该报告还应附有因该争议而产生的任何备选方案下被选任的各候选人的宣誓声明，以列明其与债务人、债权人、任何其他利益相关方、前述主体的代理律师和会计师、联邦托管人或联邦托管人办公室内的任何工作人员间的关系。在争议选任的报告被提交当日或之前，针对请求根据法典第1104条（b）召集会议或获得该报告的副本的任何利益相关方，以及根据法典第1102条被任命的任何委员会，联邦托管人应向其邮寄该报

the date on which the report of the disputed election is filed, the United States trustee shall mail a copy of the report and each verified statement to any party in interest that has made a request to convene a meeting under §1104（b）or to receive a copy of the report, and to any committee appointed under §1102 of the Code.

（c）APPROVAL OF APPOINTMENT. An order approving the appointment of a trustee or an examiner under §1104（d）of the Code shall be made on application of the United States trustee. The application shall state the name of the person appointed and, to the best of the applicant's knowledge, all the person's connections with the debtor, creditors, any other parties in interest, their respective attorneys and accountants, the United States trustee, or persons employed in the office of the United States trustee. The application shall state the names of the parties in interest with whom the United States trustee consulted regarding the appointment. The application shall be accompanied by a verified statement of the person appointed setting forth the person's connections with the debtor, creditors, any other party in interest, their respective attorneys and accountants, the United States trustee, or any person employed in the office of the United States trustee.

（Added Apr. 30, 1991, eff. Aug. 1, 1991; amended Apr. 11, 1997, eff. Dec. 1, 1997; Apr. 23, 2008,eff. Dec. 1, 2008.）

Rule 2007.2. Appointment of Patient Care Ombudsman in a Health Care Business Case

（a）ORDER TO APPOINT PATIENT CARE OMBUDSMAN. In a chapter 7, chapter 9, or chapter 11 case in which the debtor is a health care business, the court shall order the appointment of a patient care ombudsman under §333 of the Code, unless the court, on motion of the United States trustee or a party in interest filed no later than 21 days after the commencement of the case or within another time fixed by the court, finds that the appointment of a patient care ombudsman is not necessary under the specific circumstances of the case for the protection of patients.

（b）MOTION FOR ORDER TO APPOINT OMBUDSMAN. If the court has found that the appointment of an ombudsman is not necessary, or has terminated the

告的副本以及所有宣誓声明。

（c）**任命的批准**。只有在联邦托管人提出申请的情况下，法院才可根据法典第 1104 条（d）裁定批准任命托管人或检查人。该申请应载明被任命的人的姓名，以及申请人所能知道的所有此人与债务人、债权人、任何其他利益相关方、前述主体的代理律师和会计师、联邦托管人或联邦托管人办公室内的任何工作人员间的关系。该申请还应载明联邦托管人就该任命向其征求意见的利益相关方的姓名。该申请还应附有被任命的人的宣誓声明以列明其与债务人、债权人、任何其他利益相关方、前述主体的代理律师和会计师、联邦托管人或联邦托管人办公室内的任何工作人员间的关系。

（经 Apr. 30, 1991, eff. Aug. 1, 1991; amended Apr. 11, 1997, eff. Dec. 1, 1997; Apr. 23, 2008,eff. Dec. 1, 2008. 增补）

第 2007.2 条　医疗护理机构中患者护理监察员的任命

（a）**裁定任命患者护理监察员**。在第 7 章、第 9 章或第 11 章案件中，若债务人为医疗护理机构，则除非联邦托管人或利益相关方在案件启动后 21 日内或法院确定的其他期间内提出动议，且法院认为就案件的具体情形而言并无任命患者护理监察员以保护患者的必要，否则法院应裁定根据法典第 333 条任命患者护理监察员。

（b）**申请裁定任命监察员的动议**。若法院认为并无任命监察员的必要，或者已经终止该任命，则应联邦托管人或利益相关方的动议，法院可随后在认为有必

appointment, the court, on motion of the United States trustee or a party in interest, may order the appointment at a later time if it finds that the appointment has become necessary to protect patients.

(c) NOTICE OF APPOINTMENT. If a patient care ombudsman is appointed under §333, the United States trustee shall promptly file a notice of the appointment, including the name and address of the person appointed. Unless the person appointed is a State Long-Term Care Ombudsman, the notice shall be accompanied by a verified statement of the person appointed setting forth the person's connections with the debtor, creditors, patients, any other party in interest, their respective attorneys and accountants, the United States trustee, and any person employed in the office of the United States trustee.

(d) TERMINATION OF APPOINTMENT. On motion of the United States trustee or a party in interest, the court may terminate the appointment of a patient care ombudsman if the court finds that the appointment is not necessary to protect patients.

(e) MOTION. A motion under this rule shall be governed by Rule 9014. The motion shall be transmitted to the United States trustee and served on: the debtor; the trustee; any committee elected under §705 or appointed under §1102 of the Code or its authorized agent, or, if the case is a chapter 9 municipality case or a chapter 11 reorganization case and no committee of unsecured creditors has been appointed under §1102, on the creditors included on the list filed under Rule 1007 (d); and such other entities as the court may direct.

(Added Apr. 23, 2008, eff. Dec. 1, 2008; amended Mar. 26, 2009, eff. Dec. 1, 2009.)

Rule 2008. Notice to Trustee of Selection

The United States trustee shall immediately notify the person selected as trustee how to qualify and, if applicable, the amount of the trustee's bond. A trustee that has filed a blanket bond pursuant to Rule 2010 and has been selected as trustee in a chapter 7, chapter 12, or chapter 13 case that does not notify the court and the United States trustee in writing of rejection of the office within seven days after receipt of notice of selection shall be deemed to have accepted the office. Any other person selected as trustee shall notify the court and the United States trustee in writing of acceptance of the office within seven days after receipt of notice of selection or shall be deemed to have rejected the office.

要任命监察员以保护患者的情况下，裁定任命监察员。

（c）**任命的通知**。若患者护理监察员被根据法典第 333 条得以任命，则联邦托管人应及时提交任命的通知，并注明被任命的人的姓名和住址。除非被任命的人是州长期护理监察员，否则该通知还应附有被任命的人的宣誓声明以列明其与债务人、债权人、患者、任何其他利益相关方、前述主体的代理律师和会计师、联邦托管人和联邦托管人办公室内的任何工作人员间的关系。

（d）**任命的终止**。应联邦托管人或利益相关方的动议，若法院认为并无任命监察员以保护患者的必要，则法院可终止患者护理监察员的任命。

（e）**动议**。本条中的动议应符合本法第 9014 条的规定。该动议应被移交给联邦托管人并送达至：债务人、托管人；根据法典第 705 条选任或根据第 1102 条被任命的任何委员会或其授权代理机关；或者若案件为第 9 章市政机构破产案件或第 11 章重整案件，并且尚未根据法典第 1102 条任命无担保债权人委员会，则应送达至根据第 1007 条（d）被提交的名单上所列的债权人；以及法院可指定的该类其他主体。

（经 Apr. 23, 2008, eff. Dec. 1, 2008; amended Mar. 26, 2009, eff. Dec. 1, 2009. 增补）

第 2008 条　向被选任的托管人发出的通知

联邦托管人应立刻通知被选任为托管人的人如何符合相应的要求以及托管人保险金的金额（如适用）。已经根据第 2010 条申请诚实信用保险的托管人，以及已经被选任为第 7 章、第 12 章或第 13 章案件中的托管人并且未在接到被选任的通知后 7 日内书面拒绝该职位的人，应被视为已经接受该职位。任何其他被选任为托管人的人均应在接到选任通知后 7 日内以书面形式通知法院和联邦托管人其将接受该职位，否则应被视为已经拒绝该职位。

(As amended Mar. 30, 1987, eff. Aug. 1, 1987; Apr. 30, 1991, eff. Aug. 1, 1991; Mar. 26, 2009, eff.Dec. 1, 2009.)

Rule 2009. Trustees for Estates When Joint Administration Ordered

(a) ELECTION OF SINGLE TRUSTEE FOR ESTATES BEING JOINTLY ADMINISTERED. If the court orders a joint administration of two or more estates under Rule 1015 (b), creditors may elect a single trustee for the estates being jointly administered, unless the case is under subchapter V of chapter 7 of the Code.

(b) RIGHT OF CREDITORS TO ELECT SEPARATE TRUSTEE. Notwithstanding entry of an order for joint administration under Rule 1015 (b), the creditors of any debtor may elect a separate trustee for the estate of the debtor as provided in §702 of the Code, unless the case is under subchapter V of chapter 7.

(c) APPOINTMENT OF TRUSTEES FOR ESTATES BEING JOINTLY ADMINISTERED.

(1) *Chapter 7 Liquidation Cases.* Except in a case governed by subchapter V of chapter 7, the United States trustee may appoint one or more interim trustees for estates being jointly administered in chapter 7 cases.

(2) *Chapter 11 Reorganization Cases.* If the appointment of a trustee is ordered, the United States trustee may appoint one or more trustees for estates being jointly administered in chapter 11 cases.

(3) *Chapter 12 Family Farmer's Debt Adjustment Cases.* The United States trustee may appoint one or more trustees for estates being jointly administered in chapter 12 cases.

(4) *Chapter 13 Individual's Debt Adjustment Cases.* The United States trustee may appoint one or more trustees for estates being jointly administered in chapter 13 cases.

(d) POTENTIAL CONFLICTS OF INTEREST. On a showing that creditors or equity security holders of the different estates will be prejudiced by conflicts of interest of a common trustee who has been elected or appointed, the court shall order the selection of separate trustees for estates being jointly administered.

（经 Mar. 30, 1987, eff. Aug. 1, 1987; Apr. 30, 1991, eff. Aug. 1, 1991; Mar. 26, 2009, eff.Dec. 1, 2009. 修正）

第 2009 条　被裁定合并管理时多个破产实体的托管人

（a）**选任一位托管人合并管理多个破产实体**。除法典第 7 章第五附章的案件以外，若法院根据第 1015 条（b）裁定合并管理两个或两个以上的破产实体，则债权人可仅选任一位托管人以管理被合并的多个破产实体。

（b）**债权人选任单独托管人的权利**。除法典第 7 章第五附章的案件以外，即使法院根据第 1015 条（b）正式作出合并管理的裁定，各位债务人的债权人仍可根据法典第 702 条为其债务人的破产实体选任单独的托管人。

（c）**任命被合并管理的多个破产实体的托管人**。

（1）第 7 章清算案件。除第 7 章第五附章中的案件以外，针对案件均为第 7 章案件的情况下，联邦托管人可为被合并管理的多个破产实体任命一位或多位临时托管人。

（2）第 11 章重整案件。在案件均为第 11 章案件的情况下，若法院裁定任命托管人，则联邦托管人可为被合并管理的多个破产实体任命一位或多位托管人。

（3）第 12 章家庭农场主债务调整案件。在案件均为第 12 章案件的情况下，联邦托管人可为被合并管理的多个破产实体任命一位或多位托管人。

（4）第 13 章个人债务调整案件。在案件均为第 13 章案件的情况下，联邦托管人可为被合并管理的多个破产实体任命一位或多位托管人。

（d）**潜在的利益冲突**。若有证据表明不同破产实体的债权人或股本证券持有人的利益将因被选任或指定的共同托管人的利益冲突而遭受损害，则法院应裁定为被合并管理的多个破产实体分别选任单独的托管人。

(e) SEPARATE ACCOUNTS. The trustee or trustees of estates being jointly administered shall keep separate accounts of the property and distribution of each estate.

(As amended Mar. 30, 1987, eff. Aug. 1, 1987; Apr. 30, 1991, eff. Aug. 1, 1991; Mar. 27, 2003, eff.Dec. 1, 2003.)

Rule 2010. Qualification by Trustee; Proceeding on Bond

(a) BLANKET BOND. The United States trustee may authorize a blanket bond in favor of the United States conditioned on the faithful performance of official duties by the trustee or trustees to cover (1) a person who qualifies as trustee in a number of cases, and (2) a number of trustees each of whom qualifies in a different case.

(b) PROCEEDING ON BOND. A proceeding on the trustee's bond may be brought by any party in interest in the name of the United States for the use of the entity injured by the breach of the condition.

(As amended Mar. 30, 1987, eff. Aug. 1, 1987; Apr. 30, 1991, eff. Aug. 1, 1991.)

Rule 2011. Evidence of Debtor in Possession or Qualification of Trustee

(a) Whenever evidence is required that a debtor is a debtor in possession or that a trustee has qualified, the clerk may so certify and the certificate shall constitute conclusive evidence of that fact.

(b) If a person elected or appointed as trustee does not qualify within the time prescribed by §322 (a) of the Code, the clerk shall so notify the court and the United States trustee.

(As amended Apr. 30, 1991, eff. Aug. 1, 1991.)

Rule 2012. Substitution of Trustee or Successor Trustee; Accounting

(a) TRUSTEE. If a trustee is appointed in a chapter 11 case or the debtor is removed as debtor in possession in a chapter 12 case, the trustee is substituted automatically for the debtor in possession as a party in any pending action, proceeding, or matter.

（e）**独立账目**。被合并管理的破产实体的托管人（们）应对各个破产实体单独记账及分配财产。

（经 Mar. 30, 1987, eff. Aug. 1, 1987; Apr. 30, 1991, eff. Aug. 1, 1991; Mar. 27, 2003, eff.Dec. 1, 2003. 修正）

第 2010 条 托管人的资格；就保证保险提起的诉讼

（a）**保证保险**。联邦托管人可提供保证保险，该保险的受益人为美国，以托管人（们）忠实履行职务为条件，保险对象有（1）就多个案件均有资格担任托管人的人，以及（2）各个案件中合格的各位托管人。

（b）**就保证保险提起的诉讼**。任何利益相关方均可以美国的名义，为了因违反该条件而遭受损害的实体，就托管人的保证保险提起诉讼。

（经 Mar. 30, 1987, eff. Aug. 1, 1987; Apr. 30, 1991, eff. Aug. 1, 1991. 修正）

第 2011 条 经管债务人的证明或托管人的资格

（a）每当被要求提供债务人为经管债务人或托管人为合格托管人时，书记员都可出具相应的证明，而该证明应构成该事实的确凿证据。

（b）若被选任或被指定为托管人的人在法典第 322 条（a）规定的期间内仍不合格，则书记员应将该情况通知法院和联邦托管人。

（经 Apr. 30, 1991, eff. Aug. 1, 1991. 修订）

第 2012 条 托管人的取代或继任托管人；账目

（a）**托管人**。若在第 11 章案件中被任命有托管人或在第 12 章案件中债务人不再作为经管债务人，则在任何进行中的诉讼、程序或事项中，托管人都将自动取代经管债务人而作为当事人。

(b) SUCCESSOR TRUSTEE. When a trustee dies, resigns, is removed, or otherwise ceases to hold office during the pendency of a case under the Code (1) the successor is automatically substituted as a party in any pending action, proceeding, or matter; and (2) the successor trustee shall prepare, file, and transmit to the United States trustee an accounting of the prior administration of the estate.

(As amended Mar. 30, 1987, eff. Aug. 1, 1987; Apr. 30, 1991, eff. Aug. 1, 1991.)

Rule 2013. Public Record of Compensation Awarded to Trustees, Examiners, and Professionals

(a) RECORD TO BE KEPT. The clerk shall maintain a public record listing fees awarded by the court (1) to trustees and attorneys, accountants, appraisers, auctioneers and other professionals employed by trustees, and (2) to examiners. The record shall include the name and docket number of the case, the name of the individual or firm receiving the fee and the amount of the fee awarded. The record shall be maintained chronologically and shall be kept current and open to examination by the public without charge. "Trustees", as used in this rule, does not include debtors in possession.

(b) SUMMARY OF RECORD. At the close of each annual period, the clerk shall prepare a summary of the public record by individual or firm name, to reflect total fees awarded during the preceding year. The summary shall be open to examination by the public without charge. The clerk shall transmit a copy of the summary to the United States trustee.

(As amended Mar. 30, 1987, eff. Aug. 1, 1987; Apr. 30, 1991, eff. Aug. 1, 1991.)

Rule 2014. Employment of Professional Persons

(a) APPLICATION FOR AND ORDER OF EMPLOYMENT. An order approving the employment of attorneys, accountants, appraisers, auctioneers, agents, or other professionals pursuant to §327, §1103, or §1114 of the Code shall be made only on application of the trustee or committee. The application shall be filed and, unless the case is a chapter 9 municipality case, a copy of the application shall be transmitted by the applicant to the United States trustee. The application shall state the specific facts

（b）**继任托管人**。在破产法典规定的案件进行的过程中，当托管人去世、辞职、被免职或因其他原因而不再履职时（1）继任者将在任何进行中的诉讼、程序或事项中自动被替换为当事人；并且（2）继任托管人应准备、提交并向联邦托管人移交一份关于先前破产实体管理的说明。

（经 Mar. 30, 1987, eff. Aug. 1, 1987; Apr. 30, 1991, eff. Aug. 1, 1991. 修正）

第 2013 条　向托管人、监督人和专业人员给付的报酬的公共记录

（a）**应被保存的记录**。书记员应保存有公共记录，该记录应列明经法院批准而向（1）托管人和律师、会计师、评估师、拍卖师和托管人雇佣的其他专业人员，以及（2）监督人给付的报酬。该记录应载有案件的名称和档案号，收取该费用的个人或事务所的姓名或名称以及被批准给付的费用的金额。该记录应按时间顺序进行保存，并且应进行实时更新并供公众免费查阅。本条中使用的"托管人"一词不包括经管债务人。

（b）**该记录的摘要**。在每个年度结束时，书记员应按个人或事务所的姓名或名称准备该公共记录的摘要，以反映上一年度中被批准给付的总费用。该摘要应供公众免费查阅。书记员应将该摘要的副本移交给联邦托管人。

（经 Mar. 30, 1987, eff. Aug. 1, 1987; Apr. 30, 1991, eff. Aug. 1, 1991. 修正）

第 2014 条　雇佣专业人员

（a）**申请雇佣专业人员以及批准该雇佣的裁定**。仅当在托管人或委员会提出申请的情况下，法院才可根据法典第 327、1103 或 1114 条作出批准雇佣律师、会计师、评估师、拍卖师、代理人或其他专业人员的裁定。申请人应向法院提交该申请，并且除第 9 章市政机构破产案件外，还应向联邦托管人移交该申请的副本。该申请须结合具体事实说明雇佣专业人员的必要性，将被雇佣的人员的姓名，作此选任的原因，将被提供的专业服务，任何拟定的报酬安排以及申请人所能够

showing the necessity for the employment, the name of the person to be employed, the reasons for the selection, the professional services to be rendered, any proposed arrangement for compensation, and, to the best of the applicant's knowledge, all of the person's connections with the debtor, creditors, any other party in interest, their respective attorneys and accountants, the United States trustee, or any person employed in the office of the United States trustee. The application shall be accompanied by a verified statement of the person to be employed setting forth the person's connections with the debtor, creditors, any other party in interest, their respective attorneys and accountants, the United States trustee, or any person employed in the office of the United States trustee.

(b) SERVICES RENDERED BY MEMBER OR ASSOCIATE OF FIRM OF ATTORNEYS OR ACCOUNTANTS. If, under the Code and this rule, a law partnership or corporation is employed as an attorney, or an accounting partnership or corporation is employed as an accountant, or if a named attorney or accountant is employed, any partner, member, or regular associate of the partnership, corporation, or individual may act as attorney or accountant so employed, without further order of the court.

(As amended Mar. 30, 1987, eff. Aug. 1, 1987; Apr. 30, 1991, eff. Aug. 1, 1991.)

Rule 2015. Duty to Keep Records, Make Reports, and Give Notice of Case or Change of Status

(a) TRUSTEE OR DEBTOR IN POSSESSION. A trustee or debtor in possession shall:

(1) in a chapter 7 liquidation case and, if the court directs, in a chapter 11 reorganization case file and transmit to the United States trustee a complete inventory of the property of the debtor within 30 days after qualifying as a trustee or debtor in possession, unless such an inventory has already been filed;

(2) keep a record of receipts and the disposition of money and property received;

(3) file the reports and summaries required by §704 (a) (8) of the Code, which shall include a statement, if payments are made to employees, of the amounts of deductions for all taxes required to be withheld or paid for and in behalf of employees and the place where these amounts are deposited;

知道的所有此人与债务人、债权人、任何其他利益相关方、前述主体的代理律师和会计师、联邦托管人或联邦托管人办公室内的任何工作人员间的关系。该申请应附有将被雇佣的人的宣誓声明以列明其与债务人、债权人、任何其他利益相关方、前述主体的代理律师和会计师、联邦托管人或联邦托管人办公室内的任何工作人员间的关系。

（b）**由律师事务所或会计师事务所的成员或员工所提供的服务**。若根据法典和本条规定，律师合伙组织或公司被雇佣为律师，或会计师合伙组织或公司被雇佣为会计师，或者若指定雇佣某位律师或会计师，则该合伙组织、公司或个人的任何合伙人、成员或长期员工均可作为已被雇佣的律师或会计师，而无须法院作出下一步的裁定。

（经 Mar. 30, 1987, eff. Aug. 1, 1987; Apr. 30, 1991, eff. Aug. 1, 1991. 修正）

第 2015 条　保存档案、制作档案以及就案件或状态的变化发出通知的义务

（a）**托管人或经管债务人**。托管人或经管债务人应履行以下各项：

（1）在第 7 章清算案件中，以及在法院作此指示的情况下在第 11 章重整案件中，应在成为合格的托管人或经管债务人后 30 日内向法院提交并向联邦托管人移交债务人财产的完整清单，除非该清单已被提交；

（2）保存有关收取的金钱和财产的收据和处置的记录；

（3）提交法典第 704 条（a）（8）要求的报告和摘要，并且若向员工付款，则应包含一份声明，以说明就所有被要求代缴或已经为雇员或代表雇员支付的所有税款而扣除的款项以及存有这些款项的地点；

（4）as soon as possible after the commencement of the case, give notice of the case to every entity known to be holding money or property subject to withdrawal or order of the debtor, including every bank, savings or building and loan association, public utility company, and landlord with whom the debtor has a deposit, and to every insurance company which has issued a policy having a cash surrender value payable to the debtor, except that notice need not be given to any entity who has knowledge or has previously been notified of the case;

（5）in a chapter 11 reorganization case, on or before the last day of the month after each calendar quarter during which there is a duty to pay fees under 28 U.S.C. §1930（a）（6）, file and transmit to the United States trustee a statement of any disbursements made during that quarter and of any fees payable under 28 U.S.C. §1930（a）（6）for that quarter; and

（6）in a chapter 11 small business case, unless the court, for cause, sets another reporting interval, file and transmit to the United States trustee for each calendar month after the order for relief, on the appropriate Official Form, the report required by §308. If the order for relief is within the first 15 days of a calendar month, a report shall be filed for the portion of the month that follows the order for relief. If the order for relief is after the 15th day of a calendar month, the period for the remainder of the month shall be included in the report for the next calendar month. Each report shall be filed no later than 21 days after the last day of the calendar month following the month covered by the report. The obligation to file reports under this subparagraph terminates on the effective date of the plan, or conversion or dismissal of the case.

（b）CHAPTER 12 TRUSTEE AND DEBTOR IN POSSESSION. In a chapter 12 family farmer's debt adjustment case, the debtor in possession shall perform the duties prescribed in clauses（2）-（4）of subdivision（a）of this rule and, if the court directs, shall file and transmit to the United States trustee a complete inventory of the property of the debtor within the time fixed by the court. If the debtor is removed as debtor in possession, the trustee shall perform the duties of the debtor in possession prescribed in this paragraph.

（c）CHAPTER 13 TRUSTEE AND DEBTOR.

（1）*Business Cases.* In a chapter 13 individual's debt adjustment case, when the

美国联邦破产程序规则
（中英对照译本）

（4）在案件被启动后，应尽快就该案向已知的所有因代缴或债务人的裁定而持有相应的金钱或财产的各个实体发出通知，包括各银行、储蓄或房屋贷款协会、公用事业公司和债务人向其支付押金的房东，以及签发应向债务人支付退保金的保单的各家保险公司，但该通知无须向任何已经知道或先前已经就该案接到通知的任何实体发出；

（5）在第 11 章重整案件中，应在有义务根据《美国联邦法典》第 28 篇第 1930 条（a）（6）支付费用的每个日历季度后的下一个月的最后一日或之前，向法院提交并向联邦托管人移交一份声明，载明在该季度内根据《美国联邦法典》第 28 篇第 1930 条（a）（6）所支出的任何该季度内应付的费用；以及

（6）在第 11 章小企业案件中，除非法院出于特定事由确定了其他的报告频率，否则应在破产救济令被作出后的每个日历月向法院提交并向联邦托管人移交以相应的官方模板所制作的法典第 308 条所要求的报告。若破产救济令系在日历月的前 15 日内作出，则被提交的报告应针对日历月在破产救济令被作出后的剩余期间。若破产救济令系在日历月的第 15 日后作出，则该月剩余的期间也应被计入就下一日历月所作的报告中。所有报告均应在该报告所针对的月份后的下一日历月的最后一天后的 21 日内被提交。根据本款提交报告的义务将在计划生效当日或案件被转换或被驳回时被终止。

(b)**第 12 章托管人和经管债务人**。在第 12 章家庭农场主的债务调整案件中，经管债务人应履行本条(a)附条的(2)至(4)规定的义务，并且若法院作出指示，则应在法院规定的时间内向法院提交并向联邦托管人移交完整的债务人的财产清单。若债务人不再担任经管债务人，则联邦托管人应履行本款规定的经管债务人的义务。

(c)**第 13 章托管人和债务人**。
(1)商业破产案件。在第 13 章个人债务调整案件中,若债务人从事商事业务,

debtor is engaged in business, the debtor shall perform the duties prescribed by clauses (2) - (4) of subdivision (a) of this rule and, if the court directs, shall file and transmit to the United States trustee a complete inventory of the property of the debtor within the time fixed by the court.

(2) *Nonbusiness Cases.* In a chapter 13 individual's debt adjustment case, when the debtor is not engaged in business, the trustee shall perform the duties prescribed by clause (2) of subdivision (a) of this rule.

(d) FOREIGN REPRESENTATIVE. In a case in which the court has granted recognition of a foreign proceeding under chapter 15, the foreign representative shall file any notice required under §1518 of the Code within 14 days after the date when the representative becomes aware of the subsequent information.

(e) TRANSMISSION OF REPORTS. In a chapter 11 case the court may direct that copies or summaries of annual reports and copies or summaries of other reports shall be mailed to the creditors, equity security holders, and indenture trustees. The court may also direct the publication of summaries of any such reports. A copy of every report or summary mailed or published pursuant to this subdivision shall be transmitted to the United States trustee.

(As amended Mar. 30, 1987, eff. Aug. 1, 1987; Apr. 30, 1991, eff. Aug. 1, 1991; Apr. 23, 1996, eff.Dec. 1, 1996; Apr. 29, 2002, eff. Dec. 1, 2002; Apr. 23, 2008, eff. Dec. 1, 2008; Mar. 26, 2009, eff.Dec. 1, 2009; Apr. 23, 2012, eff. Dec. 1, 2012.)

Rule 2015.1. Patient Care Ombudsman

(a) REPORTS. A patient care ombudsman, at least 14 days before making a report under §333 (b) (2) of the Code, shall give notice that the report will be made to the court, unless the court orders otherwise. The notice shall be transmitted to the United States trustee, posted conspicuously at the health care facility that is the subject of the report, and served on: the debtor; the trustee; all patients; and any committee elected under §705 or appointed under §1102 of the Code or its authorized agent, or, if the case is a chapter 9 municipality case or a chapter 11 reorganization case and no committee of unsecured creditors has been appointed under §1102, on the creditors

则债务人应履行本条（a）附条的第（2）至（4）款所规定的义务，并且若法院作出指示，则应在法院规定的时间内向法院提交并向联邦托管人移交完整的债务人的财产清单。

（2）非商业破产案件。在第13章个人债务调整案件中，若债务人不从事商事业务，则联邦托管人应履行本条（a）附条的第（2）款所规定的义务。

（d）**外国代表**。当法院已经根据第15章准予承认外国程序时，外国代表应在获知任何后续信息后14日内提交法典第1518条所要求的通知。

（e）**报告的移交**。在第11章案件中，法院可指示应将年度报告的副本或摘要以及其他报告的副本或摘要邮寄给债权人、股本证券持有人以及契约受托人。法院也可指示将任何该类报告的摘要进行公告。根据本附条而被邮寄或公告的各报告的副本或摘要均应被移交给联邦托管人。

（经 Mar. 30, 1987, eff. Aug. 1, 1987; Apr. 30, 1991, eff. Aug. 1, 1991; Apr. 23, 1996, eff. Dec. 1, 1996; Apr. 29, 2002, eff. Dec. 1, 2002; Apr. 23, 2008, eff. Dec. 1, 2008; Mar. 26, 2009, eff. Dec. 1, 2009; Apr. 23, 2012, eff. Dec. 1, 2012. 修正）

第2015.1条 患者护理监察员

（a）**报告**。除非法院作出其他裁定，否则患者护理监察员至少应在根据法典第333条（b）（2）制作报告前14日以前发出通知，以说明其系为法院而制作该报告。该通知应被移交给联邦托管人，并在该报告所涉及的医疗护理机构的显著位置上张贴该通知并送达至：债务人、托管人、所有患者和任何根据法典第705条被选任或根据第1102条被指定的委员会或其授权代理机关；或者若案件为第9章市政机构破产案件或第11章重整案件，并且并未根据法典第1102条任命无担保债权人委员会，则应送达至根据第1007条（d）被提交的清单上所列明的债权人；以及法院可指定的该类其他实体。该通知应注明该报告将被得以制作的日

included on the list filed under Rule 1007（d）; and such other entities as the court may direct. The notice shall state the date and time when the report will be made, the manner in which the report will be made, and, if the report is in writing, the name, address, telephone number, email address, and website, if any, of the person from whom a copy of the report may be obtained at the debtor's expense.

（b）AUTHORIZATION TO REVIEW CONFIDENTIAL PATIENT RECORDS. A motion by a patient care ombudsman under §333（c）to review confidential patient records shall be governed by Rule 9014, served on the patient and any family member or other contact person whose name and address have been given to the trustee or the debtor for the purpose of providing information regarding the patient's health care, and transmitted to the United States trustee subject to applicable nonbankruptcy law relating to patient privacy. Unless the court orders otherwise, a hearing on the motion may not be commenced earlier than 14 days after service of the motion.

（Added Apr. 23, 2008, eff. Dec. 1, 2008; amended Mar. 26, 2009, eff. Dec. 1, 2009.）

Rule 2015.2. Transfer of Patient in Health Care Business Case

Unless the court orders otherwise, if the debtor is a health care business, the trustee may not transfer a patient to another health care business under §704（a）（12）of the Code unless the trustee gives at least 14 days' notice of the transfer to the patient care ombudsman, if any, the patient, and any family member or other contact person whose name and address has been given to the trustee or the debtor for the purpose of providing information regarding the patient's health care. The notice is subject to applicable nonbankruptcy law relating to patient privacy.

（Added Apr. 23, 2008, eff. Dec. 1, 2008; amended Mar. 26, 2009, eff. Dec. 1, 2009.）

Rule 2015.3. Reports of Financial Information on Entities in Which a Chapter 11 Estate Holds a Controlling or Substantial Interest

（a）REPORTING REQUIREMENT. In a chapter 11 case, the trustee or debtor in possession shall file periodic financial reports of the value, operations,

期、时间和方式,并且若该报告为书面报告,则应注明可提供该报告的副本并且由债务人承担费用的人的姓名、住址、电话号码、电子邮件地址和网站(如有)。

(b)**授权查阅保密的患者档案**。患者护理监察员根据法典第 333 条(c)申请查阅保密的患者档案的动议应符合第 9014 条的规定,并且在遵守有关患者隐私的相应非破产法规定的情况下,该动议应被送达至患者及其任何家庭成员或其他因提供有关患者医疗护理的信息而已经向托管人或债务人提供姓名和住址的联系人,并移交给联邦托管人。除非法院作出其他裁定,否则就该动议举行的听证不得在送达该动议后 14 日以前启动。

(经 Apr. 23, 2008, eff. Dec. 1, 2008; amended Mar. 26, 2009, eff. Dec. 1, 2009. 增补)

第 2015.2 条　医疗护理机构破产案件中患者的转移

除非法院作出其他裁定,否则若债务人为医疗护理机构,则除非托管人提前 14 日就患者的转移向患者护理监察员(如有)、患者以及任何家庭成员或其他因提供有关患者医疗护理的信息而已经向托管人或债务人提供姓名和住址的联系人发出通知,否则托管人不得根据法典第 704 条(a)(12)将患者转移至其他医疗护理机构。该通知应符合有关患者隐私的相应非破产法的规定。

(经 Apr. 23, 2008, eff. Dec. 1, 2008; amended Mar. 26, 2009, eff. Dec. 1, 2009. 增补)

第 2015.3 条　第 11 章破产实体对其享有控制权或重大利益的实体的财务信息报告

(a)**报告的要求**。在第 11 章案件中,针对破产实体对其享有控制权或重大利益的除上市公司和第 11 章债务人以外的各实体,托管人或经管债务人应就该

and profitability of each entity that is not a publicly traded corporation or a debtor in a case under title 11, and in which the estate holds a substantial or controlling interest. The reports shall be prepared as prescribed by the appropriate Official Form, and shall be based upon the most recent information reasonably available to the trustee or debtor in possession.

(b) TIME FOR FILING; SERVICE. The first report required by this rule shall be filed no later than seven days before the first date set for the meeting of creditors under §341 of the Code. Subsequent reports shall be filed no less frequently than every six months thereafter, until the effective date of a plan or the case is dismissed or converted. Copies of the report shall be served on the United States trustee, any committee appointed under §1102 of the Code, and any other party in interest that has filed a request therefor.

(c) PRESUMPTION OF SUBSTANTIAL OR CONTROLLING INTEREST; JUDICIAL DETERMINATION. For purposes of this rule, an entity of which the estate controls or owns at least a 20 percent interest, shall be presumed to be an entity in which the estate has a substantial or controlling interest. An entity in which the estate controls or owns less than a 20 percent interest shall be presumed not to be an entity in which the estate has a substantial or controlling interest. Upon motion, the entity, any holder of an interest therein, the United States trustee, or any other party in interest may seek to rebut either presumption, and the court shall, after notice and a hearing, determine whether the estate's interest in the entity is substantial or controlling.

(d) MODIFICATION OF REPORTING REQUIREMENT. The court may, after notice and a hearing, vary the reporting requirement established by subdivision (a) of this rule for cause, including that the trustee or debtor in possession is not able, after a good faith effort, to comply with those reporting requirements, or that the information required by subdivision (a) is publicly available.

(e) NOTICE AND PROTECTIVE ORDERS. No later than 14 days before filing the first report required by this rule, the trustee or debtor in possession shall send notice to the entity in which the estate has a substantial or controlling interest, and to all holders—known to the trustee or debtor in possession—of an interest in that entity,

美国联邦破产程序规则
（中英对照译本）

类实体的价值、运营以及盈利能力定期提交财务报告。该报告应按照相应官方模板的规定来制作，并且应基于托管人或经管债务人所能合理取得的最新信息。

（b）**提交期间；送达**。本条所要求的首份报告应在法典第 341 条中确定的首次债权人会议举行前 7 日内而被提交。后续报告应至少每 6 个月被提交一次，直至计划生效之日或案件被驳回或被转换时。报告的副本应被送达给联邦托管人、任何根据法典第 1102 条被任命的委员会以及任何为此已经提交请求的其他利益相关方。

（c）**重大或控制利益的推定；司法认定**。就本条而言，若破产实体控制或持有某实体至少 20% 的权益，则该实体应被推定为破产实体就其享有重大或控制利益的实体。若破产实体控制或拥有某实体的权益少于 20%，则该实体应被推定为破产实体不就其享有重大或控制利益的实体。该实体、就该实体享有权益的任何主体、联邦托管人或任何其他利益相关方均可通过提交动议以推翻前述推定，并且法院在经过通知和听证后，应就破产实体是否就该实体享有重大或控制利益作出认定。

（d）**报告要求的修改**。法院经过通知和听证后，可出于特定事由将本条（a）所规定的报告要求予以修改，该事由包括托管人或经管债务人在经过善意的努力后，仍然无法遵守该类报告要求，或者（a）附条中要求的信息可通过公开途径获得。

（e）**通知以及保护裁定**。在根据本条要求提交首份报告前 14 日以前，托管人或经管债务人应向破产实体就其享有重大或控制利益的实体以及所有就该实体享有权益的主体（托管人或经管债务人所知的主体）发出通知，以说明托管人或经管债务人将根据本条规定提交并送达与该实体有关的财务信息。破产实体就其

129

that the trustee or debtor in possession expects to file and serve financial information relating to the entity in accordance with this rule. The entity in which the estate has a substantial or controlling interest, or a person holding an interest in that entity, may request protection of the information under §107 of the Code.

(f) EFFECT OF REQUEST. Unless the court orders otherwise, the pendency of a request under subdivisions (c), (d), or (e) of this rule shall not alter or stay the requirements of subdivision (a).

(Added Apr. 23, 2008, eff. Dec. 1, 2008; amended Mar. 26, 2009, eff. Dec. 1, 2009.)

Rule 2016. Compensation for Services Rendered and Reimbursement of Expenses

(a) APPLICATION FOR COMPENSATION OR REIMBURSEMENT. An entity seeking interim or final compensation for services, or reimbursement of necessary expenses, from the estate shall file an application setting forth a detailed statement of (1) the services rendered, time expended and expenses incurred, and (2) the amounts requested. An application for compensation shall include a statement as to what payments have theretofore been made or promised to the applicant for services rendered or to be rendered in any capacity whatsoever in connection with the case, the source of the compensation so paid or promised, whether any compensation previously received has been shared and whether an agreement or understanding exists between the applicant and any other entity for the sharing of compensation received or to be received for services rendered in or in connection with the case, and the particulars of any sharing of compensation or agreement or understanding therefor, except that details of any agreement by the applicant for the sharing of compensation as a member or regular associate of a firm of lawyers or accountants shall not be required. The requirements of this subdivision shall apply to an application for compensation for services rendered by an attorney or accountant even though the application is filed by a creditor or other entity. Unless the case is a chapter 9 municipality case, the applicant shall transmit to the United States trustee a copy of the application.

(b) DISCLOSURE OF COMPENSATION PAID OR PROMISED TO

享有重大或控制利益的实体或就该实体享有权益的主体均可根据法典第 107 条申请信息保护。

（f）**申请的效力**。除非法院作出其他裁定，否则对本条的（c）、（d）或（e）附条中的申请的审理，并不会变更或冻结（a）附条中的要求。

（经 Apr. 23, 2008, eff. Dec. 1, 2008; amended Mar. 26, 2009, eff. Dec. 1, 2009. 增补）

第 2016 条　就被提供的服务而支付的报酬以及费用的报销

（a）**申请获得报酬或报销**。若某实体希望从破产实体处就其服务获得临时或最终报酬或者报销其必要费用，则该实体应提交一份申请书并详细陈述（1）所提供的服务、所花费的时间和所产生的费用，以及（2）请求的金额。请求获得报酬的申请书应载明先前向申请人就其以任何身份所提供的或将被提供的与案件有关的服务已经支付或承诺支付的款项，被支付或承诺支付的报酬的来源（无论是否已经与他人共享先前已获得的报酬，也无论申请人与就所提供的或将被提供的与案件有关的服务共享已收取的报酬或将收取报酬的任何其他实体间是否存在正式或非正式的协议），以及有关报酬的共享或因此成立的正式或非正式的协议的细节，但是若该协议系申请作为律师事务所或会计师事务所的成员或长期员工而就共享报酬所订立，则无须载明该协议的细节。本款的要求应适用于就律师或会计师所提供的服务而请求获得报酬的申请书，即使该申请书系由债权人或其他实体所提交。除第 9 章市政机构破产案件外，申请人应向联邦托管人移交该申请书的副本。

（b）**已向债务人律师支付或承诺向其支付的报酬的披露**。债务人的所有律师，

ATTORNEY FOR DEBTOR. Every attorney for a debtor, whether or not the attorney applies for compensation, shall file and transmit to the United States trustee within 14 days after the order for relief, or at another time as the court may direct, the statement required by §329 of the Code including whether the attorney has shared or agreed to share the compensation with any other entity. The statement shall include the particulars of any such sharing or agreement to share by the attorney, but the details of any agreement for the sharing of the compensation with a member or regular associate of the attorney's law firm shall not be required. A supplemental statement shall be filed and transmitted to the United States trustee within 14 days after any payment or agreement not previously disclosed.

(c) DISCLOSURE OF COMPENSATION PAID OR PROMISED TO BANKRUPTCY PETITION PREPARER. Before a petition is filed, every bankruptcy petition preparer for a debtor shall deliver to the debtor, the declaration under penalty of perjury required by §110 (h)(2). The declaration shall disclose any fee, and the source of any fee, received from or on behalf of the debtor within 12 months of the filing of the case and all unpaid fees charged to the debtor. The declaration shall also describe the services performed and documents prepared or caused to be prepared by the bankruptcy petition preparer. The declaration shall be filed with the petition. The petition preparer shall file a supplemental statement within 14 days after any payment or agreement not previously disclosed.

(As amended Mar. 30, 1987, eff. Aug. 1, 1987; Apr. 30, 1991, eff. Aug. 1, 1991; Mar. 27, 2003, eff.Dec. 1, 2003; Mar. 26, 2009, eff. Dec. 1, 2009.)

Rule 2017. Examination of Debtor's Transactions with Debtor's Attorney

(a) PAYMENT OR TRANSFER TO ATTORNEY BEFORE ORDER FOR RELIEF. On motion by any party in interest or on the court's own initiative, the court after notice and a hearing may determine whether any payment of money or any transfer of property by the debtor, made directly or indirectly and in contemplation of the filing of a petition under the Code by or against the debtor or before entry of the order for relief in an involuntary case, to an attorney for services rendered or to be rendered is excessive.

无论该律师是否申请获得报酬，均应在破产救济令被作出后 14 日内或法院可指定的其他期间内，向法院提交并向联邦托管人移交法典第 329 条所要求的声明，并载明该律师是否已经或同意与任何其他实体就报酬分成。该声明还应载明任何该类分成的细节或律师所订立的就报酬分成的协议，但是针对与律师事务所的成员或长期员工共享报酬所订立的协议，无须载明该协议的细节。任何补充声明均应在先前尚未披露的任何款项支付后或任何协议订立后 14 日内向法院提交并移交给联邦托管人。

（c）已向破产申请准备人支付或承诺向其支付的报酬的披露。在破产申请被提交前，债务人所有的破产申请准备人均应向债务人提交法典第 110 条（h）（2）所要求的伪证罚则下的声明。该声明应披露在案件被提交后 12 个月内向债务人收取或代表债务人收取的任何费用和该费用的来源以及应向债务人收取的所有尚未支付的费用。该声明还应说明由破产申请准备人所提供的服务以及已准备或将准备的文件。该声明应与破产申请被一同提交。破产申请准备人应在先前尚未披露的任何款项支付后或任何协议订立后 14 日内提交补充声明。

（经 Mar. 30, 1987, eff. Aug. 1, 1987; Apr. 30, 1991, eff. Aug. 1, 1991; Mar. 27, 2003, eff.Dec. 1, 2003; Mar. 26, 2009, eff. Dec. 1, 2009. 修正）

第 2017 条　审查债务人与其律师间的交易

（a）破产救济令被作出前向律师所作的支付或给付。应任何利益相关方的动议或法院可主动在通知和听证后，针对债务人根据法典提交破产申请或有人对其提交破产申请时，或在强制破产案件中在破产救济令被作出前，由债务人直接或间接向律师就其所提供或将提供的服务所支付的款项或所给付的财产是否超额作出认定。

(b) PAYMENT OR TRANSFER TO ATTORNEY AFTER ORDER FOR RELIEF. On motion by the debtor, the United States trustee, or on the court's own initiative, the court after notice and a hearing may determine whether any payment of money or any transfer of property, or any agreement therefor, by the debtor to an attorney after entry of an order for relief in a case under the Code is excessive, whether the payment or transfer is made or is to be made directly or indirectly, if the payment, transfer, or agreement therefor is for services in any way related to the case.

(As amended Mar. 30, 1987, eff. Aug. 1, 1987; Apr. 30, 1991, eff. Aug. 1, 1991.)

Rule 2018. Intervention; Right to Be Heard

(a) PERMISSIVE INTERVENTION. In a case under the Code, after hearing on such notice as the court directs and for cause shown, the court may permit any interested entity to intervene generally or with respect to any specified matter.

(b) INTERVENTION BY ATTORNEY GENERAL OF A STATE. In a chapter 7, 11, 12, or 13 case, the Attorney General of a State may appear and be heard on behalf of consumer creditors if the court determines the appearance is in the public interest, but the Attorney General may not appeal from any judgment, order, or decree in the case.

(c) CHAPTER 9 MUNICIPALITY CASE. The Secretary of the Treasury of the United States may, or if requested by the court shall, intervene in a chapter 9 case. Representatives of the state in which the debtor is located may intervene in a chapter 9 case with respect to matters specified by the court.

(d) LABOR UNIONS. In a chapter 9, 11, or 12 case, a labor union or employees' association, representative of employees of the debtor, shall have the right to be heard on the economic soundness of a plan affecting the interests of the employees. A labor union or employees' association which exercises its right to be heard under this subdivision shall not be entitled to appeal any judgment, order, or decree relating to the plan, unless otherwise permitted by law.

(e) SERVICE ON ENTITIES COVERED BY THIS RULE. The court may enter orders governing the service of notice and papers on entities permitted to intervene or be heard pursuant to this rule.

（b）**破产救济令被作出后向律师所作的支付或给付**。应债务人、联邦托管人的动议或法院可主动在经过通知和听证后，针对在根据法典提起的破产案件的破产救济令被作出后，由债务人向律师就其提供的与案件相关的服务所作的支付或财产的给付或因此达成的任何协议是否超额作出认定，无论该支付或给付系直接或间接作出。

（经 Mar. 30, 1987, eff. Aug. 1, 1987; Apr. 30, 1991, eff. Aug. 1, 1991. 修正）

第 2018 条　介入；发表意见的权利

（a）**许可介入**。在根据法典被提起的破产案件中，按照法院的指示进行通知和听证后，出于被主张的特定事由，法院可准予任何利益相关方介入全案或仅就某具体事项介入。

（b）**州司法部长的介入**。在第 7、11、12 或 13 章案件中，在法院认为符合公共利益的情况下，州司法部长可代表消费者债权人出席听证并发表意见，但司法部长不得就案件中的任何判决、裁定或法令提起上诉。

（c）**第 9 章市政机构破产案件**。美国财政部长可介入第 9 章案件，但若法院提出要求，则应当介入该案。债务人所在州的州代表可针对法院指定的事项介入第 9 章案件。

（d）**工会**。在第 9、11 或 12 章案件中，工会或职工联合会作为债务人的员工的代表，应有权就影响员工利益的计划的经济合理性发表意见。除非法律有其他规定对此表示许可，否则根据本附条行使其发表意见的权利的工会或职工联合会无权就与计划相关的任何判决、裁定或法令提起上诉。

（e）**向本条所述实体的送达**。法院可裁定就向根据本条被准予介入或发表意见的实体送达通知和文件作出规定。

(As amended Mar. 30, 1987, eff. Aug. 1, 1987; Apr. 30, 1991, eff. Aug. 1, 1991.)

Rule 2019. Disclosure Regarding Creditors and Equity Security Holders in Chapter 9 and Chapter 11 Cases

(a) DEFINITIONS. In this rule the following terms have the meanings indicated:

(1) "Disclosable economic interest" means any claim, interest, pledge, lien, option, participation, derivative instrument, or any other right or derivative right granting the holder an economic interest that is affected by the value, acquisition, or disposition of a claim or interest.

(2) "Represent" or "represents" means to take a position before the court or to solicit votes regarding the confirmation of a plan on behalf of another.

(b) DISCLOSURE BY GROUPS, COMMITTEES, AND ENTITIES.

(1) In a chapter 9 or 11 case, a verified statement setting forth the information specified in subdivision (c) of this rule shall be filed by every group or committee that consists of or represents, and every entity that represents, multiple creditors or equity security holders that are (A) acting in concert to advance their common interests, and (B) not composed entirely of affiliates or insiders of one another.

(2) Unless the court orders otherwise, an entity is not required to file the verified statement described in paragraph (1) of this subdivision solely because of its status as:

(A) an indenture trustee;

(B) an agent for one or more other entities under an agreement for the extension of credit;

(C) a class action representative; or

(D) a governmental unit that is not a person.

(c) INFORMATION REQUIRED. The verified statement shall include:

(1) the pertinent facts and circumstances concerning:

(A) with respect to a group or committee, other than a committee appointed under §1102 or §1114 of the Code, the formation of the group or committee, including the name of each entity at whose instance the group or committee was formed or for whom the group or committee has agreed to act; or

（经 Mar. 30, 1987, eff. Aug. 1, 1987; Apr. 30, 1991, eff. Aug. 1, 1991. 修正）

第 2019 条 针对第 9 章和第 11 章案件中的债权人和股本证券持有人所作的披露

（a）**定义**。本条以下术语适用以下定义：

（1）"可披露的经济利益"指某主体可因其而享有经济利益并且该经济利益受债权或权益的价值、取得或处置的影响的任何债权、权益、质押、财产上担保权、期权、参与权、衍生工具或任何其他权利或衍生权利。

（2）"代表"或"代表们"指在法庭上就计划的批准，代表其他人表态或征集表决权的人。

（b）**团体、委员会和实体所作的披露**。

（1）在第 9 章或第 11 章案件中，列有本条（c）附条所述信息的宣誓声明应由（A）为共同利益而共同行动，并且（B）并非完全由彼此的关联人员或内部人员组成的多名债权人或股本证券持有人所组成的各团体或委员会，或代表前述债权人或股本证券持有人的各团体、委员或各实体提交。

（2）除非法院作出其他裁定，否则任何实体不得仅因其具有以下身份而被要求提交本附条第（1）款中所述的宣誓声明：

（A）契约受托人；

（B）信用贷款协议下一位或多位其他实体的代理人；

（C）集体诉讼代表；或

（D）非个人的政府机构。

（c）**被要求提供的信息**。宣誓声明应载有以下内容：

（1）涉及以下事项的相关事实和情形：

（A）针对团体或委员会（不包括根据法典第 1102 条或第 1114 条被任命的委员会）而言，该团体或委员会的组成，包括该团体或委员会曾为其组成或曾同意为其展开行动的各实体的姓名；或

(B) with respect to an entity, the employment of the entity, including the name of each creditor or equity security holder at whose instance the employment was arranged;

(2) if not disclosed under subdivision (c)(1), with respect to an entity, and with respect to each member of a group or committee:

(A) name and address;

(B) the nature and amount of each disclosable economic interest held in relation to the debtor as of the date the entity was employed or the group or committee was formed; and

(C) with respect to each member of a group or committee that claims to represent any entity in addition to the members of the group or committee, other than a committee appointed under §1102 or §1114 of the Code, the date of acquisition by quarter and year of each disclosable economic interest, unless acquired more than one year before the petition was filed;

(3) if not disclosed under subdivision (c)(1) or (c)(2), with respect to each creditor or equity security holder represented by an entity, group, or committee, other than a committee appointed under §1102 or §1114 of the Code:

(A) name and address; and

(B) the nature and amount of each disclosable economic interest held in relation to the debtor as of the date of the statement; and

(4) a copy of the instrument, if any, authorizing the entity, group, or committee to act on behalf of creditors or equity security holders.

(d) SUPPLEMENTAL STATEMENTS. If any fact disclosed in its most recently filed statement has changed materially, an entity, group, or committee shall file a verified supplemental statement whenever it takes a position before the court or solicits votes on the confirmation of a plan. The supplemental statement shall set forth the material changes in the facts required by subdivision (c) to be disclosed.

(e) DETERMINATION OF FAILURE TO COMPLY; SANCTIONS.

(1) On motion of any party in interest, or on its own motion, the court may determine whether there has been a failure to comply with any provision of this rule.

(2) If the court finds such a failure to comply, it may:

（B）针对实体而言，该实体的雇佣情况，包括雇佣该实体的各债权人或股本证券持有人的姓名；

（2）若尚未根据（c）（1）附条作此披露，则针对于实体以及团体或委员会的各成员而言，还应载有：

（A）其姓名和住址；

（B）自该实体被雇佣或该团体或委员会组成之日起所持有的与债务人相关的各项可披露的经济利益的性质和金额；以及

（C）若某团体或委员会（不包括根据法典第 1102 条或第 1114 条被任命的委员会）除代表其成员外还主张代表其他实体，则针对该团体或委员会的成员，应载有取得各项可披露的经济利益的日期（以季度和年份划分），除非系在破产申请被提交前 1 年以前取得；

（3）若尚未根据（c）（1）或（c）（2）附条作此披露，则针对由实体、团体或委员会（不包括根据法典第 1102 条或第 1114 条而被任命的委员会）所代表的各债权人或股本证券持有人而言，还应载有：

（A）其姓名和住址；以及

（B）自出具声明之日起所持有的与债务人相关的各项可披露的经济利益的性质和金额；以及

（4）授权实体、团体或委员会代表债权人或股本证券持有人行事的文件的副本（如有）。

（d）**补充声明**。若在最近提交的声明中被披露的事实发生了重大变化，则该实体、团体或委员会在当其在法庭上就计划的批准表态或征集表决权时，应提交宣誓补充声明。该补充声明应列明根据（c）附条被要求披露的事实所发生的重大变化。

（e）**未能履行的认定；处罚**

（1）应利益相关方的动议或法院可主动就前述主体是否未能履行本条任何规定作出认定。

（2）若法院认定其未能履行本条规定，则可：

(A) refuse to permit the entity, group, or committee to be heard or to intervene in the case;

(B) hold invalid any authority, acceptance, rejection, or objection given, procured, or received by the entity, group, or committee; or

(C) grant other appropriate relief.

(As amended Mar. 30, 1987, eff. Aug. 1, 1987; Apr. 30, 1991, eff. Aug. 1, 1991; Apr. 26, 2011, eff.Dec. 1, 2011.)

Rule 2020. Review of Acts by United States Trustee

A proceeding to contest any act or failure to act by the United States trustee is governed by Rule 9014.

(Added Apr. 30, 1991, eff. Aug. 1, 1991.)

（A）拒绝该实体、团体或委员会发表意见或介入案件；

（B）使得该实体、团体或委员会给予、获得或接受的任何授权、接受、拒绝或反对均归于无效；或

（C）提供其他相应救济。

（经 Mar. 30, 1987, eff. Aug. 1, 1987; Apr. 30, 1991, eff. Aug. 1, 1991; Apr. 26, 2011, eff.Dec. 1, 2011. 修正）

第 2020 条　对联邦托管人行为的审查

因反对联邦托管人的作为或不作为而提起的程序由第 9014 条所规定。

（经 Apr. 30, 1991, eff. Aug. 1, 1991. 增补）

PART III

CLAIMS AND DISTRIBUTION TO CREDITORS AND EQUITY INTEREST HOLDERS; PLANS

Rule 3001. Proof of Claim

(a) FORM AND CONTENT. A proof of claim is a written statement setting forth a creditor's claim. A proof of claim shall conform substantially to the appropriate Official Form.

(b) WHO MAY EXECUTE. A proof of claim shall be executed by the creditor or the creditor's authorized agent except as provided in Rules 3004 and 3005.

(c) SUPPORTING INFORMATION.

(1) *Claim Based on a Writing.* Except for a claim governed by paragraph (3) of this subdivision, when a claim, or an interest in property of the debtor securing the claim, is based on a writing, a copy of the writing shall be filed with the proof of claim. If the writing has been lost or destroyed, a statement of the circumstances of the loss or destruction shall be filed with the claim.

(2) *Additional Requirements in an Individual Debtor Case; Sanctions for Failure to Comply.* In a case in which the debtor is an individual:

(A) If, in addition to its principal amount, a claim includes interest, fees, expenses, or other charges incurred before the petition was filed, an itemized statement of the interest, fees, expenses, or charges shall be filed with the proof of claim.

(B) If a security interest is claimed in the debtor's property, a statement of the amount necessary to cure any default as of the date of the petition shall be filed with the proof of claim.

(C) If a security interest is claimed in property that is the debtor's principal residence,

第 III 部分
债权以及向债权人和股本证券持有人的分配；计划

第 3001 条　债权证明

（a）**模板和内容**。债权证明是列明债权人债权的书面声明。债权证明应基本符合相应的官方模板。

（b）**可填写债权证明的主体**。除第 3004 和第 3005 条另有规定外，债权证明应由债权人或其授权代理人填写完成。

（c）**支持信息**。

（1）以书面形式确立的债权。除本附条第（3）款所规制的债权外，当债权或用于担保债权的债务人的财产权益系以书面形式确立，则在提交债权证明时应一并提交该书面证明的副本。若该书面证明已经遗失或毁损，则应在提交债权证明时一并提交一份说明该遗失或毁损情形的声明。

（2）在个人债务人破产案件中的其他要求；未能履行的处罚。在个人债务人的破产案件中：

（A）若除本金以外，该债权还包含在破产申请被提交前所产生的利息、费用、支出或其他花费，则在提交债权证明时，应一并提交逐项列明该利息、费用、支出或其他花费的声明。

（B）若主张就债务人财产享有担保权益，则在提交债权证明时，应一并提交列明自破产申请被提交之日用于纠正任何违约行为的必要费用的声明。

（C）若主张就债务人的主要住所享有担保权益，则在提交债权证明时，应一

the attachment prescribed by the appropriate Official Form shall be filed with the proof of claim. If an escrow account has been established in connection with the claim, an escrow account statement prepared as of the date the petition was filed and in a form consistent with applicable nonbankruptcy law shall be filed with the attachment to the proof of claim.

(D) If the holder of a claim fails to provide any information required by this subdivision (c), the court may, after notice and hearing, take either or both of the following actions:

(i) preclude the holder from presenting the omitted information, in any form, as evidence in any contested matter or adversary proceeding in the case, unless the court determines that the failure was substantially justified or is harmless; or

(ii) award other appropriate relief, including reasonable expenses and attorney's fees caused by the failure.

(3) *Claim Based on an Open-End or Revolving Consumer Credit Agreement.*

(A) When a claim is based on an open-end or revolving consumer credit agreement—except one for which a security interest is claimed in the debtor's real property—a statement shall be filed with the proof of claim, including all of the following information that applies to the account:

(i) the name of the entity from whom the creditor purchased the account;

(ii) the name of the entity to whom the debt was owed at the time of an account holder's last transaction on the account;

(iii) the date of an account holder's last transaction;

(iv) the date of the last payment on the account; and

(v) the date on which the account was charged to profit and loss.

(B) On written request by a party in interest, the holder of a claim based on an open-end or revolving consumer credit agreement shall, within 30 days after the request is sent, provide the requesting party a copy of the writing specified in paragraph (1) of this subdivision.

(d) EVIDENCE OF PERFECTION OF SECURITY INTEREST. If a security interest in property of the debtor is claimed, the proof of claim shall be accompanied by evidence that the security interest has been perfected.

并提交相应官方模板所规定的附件。若已经建有与债权相关的代管账户，则在提交债权证明的附件时，应一并提交根据相应非破产法规定的格式自破产申请被提交之日准备的代管账户声明。

（D）若债权人未能提交（c）附条所要求的任何信息，则法院可在通知和听证后采取以下一项或多项措施：

（i）禁止债权人在本案中的任何争议事项或对抗制诉讼程序中以任何形式将未能提交的信息作为证据呈现，除非法院认为未能提交该信息系出于正当事由或不会造成损害；或
（ii）提供其他相应救济，包括因未能提供信息而导致的合理费用和律师费。

（3）基于开放式或循环消费信贷协议的债权。
（A）当债权系基于开放式或循环消费信贷协议（但不包括就债务人的不动产主张担保权益的协议），则在提交债权证明时，应一并提交有关该账户的所有以下信息：

（i）债权人向其购得该账户的实体的姓名；
（ii）账户持有人就该账户进行最后一次交易时，向其负有债务的实体的姓名；

（iii）账户持有人进行最后一次交易的日期；
（iv）就该账户进行最后一次付款的日期；以及
（v）从该账户扣除损益的日期。
（B）应利益相关方的书面请求，其债权基于开放式或循环消费信贷协议的主体应在该请求被发出后30日内，向请求方提供本附条第（1）款所述的书面文件的副本。

（d）**担保权益的公示证明**。若主张就债务人的财产享有担保权益，则在提交债权证明时，应附有该担保权益已经公示的证明。

(e) TRANSFERRED CLAIM.

(1) *Transfer of Claim Other Than for Security Before Proof Filed.* If a claim has been transferred other than for security before proof of the claim has been filed, the proof of claim may be filed only by the transferee or an indenture trustee.

(2) *Transfer of Claim Other than for Security after Proof Filed.* If a claim other than one based on a publicly traded note, bond, or debenture has been transferred other than for security after the proof of claim has been filed, evidence of the transfer shall be filed by the transferee. The clerk shall immediately notify the alleged transferor by mail of the filing of the evidence of transfer and that objection thereto, if any, must be filed within 21 days of the mailing of the notice or within any additional time allowed by the court. If the alleged transferor files a timely objection and the court finds, after notice and a hearing, that the claim has been transferred other than for security, it shall enter an order substituting the transferee for the transferor. If a timely objection is not filed by the alleged transferor, the transferee shall be substituted for the transferor.

(3) *Transfer of Claim for Security Before Proof Filed.* If a claim other than one based on a publicly traded note, bond, or debenture has been transferred for security before proof of the claim has been filed, the transferor or transferee or both may file a proof of claim for the full amount. The proof shall be supported by a statement setting forth the terms of the transfer. If either the transferor or the transferee files a proof of claim, the clerk shall immediately notify the other by mail of the right to join in the filed claim. If both transferor and transferee file proofs of the same claim, the proofs shall be consolidated. If the transferor or transferee does not file an agreement regarding its relative rights respecting voting of the claim, payment of dividends thereon, or participation in the administration of the estate, on motion by a party in interest and after notice and a hearing, the court shall enter such orders respecting these matters as may be appropriate.

(4) *Transfer of Claim for Security after Proof Filed.* If a claim other than one based on a publicly traded note, bond, or debenture has been transferred for security after the proof of claim has been filed, evidence of the terms of the transfer shall be filed by the transferee. The clerk shall immediately notify the alleged transferor by mail of the filing of the evidence of transfer and that objection thereto, if any, must be filed

（e）**被转让的债权**。

（1）债权证明被提交前进行的并非用作担保的债权转让。若在债权证明被提交前，该债权已经基于获取担保以外的其他目的而被转让他人，则该债权证明仅可由受让人或契约受托人提交。

（2）债权证明被提交后进行的并非用作担保的债权转让。若在债权证明被提交后，该债权已经基于获取担保以外的其他目的而被转让他人（不包括基于公开交易的票据、债券或公司债券而进行的转让），则受让人应提交进行该转让的证据。书记员应立刻以邮寄的方式通知被主张的转让人在该通知被邮寄之日起21日内或法院准予的任何额外期间内提交该转让的证据以及对此提起的异议（如有）。若被主张的转让人及时提交异议并且法院在通知和听证后认为该债权已经基于获取担保以外的其他目的而转让他人，则法院应正式裁定由受让人取代转让人。若被主张为转让人的主体未能及时提交异议，则受让人应取代转让人。

（3）债权证明被提交前进行的用作担保的债权转让。若在债权证明被提交前，该债权已经基于用作担保的目的而被转让他人（不包括基于公开交易的票据、债券或公司债券而进行的转让），则转让人或受让人或二者共同均可就全部债权额而提交债权证明。该证明应由列明该转让的有关事项的声明进行补强。若转让人或受让人单方提交了债权证明，则书记员应立刻以邮寄的方式通知另一方加入被提交的债权主张的权利。若转让人和受让人均就同一债权提交了债权证明，则该证明应被合并。若转让人或受让人并未提交针对就债权参与表决、获得分配财产或参与破产实体的管理的有关权利而达成的协议，则应利益相关方的动议，经过通知和听证后，法院应就前述事项作出适当的裁定。

（4）债权证明被提交后进行的用作担保的债权转让。若在债权证明被提交后，该债权已经基于用作担保的目的而被转让他人（不包括基于公开交易的票据、债券或公司债券而进行的转让），则受让人应提交该转让有关事项的证据。书记员应立刻以邮寄的方式通知被主张为转让人的主体在该通知被邮寄之日起21日内或法院准予的任何额外期间内提交该转让的证据以及对此提起的异议（如有）。

U.S. Federal Rules of Bankruptcy Procedure
(Chinese-English bilingual version)

within 21 days of the mailing of the notice or within any additional time allowed by the court. If a timely objection is filed by the alleged transferor, the court, after notice and a hearing, shall determine whether the claim has been transferred for security. If the transferor or transferee does not file an agreement regarding its relative rights respecting voting of the claim, payment of dividends thereon, or participation in the administration of the estate, on motion by a party in interest and after notice and a hearing, the court shall enter such orders respecting these matters as may be appropriate.

(5) *Service of Objection or Motion; Notice of Hearing.* A copy of an objection filed pursuant to paragraph (2) or (4) or a motion filed pursuant to paragraph (3) or (4) of this subdivision together with a notice of a hearing shall be mailed or otherwise delivered to the transferor or transferee, whichever is appropriate, at least 30 days prior to the hearing.

(f) EVIDENTIARY EFFECT. A proof of claim executed and filed in accordance with these rules shall constitute prima facie evidence of the validity and amount of the claim.

(g) To the extent not inconsistent with the United States Warehouse Act or applicable State law, a warehouse receipt, scale ticket, or similar document of the type routinely issued as evidence of title by a grain storage facility, as defined in section 557 of title 11, shall constitute prima facie evidence of the validity and amount of a claim of ownership of a quantity of grain.

(As amended Pub. L. 98-353, title III, §354, July 10, 1984, 98 Stat. 361; Apr. 30, 1991, eff. Aug. 1,1991; Mar. 26, 2009, eff. Dec. 1, 2009; Apr. 26, 2011, eff. Dec. 1, 2011; Apr. 23, 2012, eff. Dec. 1,2012.)

Rule 3002. Filing Proof of Claim or Interest

(a) NECESSITY FOR FILING. A secured creditor, unsecured creditor, or equity security holder must file a proof of claim or interest for the claim or interest to be allowed, except as provided in Rules 1019 (3), 3003, 3004, and 3005. A lien that secures a claim against the debtor is not void due only to the failure of any entity to file a proof of claim.

(b) PLACE OF FILING. A proof of claim or interest shall be filed in accordance with Rule 5005.

若被主张为转让人的主体及时提交异议，则法院在通知和听证后，应就该债权是否以用作担保为目的而被转让作出认定。若转让人或受让人并未提交针对就债权参与表决、获得分配财产或参与破产实体的管理的有关权利而达成的协议，则应利益相关方的动议，经过通知和听证后，法院应就前述事项作出适当的裁定。

（5）异议或动议的送达；就听证发出的通知。根据本附条的第（2）或（4）款而被提交的异议的副本或者根据第（3）或（4）款而被提交的动议的副本，应在举行听证前至少30日以前，与举行听证的通知一同被邮寄或以其他方式交付给转让人或受让人（采用二者中更为适当的方式）。

（f）**证据效力**。根据本法而被填写完成并提交的债权证明即构成该债权的有效性和金额的表面证据。

（g）在不违反《美国仓库法》或相应州立法律的情况下，仓库收据、秤票或通常由谷物贮藏设施（定义见《美国联邦法典》第11篇第557条）作为所有权证明的其他类似文件，即构成主张就一定数量的谷物享有所有权的权利的有效性和所涉金额的表面证据。

（经 Pub. L. 98-353, title III, §354, July 10, 1984, 98 Stat. 361; Apr. 30, 1991, eff. Aug. 1,1991; Mar. 26, 2009, eff. Dec. 1, 2009; Apr. 26, 2011, eff. Dec. 1, 2011; Apr. 23, 2012, eff. Dec. 1,2012. 修正）

第 3002 条　提交债权或权益证明

（a）**提交的必要性**。除第1019（3）、3003、3004和3005条另有规定外，担保债权人、无担保债权人或股本证券持有人必须就债权或权益提交债权或权益证明以供确认。担保对债务人享有的债权的优先权并不仅因某实体未能提交债权证明而无效。

（b）**提交的地点**。应根据第5005条提交债权或权益证明。

U.S. Federal Rules of Bankruptcy Procedure
(Chinese-English bilingual version)

(c) TIME FOR FILING. In a voluntary chapter 7 case, chapter 12 case, or chapter 13 case, a proof of claim is timely filed if it is filed not later than 70 days after the order for relief under that chapter or the date of the order of conversion to a case under chapter 12 or chapter 13. In an involuntary chapter 7 case, a proof of claim is timely filed if it is filed not later than 90 days after the order for relief under that chapter is entered. But in all these cases, the following exceptions apply:

(1) A proof of claim filed by a governmental unit, other than for a claim resulting from a tax return filed under §1308, is timely filed if it is filed not later than 180 days after the date of the order for relief. A proof of claim filed by a governmental unit for a claim resulting from a tax return filed under §1308 is timely filed if it is filed no later than 180 days after the date of the order for relief or 60 days after the date of the filing of the tax return. The court may, for cause, enlarge the time for a governmental unit to file a proof of claim only upon motion of the governmental unit made before expiration of the period for filing a timely proof of claim.

(2) In the interest of justice and if it will not unduly delay the administration of the case, the court may extend the time for filing a proof of claim by an infant or incompetent person or the representative of either.

(3) An unsecured claim which arises in favor of an entity or becomes allowable as a result of a judgment may be filed within 30 days after the judgment becomes final if the judgment is for the recovery of money or property from that entity or denies or avoids the entity's interest in property. If the judgment imposes a liability which is not satisfied, or a duty which is not performed within such period or such further time as the court may permit, the claim shall not be allowed.

(4) A claim arising from the rejection of an executory contract or unexpired lease of the debtor may be filed within such time as the court may direct.

(5) If notice of insufficient assets to pay a dividend was given to creditors under Rule 2002 (e), and subsequently the trustee notifies the court that payment of a dividend appears possible, the clerk shall give at least 90 days' notice by mail to creditors of that fact and of the date by which proofs of claim must be filed.

(6) On motion filed by a creditor before or after the expiration of the time to file

美国联邦破产程序规则
（中英对照译本）

（c）**提交时间**。在第 7 章、第 12 章或第 13 章自愿破产案件中，若债权证明系在根据该章作出破产救济令或将案件转换至第 12 章或第 13 章案件的裁定后 70 日内即被提交，则该债权证明应被视为已被及时提交。在第 7 章强制破产案件中，若债权证明系在根据该章正式作出破产救济令后 90 日内即被提交，则该债权证明应被视为已被及时提交。但在所有该类案件中，仍适用以下例外：

（1）若政府机构系在破产救济令被作出后 180 日内提交债权证明（不包括因根据法典第 1308 条被提交的报税表而产生的债权），则该债权证明应被视为已被及时提交。针对因根据第 1308 条被提交的报税表而产生的债权，若政府机构系在破产救济令被作出后 180 日内或提交该报税表后 60 日内提交债权证明，则该债权证明应被视为已被及时提交。仅当政府机构在用于提交债权证明的期间届满前提出动议时，法院才可出于特定事由延长政府机构用于提交债权证明的时间。

（2）为了司法公正，在不会过分延误案件的实施的情况下，法院可延长婴儿或无行为能力人或其代表人用于提交债权证明的时间。

（3）若某判决系为从某实体处追回金钱或财产，或否认或撤销该实体的财产权益，则针对作为该判决的结果而支持该实体获得的无担保债权或该实体因此得以确认的无担保债权，可在该判决成为最终判决后 30 日内提交该债权证明。若该判决规定的责任或义务在该期间或法院可许可的更长期间内仍未被履行，则该债权不得被予以确认。

（4）因拒绝承继债务人的待履行合同或未完成租约而产生的债权可在法院规定的时间内而被提交。

（5）若已经根据第 2002 条（e）向债权人发出没有足够资产用于还款的通知，但随后托管人又通知法院存在还款的可能，则书记员应通过邮寄的方式在必须提交债权证明之日前至少提前 90 日就该事实和提交债权证明的日期向债权人发出通知。

（6）若债权人在提交债权证明的期间届满前或届满后提交动议，则法院可延

a proof of claim, the court may extend the time by not more than 60 days from the date of the order granting the motion. The motion may be granted if the court finds that:

(A) the notice was insufficient under the circumstances to give the creditor a reasonable time to file a proof of claim because the debtor failed to timely file the list of creditors' names and addresses required by Rule 1007 (a); or

(B) the notice was insufficient under the circumstances to give the creditor a reasonable time to file a proof of claim, and the notice was mailed to the creditor at a foreign address.

(7) A proof of claim filed by the holder of a claim that is secured by a security interest in the debtor's principal residence is timely filed if:

(A) the proof of claim, together with the attachments required by Rule 3001 (c)(2)(C), is filed not later than 70 days after the order for relief is entered; and

(B) any attachments required by Rule 3001 (c)(1) and (d) are filed as a supplement to the holder's claim not later than 120 days after the order for relief is entered.

(As amended Mar. 30, 1987, eff. Aug. 1, 1987; Apr. 30, 1991, eff. Aug. 1, 1991; Apr. 23, 1996, eff.Dec. 1, 1996; Apr. 23, 2008, eff. Dec. 1, 2008; Apr. 27, 2017, eff. Dec. 1, 2017.)

Rule 3002.1. Notice Relating to Claims Secured by Security Interest in the Debtor's Principal Residence

(a) IN GENERAL. This rule applies in a chapter 13 case to claims (1) that are secured by a security interest in the debtor's principal residence, and (2) for which the plan provides that either the trustee or the debtor will make contractual installment payments. Unless the court orders otherwise, the notice requirements of this rule cease to apply when an order terminating or annulling the automatic stay becomes effective with respect to the residence that secures the claim.

(b) NOTICE OF PAYMENT CHANGES; OBJECTION.

(1) *Notice*. The holder of the claim shall file and serve on the debtor, debtor's counsel, and the trustee a notice of any change in the payment amount, including any

长该期间，但不得超过自准予该动议的裁定被作出之日起 60 日。当法院认为存在以下情形时可准予该动议：

（A）因为债务人未能根据第 1007 条（a）的要求及时提交债权人姓名和住址的清单而导致该情形下该通知不足以为债权人提供合理时间以用于提交债权证明；或

（B）该通知系被邮寄给地址在国外的债权人，因此在该情形下该通知不足以为债权人提供合理时间以提交债权证明。

（7）针对由债务人的主要住所所担保的债权，在下列情形中，该债权证明应被视为已被及时提交：

（A）该债权证明以及第 3001 条（c）（2）（C）所要求的附件在破产救济令被作出后 70 日内即被一同提交；并且

（B）第 3001 条（c）（1）和（d）所要求的任何附件作为对该债权的补充在破产救济令作出后 120 日内即被提交。

（经 Mar. 30, 1987, eff. Aug. 1, 1987; Apr. 30, 1991, eff. Aug. 1, 1991; Apr. 23, 1996, eff.Dec. 1, 1996; Apr. 23, 2008, eff. Dec. 1, 2008; Apr. 27, 2017, eff. Dec. 1, 2017. 修正）

第 3002.1 条 与由债务人主要住所所担保的债权有关的通知

（a）一般规定。本条适用于第 13 章案件中（1）由债务人的主要住所所担保，并且（2）计划中规定托管人或债务人将按合同以分期付款的方式进行还款的债权。除非法院作出其他裁定，否则当终止或取消自动冻结的裁定针对担保该债权的住所生效时，本条中的通知要求即停止适用。

（b）还款变化的通知；异议。

（1）通知。若还款金额发生任何变化，包括因利率或代管账户的调整而引起的任何变化，则债权人应在金额发生变化的还款到期前 21 日内，向法院提交并

U.S. Federal Rules of Bankruptcy Procedure
(Chinese-English bilingual version)

change that results from an interest-rate or escrow-account adjustment, no later than 21 days before a payment in the new amount is due. If the claim arises from a home-equity line of credit, this requirement may be modified by court order.

(2) *Objection*. A party in interest who objects to the payment change may file a motion to determine whether the change is required to maintain payments in accordance with §1322(b)(5) of the Code. If no motion is filed by the day before the new amount is due, the change goes into effect, unless the court orders otherwise.

(c) NOTICE OF FEES, EXPENSES, AND CHARGES. The holder of the claim shall file and serve on the debtor, debtor's counsel, and the trustee a notice itemizing all fees, expenses, or charges (1) that were incurred in connection with the claim after the bankruptcy case was filed, and (2) that the holder asserts are recoverable against the debtor or against the debtor's principal residence. The notice shall be served within 180 days after the date on which the fees, expenses, or charges are incurred.

(d) FORM AND CONTENT. A notice filed and served under subdivision (b) or (c) of this rule shall be prepared as prescribed by the appropriate Official Form, and filed as a supplement to the holder's proof of claim. The notice is not subject to Rule 3001(f).

(e) DETERMINATION OF FEES, EXPENSES, OR CHARGES. On motion of a party in interest filed within one year after service of a notice under subdivision (c) of this rule, the court shall, after notice and hearing, determine whether payment of any claimed fee, expense, or charge is required by the underlying agreement and applicable nonbankruptcy law to cure a default or maintain payments in accordance with §1322(b)(5) of the Code.

(f) NOTICE OF FINAL CURE PAYMENT. Within 30 days after the debtor completes all payments under the plan, the trustee shall file and serve on the holder of the claim, the debtor, and debtor's counsel a notice stating that the debtor has paid in full the amount required to cure any default on the claim. The notice shall also inform the holder of its obligation to file and serve are sponse under subdivision (g). If the debtor contends that final cure payment has been made and all plan payments have been completed, and the trustee does not timely file and serve the notice required by this subdivision, the debtor may file and serve the notice.

向债务人、债务人的律师以及托管人送达就前述变化而发出的通知。若该债权系因房屋净值信贷额度而产生，则法院可裁定修改该要求。

（2）异议。就该还款变化有异议的利益相关方可提交动议以申请就该变化是否被要求根据法典第1322条（b）(5) 保持还款作出认定。若在发生变化的还款到期前无人提交动议，则除非法院作出其他裁定，否则该变化将产生效力。

（c）**费用、支出和收费的通知**。债权人应提交并向债务人、债务人的律师以及托管人送达逐项列明所有（1）在破产案件被提交后因债权而产生的，并且（2）债权人主张可向债务人或针对债务人的主要住所而追偿的费用、支出和收费的通知。该通知应在该费用、支出或收费产生后180日内而被送达。

（d）**形式和内容**。根据本条的（b）或（c）附条而被提交并送达的通知应按照相应官方模板的规定来准备，并且应作为债权人债权证明的补充而被提交。该通知不受第3001条（f）的约束。

（e）**就费用、支出或收费所作的认定**。若利益相关方在本条（c）附条的通知被送达后1年内提交动议，则法院在通知和听证后应就是否相关协议及相应的非破产法要求支付被主张的费用、支出或收费以纠正违约或根据法典第1322条（b）(5) 保持还款作出认定。

（f）**最终纠正还款的通知**。在债务人完成计划中的所有还款后30日内，托管人应向法院提交并向债权人、债务人以及债务人的律师发出通知以说明债务人已经全额支付被要求用于纠正与该债权相关的违约行为的款项。该通知还应告知债权人提交并送达（g）附条所述的答复的义务。若债务人主张其已经完成最终纠正还款以及计划中的所有还款，并且托管人未能根据本款要求及时提交并送达该通知，则债务人可提交并送达该通知。

(g) RESPONSE TO NOTICE OF FINAL CURE PAYMENT. Within 21 days after service of the notice under subdivision (f) of this rule, the holder shall file and serve on the debtor, debtor's counsel, and the trustee a statement indicating (1) whether it agrees that the debtor has paid in full the amount required to cure the default on the claim, and (2) whether the debtor is otherwise current on all payments consistent with §1322 (b)(5) of the Code. The statement shall itemize the required cure or postpetition amounts, if any, that the holder contends remain unpaid as of the date of the statement. The statement shall be filed as a supplement to the holder's proof of claim and is not subject to Rule 3001 (f).

(h) DETERMINATION OF FINAL CURE AND PAYMENT. On motion of the debtor or trustee filed within 21 days after service of the statement under subdivision (g) of this rule, the court shall, after notice and hearing, determine whether the debtor has cured the default and paid all required postpetition amounts.

(i) FAILURE TO NOTIFY. If the holder of a claim fails to provide any information as required by subdivision (b), (c), or (g) of this rule, the court may, after notice and hearing, take either or both of the following actions:

(1) preclude the holder from presenting the omitted information, in any form, as evidence in any contested matter or adversary proceeding in the case, unless the court determines that the failure was substantially justified or is harmless; or

(2) award other appropriate relief, including reasonable expenses and attorney's fees caused by the failure.

(Added Apr. 26, 2011, eff. Dec. 1, 2011; amended Apr. 28, 2016, eff. Dec. 1, 2016; Apr. 26, 2018,eff. Dec. 1, 2018.)

Rule 3003. Filing Proof of Claim or Equity Security Interest in Chapter 9 Municipality or Chapter 11 Reorganization Cases

(a) APPLICABILITY OF RULE. This rule applies in chapter 9 and 11 cases.

(b) SCHEDULE OF LIABILITIES AND LIST OF EQUITY SECURITY HOLDERS.

(1) *Schedule of Liabilities*. The schedule of liabilities filed pursuant to §521 (1)

（g）**就最终纠正还款通知所作的答复**。在本条（f）附条中的通知被送达后21日内，债权人应向法院提交并向债务人、债务人的律师以及托管人送达一份声明以说明（1）是否其对债务人已经完全纠正与该债权相关的违约行为表示认同，以及（2）债务人是否就所有还款均符合第1322条（b）（6）的规定。该声明应逐项列出债权人认为截至该声明出具之日仍未支付的被要求纠正违约或提交破产申请后成立的债权的金额（如有）。该声明应作为债权人的债权证明的补充而被提交至法院并且不受第3001条（f）的约束。

（h）**最终纠正和还款的认定**。当债务人或托管人在本条（g）附条中的声明被送达后21日内提交动议时，法院在通知和听证后应就债务人是否已经纠正违约行为并清偿所有被主张的提交破产申请后成立的债权金额作出认定。

（i）**未能通知**。若债权人未能提供本条（b）、（c）或（g）附条所要求的任何信息，则法院在通知和听证后可采取以下任意或全部措施：

（1）禁止债权人在本案中的任何争议事项或对抗制诉讼程序中以任何形式将未能提交的信息作为证据呈现，除非法院认为未能提交该信息系出于正当事由或不会造成损害；或

（2）提供其他相应救济，包括因未能提供信息而导致的合理费用和律师费。

（经 Apr. 26, 2011, eff. Dec. 1, 2011; amended Apr. 28, 2016, eff. Dec. 1, 2016; Apr. 26, 2018,eff. Dec. 1, 2018. 增补）

第3003条　在第9章市政机构破产案件或第11章重整案件中提交债权或股本权益证明

（a）**本条的适用范围**。本条适用于第9章和第11章案件。

（b）**债务清单和股本权益持有人名单**。

（1）**债务清单**。根据法典第521条（1）而被提交的债务清单即构成债权人

of the Code shall constitute prima facie evidence of the validity and amount of the claims of creditors, unless they are scheduled as disputed, contingent, or unliquidated. It shall not be necessary for a creditor or equity security holder to file a proof of claim or interest except as provided in subdivision (c)(2) of this rule.

(2) *List of Equity Security Holders*. The list of equity security holders filed pursuant to Rule 1007 (a)(3) shall constitute prima facie evidence of the validity and amount of the equity security interests and it shall not be necessary for the holders of such interests to file a proof of interest.

(c) FILING PROOF OF CLAIM.

(1) *Who May File*. Any creditor or indenture trustee may file a proof of claim within the time prescribed by subdivision (c)(3) of this rule.

(2) *Who Must File*. Any creditor or equity security holder whose claim or interest is not scheduled or scheduled as disputed, contingent, or unliquidated shall file a proof of claim or interest within the time prescribed by subdivision (c)(3) of this rule; any creditor who fails to do so shall not be treated as a creditor with respect to such claim for the purposes of voting and distribution.

(3) *Time for Filing*. The court shall fix and for cause shown may extend the time within which proofs of claim or interest may be filed. Notwithstanding the expiration of such time, a proof of claim may be filed to the extent and under the conditions stated in Rule 3002 (c)(2), (c)(3), (c)(4), and (c)(6).

(4) *Effect of Filing Claim or Interest*. A proof of claim or interest executed and filed in accordance with this subdivision shall supersede any scheduling of that claim or interest pursuant to §521 (a)(1) of the Code.

(5) *Filing by Indenture Trustee*. An indenture trustee may file a claim on behalf of all known or unknown holders of securities issued pursuant to the trust instrument under which it is trustee.

(d) PROOF OF RIGHT TO RECORD STATUS. For the purposes of Rules 3017, 3018 and 3021 and for receiving notices, an entity who is not the record holder of a security may file a statement setting forth facts which entitle that entity to be treated as the record holder. An objection to the statement may be filed by any party in interest.

债权的有效性和金额的表面证据,除非其被列为有争议的、或然的或数额不确定的债权。除本条(c)(2)另有规定外,债权人或股本权益持有人并无提交债权证明或权益证明的必要。

(2)股本证券持有人名单。根据第1007条(a)(3)而被提交的股本证券持有人名单即构成股本权益的有效性和金额的表面证据,并且股本证券持有人并无提交权益证明的必要。

(c)**提交债权证明**。
(1)可提交债权证明的主体。任何债权人或契约受托人均可在本条(c)(3)规定的时间内提交债权证明。
(2)必须提交债权证明的主体。其债权或权益并未被列入清单或被列为有争议的、或然的或数额不确定的债权或权益的任何债权人或股本证券持有人均应在本条(c)(3)规定的时间内提交债权或权益证明;任何未能履行该要求的债权人不得在参与表决和分配时而被视为该债权的债权人。

(3)提交的时间。法院应确定用于提交债权或权益证明的时间并且出于被主张的特定事由,法院还可延长该期间。即使该期间已经届满,债权证明仍可在第3002条(c)(2)、(c)(3)、(c)(4)和(c)(6)规定的情形下而被提交。

(4)提交债权或权益的效力。已经填写完成并根据本款规定而被提交的债权或权益证明应取代根据法典第521条(a)(1)而就该债权或权益所作的任何记录。

(5)由契约受托人提交。契约受托人可代表所有已知或未知的,持有该信托证书所签发的证券的主体提交债权。

(d)**有权享有已登记地位的证明**。在第3017、3018和3021条中以及出于获得通知的目的,即使某实体不是已登记的证券持有人,其仍可提交声明以列明该实体有权被视为已登记持有人的相关事实。任何利益相关方均可就该声明提交异议。

U.S. Federal Rules of Bankruptcy Procedure
(Chinese-English bilingual version)

(As amended Mar. 30, 1987, eff. Aug. 1, 1987; Apr. 30, 1991, eff. Aug. 1, 1991; Apr. 23, 2008, eff.Dec. 1, 2008.)

Rule 3004. Filing of Claims by Debtor or Trustee

If a creditor does not timely file a proof of claim under Rule 3002(c)or 3003(c), the debtor or trustee may file a proof of the claim within 30 days after the expiration of the time for filing claims prescribed by Rule 3002 (c) or 3003 (c) , whichever is applicable. The clerk shall forthwith give notice of the filing to the creditor, the debtor and the trustee.

(As amended Mar. 30, 1987, eff. Aug. 1, 1987; Apr. 25, 2005, eff. Dec. 1, 2005.)

Rule 3005. Filing of Claim, Acceptance, or Rejection by Guarantor, Surety, Indorser, or Other Codebtor

(a) FILING OF CLAIM. If a creditor does not timely file a proof of claim under Rule 3002 (c) or 3003 (c) , any entity that is or may be liable with the debtor to that creditor, or who has secured that creditor, may file a proof of the claim within 30 days after the expiration of the time for filing claims prescribed by Rule 3002 (c) or Rule 3003 (c) whichever is applicable. No distribution shall be made on the claim except on satisfactory proof that the original debt will be diminished by the amount of distribution.

(b) FILING OF ACCEPTANCE OR REJECTION; SUBSTITUTION OF CREDITOR. An entity which has filed a claim pursuant to the first sentence of subdivision (a) of this rule may file an acceptance or rejection of a plan in the name of the creditor, if known, or if unknown, in the entity's own name but if the creditor files a proof of claim within the time permitted by Rule 3003 (c) or files a notice prior to confirmation of a plan of the creditor's intention to act in the creditor's own behalf, the creditor shall be substituted for the obligor with respect to that claim.

(As amended Mar. 30, 1987, eff. Aug. 1, 1987; Apr. 30, 1991, eff. Aug. 1, 1991; Apr. 25, 2005, eff.Dec. 1, 2005.)

（经 Mar. 30, 1987, eff. Aug. 1, 1987; Apr. 30, 1991, eff. Aug. 1, 1991; Apr. 23, 2008, eff.Dec. 1, 2008. 增补）

第 3004 条　由债务人或托管人提交债权

若债权人未能根据第 3002（c）或 3003（c）条及时提交债权证明，则债务人或托管人可在第 3002（c）或 3003（c）条（以二者中所适用者为准）规定的用于提交债权的期间届满后 30 日内提交债权证明。书记员应立刻就该债权证明的提交向债权人、债务人及托管人发出通知。

（经 Mar. 30, 1987, eff. Aug. 1, 1987; Apr. 25, 2005, eff. Dec. 1, 2005. 修正）

第 3005 条　由连带保证人、一般保证人、背书人或其他共同债务人提交债权、接受或拒绝计划

（a）提交债权。若债权人未能根据第 3002（c）或 3003（c）条及时提交债权证明，则任何与债务人共同向该债权人承担责任或对该债权人提供担保的实体均可在第 3002（c）或 3003（c）条（以二者中所适用者为准）所规定的用于提交债权的期间届满后 30 日内提交债权证明。除非有充足的证据表明原始债务将因分配所得的金额而有所减少，否则不得就该债权进行分配。

（b）接受或拒绝意见的提交；债权人的替换。已经根据本条（a）附条首句的规定提交债权的实体若已知债权人的姓名，则可以债权人的名义就计划提交接受或拒绝意见；若并未知悉债权人的姓名，则可以自己的名义提交接受或拒绝意见，但若债权人在第 3003 条（c）规定的时间内提交债权证明或在计划得到批准前提交通知以说明其以自身名义亲自行事的意图，则债权人应就该债权取代该实体。

（经 Mar. 30, 1987, eff. Aug. 1, 1987; Apr. 30, 1991, eff. Aug. 1, 1991; Apr. 25, 2005, eff.Dec. 1, 2005. 修正）

U.S. Federal Rules of Bankruptcy Procedure
(Chinese-English bilingual version)

Rule 3006. Withdrawal of Claim; Effect on Acceptance or Rejection of Plan

A creditor may withdraw a claim as of right by filing a notice of withdrawal, except as provided in this rule. If after a creditor has filed a proof of claim an objection is filed thereto or a complaint is filed against that creditor in an adversary proceeding, or the creditor has accepted or rejected the plan or otherwise has participated significantly in the case, the creditor may not withdraw the claim except on order of the court after a hearing on notice to the trustee or debtor in possession, and any creditors' committee elected pursuant to §705 (a) or appointed pursuant to §1102 of the Code. The order of the court shall contain such terms and conditions as the court deems proper. Unless the court orders otherwise, an authorized withdrawal of a claim shall constitute withdrawal of any related acceptance or rejection of a plan.

(As amended Apr. 30, 1991, eff. Aug. 1, 1991.)

Rule 3007. Objections to Claims

(a) TIME AND MANNER OF SERVICE.

(1) *Time of Service.* An objection to the allowance of a claim and a notice of objection that substantially conforms to the appropriate Official Form shall be filed and served at least 30 days before any scheduled hearing on the objection or any deadline for the claimant to request a hearing.

(2) *Manner of Service.*

(A) The objection and notice shall be served on a claimant by first-class mail to the person most recently designated on the claimant's original or amended proof of claim as the person to receive notices, at the address so indicated; and

(i) if the objection is to a claim of the United States, or any of its officers or agencies, in the manner provided for service of a summons and complaint by Rule 7004 (b)(4) or (5); or

(ii) if the objection is to a claim of an insured depository institution as defined in section 3 of the Federal Deposit Insurance Act, in the manner provided by Rule 7004(h).

(B) Service of the objection and notice shall also be made by first-class mail

第 3006 条　撤回债权主张；接受或拒绝计划的效力

除本条另有规定外，债权人可通过提交撤回通知而撤回其债权主张。若债权人已经提交债权证明，并且有人就该债权证明提交异议或在对抗制诉讼程序中就该债权人提交诉讼主张，或者债权人已经就计划发表接受或拒绝意见或者以其他方式深入参与案件，则债权人不得撤回其债权主张，除非法院在向托管人或经管债务人以及根据法典第 705 条（a）选任或根据第 1102 条被任命的任何债权人委员会发出通知并举行听证后，裁定准予其撤回。法院作出的该项裁定应载有法院认为适当的条款和条件。除非法院作出其他裁定，否则被准予的债权主张的撤回即构成与所涉的对计划的接受或拒绝意见的撤回。

（经 Apr. 30, 1991, eff. Aug. 1, 1991. 修正）

第 3007 条　对债权的异议

（a）送达的时间和方式。

（1）送达的时间。就债权的确认而提出的异议以及与相应的官方模板基本相符的异议通知均应在就该异议安排的听证得以举行前或债权人申请举行听证的截止日前至少提前 30 日提交并送达。

（2）送达的方式。

（A）该异议和通知应通过以一级邮件的方式向在债权人原始或修正后的债权证明上最新指定的地址邮寄给同样被指定的接收通知的人从而送达给债权人；并且

（i）若该异议针对的是美国享有的债权或者其官员或代理机关的债权，则应采用第 7004 条（b）（4）或（5）规定的适用于传票和起诉状的送达方式；或

（ii）若该异议针对的是受保存款机构（定义见《联邦存款保险法》第 3 条）享有的债权，则应采用第 7004 条（h）规定的方式。

（B）该异议和通知也应以一级邮件或其他所允许的方式送达给债务人或经管

or other permitted means on the debtor or debtor in possession, the trustee, and, if applicable, the entity filing the proof of claim under Rule 3005.

(b) DEMAND FOR RELIEF REQUIRING AN ADVERSARY PROCEEDING. A party in interest shall not include a demand for relief of a kind specified in Rule 7001 in an objection to the allowance of a claim, but may include the objection in an adversary proceeding.

(c) LIMITATION ON JOINDER OF CLAIMS OBJECTIONS. Unless otherwise ordered by the court or permitted by subdivision (d), objections to more than one claim shall not be joined in a single objection.

(d) OMNIBUS OBJECTION. Subject to subdivision (e), objections to more than one claim may be joined in an omnibus objection if all the claims were filed by the same entity, or the objections are based solely on the grounds that the claims should be disallowed, in whole or in part, because:

(1) they duplicate other claims;

(2) they have been filed in the wrong case;

(3) they have been amended by subsequently filed proofs of claim;

(4) they were not timely filed;

(5) they have been satisfied or released during the case in accordance with the Code, applicable rules, or a court order;

(6) they were presented in a form that does not comply with applicable rules, and the objection states that the objector is unable to determine the validity of the claim because of the noncompliance;

(7) they are interests, rather than claims; or

(8) they assert priority in an amount that exceeds the maximum amount under §507 of the Code.

(e) REQUIREMENTS FOR OMNIBUS OBJECTION. An omnibus objection shall:

(1) state in a conspicuous place that claimants receiving the objection should locate their names and claims in the objection;

(2) list claimants alphabetically, provide a cross-reference to claim numbers, and, if appropriate, list claimants by category of claims;

债务人、托管人以及根据第 3005 条提交债权证明的实体（如适用）。

（b）**要求进行对抗制诉讼程序的救济请求**。利益相关方在就债权的确认提交的异议中不得请求第 7001 条所规定的救济，但可在对抗制诉讼程序中提出该异议。

（c）**债权异议合并的限制**。除非法院作出其他裁定或（d）附条有其他规定，否则就多项债权提出的异议不得被合并为一项异议。

（d）**综合异议**。在符合（e）附条规定的情况下，就多项债权提出的多项异议可被合并在综合异议中，但前述债权必须均由同一实体所提交或前述异议仅主张前述债权因以下原因而不得被全部或部分予以确认：

（1）其与其他债权有所重复；
（2）其系被错误提交；
（3）其已由随后被提交的债权证明所修正；
（4）其未被及时提交；
（5）其在案件实施过程中已经被根据法典、相应规则或法院裁定而被清偿或解除；
（6）提出主张该类债权的形式并不符合相应规则，并且该异议载明异议方系因该违规行为而无法判断债权的有效性；
（7）其为权益，而并非债权；或
（8）其主张优先权的数额已经超过法典第 507 条规定的最大金额。

（e）**综合异议的要求**。综合异议应满足以下要求：
（1）在显眼的位置注明收到该异议的债权人应在该异议中定位到其姓名和债权；
（2）按字母顺序列明债权人，提供与债权编号间的交叉引用，并在适当的情况下按债权类别列明债权人；

(3) state the grounds of the objection to each claim and provide a cross-reference to the pages in the omnibus objection pertinent to the stated grounds;

(4) state in the title the identity of the objector and the grounds for the objections;

(5) be numbered consecutively with other omnibus objections filed by the same objector; and

(6) contain objections to no more than 100 claims.

(f) FINALITY OF OBJECTION. The finality of any order regarding a claim objection included in an omnibus objection shall be determined as though the claim had been subject to an individual objection.

(As amended Apr. 30, 1991, eff. Aug. 1, 1991; Apr. 30, 2007, eff. Dec. 1, 2007; Apr. 27, 2017, eff.Dec. 1, 2017; Apr. 14, 2021, eff. Dec. 1, 2021.)

Rule 3008. Reconsideration of Claims

A party in interest may move for reconsideration of an order allowing or disallowing a claim against the estate. The court after a hearing on notice shall enter an appropriate order.

Rule 3009. Declaration and Payment of Dividends in a Chapter 7 Liquidation Case

In a chapter 7 case, dividends to creditors shall be paid as promptly as practicable. Dividend checks shall be made payable to and mailed to each creditor whose claim has been allowed, unless a power of attorney authorizing another entity to receive dividends has been executed and filed in accordance with Rule 9010. In that event, dividend checks shall be made payable to the creditor and to the other entity and shall be mailed to the other entity.

(As amended Mar. 30, 1987, eff. Aug. 1, 1987; Apr. 22, 1993, eff. Aug. 1, 1993.)

Rule 3010. Small Dividends and Payments in Chapter 7 Liquidation, Chapter 12 Family Farmer's Debt Adjustment, and Chapter 13 Individual's Debt Adjustment Cases

(a) CHAPTER 7 CASES. In a chapter 7 case no dividend in an amount less than

（3）注明就各项债权提出的异议的依据并在综合异议中提供与异议依据间的交叉引用；

（4）在标题中注明异议方的身份和提出异议的理由；

（5）与同一异议方提交的其他综合异议进行连续编号；并且

（6）其异议所针对的债权不得超过 100 项。

（f）**终局异议**。就综合异议中的某项债权异议所作的裁定应被视为就该债权而提出的单独异议从而就该裁定的终局性作出认定。

（经 Apr. 30, 1991, eff. Aug. 1, 1991; Apr. 30, 2007, eff. Dec. 1, 2007; Apr. 27, 2017, eff.Dec. 1, 2017; Apr. 14, 2021, eff. Dec. 1, 2021. 修正）

第 3008 条　债权的复议

针对就破产实体享有的债权予以确认或不予确认的裁定，利益相关方可提出动议申请对其复议。法院经过通知和听证后应作出适当的裁定。

第 3009 条　在第 7 章清算案件中的还款宣告和支付

在第 7 章案件中，应在切实可行的情况下尽快向债权人还款。还款支票应被邮寄给享有经确认债权的各主体并可由其支取，除非已经根据第 9010 条完成并提交了授权书以授权其他实体接收该还款。在该情形下，还款支票应被邮寄给其他实体，但可由该实体和债权人所支取。

（经 Mar. 30, 1987, eff. Aug. 1, 1987; Apr. 22, 1993, eff. Aug. 1, 1993. 修正）

第 3010 条　在第 7 章清算案件、第 12 章家庭农场主债务调整案件和第 13 章个人债务调整案件中的小额还款

（a）**第 7 章案件**。在第 7 章案件中，除非当地法律或法院裁定作此授权，否

$5 shall be distributed by the trustee to any creditor unless authorized by local rule or order of the court. Any dividend not distributed to a creditor shall be treated in the same manner as unclaimed funds as provided in §347 of the Code.

(b) CHAPTER 12 AND CHAPTER 13 CASES. In a chapter 12 or chapter 13 case no payment in an amount less than $15 shall be distributed by the trustee to any creditor unless authorized by local rule or order of the court. Funds not distributed because of this subdivision shall accumulate and shall be paid whenever the accumulation aggregates $15. Any funds remaining shall be distributed with the final payment.

(As amended Mar. 30, 1987, eff. Aug. 1, 1987; Apr. 30, 1991, eff. Aug. 1, 1991.)

Rule 3011. Unclaimed Funds in Chapter 7 Liquidation, Chapter 12 Family Farmer's Debt Adjustment, and Chapter 13 Individual's Debt Adjustment Cases

The trustee shall file a list of all known names and addresses of the entities and the amounts which they are entitled to be paid from remaining property of the estate that is paid into court pursuant to §347 (a) of the Code.

(As amended Mar. 30, 1987, eff. Aug. 1, 1987; Apr. 30, 1991, eff. Aug. 1, 1991.)

Rule 3012. Determining the Amount of Secured and Priority Claims

(a) DETERMINATION OF AMOUNT OF CLAIM. On request by a party in interest and after notice—to the holder of the claim and any other entity the court designates—and a hearing, the court may determine:

(1) the amount of a secured claim under §506 (a) of the Code; or

(2) the amount of a claim entitled to priority under §507 of the Code.

(b) REQUEST FOR DETERMINATION; HOW MADE. Except as provided in subdivision (c) , a request to determine the amount of a secured claim may be made by motion, in a claim objection, or in a plan filed in a chapter 12 or chapter 13 case. When the request is made in a chapter 12 or chapter 13 plan, the plan shall be served on the holder of the claim and any other entity the court designates in the manner provided

则托管人不得向任何债权人分配金额少于 5 美元的还款。任何未能分配给债权人的资金均应被视为法典第 347 条中无人主张的资金而进行处理。

（b）**第 12 章和第 13 章案件**。在第 12 章或第 13 章案件中，除非当地法律或法院裁定作此授权，否则托管人不得向任何债权人分配金额少于 15 美元的还款。因本附条规定而未能得以分配的资金应进行累计并且每当累计达到 15 美元时即应进行支付。剩余资金应在最终还款时进行分配。

（经 Mar. 30, 1987, eff. Aug. 1, 1987; Apr. 30, 1991, eff. Aug. 1, 1991. 修正）

第 3011 条　第 7 章清算案件、第 12 章家庭农场主债务调整案件和第 13 章个人债务调整案件中无人主张的资金

托管人应提交一份清单以列明所有已知的各实体的姓名和住址以及其有权就根据法典第 347 条（a）交予法院的剩余破产财产得以分配的金额。

（经 Mar. 30, 1987, eff. Aug. 1, 1987; Apr. 30, 1991, eff. Aug. 1, 1991. 修正）

第 3012 条　就担保和优先债权的金额认定

（a）**就债权金额的认定**。应利益相关方的请求，在向债权人和法院指定的任何其他实体发出通知并举行听证后，法院可就以下各项作出认定：

（1）法典第 506 条（a）中担保债权的金额；或
（2）法典第 507 条中具有优先顺位的债权的金额。

（b）**申请作此认定的请求；如何作出**。除（c）附条另有规定外，可通过动议或者在债权异议或第 12 章或第 13 章案件中被提交的计划里申请就担保债权的金额作出认定。当系在第 12 章或第 13 章计划中提出该请求，则该计划应按照第 7004 条规定的适用于传票和起诉状的送达方式而被送达给债权人以及法院指定任何其他实体。针对就具有优先顺位的债权的金额的认定，仅可通过在债权被提

for service of a summons and complaint by Rule 7004. A request to determine the amount of a claim entitled to priority may be made only by motion after a claim is filed or in a claim objection.

(c) CLAIMS OF GOVERNMENTAL UNITS. A request to determine the amount of a secured claim of a governmental unit may be made only by motion or in a claim objection after the governmental unit files a proof of claim or after the time for filing one under Rule 3002 (c)(1) has expired.

(As amended Mar. 30, 1987, eff. Aug. 1, 1987; Apr. 27, 2017, eff. Dec. 1, 2017.)

Rule 3013. Classification of Claims and Interests

For the purposes of the plan and its acceptance, the court may, on motion after hearing on notice as the court may direct, determine classes of creditors and equity security holders pursuant to §§1122, 1222 (b)(1), and 1322 (b)(1) of the Code.

(As amended Apr. 30, 1991, eff. Aug. 1, 1991.)

Rule 3014. Election Under §1111 (b) by Secured Creditor in Chapter 9 Municipality or Chapter 11 Reorganization Case

An election of application of §1111 (b)(2) of the Code by a class of secured creditors in a chapter 9 or 11 case may be made at any time prior to the conclusion of the hearing on the disclosure statement or within such later time as the court may fix. If the disclosure statement is conditionally approved pursuant to Rule 3017.1, and a final hearing on the disclosure statement is not held, the election of application of §1111 (b)(2) may be made not later than the date fixed pursuant to Rule 3017.1 (a)(2) or another date the court may fix. The election shall be in writing and signed unless made at the hearing on the disclosure statement. The election, if made by the majorities required by §1111 (b)(1)(A)(i), shall be binding on all members of the class with respect to the plan.

(As amended Apr. 11, 1997, eff. Dec. 1, 1997.)

交后提交动议或在债权异议中申请作此认定。

（c）**政府机构的债权**。针对就政府机构的担保债权的金额的认定，仅可在政府机构提交债权证明后或第 3002 条（c）（1）规定的用于提交债权证明的期间届满后通过动议或在债权异议中申请作此认定。

（经 Mar. 30, 1987, eff. Aug. 1, 1987; Apr. 27, 2017, eff. Dec. 1, 2017. 修正）

第 3013 条　债权和权益分组

就计划及其接受意见而言，在有人提出动议的情况下，按照法院可作出的指示发出通知并举行听证后，法院可根据法典第 1122、1222（b）（1）和 1322（b）（1）条决定债权人和股本证券持有人的分组。

（经 Apr. 30, 1991, eff. Aug. 1, 1991. 修正）

第 3014 条　在第 9 章市政机构破产案件或第 11 章重整案件中担保债权人根据第 1111 条（b）所作的选择

在就披露声明举行的听证结束前或在法院可确定的更长期间内的任意时间，在第 9 章或第 11 章案件中，担保债权人小组可随时选择适用法典第 1111 条（b）（2）的规定。若披露声明被根据本法第 3017.1 条有条件批准通过，并且并未就披露声明举行最终听证，则可在根据第 3017.1 条（a）（2）确定的日期或法院可确定的其他日期前选择适用法典第 1111 条（b）（2）的规定。除非系在就披露声明举行的听证上而作出该选择，否则该选择应以书面形式作出并签署。若该选择系根据第 1111 条（b）（1）（A）（i）的要求而经多数作出，则其就该计划而言应约束该小组内的所有成员。

（经 Apr. 11, 1997, eff. Dec. 1, 1997. 修正）

U.S. Federal Rules of Bankruptcy Procedure
(Chinese-English bilingual version)

Rule 3015. Filing, Objection to Confirmation, Effect of Confirmation, and Modification of a Plan in a Chapter 12 or a Chapter 13 Case

(a) FILING A CHAPTER 12 PLAN. The debtor may file a chapter 12 plan with the petition. If a plan is not filed with the petition, it shall be filed within the time prescribed by §1221 of the Code.

(b) FILING A CHAPTER 13 PLAN. The debtor may file a chapter 13 plan with the petition. If a plan is not filed with the petition, it shall be filed within 14 days thereafter, and such time may not be further extended except for cause shown and on notice as the court may direct. If a case is converted to chapter 13, a plan shall be filed within 14 days thereafter, and such time may not be further extended except for cause shown and on notice as the court may direct.

(c) FORM OF CHAPTER 13 PLAN. If there is an Official Form for a plan filed in a chapter 13 case, that form must be used unless a Local Form has been adopted in compliance with Rule 3015.1. With either the Official Form or a Local Form, a nonstandard provision is effective only if it is included in a section of the form designated for nonstandard provisions and is also identified in accordance with any other requirements of the form. As used in this rule and the Official Form or a Local Form, "nonstandard provision" means a provision not otherwise included in the Official or Local Form or deviating from it.

(d) NOTICE. If the plan is not included with the notice of the hearing on confirmation mailed under Rule 2002, the debtor shall serve the plan on the trustee and all creditors when it is filed with the court.

(e) TRANSMISSION TO UNITED STATES TRUSTEE. The clerk shall forthwith transmit to the United States trustee a copy of the plan and any modification thereof filed under subdivision (a) or (b) of this rule.

(f) OBJECTION TO CONFIRMATION; DETERMINATION OF GOOD FAITH IN THE ABSENCE OF AN OBJECTION. An objection to confirmation of a plan shall be filed and served on the debtor, the trustee, and any other entity designated by the court, and shall be transmitted to the United States trustee, at

美国联邦破产程序规则
（中英对照译本）

第 3015 条　在第 12 章或第 13 章案件中提交计划、对计划的批准提出异议、批准的效力以及计划的修改

（a）**提交第 12 章计划**。债务人可在提交破产申请时一并提交第 12 章计划。若该计划未与破产申请被一同提交，则其应在法典第 1221 条规定的期间内而被提交。

（b）**提交第 13 章计划**。债务人可在提交破产申请一并提交第 13 章计划。若该计划未与破产申请被一同提交，则应在破产申请被提交后 14 日内而被提交，并且除非基于被主张的特定事由并且按照法院可作出的指示发出通知，否则该期间不得被予以延长。若该案系被转换至第 13 章案件，则该计划应在被转换后 14 日内而被提交，并且除非基于被主张的特定事由并按照法院可作出的指示发出通知，否则该期间不得被予以延长。

（c）**第 13 章计划的模板**。若就第 13 章案件中被提交的计划存在官方模板，则除非已经采用符合第 3015.1 条规定的地方模板，否则应采用该官方模板。无论系采用官方模板抑或是地方模板，非格式条款仅当其被载于该模板中为非格式条款所指定的区域时才有效，并且还应根据该模板中的任何其他要求予以标识。就本条规定以及官方模板或地方模板而言，"非格式条款"指本未被载于官方模板或地方模板，或者与前述模板存在差异的规定。

（d）**通知**。若该计划并未含有根据第 2002 条邮寄的就批准计划举行听证的通知，则债务人应在向法院提交该计划时，将其送达给托管人和全体债权人。

（e）**向联邦托管人移交**。书记员应立刻向联邦托管人移交该计划的副本以及根据本条的（a）或（b）附条而被提交的任何计划的修改。

（f）**就计划的批准提出的异议；在无人提出异议的情况下对善意的认定**。除非法院作出其他裁定，否则就计划的批准而提出的异议应至少在就计划的批准而举行的听证前 7 日以前而向法院提交并送达给债务人、托管人以及法院可指定的任何其他实体，并且应移交给联邦托管人。就计划的批准提出异议应遵守第

least seven days before the date set for the hearing on confirmation, unless the court orders otherwise. An objection to confirmation is governed by Rule 9014. If no objection is timely filed, the court may determine that the plan has been proposed in good faith and not by any means forbidden by law without receiving evidence on such issues.

(g) EFFECT OF CONFIRMATION. Upon the confirmation of a chapter 12 or chapter 13 plan:

(1) any determination in the plan made under Rule 3012 about the amount of a secured claim is binding on the holder of the claim, even if the holder files a contrary proof of claim or the debtor schedules that claim, and regardless of whether an objection to the claim has been filed; and

(2) any request in the plan to terminate the stay imposed by §362(a), §1201(a), or §1301(a) is granted.

(h) MODIFICATION OF PLAN AFTER CONFIRMATION. A request to modify a plan under §1229 or §1329 of the Code shall identify the proponent and shall be filed together with the proposed modification. The clerk, or some other person as the court may direct, shall give the debtor, the trustee, and all creditors not less than 21 days' notice by mail of the time fixed for filing objections and, if an objection is filed, the hearing to consider the proposed modification, unless the court orders otherwise with respect to creditors who are not affected by the proposed modification. A copy of the notice shall be transmitted to the United States trustee. A copy of the proposed modification, or a summary thereof, shall be included with the notice. Any objection to the proposed modification shall be filed and served on the debtor, the trustee, and any other entity designated by the court, and shall be transmitted to the United States trustee. An objection to a proposed modification is governed by Rule 9014.

(As amended Apr. 30, 1991, eff. Aug. 1, 1991; Apr. 22, 1993, eff. Aug. 1, 1993; Mar. 26, 2009, eff.Dec. 1, 2009; Apr. 27, 2017, eff. Dec. 1, 2017.)

9014 条的规定。若在规定的时间内无人提交异议，则法院可认定该计划系基于善意而提出并且在没有相反证据的情况下，该计划并非系以法律所禁止的任何方式而被提出。

（g）**批准的效力**。在第 12 章或第 13 章计划得到批准时：

（1）根据第 3012 条在计划中就担保债权的金额所作的任何认定对债权人均具有约束力，即使该债权人提交了不同的债权证明或债务人将该债权计入报表，也无论是否有人就已被提交的债权提出异议；并且

（2）在计划中任何申请终止第 362（a）、1201（a）或 1301（a）条所规定的冻结均将得到准予。

（h）**批准后计划的修改**。根据法典第 1229 条或第 1329 条申请修改计划的请求应载明提议者的身份，并且在提交该请求时应一并提交拟议的修改。除非法院针对未受拟议修改所影响的债权人作出其他规定，否则书记员或法院可指定的其他人应以邮寄的方式至少提前 21 日向债务人、托管人以及全体债权人发出通知以告知其确定的用于提交异议的期间，并且若有人提交异议，还应告知其确定的就审议拟议的修改而举行听证的时间。该通知的副本还应被移交给联邦托管人。该通知应附有拟议修改的副本或其摘要。就拟议修改的任何异议均应向法院提交并被送达给债务人、托管人和法院指定的任何其他实体，并且应被移交给联邦托管人。就拟议修改提出异议应遵守第 9014 条的规定。

（经 Apr. 30, 1991, eff. Aug. 1, 1991; Apr. 22, 1993, eff. Aug. 1, 1993; Mar. 26, 2009, eff.Dec. 1, 2009; Apr. 27, 2017, eff. Dec. 1, 2017. 修正）

Rule 3015.1. Requirements for a Local Form for Plans Filed in a Chapter 13 Case

Notwithstanding Rule 9029（a）（1）, a district may require that a Local Form for a plan filed in a chapter 13 case be used instead of an Official Form adopted for that purpose if the following conditions are satisfied:

（a）a single Local Form is adopted for the district after public notice and an opportunity for public comment;

（b）each paragraph is numbered and labeled in boldface type with a heading stating the general subject matter of the paragraph;

（c）the Local Form includes an initial paragraph for the debtor to indicate that the plan does or does not:

（1）contain any nonstandard provision;

（2）limit the amount of a secured claim based on a valuation of the collateral for the claim; or

（3）avoid a security interest or lien;

（d）the Local Form contains separate paragraphs for:

（1）curing any default and maintaining payments on a claim secured by the debtor's principal residence;

（2）paying a domestic-support obligation;

（3）paying a claim described in the final paragraph of §1325（a）of the Bankruptcy Code; and

（4）surrendering property that secures a claim with a request that the stay under §§362（a）and 1301（a）be terminated as to the surrendered collateral; and

（e）the Local Form contains a final paragraph for:

（1）the placement of nonstandard provisions, as defined in Rule 3015（c）, along with a statement that any nonstandard provision placed elsewhere in the plan is void; and

（2）certification by the debtor's attorney or by an unrepresented debtor that the plan contains no nonstandard provision other than those set out in the final paragraph.

（Added Apr. 27, 2017, eff. Dec. 1, 2017.）

第 3015.1 条　第 13 章计划适用地方模板的条件

即使存在第 9029 条（a）（1）的规定，若符合下列条件，则某辖区可要求在第 13 章案件中被提交的计划采用地方模板，而不采用相应的官方模板：

（a）在向公众发出通知并听取公众意见后，该辖区才被决定适用单项地方模板；

（b）每段均以黑体字标明编号以及标题，并且该标题能表明该段的主要事项；

（c）该地方模板的首段即向债务人说明该计划是否：

（1）含有任何非格式条款；
（2）基于债权所涉担保物的价值来限制担保债权的金额；或

（3）撤销担保权益或物上担保权；
（d）该地方模板设置有单独段落以说明以下事项：
（1）就由债务人的主要住所所担保的债权纠正违约并保持还款；

（2）支付家庭抚养费；
（3）《清偿破产法典》第 1325 条（a）的最后一段所述的债权；以及

（4）在申请终止根据第 362（a）和 1301（a）条而对担保债权的财产所施加的冻结时，移交该担保物；并且
（e）地方模板的最后一段设置有填写以下内容的区域：
（1）第 3015 条（c）所述的非格式条款，并注明在该计划中其他部分所出现的非格式条款均无效；以及

（2）债务人的律师或没有律师代表的债务人证明该计划除最后一段所列明的非格式条款外不存在其他非格式条款。

（经 Apr. 27, 2017, eff. Dec. 1, 2017. 增补）

Rule 3016. Filing of Plan and Disclosure Statement in a Chapter 9 Municipality or Chapter 11 Reorganization Case

(a) IDENTIFICATION OF PLAN. Every proposed plan and any modification thereof shall be dated and, in a chapter 11 case, identified with the name of the entity or entities submitting or filing it.

(b) DISCLOSURE STATEMENT. In a chapter 9 or 11 case, a disclosure statement under §1125 of the Code or evidence showing compliance with §1126 (b) shall be filed with the plan or within a time fixed by the court, unless the plan is intended to provide adequate information under §1125 (f)(1). If the plan is intended to provide adequate information under §1125 (f)(1), it shall be so designated and Rule 3017.1 shall apply as if the plan is a disclosure statement.

(c) INJUNCTION UNDER A PLAN. If a plan provides for an injunction against conduct not otherwise enjoined under the Code, the plan and disclosure statement shall describe in specific and conspicuous language (bold, italic, or underlined text) all acts to be enjoined and identify the entities that would be subject to the injunction.

(d) STANDARD FORM SMALL BUSINESS DISCLOSURE STATEMENT AND PLAN. In a small business case, the court may approve a disclosure statement and may confirm a plan that conform substantially to the appropriate Official Forms or other standard forms approved by the court.

(As amended Mar. 30, 1987, eff. Aug. 1, 1987; Apr. 30, 1991, eff. Aug. 1, 1991; Apr. 23, 1996, eff.Dec. 1, 1996; Apr. 23, 2001, eff. Dec. 1, 2001; Apr. 23, 2008, eff. Dec. 1, 2008.)

Rule 3017. Court Consideration of Disclosure Statement in a Chapter 9 Municipality or Chapter 11 Reorganization Case

(a) HEARING ON DISCLOSURE STATEMENT AND OBJECTIONS. Except as provided in Rule 3017.1, after a disclosure statement is filed in accordance with Rule 3016 (b), the court shall hold a hearing on at least 28 days' notice to the debtor, creditors, equity security holders and other parties in interest as provided in Rule 2002 to consider the disclosure statement and any objections or modifications thereto. The

第 3016 条　在第 9 章市政机构破产案件或第 11 章重整案件中计划和披露声明的提交

（a）**计划的标注**。所有被提出的计划和任何修改都应注明日期，并且在第 11 章案件中，还应注明提交该计划的实体（们）的姓名。

（b）**披露声明**。在第 9 章或第 11 章案件中，法典第 1125 条中的披露声明或用于说明符合第 1126 条（b）的规定的证明应在计划被提交时或法院规定的时间内而被提交，除非提出者意图通过计划本身而根据第 1125 条（f）（1）提供充分信息。若提出者意图通过计划本身而根据第 1125 条（f）（1）提供充分信息，则该计划应被认定为披露声明并适用第 3017.1 条的规定。

（c）**计划中的禁令**。若该计划针对并不为法典所禁止的行为规定有禁令，则该计划及披露声明应以明确且显眼的语言（粗体、斜体或下画线）说明其将禁止的所有行为并注明该禁令所将针对的实体。

（d）**小企业披露声明和计划的标准格式**。在小企业破产案件中，法院可批准基本符合相应官方模板或法院所批准的其他标准格式的披露声明和计划。

（经 Mar. 30, 1987, eff. Aug. 1, 1987; Apr. 30, 1991, eff. Aug. 1, 1991; Apr. 23, 1996, eff.Dec. 1, 1996; Apr. 23, 2001, eff. Dec. 1, 2001; Apr. 23, 2008, eff. Dec. 1, 2008. 修正）

第 3017 条　在第 9 章市政机构破产案件或第 11 章重整案件中法院对披露声明的审议

（a）**就披露声明和异议所举行的听证**。除第 3017.1 条另有规定外，在披露声明被根据第 3016 条（b）提交后，法院应提前 28 日根据第 2002 条向债务人、债权人、股本证券持有人以及其他利益相关方发出通知并举行听证以审议披露声明以及对披露声明的任何异议和修改。在向债务人、任何托管人或根据法典而被任命的委员会、证券交易委员会以及任何书面请求获得声明或计划的副本的利益相

plan and the disclosure statement shall be mailed with the notice of the hearing only to the debtor, any trustee or committee appointed under the Code, the Securities and Exchange Commission and any party in interest who requests in writing a copy of the statement or plan. Objections to the disclosure statement shall be filed and served on the debtor, the trustee, any committee appointed under the Code, and any other entity designated by the court, at any time before the disclosure statement is approved or by an earlier date as the court may fix. In a chapter 11 reorganization case, every notice, plan, disclosure statement, and objection required to be served or mailed pursuant to this subdivision shall be transmitted to the United States trustee within the time provided in this subdivision.

(b) DETERMINATION ON DISCLOSURE STATEMENT. Following the hearing the court shall determine whether the disclosure statement should be approved.

(c) DATES FIXED FOR VOTING ON PLAN AND CONFIRMATION. On or before approval of the disclosure statement, the court shall fix a time within which the holders of claims and interests may accept or reject the plan and may fix a date for the hearing on confirmation.

(d) TRANSMISSION AND NOTICE TO UNITED STATES TRUSTEE, CREDITORS, AND EQUITY SECURITY HOLDERS. Upon approval of a disclosure statement,— except to the extent that the court orders otherwise with respect to one or more unimpaired classes of creditors or equity security holders—the debtor in possession, trustee, proponent of the plan, or clerk as the court orders shall mail to all creditors and equity security holders, and in a chapter 11 reorganization case shall transmit to the United States trustee,

(1) the plan or a court-approved summary of the plan;

(2) the disclosure statement approved by the court;

(3) notice of the time within which acceptances and rejections of the plan may be filed; and

(4) any other information as the court may direct, including any court opinion approving the disclosure statement or a court-approved summary of the opinion.

In addition, notice of the time fixed for filing objections and the hearing on confirmation shall be mailed to all creditors and equity security holders in accordance

美国联邦破产程序规则
（中英对照译本）

关方就听证发出通知时，还应向其邮寄该计划以及披露声明。就披露声明而提出的异议应在披露声明被批准前或法院可确定的更早日期前的任意时间而向法院提交并被送达给债务人、托管人、根据法典而被任命的任何委员会以及法院指定的任何实体。在第 11 章重整案件中，所有根据本附条规定被要求送达或邮寄的通知、计划、披露声明和异议均应在本附条规定的时间内移交给联邦托管人。

（b）**就披露声明的认定**。在听证后法院应就该披露声明是否应被批准而作出认定。

（c）**为计划的表决和批准而确定的日期**。在披露声明被批准时或之前，法院应确定享有债权和权益的主体可接受或拒绝计划的期间并且可确定就计划的批准举行听证的日期。

（d）**向联邦托管人、债权人以及股本证券持有人移交并发出通知**。除非法院针对未受调整的一个或多个债权人或股本证券持有人小组作出其他裁定，否则在披露声明得到批准时，经管债务人、托管人、计划的提出者或法院裁定的书记员应向全体债权人和股本证券持有人，以及在第 11 章重整案件中还应向联邦托管人移交以下各项：

（1）计划或经法院批准的计划的摘要；

（2）经法院批准的披露声明；

（3）告知确定的用于提交计划的接受和拒绝意见的期间的通知；以及

（4）法院可规定的任何其他信息，包括批准披露声明的法院意见或经法院批准的意见的摘要。

除此之外，还应根据第 2002 条（b）向全体债权人和股本证券持有人邮寄通知以告知其确定的用于提交异议以及就批准举行听证的时间，并且还应向有权就

with Rule 2002 (b), and a form of ballot conforming to the appropriate Official Form shall be mailed to creditors and equity security holders entitled to vote on the plan. If the court opinion is not transmitted or only a summary of the plan is transmitted, the court opinion or the plan shall be provided on request of a party in interest at the plan proponent's expense. If the court orders that the disclosure statement and the plan or a summary of the plan shall not be mailed to any unimpaired class, notice that the class is designated in the plan as unimpaired and notice of the name and address of the person from whom the plan or summary of the plan and disclosure statement may be obtained upon request and at the plan proponent's expense, shall be mailed to members of the unimpaired class together with the notice of the time fixed for filing objections to and the hearing on confirmation. For the purposes of this subdivision, creditors and equity security holders shall include holders of stock, bonds, debentures, notes, and other securities of record on the date the order approving the disclosure statement is entered or another date fixed by the court, for cause, after notice and a hearing.

(e) TRANSMISSION TO BENEFICIAL HOLDERS OF SECURITIES. At the hearing held pursuant to subdivision (a) of this rule, the court shall consider the procedures for transmitting the documents and information required by subdivision (d) of this rule to beneficial holders of stock, bonds, debentures, notes, and other securities, determine the adequacy of the procedures, and enter any orders the court deems appropriate.

(f) NOTICE AND TRANSMISSION OF DOCUMENTS TO ENTITIES SUBJECT TO AN INJUNCTION UNDER A PLAN. If a plan provides for an injunction against conduct not otherwise enjoined under the Code and an entity that would be subject to the injunction is not a creditor or equity security holder, at the hearing held under Rule 3017 (a), the court shall consider procedures for providing the entity with:

(1) at least 28 days' notice of the time fixed for filing objections and the hearing on confirmation of the plan containing the information described in Rule 2002 (c) (3); and

(2) to the extent feasible, a copy of the plan and disclosure statement.

(As amended Mar. 30, 1987, eff. Aug. 1, 1987; Apr. 30, 1991, eff. Aug. 1, 1991; Apr. 11, 1997, eff.Dec. 1, 1997; Apr. 23, 2001, eff. Dec. 1, 2001; Mar. 26, 2009, eff. Dec. 1, 2009.)

美国联邦破产程序规则
（中英对照译本）

计划参与表决的债权人和股本证券持有人邮寄根据相应官方模板而制作的表决票。若法院意见未被移交或仅移交了计划的摘要，则在利益相关方提出请求的情况下，应向其提供法院意见或计划，并由计划的提出者承担费用。若法院裁定披露声明和计划或计划的摘要不得被邮寄给任何未受调整的小组，则在向未受调整的小组的成员邮寄就确定的用于提交异议以及举行批准听证的时间而发出的通知时，应一并邮寄其他通知以告知其该小组在计划中被认定为未受调整的小组，以及可向其请求获得计划或计划的摘要以及披露声明并由计划的提出者承担费用的主体的姓名和住址。就本款而言，债权人和股本证券持有人应当包括在批准披露声明的裁定被正式作出之日或法院出于特定事由经过通知和听证后确定的其他日期持有已登记的股票、债券、公司债券、票据以及其他证券的主体。

（e）**向证券的实益持有人移交**。在根据本条（a）附条举行的听证上，法院应审议向股票、债券、公司债券、票据以及其他证券的实益持有人移交本条（d）附条所要求的文件和信息的程序，就该程序是否适当作出认定并作出其认为适当的裁定。

（f）**向计划中的禁令所针对的实体发出通知和移交文件**。若该计划针对并不为法典所禁止的行为规定有禁令并且该禁令所将针对的实体并非债权人或股本证券持有人，则在根据第3017条（a）举行的听证上，法院应审议向该实体提供以下各项的程序：

（1）提前28日发出的通知以告知其确定的用于提交异议和举行批准计划的听证的时间，并应载有第2002条（c）（3）所述的信息；以及
（2）在切实可行的情况下，提供计划和披露声明的副本。

（经 Mar. 30, 1987, eff. Aug. 1, 1987; Apr. 30, 1991, eff. Aug. 1, 1991; Apr. 11, 1997, eff.Dec. 1, 1997; Apr. 23, 2001, eff. Dec. 1, 2001; Mar. 26, 2009, eff. Dec. 1, 2009. 修正）

Rule 3017.1. Court Consideration of Disclosure Statement in a Small Business Case

(a) CONDITIONAL APPROVAL OF DISCLOSURE STATEMENT. In a small business case, the court may, on application of the plan proponent or on its own initiative, conditionally approve a disclosure statement filed in accordance with Rule 3016. On or before conditional approval of the disclosure statement, the court shall:

(1) fix a time within which the holders of claims and interests may accept or reject the plan;

(2) fix a time for filing objections to the disclosure statement;

(3) fix a date for the hearing on final approval of the disclosure statement to be held if a timely objection is filed; and

(4) fix a date for the hearing on confirmation.

(b) APPLICATION OF RULE 3017. Rule 3017 (a), (b), (c), and (e) do not apply to a conditionally approved disclosure statement. Rule 3017 (d) applies to a conditionally approved disclosure statement, except that conditional approval is considered approval of the disclosure statement for the purpose of applying Rule 3017 (d).

(c) FINAL APPROVAL.

(1) *Notice*. Notice of the time fixed for filing objections and the hearing to consider final approval of the disclosure statement shall be given in accordance with Rule 2002 and may be combined with notice of the hearing on confirmation of the plan.

(2) *Objections*. Objections to the disclosure statement shall be filed, transmitted to the United States trustee, and served on the debtor, the trustee, any committee appointed under the Code and any other entity designated by the court at any time before final approval of the disclosure statement or by an earlier date as the court may fix.

(3) *Hearing*. If a timely objection to the disclosure statement is filed, the court shall hold a hearing to consider final approval before or combined with the hearing on confirmation of the plan.

(Added Apr. 11, 1997, eff. Dec. 1, 1997; amended Apr. 23, 2008, eff. Dec. 1, 2008.)

第 3017.1 条　在小企业案件中法院就披露声明的审议

（a）**披露声明的有条件批准**。在小企业案件中，法院可在计划的提出者提出申请的情况下或主动有条件地批准根据第 3016 条被提交的披露声明。在有条件地批准披露声明时或之前，法院应履行以下各项：

（1）确定享有债权和权益的主体可接受或拒绝计划的时间；

（2）确定就披露声明提交异议的期间；
（3）在有人及时提出异议的情况下，确定就披露声明的最终批准举行听证的日期；以及
（4）确定就计划的批准举行听证的日期。

（b）**第 3017 条的适用**。第 3017 条（a）、（b）、（c）和（e）并不适用于被有条件批准的披露声明。第 3017 条（d）适用于被有条件批准的披露声明，除非有条件的批准系基于适用第 3017 条（d）的目的而被视为对披露声明的批准。

（c）**最终批准**。
（1）通知。就确定的用于提交异议以及就披露声明的最终批准举行听证的时间的通知应根据第 2002 条而发出并应附有就举行计划批准听证而应发出的通知。

（2）异议。就披露声明而提出的异议应在披露声明得到最终批准或法院可确定的更早日期前的任意时间内，被提交至法院、移送给联邦托管人并送达给债务人、托管人、任何根据法典被任命的委员会以及法院可指定的任何其他实体。

（3）听证。若有人及时就披露声明提交了异议，则法院应在就计划的批准举行听证前举行听证以对披露声明的最终批准进行审议，前述听证也可进行合并。

（经 Apr. 11, 1997, eff. Dec. 1, 1997; amended Apr. 23, 2008, eff. Dec. 1, 2008. 增补）

U.S. Federal Rules of Bankruptcy Procedure
(Chinese-English bilingual version)

Rule 3018. Acceptance or Rejection of Plan in a Chapter 9 Municipality or a Chapter 11 Reorganization Case

(a) ENTITIES ENTITLED TO ACCEPT OR REJECT PLAN; TIME FOR ACCEPTANCE OR REJECTION. A plan may be accepted or rejected in accordance with §1126 of the Code within the time fixed by the court pursuant to Rule 3017. Subject to subdivision (b) of this rule, an equity security holder or creditor whose claim is based on a security of record shall not be entitled to accept or reject a plan unless the equity security holder or creditor is the holder of record of the security on the date the order approving the disclosure statement is entered or on another date fixed by the court, for cause, after notice and a hearing. For cause shown, the court after notice and hearing may permit a creditor or equity security holder to change or withdraw an acceptance or rejection. Notwithstanding objection to a claim or interest, the court after notice and hearing may temporarily allow the claim or interest in an amount which the court deems proper for the purpose of accepting or rejecting a plan.

(b) ACCEPTANCES OR REJECTIONS OBTAINED BEFORE PETITION. An equity security holder or creditor whose claim is based on a security of record who accepted or rejected the plan before the commencement of the case shall not be deemed to have accepted or rejected the plan pursuant to §1126 (b) of the Code unless the equity security holder or creditor was the holder of record of the security on the date specified in the solicitation of such acceptance or rejection for the purposes of such solicitation. A holder of a claim or interest who has accepted or rejected a plan before the commencement of the case under the Code shall not be deemed to have accepted or rejected the plan if the court finds after notice and hearing that the plan was not transmitted to substantially all creditors and equity security holders of the same class, that an unreasonably short time was prescribed for such creditors and equity security holders to accept or reject the plan, or that the solicitation was not in compliance with §1126 (b) of the Code.

(c) FORM OF ACCEPTANCE OR REJECTION. An acceptance or rejection shall be in writing, identify the plan or plans accepted or rejected, be signed by the creditor or equity security holder or an authorized agent, and conform to the

第 3018 条　第 9 章市政机构破产案件或第 11 章重整案件中对计划的接受或拒绝

（a）**有权接受或拒绝计划的实体；接受或拒绝的时间**。该计划可在法院根据第 3017 条确定的时间内由实体根据法典第 1126 条予以接受或拒绝。在符合本条（b）附条规定的情况下，股本证券持有人或其债权基于已登记的证券的债权人无权就计划发表接受或拒绝意见，除非该股本证券持有人或债权人在批准披露声明的裁定被正式作出之日或法院出于特定事由经过通知和听证后确定的其他日期是已登记的证券的持有人。出于被主张的特定事由，经过通知和听证后，法院可准予债权人或股本证券持有人变更或撤销其接受或拒绝意见。即使有人就债权或权益提出异议，法院出于征集计划的接受或拒绝意见的目的，经过通知和听证后可暂时在其认为适当的金额内对债权或权益予以确认。

（b）**破产申请被提交前已征集的接受或拒绝意见**。在破产案件启动前已经接受或拒绝计划的股本证券持有人或其债权基于已登记的证券的债权人不得被视为已经根据法典第 1126 条（b）接受或拒绝计划，除非该股本证券持有人或债权人在接受或拒绝意见的征集中为该征集而确定的日期当日系已登记的证券的持有人。若法院在通知和听证后认定计划并未被移交给同一小组内几乎全部债权人以及股本证券持有人，为该类债权人和股本证券持有人规定的用于接受或拒绝计划的时间过短，或者对接受或拒绝意见的征集并不符合法典第 1126 条（b）的规定，则在破产案件被根据法典启动前已经接受或拒绝计划的享有债权或权益的主体，不得被视为已经接受或拒绝该计划。

（c）**接受或拒绝意见的格式**。接受或拒绝意见应被根据相应的官方模板以书面形式作出，注明被接受或拒绝的计划（们）并由债权人或股本证券持有人或者授权代理人签署。若有不止一项计划根据第 3017 条而被移交，则各债权人或股

appropriate Official Form. If more than one plan is transmitted pursuant to Rule 3017, an acceptance or rejection may be filed by each creditor or equity security holder for any number of plans transmitted and if acceptances are filed for more than one plan, the creditor or equity security holder may indicate a preference or preferences among the plans so accepted.

(d) ACCEPTANCE OR REJECTION BY PARTIALLY SECURED CREDITOR. A creditor whose claim has been allowed in part as a secured claim and in part as an unsecured claim shall be entitled to accept or reject a plan in both capacities.

(As amended Mar. 30, 1987, eff. Aug. 1, 1987; Apr. 30, 1991, eff. Aug. 1, 1991; Apr. 22, 1993, eff.Aug. 1, 1993; Apr. 11, 1997, eff. Dec. 1, 1997.)

Rule 3019. Modification of Accepted Plan in a Chapter 9 Municipality or a Chapter 11 Reorganization Case

(a) MODIFICATION OF PLAN BEFORE CONFIRMATION. In a chapter 9 or chapter 11 case, after a plan has been accepted and before its confirmation, the proponent may file a modification of the plan. If the court finds after hearing on notice to the trustee, any committee appointed under the Code, and any other entity designated by the court that the proposed modification does not adversely change the treatment of the claim of any creditor or the interest of any equity security holder who has not accepted in writing the modification, it shall be deemed accepted by all creditors and equity security holders who have previously accepted the plan.

(b) MODIFICATION OF PLAN AFTER CONFIRMATION IN INDIVIDUAL DEBTOR CASE. If the debtor is an individual, a request to modify the plan under §1127 (e) of the Code is governed by Rule 9014. The request shall identify the proponent and shall be filed together with the proposed modification. The clerk, or some other person as the court may direct, shall give the debtor, the trustee, and all creditors not less than 21 days' notice by mail of the time fixed to file objections and, if an objection is filed, the hearing to consider the proposed modification, unless the court orders otherwise with respect to creditors who are not affected by the proposed modification. A copy of the notice shall be transmitted to the United States trustee, together with a copy of the

本证券持有人针对已被移交的任意数量的计划均可提交接受或拒绝意见，并且若针对多项计划提交了接受意见，则债权人或股本证券持有人可注明在被其接受的计划中其更偏好哪（些）项计划。

（d）**不完全担保债权人的接受或拒绝意见。**其债权一部分被确认为担保债权而另一部分被确认为无担保债权的债权人应有权就两种身份而接受或拒绝计划。

（经 Mar. 30, 1987, eff. Aug. 1, 1987; Apr. 30, 1991, eff. Aug. 1, 1991; Apr. 22, 1993, eff. Aug. 1, 1993; Apr. 11, 1997, eff. Dec. 1, 1997. 修正）

第 3019 条　第 9 章市政机构破产案件或第 11 章重整案件中已被接受的计划的修改

（a）**批准前对计划的修改。**在第 9 章或第 11 章案件中，在计划得到接受后、得到批准前，计划的提出者可提交计划的修改方案。若法院在向托管人、任何根据法典而被任命的委员会以及法院所指定的任何其他实体发出通知并举行听证后，认为拟议的修改方案并未实质改变尚未书面接受修改方案的任何债权人的债权或任何股本证券持有人的权益所受的待遇，则其应被视为已由先前接受该计划的所有债权人及股本证券持有人所接受。

（b）**个人债务人案件中批准后对计划的修改。**若债务人为自然人，则根据法典第 1127 条（e）申请修改计划的请求应符合第 9014 条的规定。该请求应注明提出者的身份并应与拟议的修改方案被一同提交。除非法院针对未受拟议修改方案影响的债权人作出其他裁定，否则书记员或法院可指定的其他人，应以邮寄的方式至少提前 21 日向债务人、托管人以及全体债权人发出通知以告知其确定的用于提交异议的期间以及在有人提交异议的情况下，告知其确定的用于举行听证以审议拟议修改方案的时间。该通知的副本应与拟议修改方案的副本被一同移交给联邦托管人。对拟议修改方案的任何异议均应被提交至法院并送达给债务人、修改方案的提出者、托管人以及法院所指定的任何其他实体，并且

proposed modification. Any objection to the proposed modification shall be filed and served on the debtor, the proponent of the modification, the trustee, and any other entity designated by the court, and shall be transmitted to the United States trustee.

(As amended Mar. 30, 1987, eff. Aug. 1, 1987; Apr. 22, 1993, eff. Aug. 1, 1993; Apr. 23, 2008, eff.Dec. 1, 2008; Mar. 26, 2009, eff. Dec. 1, 2009.)

Rule 3020. Deposit; Confirmation of Plan in a Chapter 9 Municipality or Chapter 11 Reorganization Case

(a) DEPOSIT. In a chapter 11 case, prior to entry of the order confirming the plan, the court may order the deposit with the trustee or debtor in possession of the consideration required by the plan to be distributed on confirmation. Any money deposited shall be kept in a special account established for the exclusive purpose of making the distribution.

(b) OBJECTION TO AND HEARING ON CONFIRMATION IN A CHAPTER 9 OR CHAPTER 11 CASE.

(1) *Objection*. An objection to confirmation of the plan shall be filed and served on the debtor, the trustee, the proponent of the plan, any committee appointed under the Code, and any other entity designated by the court, within a time fixed by the court. Unless the case is a chapter 9 municipality case, a copy of every objection to confirmation shall be transmitted by the objecting party to the United States trustee within the time fixed for filing objections. An objection to confirmation is governed by Rule 9014.

(2) *Hearing*. The court shall rule on confirmation of the plan after notice and hearing as provided in Rule 2002. If no objection is timely filed, the court may determine that the plan has been proposed in good faith and not by any means forbidden by law without receiving evidence on such issues.

(c) ORDER OF CONFIRMATION.

(1) The order of confirmation shall conform to the appropriate Official Form. If the plan provides for an injunction against conduct not otherwise enjoined under the Code, the order of confirmation shall (1) describe in reasonable detail all acts enjoined; (2) be specific in its terms regarding the injunction; and (3) identify the entities subject to the injunction.

应被移交给联邦托管人。

（经 Mar. 30, 1987, eff. Aug. 1, 1987; Apr. 22, 1993, eff. Aug. 1, 1993; Apr. 23, 2008, eff.Dec. 1, 2008; Mar. 26, 2009, eff. Dec. 1, 2009. 修正）

第 3020 条 交存；第 9 章市政机构破产案件或第 11 章重整案件中计划的批准

（a）**交存**。在第 11 章案件中，在正式裁定批准计划前，法院可裁定向托管人或经管债务人交存计划所要求的对价以在得到批准时进行分配。所交存的任何款项均应被存放在仅用于分配的专用账户中。

（b）**就第 9 章或第 11 章计划的批准提出的异议和举行的听证**。

（1）异议。就计划的批准而提出的异议应在法院所确定的时间内被提交至法院并送达给债务人、托管人、计划的提出者、任何根据法典而被任命的委员会以及法院指定的任何其他实体。除第 9 章市政机构破产案件外，就计划的批准而提出的异议的副本应由提出者在确定的用于提交异议的期间内移交给联邦托管人。就计划的批准提出异议应遵守第 9014 条的规定。

（2）听证。在根据第 2002 条发出通知和举行听证后，法院应就计划的批准作出裁定。若在规定的时间内无人提交异议，则法院可认定该计划系被基于善意而提出并且在没有相反证据的情况下，该计划并非系以法律所禁止的任何方式而被提出。

（c）**批准的裁定**。
（1）批准计划的裁定应符合相应官方模板的规定。若该计划针对并未由法典所禁止的行为规定有禁令,则批准的裁定应（1）合理详细地描述所有禁止的行为；（2）明确涉及该禁令的各术语的含义；并（3）注明该禁令所针对的实体。

(2) Notice of entry of the order of confirmation shall be mailed promptly to the debtor, the trustee, creditors, equity security holders, other parties in interest, and, if known, to any identified entity subject to an injunction provided for in the plan against conduct not otherwise enjoined under the Code.

(3) Except in a chapter 9 municipality case, notice of entry of the order of confirmation shall be transmitted to the United States trustee as provided in Rule 2002(k).

(d) RETAINED POWER. Notwithstanding the entry of the order of confirmation, the court may issue any other order necessary to administer the estate.

(e) STAY OF CONFIRMATION ORDER. An order confirming a plan is stayed until the expiration of 14 days after the entry of the order, unless the court orders otherwise.

(As amended Mar. 30, 1987, eff. Aug. 1, 1987; Apr. 30, 1991, eff. Aug. 1, 1991; Apr. 22, 1993, eff.Aug. 1, 1993; Apr. 26, 1999, eff. Dec. 1, 1999; Apr. 23, 2001, eff. Dec. 1, 2001; Mar. 26, 2009, eff.Dec. 1, 2009.)

Rule 3021. Distribution under Plan

Except as provided in Rule 3020(e), after a plan is confirmed, distribution shall be made to creditors whose claims have been allowed, to interest holders whose interests have not been disallowed, and to indenture trustees who have filed claims under Rule 3003(c)(5) that have been allowed. For purposes of this rule, creditors include holders of bonds, debentures, notes, and other debt securities, and interest holders include the holders of stock and other equity securities, of record at the time of commencement of distribution, unless a different time is fixed by the plan or the order confirming the plan.

(As amended Apr. 11, 1997, eff. Dec. 1, 1997; Apr. 26, 1999, eff. Dec. 1, 1999.)

Rule 3022. Final Decree in Chapter 11 Reorganization Case

After an estate is fully administered in a chapter 11 reorganization case, the court, on its own motion or on motion of a party in interest, shall enter a final decree closing the case.

(As amended Mar. 30, 1987, eff. Aug. 1, 1987; Apr. 30, 1991, eff. Aug. 1, 1991.)

（2）就批准计划的裁定的正式作出而发出的通知应被立刻邮寄给债务人、托管人、债权人、股本证券持有人、其他利益相关方以及若计划针对并未由法典所禁止的行为规定有禁令，则还应邮寄给已知的该禁令所针对的实体。

（3）除第 9 章市政机构破产案件另有规定外，就批准计划的裁定的正式作出而发出的通知应根据第 2002 条（k）的规定移交给联邦托管人。

（d）**保留的权力**。即使正式作出批准计划的裁定，法院仍可签发任何其他必要的裁定以管理破产实体。

（e）**批准裁定的冻结**。除非法院作出其他裁定，否则批准计划的裁定将在该裁定被正式作出后 14 日内被冻结。

（经 Mar. 30, 1987, eff. Aug. 1, 1987; Apr. 30, 1991, eff. Aug. 1, 1991; Apr. 22, 1993, eff.Aug. 1, 1993; Apr. 26, 1999, eff. Dec. 1, 1999; Apr. 23, 2001, eff. Dec. 1, 2001; Mar. 26, 2009, eff.Dec. 1, 2009. 修正）

第 3021 条　根据计划进行的分配

除第 3020 条（e）另有规定外，计划得到批准后，应向其债权已经确认的债权人、其权益未被拒绝确认的权益人以及根据第 3003 条（c）（5）提交债权且得到确认的契约受托人进行分配。就本条而言，债权人和权益人分别包括启动分配时（除非计划或批准计划的裁定规定了其他时间）持有已登记的债券、公司债券、票据以及其他债务凭证的主体，以及持有已登记的股票或其他股权凭证的主体。

（经 Apr. 11, 1997, eff. Dec. 1, 1997; Apr. 26, 1999, eff. Dec. 1, 1999. 修正）

第 3022 条　第 11 章重整案件中的终局裁定

在第 11 章重整案件中，当破产实体得到完全管理后，法院在其自身动议或利益相关方的动议下，应终局裁定结案。

（经 Mar. 30, 1987, eff. Aug. 1, 1987; Apr. 30, 1991, eff. Aug. 1, 1991. 修正）

PART IV

THE DEBTOR: DUTIES AND BENEFITS

Rule 4001. Relief from Automatic Stay; Prohibiting or Conditioning the Use, Sale, or Lease of Property; Use of Cash Collateral; Obtaining Credit; Agreements

(a) RELIEF FROM STAY; PROHIBITING OR CONDITIONING THE USE, SALE, OR LEASE OF PROPERTY.

(1) *Motion.* A motion for relief from an automatic stay provided by the Code or a motion to prohibit or condition the use, sale, or lease of property pursuant to §363 (e) shall be made in accordance with Rule 9014 and shall be served on any committee elected pursuant to §705 or appointed pursuant to §1102 of the Code or its authorized agent, or, if the case is a chapter 9 municipality case or a chapter 11 reorganization case and no committee of unsecured creditors has been appointed pursuant to §1102, on the creditors included on the list filed pursuant to Rule 1007 (d), and on such other entities as the court may direct.

(2) *Ex Parte Relief.* Relief from a stay under §362 (a) or a request to prohibit or condition the use, sale, or lease of property pursuant to §363 (e) may be granted without prior notice only if (A) it clearly appears from specific facts shown by affidavit or by a verified motion that immediate and irreparable injury, loss, or damage will result to the movant before the adverse party or the attorney for the adverse party can be heard in opposition, and (B) the movant's attorney certifies to the court in writing the efforts, if any, which have been made to give notice and the reasons why notice should not be required. The party obtaining relief under this subdivision and §362 (f) or §363 (e) shall immediately give oral notice thereof to the trustee or

第 IV 部分
债务人：义务和利益

第 4001 条　自动冻结的解除；禁止或附条件使用、出售或出租财产；现金担保物的使用；获取信贷；协议

（a）冻结的解除；禁止或附条件使用、出售或出租财产。

（1）动议。申请解除法典所规定的自动冻结或申请禁止或附条件根据第 363 条（e）使用、出售或出租财产的动议应根据第 9014 条的规定而被作出，并且应将其送达给根据法典第 705 条被选任或根据第 1102 条被指定的任何委员会或其授权代理机关，若在第 9 章市政机构破产案件或第 11 章重整案件中并未根据第 1102 条任命无担保债权人委员会，则应送达给根据第 1007 条（d）而被提交的清单中所列明的债权人，以及法院可指定的该类其他实体。

（2）单方救济。若（A）宣誓书或宣誓动议所主张的具体事实能够充分证明在他方当事人或他方当事人的律师提出异议前动议方即会遭受直接且不可弥补的伤害、损失或损害，并且（B）动议方的律师向法院以书面形式证明其就发出通知所作的努力（如有）以及不应要求其发出通知的原因，则在不进行事先通知的情况下法院即可准予解除第 362 条（a）所规定的冻结或申请禁止或附条件根据第 363 条（e）使用、出售或出租财产的请求。根据本附条以及第 362（f）或 363（e）条获得救济的主体应立刻就此向托管人或经管债务人以及债务人发出口头通知，并立刻以邮寄或其他方式将准予救济的裁定的副本移交给他方当事人（们）。在提前两日向未经通知即被准予解除冻结的主体发出通知或者在法院可规定的更短

debtor in possession and to the debtor and forthwith mail or otherwise transmit to such adverse party or parties a copy of the order granting relief. On two days notice to the party who obtained relief from the stay without notice or on shorter notice to that party as the court may prescribe, the adverse party may appear and move reinstatement of the stay or reconsideration of the order prohibiting or conditioning the use, sale, or lease of property. In that event, the court shall proceed expeditiously to hear and determine the motion.

(3) *Stay of Order.* An order granting a motion for relief from an automatic stay made in accordance with Rule 4001 (a)(1) is stayed until the expiration of 14 days after the entry of the order, unless the court orders otherwise.

(b) USE OF CASH COLLATERAL.

(1) *Motion; Service.*

(A) *Motion.* A motion for authority to use cash collateral shall be made in accordance with Rule 9014 and shall be accompanied by a proposed form of order.

(B) *Contents.* The motion shall consist of or (if the motion is more than five pages in length) begin with a concise statement of the relief requested, not to exceed five pages, that lists or summarizes, and sets out the location within the relevant documents of, all material provisions, including:

(i) the name of each entity with an interest in the cash collateral;

(ii) the purposes for the use of the cash collateral;

(iii) the material terms, including duration, of the use of the cash collateral; and

(iv) any liens, cash payments, or other adequate protection that will be provided to each entity with an interest in the cash collateral or, if no additional adequate protection is proposed, an explanation of why each entity's interest is adequately protected.

(C) *Service.* The motion shall be served on: (1) any entity with an interest in the cash collateral; (2) any committee elected under §705 or appointed under §1102 of the Code, or its authorized agent, or, if the case is a chapter 9 municipality case or a chapter 11 reorganization case and no committee of unsecured creditors has been appointed under §1102, the creditors included on the list filed under Rule 1007 (d); and (3) any other entity that the court directs.

(2) *Hearing.* The court may commence a final hearing on a motion for authorization

美国联邦破产程序规则
（中英对照译本）

时间内向法院可指定的主体发出通知后，他方当事人可出庭并提出动议以申请恢复冻结或重新审议禁止或附条件使用、出售或出租财产的裁定。在该情形下，法院应迅速举行听证并就该动议作出决定。

（3）裁定的冻结。除非法院作出其他裁定，否则准予根据第4001条（a）（1）所作的申请解除自动冻结的动议的裁定在该裁定被正式作出后14日内将被冻结。

（b）现金担保物的使用。
（1）动议；送达。
（A）动议。申请被准予使用现金担保物的动议应根据第9014条的规定而作出并且应附有拟议的裁定模板。
（B）内容。该动议应载有对所请求的救济的简要陈述（不超过5页），或者（若该动议超过5页）以该陈述作为开头，该陈述应列明或总结相关文件中的所有重要规定并标明其位置，包括以下事项：

（i）就现金担保物享有权益的各实体的姓名；
（ii）使用该现金担保物的目的；
（iii）有关使用该现金担保物的重要事项，包括使用期间；以及
（iv）针对就现金担保物享有权益的各实体，将向其提供的任何优先权、现金支付或其他充分保护；或者在未另行提供充分保护的情况下，说明各实体的权益已得到充分保护的解释。
（C）送达。该动议应被送达给：（1）就现金担保物享有权益的任何实体；（2）根据法典第705条被选任或根据第1102条被指定的任何委员或其授权代理机关，若在第9章市政机构破产案件或第11章重整案件中并未根据第1102条任命无担保债权人委员会，则应送达给根据第1007条（d）而被提交的清单中所列明的债权人，以及（3）法院指定的任何其他实体。

（2）听证。法院可在申请被准予使用现金担保物的动议被送达后的14日后

to use cash collateral no earlier than 14 days after service of the motion. If the motion so requests, the court may conduct a preliminary hearing before such 14-day period expires, but the court may authorize the use of only that amount of cash collateral as is necessary to avoid immediate and irreparable harm to the estate pending a final hearing.

(3) *Notice*. Notice of hearing pursuant to this subdivision shall be given to the parties on whom service of the motion is required by paragraph (1) of this subdivision and to such other entities as the court may direct.

(c) OBTAINING CREDIT.

(1) *Motion; Service.*

(A) *Motion*. A motion for authority to obtain credit shall be made in accordance with Rule 9014 and shall be accompanied by a copy of the credit agreement and a proposed form of order.

(B) *Contents*. The motion shall consist of or (if the motion is more than five pages in length) begin with a concise statement of the relief requested, not to exceed five pages, that lists or summarizes, and sets out the location within the relevant documents of, all material provisions of the proposed credit agreement and form of order, including interest rate, maturity, events of default, liens, borrowing limits, and borrowing conditions. If the proposed credit agreement or form of order includes any of the provisions listed below, the concise statement shall also: briefly list or summarize each one; identify its specific location in the proposed agreement and form of order; and identify any such provision that is proposed to remain in effect if interim approval is granted, but final relief is denied, as provided under Rule 4001 (c)(2). In addition, the motion shall describe the nature and extent of each provision listed below:

(i) a grant of priority or a lien on property of the estate under §364 (c) or (d);

(ii) the providing of adequate protection or priority for a claim that arose before the commencement of the case, including the granting of a lien on property of the estate to secure the claim, or the use of property of the estate or credit obtained under §364 to make cash payments on account of the claim;

(iii) a determination of the validity, enforceability, priority, or amount of a claim that arose before the commencement of the case, or of any lien securing the claim;

就该动议启动最终听证。若有动议作此申请，则法院可在该14日期间届满前举行初步听证，但若现金担保物的使用对于避免对破产实体造成直接且不可弥补的损害是必要的，则在举行最终听证期间，法院可准予使用必要金额内的现金担保物。

（3）通知。根据本款举行听证的通知应向本附条第（1）款要求向其送达动议的主体以及法院可指定的该类其他实体发出。

（c）获取信贷。
（1）动议；送达。
（A）动议。申请被准予获取信贷的动议应根据第9014条的规定而作出并应附有贷款协议的副本以及拟议的裁定模板。

（B）内容。该动议应载有对所请求的救济的简要陈述（不超过5页），或者（若该动议超过5页）以该陈述作为开头，该陈述应列明或总结相关文件中的所有拟议贷款协议以及裁定模板的重要规定并标明其位置，包括利率、到期日、违约事件、优先权、借款限额和借款条件。若拟议的贷款协议或裁定模板含有以下规定，则该简要陈述还应：简要列明各项并进行总结；标明其在拟议协议以及裁定模板中所在的具体位置；并且列明在根据第4001条（c）（2）获得临时批准但被拒绝授予最终救济的情况下仍将有效的任何该类规定。除此之外，该动议还应说明以下各项规定的性质以及范围：

（i）根据第364条（c）或（d）授予优先顺位或破产财产上的担保权；

（ii）为破产案件启动前成立的债权提供充分保护或优先顺位，包括授予破产财产上的担保权以担保债权或者使用破产财产或根据第364条规定获取信贷从而就该债权进行清偿；

（iii）就破产案件启动前成立的债权或担保该债权的担保权的有效性、可执行性或金额所作的认定；

(iv) a waiver or modification of Code provisions or applicable rules relating to the automatic stay;

(v) a waiver or modification of any entity's authority or right to file a plan, seek an extension of time in which the debtor has the exclusive right to file a plan, request the use of cash collateral under §363 (c), or request authority to obtain credit under §364;

(vi) the establishment of deadlines for filing a plan of reorganization, for approval of a disclosure statement, for a hearing on confirmation, or for entry of a confirmation order;

(vii) a waiver or modification of the applicability of nonbankruptcy law relating to the perfection of a lien on property of the estate, or on the foreclosure or other enforcement of the lien;

(viii) a release, waiver, or limitation on any claim or other cause of action belonging to the estate or the trustee, including any modification of the statute of limitations or other deadline to commence an action;

(ix) the indemnification of any entity;

(x) a release, waiver, or limitation of any right under §506 (c); or

(xi) the granting of a lien on any claim or cause of action arising under §§544, 545, 547, 548, 549, 553 (b), 723 (a), or 724 (a).

(C) *Service*. The motion shall be served on: (1) any committee elected under §705 or appointed under §1102 of the Code, or its authorized agent, or, if the case is a chapter 9 municipality case or a chapter 11 reorganization case and no committee of unsecured creditors has been appointed under §1102, on the creditors included on the list filed under Rule 1007 (d); and (2) on any other entity that the court directs.

(2) *Hearing*. The court may commence a final hearing on a motion for authority to obtain credit no earlier than 14 days after service of the motion. If the motion so requests, the court may conduct a hearing before such 14-day period expires, but the court may authorize the obtaining of credit only to the extent necessary to avoid immediate and irreparable harm to the estate pending a final hearing.

(3) *Notice*. Notice of hearing pursuant to this subdivision shall be given to the parties on whom service of the motion is required by paragraph (1) of this subdivision and to such other entities as the court may direct.

（iv）放弃或修改与自动冻结相关的法典中的规定或相应规则；

（v）放弃或修改任何实体提交计划、寻求延长债务人享有提交计划的专属权利的期间、根据第363条（c）申请使用现金担保物或根据第364条申请获取信贷的许可的权利；

（vi）设置提交重整计划、批准披露声明、就计划的批准举行听证或正式裁定批准计划的截止日期；

（vii）放弃或修改与破产财产上担保权的公示相关的或者针对取消抵押品赎回权或优先权的其他强制措施的非破产法的适用；

（viii）放弃或限制属于破产实体或托管人的任何债权或其他诉因，包括对提起诉讼的诉讼时效或其他截止日期的任何修改；

（ix）任何实体的赔偿；

（x）对第506条（c）项下权利的放弃或限制；或

（xi）就根据第544、545、547、548、549、553（b）、723（a）或724（a）条而成立的任何债权或诉因设立财产上担保权。

（C）送达。该动议应被送达给：（1）根据法典第705条被选任或根据第1102条被指定的任何委员或其授权代理机关，若在第9章市政机构破产案件或第11章重整案件中并未根据第1102条任命无担保债权人委员会，则应送达给根据第1007条（d）而被提交的清单中所列明的债权人；以及（2）法院指定的任何其他实体。

（2）听证。法院可在申请被准予获取信贷的动议被送达后的14日后就该动议启动最终听证。法院可应动议在该14日期间届满前举行初步听证，但若信贷的获取对于避免对破产实体造成直接且不可弥补的损害是必要的，则在举行最终听证期间，法院可准予其在必要范围内获取信贷。

（3）通知。根据本款举行听证的通知应向本附条第（1）款要求向其送达动议的主体以及法院可指定的该类其他实体发出。

U.S. Federal Rules of Bankruptcy Procedure
(Chinese-English bilingual version)

(4) *Inapplicability in a Chapter 13 Case.* This subdivision (c) does not apply in a chapter 13 case.

(d) AGREEMENT RELATING TO RELIEF FROM THE AUTOMATIC STAY, PROHIBITING OR CONDITIONING THE USE, SALE, OR LEASE OF PROPERTY, PROVIDING ADEQUATE PROTECTION, USE OF CASH COLLATERAL, AND OBTAINING CREDIT.

(1) *Motion; Service.*

(A) *Motion.* A motion for approval of any of the following shall be accompanied by a copy of the agreement and a proposed form of order:

(i) an agreement to provide adequate protection;

(ii) an agreement to prohibit or condition the use, sale, or lease of property;

(iii) an agreement to modify or terminate the stay provided for in §362;

(iv) an agreement to use cash collateral; or

(v) an agreement between the debtor and an entity that has a lien or interest in property of the estate pursuant to which the entity consents to the creation of a lien senior or equal to the entity's lien or interest in such property.

(B) *Contents.* The motion shall consist of or (if the motion is more than five pages in length) begin with a concise statement of the relief requested, not to exceed five pages, that lists or summarizes, and sets out the location within the relevant documents of, all material provisions of the agreement. In addition, the concise statement shall briefly list or summarize, and identify the specific location of, each provision in the proposed form of order, agreement, or other document of the type listed in subdivision (c)(1)(B). The motion shall also describe the nature and extent of each such provision.

(C) *Service.* The motion shall be served on: (1) any committee elected under §705 or appointed under §1102 of the Code, or its authorized agent, or, if the case is a chapter 9 municipality case or a chapter 11 reorganization case and no committee of unsecured creditors has been appointed under §1102, on the creditors included on the list filed under Rule 1007 (d); and (2) on any other entity the court directs.

(2) *Objection.* Notice of the motion and the time within which objections may be filed and served on the debtor in possession or trustee shall be mailed to the parties

（4）不适用于第13章案件。附条（c）不适用于第13章案件。

（d）与自动冻结的解除，禁止或附条件使用、出售或出租财产，提供充分保护，使用现金担保物以及获取信贷相关的协议。

（1）动议；送达。
（A）动议。申请批准以下各项的动议均应附有协议的副本以及拟议的裁定模板：
（i）提供充分保护的协议；
（ii）禁止或附条件使用、出售或出租财产的协议；
（iii）变更或终止法典第362条所规定的冻结；
（iv）使用现金担保物的协议；或
（v）就破产财产享有担保权或其他权益的实体同意在该财产上创设优先于或与其担保权或其他权益同级的担保权而与债务人间达成的协议。

（B）内容。该动议应载有对所请求的救济的简要陈述（不超过5页），或者（若该动议超过5页）以该陈述作为开头。该陈述应列明或总结相关文件中的重要规定，并列明其位置。除此之外，该简要陈述还应简要列明或总结拟议的裁定模板、协议或（c）(1)(B)款所列类型的其他文件中的各项规定并标明其具体位置，该动议还应说明前述各项规定的性质以及范围。

（C）送达。该动议应被送达给：(1)根据法典第705条被选任或根据第1102条被指定的任何委员会或其授权代理机关，若在第9章市政机构破产案件或第11章重整案件中并未根据第1102条任命无担保债权人委员会，则应送达给根据第1007条（d）而被提交的清单中所列明的债权人；以及（2）法院指定的任何其他实体。

（2）异议。就动议以及规定的用于提交并向经管债务人或托管人送达异议的时间而发出的通知应被邮寄给本附条第（1）款要求向其送达的主体以及法院可

on whom service is required by paragraph (1) of this subdivision and to such other entities as the court may direct. Unless the court fixes a different time, objections may be filed within 14 days of the mailing of the notice.

(3) *Disposition; Hearing.* If no objection is filed, the court may enter an order approving or disapproving the agreement without conducting a hearing. If an objection is filed or if the court determines a hearing is appropriate, the court shall hold a hearing on no less than seven days' notice to the objector, the movant, the parties on whom service is required by paragraph (1) of this subdivision and such other entities as the court may direct.

(4) *Agreement in Settlement of Motion.* The court may direct that the procedures prescribed in paragraphs (1), (2), and (3) of this subdivision shall not apply and the agreement may be approved without further notice if the court determines that a motion made pursuant to subdivisions (a), (b), or (c) of this rule was sufficient to afford reasonable notice of the material provisions of the agreement and opportunity for a hearing.

(As amended Mar. 30, 1987, eff. Aug. 1, 1987; Apr. 30, 1991, eff. Aug. 1, 1991; Apr. 26, 1999, eff. Dec. 1, 1999; Apr. 30, 2007, eff. Dec. 1, 2007; Mar. 26, 2009, eff. Dec. 1, 2009; Apr. 28, 2010, eff. Dec. 1, 2010; Apr. 25, 2019, eff. Dec. 1, 2019.)

Rule 4002. Duties of Debtor

(a) IN GENERAL. In addition to performing other duties prescribed by the Code and rules, the debtor shall:

(1) attend and submit to an examination at the times ordered by the court;

(2) attend the hearing on a complaint objecting to discharge and testify, if called as a witness;

(3) inform the trustee immediately in writing as to the location of real property in which the debtor has an interest and the name and address of every person holding money or property subject to the debtor's withdrawal or order if a schedule of property has not yet been filed pursuant to Rule 1007;

(4) cooperate with the trustee in the preparation of an inventory, the examination of proofs of claim, and the administration of the estate; and

指定的该类其他实体发出。除非法院对期间另有规定，否则该异议可在该通知被邮寄后 14 日内而被提交。

（3）处置；听证。若无人提交动议，则法院可不经听证而正式裁定批准或不批准协议。若有人提交异议或者法院认定举行听证更为适当，则法院应在至少提前 7 日向异议方、动议方、本附条第（1）款要求向其送达的主体以及法院可指定的该类其他实体发出通知后举行听证。

（4）就动议达成的和解协议。若法院认定根据本条（a）、（b）或（c）所作的动议足以对协议的重要条款给予合理的通知而提供听证的机会则法院可决定对本附条第（1）、（2）及（3）款所规定的程序不予适用并在不进行额外通知的情况下即可批准该协议。

（经 Mar. 30, 1987, eff. Aug. 1, 1987; Apr. 30, 1991, eff. Aug. 1, 1991; Apr. 26, 1999, eff. Dec. 1, 1999; Apr. 30, 2007, eff. Dec. 1, 2007; Mar. 26, 2009, eff. Dec. 1, 2009; Apr. 28, 2010, eff. Dec. 1, 2010; Apr. 25, 2019, eff. Dec. 1, 2019. 增补）

第 4002 条　债务人的义务

（a）**一般规定**。除履行法典和相应规则所规定的其他义务外，债务人还应履行以下各项：

（1）在法院规定的时间内出席并接受质询；

（2）出席就免责的异议而举行的听证并作证（若以证人身份而被传唤）；

（3）若尚未根据第 1007 条提交财产清单，则应立刻以书面形式告知托管人债权人享有权益的不动产所在地以及持有受债务人的取款行为或裁定所约束的金钱或财产的各主体的姓名和住址；

（4）协助托管人准备财产清单、审查债权证明以及管理破产实体；以及

U.S. Federal Rules of Bankruptcy Procedure
(Chinese-English bilingual version)

(5) file a statement of any change of the debtor's address.

(b) INDIVIDUAL DEBTOR'S DUTY TO PROVIDE DOCUMENTATION.

(1) *Personal Identification*. Every individual debtor shall bring to the meeting of creditors under §341:

(A) a picture identification issued by a governmental unit, or other personal identifying information that establishes the debtor's identity; and

(B) evidence of social-security number (s), or a written statement that such documentation does not exist.

(2) *Financial Information*. Every individual debtor shall bring to the meeting of creditors under §341, and make available to the trustee, the following documents or copies of them, or provide a written statement that the documentation does not exist or is not in the debtor's possession:

(A) evidence of current income such as the most recent payment advice;

(B) unless the trustee or the United States trustee instructs otherwise, statements for each of the debtor's depository and investment accounts, including checking, savings, and money market accounts, mutual funds and brokerage accounts for the time period that includes the date of the filing of the petition; and

(C) documentation of monthly expenses claimed by the debtor if required by §707 (b) (2) (A) or (B).

(3) *Tax Return*. At least 7 days before the first date set for the meeting of creditors under §341, the debtor shall provide to the trustee a copy of the debtor's federal income tax return for the most recent tax year ending immediately before the commencement of the case and for which a return was filed, including any attachments, or a transcript of the tax return, or provide a written statement that the documentation does not exist.

(4) *Tax Returns Provided to Creditors*. If a creditor, at least 14 days before the first date set for the meeting of creditors under §341, requests a copy of the debtor's tax return that is to be provided to the trustee under subdivision (b) (3), the debtor, at least 7 days before the first date set for the meeting of creditors under §341, shall provide to the requesting creditor a copy of the return, including any attachments, or a transcript of the tax return, or provide a written statement that the documentation does not exist.

（5）提交声明以说明债务人住址的任何变化。

（b）**个人债务人提供材料的义务**。

（1）个人身份信息。所有个人债务人均应将以下材料带至第341条中的债权人会议：

（A）政府部门签发的照片证明，或其他可确定债务人身份的个人身份信息；以及

（B）社保账号的证明，或说明并不存在该文件的书面声明。

（2）财务信息。所有个人债务人均应将以下材料或其副本带至第341条中的债权人会议并提供给托管人；若不存在以下材料或债务人并未持有以下材料，则应提供书面声明以说明该情况：

（A）当前收入的证明，如最新的付款通知书；

（B）除非托管人或联邦托管人作出其他指示，否则应提供债务人的所有存托和投资账户（包括支票、储蓄和货币市场账户，共同基金以及经纪账户）的报表，该报表的期间应涵盖有提交破产申请的当日；以及

（C）根据法典第707条（b）（2）（A）或（B）的要求（如有），债务人所主张的月支出的相关材料。

（3）报税表。在确定的首次举行第341条中的债权人会议之日至少7日以前，债务人应向托管人提供就破产案件启动前刚刚结束的最近一个纳税年度而提交的联邦收入报税表的副本，包括其各种附件，或该报税表的报告单，或者说明并不存在该材料的书面声明。

（4）向债权人提供的报税表。若债权人在确定的首次举行第341条中的债权人会议之日至少14日以前请求获得附条（b）（3）中将被提供给托管人的债务人的报税表的副本，则债务人应在确定的首次举行第341条中的债权人会议至少7日以前向提出请求的债权人提供该报税表的副本，包括各种附件，或该报税表的报告单，或者说明并不存在该材料的书面声明。

U.S. Federal Rules of Bankruptcy Procedure
(Chinese-English bilingual version)

(5) *Confidentiality of Tax Information*. The debtor's obligation to provide tax returns under Rule 4002 (b)(3) and (b)(4) is subject to procedures for safeguarding the confidentiality of tax information established by the Director of the Administrative Office of the United States Courts.

(As amended Mar. 30, 1987, eff. Aug. 1, 1987; Apr. 23, 2008, eff. Dec. 1 2008; Mar. 26, 2009, eff. Dec. 1, 2009.)

Rule 4003. Exemptions

(a) CLAIM OF EXEMPTIONS. A debtor shall list the property claimed as exempt under §522 of the Code on the schedule of assets required to be filed by Rule 1007. If the debtor fails to claim exemptions or file the schedule within the time specified in Rule 1007, a dependent of the debtor may file the list within 30 days thereafter.

(b) OBJECTING TO A CLAIM OF EXEMPTIONS.

(1) Except as provided in paragraphs (2) and (3), a party in interest may file an objection to the list of property claimed as exempt within 30 days after the meeting of creditors held under §341 (a) is concluded or within 30 days after any amendment to the list or supplemental schedules is filed, whichever is later. The court may, for cause, extend the time for filing objections if, before the time to object expires, a party in interest files a request for an extension.

(2) The trustee may file an objection to a claim of exemption at any time prior to one year after the closing of the case if the debtor fraudulently asserted the claim of exemption. The trustee shall deliver or mail the objection to the debtor and the debtor's attorney, and to any person filing the list of exempt property and that person's attorney.

(3) An objection to a claim of exemption based on §522 (q) shall be filed before the closing of the case. If an exemption is first claimed after a case is reopened, an objection shall be filed before the reopened case is closed.

(4) A copy of any objection shall be delivered or mailed to the trustee, the debtor and the debtor's attorney, and the person filing the list and that person's attorney.

(c) BURDEN OF PROOF. In any hearing under this rule, the objecting party has the burden of proving that the exemptions are not properly claimed. After hearing on

（5）税务信息的机密性。债务人根据第4002条（b）（3）和（b）（4）履行提供报税表的义务应按照美国法院行政办公室主任规定的用于确保税务信息的机密性的程序来进行。

（经 Mar. 30, 1987, eff. Aug. 1, 1987; Apr. 23, 2008, eff. Dec. 1 2008; Mar. 26, 2009, eff. Dec. 1, 2009. 增补）

第4003条　豁免

（a）**豁免的主张**。债务人应在根据第1007条而被要求提交的财产清单上列明根据法典第522条主张豁免的财产。若债务人未能主张豁免或未能在第1007条规定的时间内提交该清单，则债务人的被抚/扶养人可在其后30日内提交该清单。

（b）**对豁免主张的异议**。

（1）除第（2）款和第（3）款另有规定外，利益相关方可在根据第341条（a）而被举行的债权人会议结束后30日内或就前述豁免财产清单或补充财产清单的修正被提交后30日内(以二者中较晚者为准)就被主张豁免的财产清单提交异议。若在提交异议的期间届满前利益相关方提交请求申请延长该期间，则法院出于特定事由可延长用于提交异议的期间。

（2）若债务人系以欺诈方式主张豁免，则托管人可在结案后一年之前的任何时间内就豁免请求提交异议。托管人应将该异议交付或邮寄给债务人及其律师，以及提交豁免财产清单的任何人及其律师。

（3）就根据法典第522条（q）而主张的豁免的异议应在案件结案前被提交。若该豁免系在该案重启后才被首次主张，则相应动议应在重启案件结案前被提交。

（4）任何异议的副本均应被交付或邮寄给托管人、债务人及其律师以及提交豁免财产清单的任何人及其律师。

（c）**举证责任**。在本条中的任何听证中，异议方有责任证明该豁免主张并不适当。经过通知和听证后，法院应就该异议所提出的事项作出认定。

notice, the court shall determine the issues presented by the objections.

(d) AVOIDANCE BY DEBTOR OF TRANSFERS OF EXEMPT PROPERTY. A proceeding under §522 (f) to avoid a lien or other transfer of property exempt under the Code shall be commenced by motion in the manner provided by Rule 9014, or by serving a chapter 12 or chapter 13 plan on the affected creditors in the manner provided by Rule 7004 for service of a summons and complaint. Notwithstanding the provisions of subdivision (b), a creditor may object to a request under §522 (f) by challenging the validity of the exemption asserted to be impaired by the lien.

(As amended Mar. 30, 1987, eff. Aug. 1, 1987; Apr. 30, 1991, eff. Aug. 1, 1991; Apr. 17, 2000, eff. Dec. 1, 2000; Apr. 23, 2008, eff. Dec. 1, 2008; Apr. 27, 2017, eff. Dec. 1, 2017.)

Rule 4004. Grant or Denial of Discharge

(a) TIME FOR OBJECTING TO DISCHARGE; NOTICE OF TIME FIXED. In a chapter 7 case, a complaint, or a motion under §727 (a)(8) or (a)(9) of the Code, objecting to the debtor's discharge shall be filed no later than 60 days after the first date set for the meeting of creditors under §341 (a). In a chapter 11 case, the complaint shall be filed no later than the first date set for the hearing on confirmation. In a chapter 13 case, a motion objecting to the debtor's discharge under §1328 (f) shall be filed no later than 60 days after the first date set for the meeting of creditors under §341 (a). At least 28 days' notice of the time so fixed shall be given to the United States trustee and all creditors as provided in Rule 2002 (f) and (k) and to the trustee and the trustee's attorney.

(b) EXTENSION OF TIME.

(1) On motion of any party in interest, after notice and hearing, the court may for cause extend the time to object to discharge. Except as provided in subdivision (b)(2), the motion shall be filed before the time has expired.

(2) A motion to extend the time to object to discharge may be filed after the time for objection has expired and before discharge is granted if (A) the objection is based on facts that, if learned after the discharge, would provide a basis for revocation under

（d）**由债务人撤销豁免财产的给付**。为启动根据法典第522条（f）撤销根据法典得以豁免的财产上的担保权或就该财产所作的其他转让的程序，应以第9014条规定的方式提出动议或以第7004条规定的用于送达传票和诉状的方式向受影响的债权人送达第12章或第13章计划来启动。即使存在附条（b）的规定，债权人仍可通过对受该财产上担保权所影响的豁免的有效性提出质疑从而对第522条（f）中的请求提出异议。

（经 Mar. 30, 1987, eff. Aug. 1, 1987; Apr. 30, 1991, eff. Aug. 1, 1991; Apr. 17, 2000, eff. Dec. 1, 2000; Apr. 23, 2008, eff. Dec. 1, 2008; Apr. 27, 2017, eff. Dec. 1, 2017. 修正）

第4004条　免责的授予或拒绝

（a）**就免责提出异议的时间；就规定的期间而发出的通知**。在第7章案件中，为就债务人的免责提出异议而根据法典第727条（a）（8）或（a）（9）提出的申诉或动议应在确定的首次举行第341条（a）中的债权人会议之日后的60日内而被提交。在第11章案件中，该申诉应在不迟于首次就计划的批准举行听证之日而被提交。在第13章案件中，为就债务人的免责提出异议而根据法典第1328条（f）提出的动议应在确定的首次举行第341条（a）中的债权人会议之日后的60日内而被提交。应至少提前28日向联邦托管人、第2002条（f）和（k）规定的全体债权人以及托管人及其律师发出通知以告知其确定的前述期间。

（b）**期间的延长**。

（1）应利益相关方的动议，经过通知和听证后，法院出于特定事由可延长就免责提出异议的期间。除附条（b）（2）另有规定外，该动议应在该期间届满前而被提交。

（2）针对申请延长就免责提出异议的期间的动议，若（A）该异议所基于的事实在免责后而被获悉，则将为根据法典第727条（d）撤销免责提供依据，并且（B）动议方在规定的提交异议的期间内对此并不知情，则在提交异议的期间届满后、

§727（d）of the Code, and (B) the movant did not have knowledge of those facts in time to permit an objection. The motion shall be filed promptly after the movant discovers the facts on which the objection is based.

(c) GRANT OF DISCHARGE.

(1) In a chapter 7 case, on expiration of the times fixed for objecting to discharge and for filing a motion to dismiss the case under Rule 1017 (e), the court shall forthwith grant the discharge, except that the court shall not grant the discharge if:

(A) the debtor is not an individual;

(B) a complaint, or a motion under §727 (a)(8) or (a)(9), objecting to the discharge has been filed and not decided in the debtor's favor;

(C) the debtor has filed a waiver under §727 (a)(10);

(D) a motion to dismiss the case under §707 is pending;

(E) a motion to extend the time for filing a complaint objecting to the discharge is pending;

(F) a motion to extend the time for filing a motion to dismiss the case under Rule 1017 (e)(1) is pending;

(G) the debtor has not paid in full the filing fee prescribed by 28 U.S.C. §1930(a) and any other fee prescribed by the Judicial Conference of the United States under 28 U.S.C. §1930 (b) that is payable to the clerk upon the commencement of a case under the Code, unless the court has waived the fees under 28 U.S.C. §1930 (f);

(H) the debtor has not filed with the court a statement of completion of a course concerning personal financial management if required by Rule 1007 (b)(7);

(I) a motion to delay or postpone discharge under §727 (a)(12) is pending;

(J) a motion to enlarge the time to file a reaffirmation agreement under Rule 4008 (a) is pending;

(K) a presumption is in effect under §524 (m) that a reaffirmation agreement is an undue hardship and the court has not concluded a hearing on the presumption; or

(L) a motion is pending to delay discharge because the debtor has not filed with the court all tax documents required to be filed under §521 (f).

(2) Notwithstanding Rule 4004 (c)(1), on motion of the debtor, the court

免责被授予前，仍可提交该动议。动议方应在发现其异议所依据的事实后立刻提交动议。

（c）免责的授予。

（1）在第 7 章案件中，在规定的用于就免责提出异议以及用于提交动议以申请驳回案件的期间届满时，法院应立刻授予免责，但在下列情形中法院不应授予免责：

（A）债务人并非自然人；

（B）已经有人根据法典第 727 条（a）(8) 或（a）(9) 提交申诉或动议以就免责提出动议，并且债务人并未得到支持；

（C）债务人已经根据法典第 727 条（a）(10) 提交了放弃免责的声明；

（D）就根据第 707 条申请驳回案件的动议的审理正在进行中；

（E）就申请延长用于就免责提出异议的期间的动议的审理正在进行中；

（F）就申请延长用于根据第 1017 条（e）(1) 提交动议以申请驳回案件的动议的审理正在进行中；

（G）债务人未能全额支付应在根据法典提交的案件启动时向书记员支付的《美国联邦法典》第 28 篇第 1930 条（a）所规定的申请费以及美国司法会议根据《美国联邦法典》第 28 篇第 1930 条（b）所规定的任何其他费用，除非法院根据《美国联邦法典》第 28 篇第 1930 条（f）放弃收取前述费用；

（H）在根据第 1007 条（b）(7) 债务人被要求向法院提交已经完成有关个人财务管理课程的声明的情况下，债务人未能向法院提交该声明；

（I）就根据第 727 条（a）(12) 申请延后授予免责的动议的审理正在进行中；

（J）就根据第 4008 条（a）申请延长用于提交再认协议的期间的动议的审理正在进行中；

（K）根据第 524 条（m）的规定，再认协议被推定为造成不当负担，并且法院就该推定而举行的听证尚未结束；或

（L）针对因债务人未能向法院提交第 521 条（f）所要求的所有税务材料的情况而申请延后授予免责的动议，就该动议的审理尚在进行中。

（2）即使存在第 4004 条（c）(1) 的规定，应债务人的动议，法院可延后 30

213

may defer the entry of an order granting a discharge for 30 days and, on motion within that period, the court may defer entry of the order to a date certain.

(3) If the debtor is required to file a statement under Rule 1007 (b)(8), the court shall not grant a discharge earlier than 30 days after the statement is filed.

(4) In a chapter 11 case in which the debtor is an individual, or a chapter 13 case, the court shall not grant a discharge if the debtor has not filed any statement required by Rule 1007 (b)(7).

(d) APPLICABILITY OF RULES IN PART VII AND RULE 9014. An objection to discharge is governed by Part VII of these rules, except that an objection to discharge under §§727 (a)(8), (a)(9), or 1328 (f) is commenced by motion and governed by Rule 9014.

(e) ORDER OF DISCHARGE. An order of discharge shall conform to the appropriate Official Form.

(f) REGISTRATION IN OTHER DISTRICTS. An order of discharge that has become final may be registered in any other district by filing a certified copy of the order in the office of the clerk of that district. When so registered the order of discharge shall have the same effect as an order of the court of the district where registered.

(g) NOTICE OF DISCHARGE. The clerk shall promptly mail a copy of the final order of discharge to those specified in subdivision (a) of this rule.

(As amended Mar. 30, 1987, eff. Aug. 1, 1987; Apr. 30, 1991, eff. Aug. 1, 1991; Apr. 23, 1996, eff. Dec. 1, 1996; Apr. 26, 1999, eff. Dec. 1, 1999; Apr. 17, 2000, eff. Dec. 1, 2000; Apr. 29, 2002, eff. Dec. 1, 2002; Apr. 23, 2008, eff. Dec. 1, 2008; Mar. 26, 2009, eff. Dec. 1, 2009; Apr. 28, 2010, eff. Dec. 1, 2010; Apr. 26, 2011, eff. Dec. 1, 2011; Apr. 16, 2013, eff. Dec. 1, 2013.)

Rule 4005. Burden of Proof in Objecting to Discharge

At the trial on a complaint objecting to a discharge, the plaintiff has the burden of proving the objection.

(As amended Mar. 30, 1987, eff. Aug. 1, 1987.)

日而裁定授予免责，并且应该期间内所作出的动议，法院还可将该裁定延后至特定日期而作出。

（3）若根据第1007条（b）(8）规定债务人被要求提交相应声明，则法院在该声明被提交后30日内不得授予免责。

（4）在第11章个人债务人案件或第13章案件中，若债务人未能提交第1007条（b）(7）所要求的任何声明，则法院不得授予免责。

（d）**第 VII 部分的规则及第 9014 条的适用**。就免责提出异议应遵守第 VII 部分的规定，但通过提交动议而根据第 727 条（a）(8)、(a)(9）或 1328（f）节就免责提出异议应遵守第 9014 条的规定。

（e）**免责裁定**。免责裁定应按照相应的官方模板而作出。

（f）**在其他辖区的登记**。终局的免责裁定可通过向任何其他辖区的书记员办公室提交该裁定的核证副本而在该辖区进行登记。登记后的免责裁定在被登记辖区内与法院裁定具有同等效力。

（g）**免责通知**。书记员应立刻向附条（a）所述主体邮寄免责的终局裁定的副本。

（经 Mar. 30, 1987, eff. Aug. 1, 1987; Apr. 30, 1991, eff. Aug. 1, 1991; Apr. 23, 1996, eff. Dec. 1, 1996; Apr. 26, 1999, eff. Dec. 1, 1999; Apr. 17, 2000, eff. Dec. 1, 2000; Apr. 29, 2002, eff. Dec. 1, 2002; Apr. 23, 2008, eff. Dec. 1, 2008; Mar. 26, 2009, eff. Dec. 1, 2009; Apr. 28, 2010, eff. Dec. 1, 2010; Apr. 26, 2011, eff. Dec. 1, 2011; Apr. 16, 2013, eff. Dec. 1, 2013. 修正）

第 4005 条　就免责提出异议的举证责任

在审理就免责提出的异议中，原告须承担证明该异议的举证责任。

（经 Mar. 30, 1987, eff. Aug. 1, 1987. 修正）

Rule 4006. Notice of No Discharge

If an order is entered: denying a discharge; revoking a discharge; approving a waiver of discharge; or, in the case of an individual debtor, closing the case without the entry of a discharge, the clerk shall promptly notify all parties in interest in the manner provided by Rule 2002.

(As amended Mar. 30, 1987, eff. Aug. 1, 1987; Apr. 23, 2008, eff. Dec. 1, 2008.)

Rule 4007. Determination of Dischargeability of a Debt

(a) PERSONS ENTITLED TO FILE COMPLAINT. A debtor or any creditor may file a complaint to obtain a determination of the dischargeability of any debt.

(b) TIME FOR COMMENCING PROCEEDING OTHER THAN UNDER §523 (c) OF THE CODE. A complaint other than under §523 (c) may be filed at any time. A case may be reopened without payment of an additional filing fee for the purpose of filing a complaint to obtain a determination under this rule.

(c) TIME FOR FILING COMPLAINT UNDER §523 (c) IN A CHAPTER 7 LIQUIDATION, CHAPTER 11 REORGANIZATION, CHAPTER 12 FAMILY FARMER'S DEBT ADJUSTMENT CASE, OR CHAPTER 13 INDIVIDUAL'S DEBT ADJUSTMENT CASE; NOTICE OF TIME FIXED. Except as otherwise provided in subdivision (d) , a complaint to determine the dischargeability of a debt under §523 (c) shall be filed no later than 60 days after the first date set for the meeting of creditors under §341 (a) . The court shall give all creditors no less than 30 days' notice of the time so fixed in the manner provided in Rule 2002. On motion of a party in interest, after hearing on notice, the court may for cause extend the time fixed under this subdivision. The motion shall be filed before the time has expired.

(d) TIME FOR FILING COMPLAINT UNDER §523 (a) (6) IN A CHAPTER 13 INDIVIDUAL'S DEBT ADJUSTMENT CASE; NOTICE OF TIME FIXED. On motion by a debtor for a discharge under §1328 (b) , the court shall enter an order fixing the time to file a complaint to determine the dischargeability of any debt under §523 (a) (6) and shall give no less than 30 days' notice of the time fixed to all

第4006条　不予免责的通知

若法院正式裁定：拒绝授予免责；撤销免责；批准债务人放弃免责；或在个人债务人案件中，在尚未裁定授予免责的情况下即结案，则书记员应立刻以第2002条所规定的方式通知所有利益相关方。

（经 Mar. 30, 1987, eff. Aug. 1, 1987; Apr. 23, 2008, eff. Dec. 1, 2008. 修正）

第4007条　就债务不可免责所作的认定

（a）**有权提交申诉的主体**。债务人或任何债权人均可提交申诉以获得就债务不可免责所作的认定。

（b）**除根据法典第523条（c）外启动程序的时间**。除根据法典第523条（c）外，其他申诉可在任何时间内而被提交。为实现本条中提交申诉以获得认定的裁定，案件可被予以重启且无须支付任何额外费用。

（c）**在第7章清算案件、第11章重整案件、第12章家庭农场主债务调整案件或第13章个人债务调整案件中根据第523条（c）提交申诉的时间；就规定的期间而发出的通知**。除附条（d）另有规定外，申请根据第523条（c）就债务不可免责作出认定的申诉应在确定的首次举行第341条（a）中债权人会议之日后的60日内而被提交。法院应以第2002条规定的方式提前30日向全体债权人发出通知以告知该期间。应利益相关方的动议，经过通知和听证后，法院可出于特定事由延长本款所规定的期间。该动议应在该期间届满前而被提交。

（d）**在第13章个人债务调整案件中根据第523条（a）(6)提交申诉的期间；就规定的期间而发出的通知**。若债务人根据第1328条（b）提交动议申请免责，则法院应裁定规定用于提交申诉以申请根据第523条（a）(6)就任何债务不可免责作出认定的期间，并且应以第2002条规定的方式至少提前30日向全体债权人发出通知以告知该期间。应利益相关方的动议，经过通知和听证，法院可出于

creditors in the manner provided in Rule 2002. On motion of any party in interest, after hearing on notice, the court may for cause extend the time fixed under this subdivision. The motion shall be filed before the time has expired.

(e) APPLICABILITY OF RULES IN PART VII. A proceeding commenced by a complaint filed under this rule is governed by Part VII of these rules.

(As amended Mar. 30, 1987, eff. Aug. 1, 1987; Apr. 30, 1991, eff. Aug. 1, 1991; Apr. 26, 1999, eff. Dec. 1, 1999; Apr. 23, 2008, eff. Dec. 1, 2008.)

Rule 4008. Filing of Reaffirmation Agreement; Statement in Support of Reaffirmation Agreement

(a) FILING OF REAFFIRMATION AGREEMENT. A reaffirmation agreement shall be filed no later than 60 days after the first date set for the meeting of creditors under §341 (a) of the Code. The reaffirmation agreement shall be accompanied by a cover sheet, prepared as prescribed by the appropriate Official Form. The court may, at any time and in its discretion, enlarge the time to file a reaffirmation agreement.

(b) STATEMENT IN SUPPORT OF REAFFIRMATION AGREEMENT. The debtor's statement required under §524 (k) (6) (A) of the Code shall be accompanied by a statement of the total income and expenses stated on schedules I and J. If there is a difference between the total income and expenses stated on those schedules and the statement required under §524 (k) (6) (A), the statement required by this subdivision shall include an explanation of the difference.

(As amended Apr. 30, 1991, eff. Aug. 1, 1991; Apr. 23, 2008, eff. Dec. 1, 2008; Mar. 26, 2009, eff. Dec. 1, 2009.)

特定事由延长本款所规定的期间。该动议应在该期间届满前而被提交。

（e）**第 VII 部分的规则的适用**。由根据本条而被提交的申诉所启动的程序由第 VII 部分所规定。

（经 Mar. 30, 1987, eff. Aug. 1, 1987; Apr. 30, 1991, eff. Aug. 1, 1991; Apr. 26, 1999, eff. Dec. 1, 1999; Apr. 23, 2008, eff. Dec. 1, 2008. 修正）

第 4008 条　再认协议的提交；支持再认协议的声明

（a）**再认协议的提交**。再认协议应在确定的首次举行第 341 条（a）中债权人会议之日后的 60 日内而被提交。再认协议应附有根据相应官方模板的规定而准备的封面。法院可随时自主决定延长用于提交再认协议的期间。

（b）**支持再认协议的声明**。法典第 524 条（k）（6）（A）所要求的债务人的声明应附有载有报表 I 和 J 中载明的总收入及支出的声明。若在前述报表中和第 524 条（k）（6）（A）所要求的声明中分别载明的总收入及支出间存在差异，则本附条所要求的声明中应就该差异作出解释。

（经 Apr. 30, 1991, eff. Aug. 1, 1991; Apr. 23, 2008, eff. Dec. 1, 2008; Mar. 26, 2009, eff. Dec. 1, 2009. 修正）

PART V
COURTS AND CLERKS

Rule 5001. Courts and Clerks' Offices

(a) COURTS ALWAYS OPEN. The courts shall be deemed always open for the purpose of filing any pleading or other proper paper, issuing and returning process, and filing, making, or entering motions, orders and rules.

(b) TRIALS AND HEARINGS; ORDERS IN CHAMBERS. All trials and hearings shall be conducted in open court and so far as convenient in a regular court room. Except as otherwise provided in 28 U.S.C. §152 (c), all other acts or proceedings may be done or conducted by a judge in chambers and at any place either within or without the district; but no hearing, other than one ex parte, shall be conducted outside the district without the consent of all parties affected thereby.

(c) CLERK'S OFFICE. The clerk's office with the clerk or a deputy in attendance shall be open during business hours on all days except Saturdays, Sundays and the legal holidays listed in Rule 9006 (a).

(As amended Mar. 30, 1987, eff. Aug. 1, 1987; Apr. 30, 1991, eff. Aug. 1, 1991; Apr. 23, 2008, eff. Dec. 1, 2008.)

Rule 5002. Restrictions on Approval of Appointments

(a) APPROVAL OF APPOINTMENT OF RELATIVES PROHIBITED. The appointment of an individual as a trustee or examiner pursuant to §1104 of the Code shall not be approved by the court if the individual is a relative of the bankruptcy judge approving the appointment or the United States trustee in the region in which the case is pending. The employment of an individual as an attorney, accountant, appraiser,

第 V 部分
法院和书记员

第 5001 条　法院和书记员办公室

（a）**法院保持开放**。就提交任何诉状或其他适当的文件，签发及归还司法文书，以及提交、制作或正式作出动议、裁定及规则而言，法院应被视为始终保持开放状态。

（b）**审判及听证；在法官办公室所作的裁定**。所有的审判及听证均应在公开法庭上进行，并且应尽量在常规审判室中进行。除《美国联邦法典》第 28 篇第 152 条（c）另有规定外，所有其他行为或程序均可由法官在其办公室以及所在辖区内或辖区外的任何地点完成或作出；但是除单方听证外，任何听证在未经所有受影响的当事方同意的情况下均不得在辖区外进行。

（c）**书记员办公室**。除第 9006 条（a）所列的周六、周日以及法定节假日外，书记员或其助理所在的书记员办公室在办公时间均保持开放。

（经 Mar. 30, 1987, eff. Aug. 1, 1987; Apr. 30, 1991, eff. Aug. 1, 1991; Apr. 23, 2008, eff. Dec. 1, 2008. 修正）

第 5002 条　就任命批准的限制

（a）**批准任命所禁止的亲属**。若某自然人为批准任命托管人或监督人的破产法官或破产案件所在辖区内任职的联邦托管人的亲属，则法院不得批准该自然人根据法典第 1104 条被任命为托管人或监督人。若某自然人为批准雇佣律师、会计师、评估师或拍卖师或其他专业人员的破产法官的亲属，则法院不得批准该自然人根据第 327、1103 或 1114 条被雇佣为律师、会计师、评估师、拍卖师或其

U.S. Federal Rules of Bankruptcy Procedure
(Chinese-English bilingual version)

auctioneer, or other professional person pursuant to §§327, 1103, or 1114 shall not be approved by the court if the individual is a relative of the bankruptcy judge approving the employment. The employment of an individual as attorney, accountant, appraiser, auctioneer, or other professional person pursuant to §§327, 1103, or 1114 may be approved by the court if the individual is a relative of the United States trustee in the region in which the case is pending, unless the court finds that the relationship with the United States trustee renders the employment improper under the circumstances of the case. Whenever under this subdivision an individual may not be approved for appointment or employment, the individual's firm, partnership, corporation, or any other form of business association or relationship, and all members, associates and professional employees thereof also may not be approved for appointment or employment.

(b) JUDICIAL DETERMINATION THAT APPROVAL OF APPOINTMENT OR EMPLOYMENT IS IMPROPER. A bankruptcy judge may not approve the appointment of a person as a trustee or examiner pursuant to §1104 of the Code or approve the employment of a person as an attorney, accountant, appraiser, auctioneer, or other professional person pursuant to §§327, 1103, or 1114 of the Code if that person is or has been so connected with such judge or the United States trustee as to render the appointment or employment improper.

(As amended Apr. 29, 1985, eff. Aug. 1, 1985; Apr. 30, 1991, eff. Aug. 1, 1991.)

Rule 5003. Records Kept by the Clerk

(a) BANKRUPTCY DOCKETS. The clerk shall keep a docket in each case under the Code and shall enter thereon each judgment, order, and activity in that case as prescribed by the Director of the Administrative Office of the United States Courts. The entry of a judgment or order in a docket shall show the date the entry is made.

(b) CLAIMS REGISTER. The clerk shall keep in a claims register a list of claims filed in a case when it appears that there will be a distribution to unsecured creditors.

(c) JUDGMENTS AND ORDERS. The clerk shall keep, in the form and manner as the Director of the Administrative Office of the United States Courts may prescribe, a correct copy of every final judgment or order affecting title to or lien on real property

他专业人员。若某自然人为破产案件所在辖区内任职的联邦托管人的亲属，则除非法院认为就案件情形其与联邦托管人间的关系将使该雇佣有所不当，否则法院可批准该自然人根据第 327 条、1103 条或 1114 条被雇佣为律师、会计师、评估师、拍卖师或其他专业人员。若根据本附条某自然人不得被批准、被任命或被雇佣，则该自然人的事务所、合伙、公司或任何其他形式的商业协会或组织以及前述组织的全体成员、职工及专业员工也均不得被批准、被任命或被雇佣。

（b）**就任命或雇佣有所不当所作的司法认定**。若某人现在或曾经与该法官或联邦托管人有一定关系以致该任命或雇佣有所不当，则破产法官不得批准此人根据法典第 1104 条被任命为托管人或监督人或者批准此人根据法典第 327 条、1103 条或 1114 条被雇佣为律师、会计师、评估师、拍卖师或其他专业人员。

（经 Apr. 29, 1985, eff. Aug. 1, 1985; Apr. 30, 1991, eff. Aug. 1, 1991. 修正）

第 5003 条　由书记员所保存的档案

（a）**破产案卷**。书记员应保留根据法典而提交的所有案件的案卷，并应按照美国法院行政办公室主任的规定载入在该案中所作的所有判决、裁定及活动。在案卷中载明的判决或裁定均应注明将其载入的日期。

（b）**债权登记册**。若存在向无担保债权人进行分配的可能，则书记员应在债权登记册中保存在破产案件中被提交的债权清单。

（c）**判决及裁定**。书记员应按照美国法院行政办公室主任可规定的形式及方式保存所有影响不动产的所有权或担保权或者追偿金钱或财产的终局判决或裁定，以及法院可指定进行保存的任何其他裁定的正确副本。应胜诉方的请求，所

U.S. Federal Rules of Bankruptcy Procedure
(Chinese-English bilingual version)

or for the recovery of money or property, and any other order which the court may direct to be kept. On request of the prevailing party, a correct copy of every judgment or order affecting title to or lien upon real or personal property or for the recovery of money or property shall be kept and indexed with the civil judgments of the district court.

(d) INDEX OF CASES; CERTIFICATE OF SEARCH. The clerk shall keep indices of all cases and adversary proceedings as prescribed by the Director of the Administrative Office of the United States Courts. On request, the clerk shall make a search of any index and papers in the clerk's custody and certify whether a case or proceeding has been filed in or transferred to the court or if a discharge has been entered in its records.

(e) REGISTER OF MAILING ADDRESSES OF FEDERAL AND STATE GOVERNMENTAL UNITS AND CERTAIN TAXING AUTHORITIES. The United States or the state or territory in which the court is located may file a statement designating its mailing address. The United States, state, territory, or local governmental unit responsible for collecting taxes within the district in which the case is pending may also file a statement designating an address for service of requests under §505(b) of the Code, and the designation shall describe where further information concerning additional requirements for filing such requests may be found. The clerk shall keep, in the form and manner as the Director of the Administrative Office of the United States Courts may prescribe, a register that includes the mailing addresses designated under the first sentence of this subdivision, and a separate register of the addresses designated for the service of requests under §505(b) of the Code. The clerk is not required to include in any single register more than one mailing address for each department, agency, or instrumentality of the United States or the state or territory. If more than one address for a department, agency, or instrumentality is included in the register, the clerk shall also include information that would enable a user of the register to determine the circumstances when each address is applicable, and mailing notice to only one applicable address is sufficient to provide effective notice. The clerk shall update the register annually, effective January 2 of each year. The mailing address in the register is conclusively presumed to be a proper address for the governmental unit, but the failure to use that mailing address does not invalidate any notice that is otherwise effective under applicable law.

有影响不动产或动产的所有权或担保权或者追偿金钱或财产的各判决或裁定的正确副本均应被保存并与地方法院的民事判决间建立索引。

（d）**案件的索引；搜索证明**。书记员应按照美国法院行政办公室主任的规定保存所有案件和对抗制诉讼程序的索引。若有人提出请求，则书记员应搜索其保管的任何索引和文件，并开具相应证明以说明案件或程序是否已被提交至或移交至法院，或者在该案的档案中是否记载有免责。

（e）**联邦及州政府机构以及特定税务机关的邮寄地址的登记**。美国或法院所在的州或地区可提交声明以指定其邮寄地址。在破产案件所在辖区内负责征收税款的联邦、州、地区或地方政府机构也可提交声明以根据法典第 505 条（b）指定送达请求的地址，并且该指定声明应说明可获得与提交该请求的额外要求有关的更多信息的途径。书记员应以美国法院行政办公室主任可规定的形式及方式保存载有根据本附条前述规定而被指定的邮寄地址的登记册以及单独载有根据法典第 505 条（b）而指定的用于送达请求的地址的登记册。书记员无须在任何单独的登记册中载入美国或者州或地区的各部门、机构或机关的一个以上的地址。若某部门、机构或机关有不止一个地址被登记在册，则书记员还应载明其他信息以使该登记册的使用者能够认定各地址所适用的情形并说明将通知邮寄给一个可适用的地址即足以构成有效的通知。书记员应每年更新登记册，并于每年 1 月 2 日生效。登记册中的邮寄地址即被确定性地推定为政府机构的适当地址，但未能使用该邮寄地址并不会使根据相应法律规定而仍将有效的通知归于无效。

U.S. Federal Rules of Bankruptcy Procedure
(Chinese-English bilingual version)

(f) OTHER BOOKS AND RECORDS OF THE CLERK. The clerk shall keep any other books and records required by the Director of the Administrative Office of the United States Courts.

(As amended Mar. 30, 1987, eff. Aug. 1, 1987; Apr. 17, 2000, eff. Dec. 1, 2000; Apr. 23, 2008, eff. Dec. 1, 2008.)

Rule 5004. Disqualification

(a) DISQUALIFICATION OF JUDGE. A bankruptcy judge shall be governed by 28 U.S.C. §455, and disqualified from presiding over the proceeding or contested matter in which the disqualifying circumstances arises or, if appropriate, shall be disqualified from presiding over the case.

(b) DISQUALIFICATION OF JUDGE FROM ALLOWING COMPENSATION. A bankruptcy judge shall be disqualified from allowing compensation to a person who is a relative of the bankruptcy judge or with whom the judge is so connected as to render it improper for the judge to authorize such compensation.

(As amended Apr. 29, 1985, eff. Aug. 1, 1985; Mar. 30, 1987, eff. Aug. 1, 1987.)

Rule 5005. Filing and Transmittal of Papers

(a) FILING.

(1) *Place of Filing.* The lists, schedules, statements, proofs of claim or interest, complaints, motions, applications, objections and other papers required to be filed by these rules, except as provided in 28 U.S.C. §1409, shall be filed with the clerk in the district where the case under the Code is pending. The judge of that court may permit the papers to be filed with the judge, in which event the filing date shall be noted thereon, and they shall be forthwith transmitted to the clerk. The clerk shall not refuse to accept for filing any petition or other paper presented for the purpose of filing solely because it is not presented in proper form as required by these rules or any local rules or practices.

(2) *Electronic Filing and Signing.*

(A) *By a Represented Entity—Generally Required; Exceptions.* An entity

（f）**书记员的其他材料及档案**。书记员应保存美国法院行政办公室主任所要求的任何其他材料及档案。

（经 Mar. 30, 1987, eff. Aug. 1, 1987; Apr. 17, 2000, eff. Dec. 1, 2000; Apr. 23, 2008, eff. Dec. 1, 2008. 修正）

第5004条 丧失资格

（a）**法官资格的丧失**。破产法官应受《美国联邦法典》第28篇第455条的规制，并且在导致其丧失相应资格的情形所在的程序或争议事项中，法院将丧失主持该程序或事项的资格，甚至在适当情形下，法官将丧失主持全案的资格。

（b）**法官丧失准予提供报酬的资格**。针对破产法官的亲属或与破产法官具有一定关系以使法官准予其获得报酬有所不当的人，该破产法官无权授予此人报酬。

（经 Apr. 29, 1985, eff. Aug. 1, 1985; Mar. 30, 1987, eff. Aug. 1, 1987. 修正）

第5005条 材料的提交和移送

（a）**提交**。

（1）提交的地点。除《美国联邦法典》第28篇第1409条另有规定外，根据本法被要求提交的清单、报表、声明、债权或权益证明、申诉、动议、申请、异议以及其他材料，应被提交至根据法典所提交的案件所在辖区内的书记员。该法院的法官也可允许提交至该法官的材料，但在该情形中应在该材料上注明提交日期并应立刻移交给书记员。书记员不得仅因任何破产申请或被提交的其他材料未能按照本法或任何地方规则或实践所规定的适当方式被提交而拒绝接受前述材料。

（2）电子提交和签名。

（A）被代表实体——一般要求；例外规定。由律师所代表的实体应以电子

U.S. Federal Rules of Bankruptcy Procedure
(Chinese-English bilingual version)

represented by an attorney shall file electronically, unless nonelectronic filing is allowed by the court for good cause or is allowed or required by local rule.

(B) *By an Unrepresented Individual—When Allowed or Required.* An individual not represented by an attorney:

(i) may file electronically only if allowed by court order or by local rule; and

(ii) may be required to file electronically only by court order, or by a local rule that includes reasonable exceptions.

(C) *Signing.* A filing made through a person's electronic-filing account and authorized by that person, together with that person's name on a signature block, constitutes the person's signature.

(D) *Same as a Written Paper.* A paper filed electronically is a written paper for purposes of these rules, the Federal Rules of Civil Procedure made applicable by these rules, and §107 of the Code.

(b) TRANSMITTAL TO THE UNITED STATES TRUSTEE.

(1) The complaints, motions, applications, objections and other papers required to be transmitted to the United States trustee by these rules shall be mailed or delivered to an office of the United States trustee, or to another place designated by the United States trustee, in the district where the case under the Code is pending.

(2) The entity, other than the clerk, transmitting a paper to the United States trustee shall promptly file as proof of such transmittal a verified statement identifying the paper and stating the date on which it was transmitted to the United States trustee.

(3) Nothing in these rules shall require the clerk to transmit any paper to the United States trustee if the United States trustee requests in writing that the paper not be transmitted.

(c) ERROR IN FILING OR TRANSMITTAL. A paper intended to be filed with the clerk but erroneously delivered to the United States trustee, the trustee, the attorney for the trustee, a bankruptcy judge, a district judge, the clerk of the bankruptcy appellate panel, or the clerk of the district court shall, after the date of its receipt has been noted thereon, be transmitted forthwith to the clerk of the bankruptcy court. A paper intended to be transmitted to the United States trustee but erroneously delivered to the clerk, the

方式提交，除非法院出于正当事由准予其以非电子方式提交或地方规则准予或要求其以非电子方式提交。

（B）未被代表的自然人——当被准许或要求时。未由律师所代表的自然人：

（i）仅当法院裁定或地方规则准许时才可以电子方式提交；以及

（ii）仅当法院裁定或地方规则作此要求并且载有合理的例外规定时，才可被要求以电子方式提交。

（C）签名。通过某人的电子提交账户所制作的并经此人授权的文件，与此人在签名栏上的姓名一同构成此人的签名。

（D）作为书面材料。就本法、因本法而得以适用的《联邦民事诉讼规则》以及法典第107条而言，以电子方式而被提交的材料即为书面材料。

（b）向联邦托管人移送。
（1）根据本法被要求向联邦托管人移送的申诉、动议、申请、异议以及其他材料均应被邮寄或交付给根据法典所提交的案件所在辖区内联邦托管人的办公室或联邦托管人所指定的其他地点。

（2）除书记员外其他向联邦托管人移交材料的实体应及时提交宣誓声明以作为移交的证据，并注明该材料的信息以及被移交给联邦托管人的日期。

（3）本条并未要求书记员在联邦托管人书面请求获得未经移送的材料的情况下向其移送任何材料。

（c）**提交或移送中的错误。**拟向书记员提交但被错误地交付给联邦托管人、托管人、托管人的律师、破产法官、地区法官、破产上诉合议庭的书记员或地区法院的书记员的材料应在收据上注明日期后立刻被移交给破产法院的书记员。拟向联邦托管人移交但被错误地交付给书记员、托管人、托管人的律师、破产法官、地区法官、破产上诉合议庭的书记员或地区法院的书记员的材料应在收据上注明日期后立刻被移交给联邦托管人。为了司法公正，法院可裁定被错误交付的材料

trustee, the attorney for the trustee, a bankruptcy judge, a district judge, the clerk of the bankruptcy appellate panel, or the clerk of the district court shall, after the date of its receipt has been noted thereon, be transmitted forthwith to the United States trustee. In the interest of justice, the court may order that a paper erroneously delivered shall be deemed filed with the clerk or transmitted to the United States trustee as of the date of its original delivery.

(As amended Mar. 30, 1987, eff. Aug. 1, 1987; Apr. 30, 1991, eff. Aug. 1, 1991; Apr. 22, 1993, eff. Aug. 1, 1993; Apr. 23, 1996, eff. Dec. 1, 1996; Apr. 12, 2006, eff. Dec. 1, 2006; Apr. 26, 2018, eff. Dec. 1, 2018.)

Rule 5006. Certification of Copies of Papers

The clerk shall issue a certified copy of the record of any proceeding in a case under the Code or of any paper filed with the clerk on payment of any prescribed fee.

(As amended Apr. 30, 1991, eff. Aug. 1, 1991.)

Rule 5007. Record of Proceedings and Transcripts

(a) FILING OF RECORD OR TRANSCRIPT. The reporter or operator of a recording device shall certify the original notes of testimony, tape recording, or other original record of the proceeding and promptly file them with the clerk. The person preparing any transcript shall promptly file a certified copy.

(b) TRANSCRIPT FEES. The fees for copies of transcripts shall be charged at rates prescribed by the Judicial Conference of the United States. No fee may be charged for the certified copy filed with the clerk.

(c) ADMISSIBILITY OF RECORD IN EVIDENCE. A certified sound recording or a transcript of a proceeding shall be admissible as prima facie evidence to establish the record.

(As amended Mar. 30, 1987, eff. Aug. 1, 1987; Apr. 30, 1991, eff. Aug. 1, 1991.)

Rule 5008. Notice Regarding Presumption of Abuse in Chapter 7 Cases of Individual Debtors

If a presumption of abuse has arisen under §707 (b) in a chapter 7 case of an

应自其原始交付之日起即被视为已被提交给书记员或被移交给联邦托管人。

（经 Mar. 30, 1987, eff. Aug. 1, 1987; Apr. 30, 1991, eff. Aug. 1, 1991; Apr. 22, 1993, eff. Aug. 1, 1993; Apr. 23, 1996, eff. Dec. 1, 1996; Apr. 12, 2006, eff. Dec. 1, 2006; Apr. 26, 2018, eff. Dec. 1, 2018. 修正）

第 5006 条　材料副本的证明

在被支付任何规定的费用后，针对根据法典而提起的破产案件中任何程序的档案或向书记员提交的任何材料，书记员均应签发前述材料的核证副本。

（经 Apr. 30, 1991, eff. Aug. 1, 1991. 修正）

第 5007 条　程序记录和报告单

（a）**记录或报告单的提交**。记录设备的报告者或操作者应核证证词原件、录音带或程序的其他原始记录并及时向书记员提交。准备任何报告单的人应及时提交其核证副本。

（b）**报告单费用**。就报告单的副本所收取的费用应按照美国司法会议所规定的费率来收取。不得就向书记员提交的核证副本收费。

（c）**录音证据的可采性**。经核证的录音或程序的报告单应作为表面证据而被采信以证实该录音。

（经 Mar. 30, 1987, eff. Aug. 1, 1987; Apr. 30, 1991, eff. Aug. 1, 1991. 修正）

第 5008 条　在第 7 章个人债务人案件中就滥用推定而发出的通知

在第 7 章其主要债务为消费债务的个人债务人案件中，若根据第 707 条（b）

individual with primarily consumer debts, the clerk shall within 10 days after the date of the filing of the petition notify creditors of the presumption of abuse in accordance with Rule 2002. If the debtor has not filed a statement indicating whether a presumption of abuse has arisen, the clerk shall within 10 days after the date of the filing of the petition notify creditors that the debtor has not filed the statement and that further notice will be given if a later filed statement indicates that a presumption of abuse has arisen. If a debtor later files a statement indicating that a presumption of abuse has arisen, the clerk shall notify creditors of the presumption of abuse as promptly as practicable.

(Added Apr. 23, 2008, eff. Dec. 1, 2008.)

Rule 5009. Closing Chapter 7, Chapter 12, Chapter 13, and Chapter 15 Cases;Order Declaring Lien Satisfied

(a) CLOSING OF CASES UNDER CHAPTERS 7, 12, AND 13. If in a chapter 7, chapter 12, or chapter 13 case the trustee has filed a final report and final account and has certified that the estate has been fully administered, and if within 30 days no objection has been filed by the United States trustee or a party in interest, there shall be a presumption that the estate has been fully administered.

(b) NOTICE OF FAILURE TO FILE RULE 1007 (b) (7) STATEMENT. If an individual debtor in a chapter 7 or 13 case is required to file a statement under Rule 1007 (b) (7) and fails to do so within 45 days after the first date set for the meeting of creditors under §341 (a) of the Code, the clerk shall promptly notify the debtor that the case will be closed without entry of a discharge unless the required statement is filed within the applicable time limit under Rule 1007 (c).

(c) CASES UNDER CHAPTER 15. A foreign representative in a proceeding recognized under §1517 of the Code shall file a final report when the purpose of the representative's appearance in the court is completed. The report shall describe the nature and results of the representative's activities in the court. The foreign representative shall transmit the report to the United States trustee, and give notice of its filing to the debtor, all persons or bodies authorized to administer foreign proceedings

已经成立滥用推定，则书记员应在申请被提交后 10 日内根据第 2002 条的规定向债权人通知滥用推定的成立。若债务人尚未提交声明以表明滥用推定是否成立，则书记员应在申请被提交后 10 日内通知债权人债务人尚未提交声明，并且若其后债务人提交声明并表明滥用推定成立，则还应就此发出通知。若债务人此后提交的声明表明滥用推定成立，则书记员应在切实可行的情况下尽快向债权人通知滥用推定的成立。

（经 Apr. 23, 2008, eff. Dec. 1, 2008. 增补）

第 5009 条　第 7 章、第 12 章、第 13 章及第 15 章案件结案；宣告解除优先权

（a）**第 7 章、第 12 章及第 13 章案件的结案**。在第 7 章、第 12 章或第 13 章案件中，若托管人已经提交最终报告以及最终账目并且证明破产实体已经得到完全管理，并且在 30 日内联邦托管人或利益相关方并未提交异议，则破产实体应被推定为得到完全管理。

（b）**未能提交第 1007 条（b）（7）所述声明的通知**。若第 7 章或第 13 章案件中个人债务人根据第 1007 条（b）（7）被要求提交声明，但在确定的首次举行法典第 341 条（a）中债权人会议后 45 日内仍未提交，则书记员应立刻通知债务人除非其在第 1007 条（c）中规定的相应时间内提交所要求的声明，否则本案将在不授予免责的情况下而结案。

（c）**第 15 章案件**。根据法典第 1517 条得以承认的程序的外国代表应在完成以代表身份而出庭的目的时提交最终报告。该报告应说明该代表在法院进行的活动的性质和结果。外国代表应将该报告移交给联邦托管人并向债务人、所有被授权处理债务人外国程序的人或机构、破产申请被提交时债务人作为当事人而在美国进行中的诉讼的所有当事人以及法院可指定的该类其他实体发出通知以说明其已提交该报告。外国代表还应向法院提交证明文件以说明其已发出该通知。若该

of the debtor, all parties to litigation pending in the United States in which the debtor was a party at the time of the filing of the petition, and such other entities as the court may direct. The foreign representative shall file a certificate with the court that notice has been given. If no objection has been filed by the United States trustee or a party in interest within 30 days after the certificate is filed, there shall be a presumption that the case has been fully administered.

(d) ORDER DECLARING LIEN SATISFIED. In a chapter 12 or chapter 13 case, if a claim that was secured by property of the estate is subject to a lien under applicable nonbankruptcy law, the debtor may request entry of an order declaring that the secured claim has been satisfied and the lien has been released under the terms of a confirmed plan. The request shall be made by motion and shall be served on the holder of the claim and any other entity the court designates in the manner provided by Rule 7004 for service of a summons and complaint.

(As amended Apr. 30, 1991, eff. Aug. 1, 1991; Apr. 28, 2010, eff. Dec. 1, 2010; Apr. 16, 2013, eff. Dec. 1, 2013; Apr. 27, 2017, eff. Dec. 1, 2017.)

Rule 5010. Reopening Cases

A case may be reopened on motion of the debtor or other party in interest pursuant to §350 (b) of the Code. In a chapter 7, 12, or 13 case a trustee shall not be appointed by the United States trustee unless the court determines that a trustee is necessary to protect the interests of creditors and the debtor or to insure efficient administration of the case.

(As amended Mar. 30, 1987, eff. Aug. 1, 1987; Apr. 30, 1991, eff. Aug. 1, 1991.)

Rule 5011. Withdrawal and Abstention from Hearing a Proceeding

(a) WITHDRAWAL. A motion for withdrawal of a case or proceeding shall be heard by a district judge.

(b) ABSTENTION FROM HEARING A PROCEEDING. A motion for abstention pursuant to 28 U.S.C. §1334 (c) shall be governed by Rule 9014 and shall be served on the parties to the proceeding.

(c) EFFECT OF FILING OF MOTION FOR WITHDRAWAL OR

证明文件被提交后 30 日内联邦托管人或利益相关方并未提交异议，则本案应被推定为已被完全实施。

（d）宣告解除财产上担保权的裁定。在第 12 章或第 13 章案件中，若根据相应的非破产法由破产财产所担保的债权系担保权的客体，则债务人可请求裁定宣告担保债权已得到完全清偿并且根据经批准的计划的条款该担保权也已被解除。应通过提交动议而作出该请求并且该动议应按照第 7004 条规定的送达传票和申诉的方式而被送达给债权人及法院所指定的任何其他实体。

（经 Apr. 30, 1991, eff. Aug. 1, 1991; Apr. 28, 2010, eff. Dec. 1, 2010; Apr. 16, 2013, eff. Dec. 1, 2013; Apr. 27, 2017, eff. Dec. 1, 2017. 修正）

第 5010 条　案件的重启

若债务人或其他利益相关方根据法典第 350 条（b）提出动议，则可重启破产案件。在第 7 章、第 12 章或第 13 章案件中，除非法院认为出于保护债权人及债务人或确保高效实施案件的目的有必要任命托管人，否则联邦托管人不得指定托管人。

（经 Mar. 30, 1987, eff. Aug. 1, 1987; Apr. 30, 1991, eff. Aug. 1, 1991. 修正）

第 5011 条　撤回及放弃就程序举行听证

（a）撤回。地区法官应就申请撤回案件或程序的动议举行听证。

（b）放弃就程序举行听证。根据《美国联邦法典》的第 28 篇第 1334 条（c）申请放弃举行听证的动议应符合第 9014 条的规定并应被送达给该程序的各当事人。

（c）提交申请撤回或放弃的动议的效力。申请撤回案件或程序或者根据《美

ABSTENTION. The filing of a motion for withdrawal of a case or proceeding or for abstention pursuant to 28 U.S.C. §1334 (c) shall not stay the administration of the case or any proceeding therein before the bankruptcy judge except that the bankruptcy judge may stay, on such terms and conditions as are proper, proceedings pending disposition of the motion. A motion for a stay ordinarily shall be presented first to the bankruptcy judge. A motion for a stay or relief from a stay filed in the district court shall state why it has not been presented to or obtained from the bankruptcy judge. Relief granted by the district judge shall be on such terms and conditions as the judge deems proper.

(Added Mar. 30, 1987, eff. Aug. 1, 1987; amended Apr. 30, 1991, eff. Aug. 1, 1991.)

Rule 5012. Agreements Concerning Coordination of Proceedings in Chapter 15 Cases

Approval of an agreement under §1527 (4) of the Code shall be sought by motion. The movant shall attach to the motion a copy of the proposed agreement or protocol and, unless the court directs otherwise, give at least 30 days' notice of any hearing on the motion by transmitting the motion to the United States trustee, and serving it on the debtor, all persons or bodies authorized to administer foreign proceedings of the debtor, all entities against whom provisional relief is being sought under §1519, all parties to litigation pending in the United States in which the debtor was a party at the time of the filing of the petition, and such other entities as the court may direct.

(Added Apr. 28, 2010, eff. Dec. 1, 2010.)

国联邦法典》第 28 篇第 1334 条（c）放弃举行听证的动议的提交，不得冻结案件或任何在破产法官前进行的程序，但在处理该动议期间破产法官可在适当的条件和情况下冻结该程序。通常情况下，申请冻结的动议应首先被提交给破产法官。向地区法院提交的申请冻结或解除冻结的动议应注明未向破产法官提交的原因或破产法官未准予冻结或解除冻结的原因。地区法官应在其认为适当的条件和情况下准予解除冻结。

（经 Mar. 30, 1987, eff. Aug. 1, 1987; amended Apr. 30, 1991, eff. Aug. 1, 1991. 增补）

第 5012 条　在第 15 章案件中有关程序间协调的协议

应通过提交动议以申请批准根据法典第 1527 条（4）而达成的协议。动议方应将拟议的协议或议定书的副本附于该动议；该动议应被移交给联邦托管人，并且除非法院作出其他指示，否则应提前 30 日针对就该动议而举行的任何听证发出通知，并送达给债务人、被授权处理债务人外国程序的所有人或机构、根据法典第 1519 条而寻求的临时救济所针对的所有实体、破产申请被提交时债务人作为当事人而在美国进行中的诉讼的所有其他当事人以及法院可指定的该类其他实体。

（经 Apr. 28, 2010, eff. Dec. 1, 2010. 增补）

PART VI

COLLECTION AND LIQUIDATION OF THE ESTATE

Rule 6001. Burden of Proof As to Validity of Postpetition Transfer

Any entity asserting the validity of a transfer under §549 of the Code shall have the burden of proof.

Rule 6002. Accounting by Prior Custodian of Property of the Estate

(a) ACCOUNTING REQUIRED. Any custodian required by the Code to deliver property in the custodian's possession or control to the trustee shall promptly file and transmit to the United States trustee a report and account with respect to the property of the estate and the administration thereof.

(b) EXAMINATION OF ADMINISTRATION. On the filing and transmittal of the report and account required by subdivision (a) of this rule and after an examination has been made into the superseded administration, after notice and a hearing, the court shall determine the propriety of the administration, including the reasonableness of all disbursements.

(As amended Mar. 30, 1987, eff. Aug. 1, 1987; Apr. 30, 1991, eff. Aug. 1, 1991; Apr. 22, 1993, eff. Aug. 1, 1993.)

Rule 6003. Interim and Final Relief Immediately Following the Commencement of the Case—Applications for Employment; Motions for Use, Sale, or Lease of Property; and Motions for Assumption or Assignment of Executory Contracts

Except to the extent that relief is necessary to avoid immediate and irreparable

第 VI 部分
破产实体的收集和清算

第 6001 条　申请后转让的合法性的举证责任

任何根据法典第 549 条主张转让的合法性的实体应承担举证责任。

第 6002 条　破产财产先前保管人所作的核算

（a）**核算要求**。任何根据法典被要求向托管人交付其占有或控制的财产的保管人应及时向法院提交并向联邦托管人移交其就破产财产及破产财产的管理而制作的报告及账目。

（b）**管理的审查**。在根据本条的附条（a）的要求提交并移交报告和账目并对原破产财产管理事项进行审查后，经过通知和听证，法院应就原管理行为是否适当（包括所有支出的合理性）作出认定。

（经 Mar. 30, 1987, eff. Aug. 1, 1987; Apr. 30, 1991, eff. Aug. 1, 1991; Apr. 22, 1993, eff. Aug. 1, 1993. 修正）

第 6003 条　案件启动后即进行的临时及最终救济——申请雇佣；申请使用、出售或出租财产的动议；以及申请确认或拒绝确认待履行合同的动议

除非出于避免造成直接且难以弥补的损害的必要，否则法院在破产申请被提

harm, the court shall not, within 21 days after the filing of the petition, issue an order granting the following:

(a) an application under Rule 2014;

(b) a motion to use, sell, lease, or otherwise incur an obligation regarding property of the estate, including a motion to pay all or part of a claim that arose before the filing of the petition, but not a motion under Rule 4001; or

(c) a motion to assume or assign an executory contract or unexpired lease in accordance with §365.

(Added Apr. 30, 2007, eff. Dec. 1, 2007; amended Mar. 26, 2009, eff. Dec. 1, 2009; Apr. 26, 2011, eff. Dec. 1, 2011.)

Rule 6004. Use, Sale, or Lease of Property

(a) NOTICE OF PROPOSED USE, SALE, OR LEASE OF PROPERTY. Notice of a proposed use, sale, or lease of property, other than cash collateral, not in the ordinary course of business shall be given pursuant to Rule 2002 (a)(2), (c)(1), (i), and (k) and, if applicable, in accordance with §363 (b)(2) of the Code.

(b) OBJECTION TO PROPOSAL. Except as provided in subdivisions (c) and (d) of this rule, an objection to a proposed use, sale, or lease of property shall be filed and served not less than seven days before the date set for the proposed action or within the time fixed by the court. An objection to the proposed use, sale, or lease of property is governed by Rule 9014.

(c) SALE FREE AND CLEAR OF LIENS AND OTHER INTERESTS. A motion for authority to sell property free and clear of liens or other interests shall be made in accordance with Rule 9014 and shall be served on the parties who have liens or other interests in the property to be sold. The notice required by subdivision (a) of this rule shall include the date of the hearing on the motion and the time within which objections may be filed and served on the debtor in possession or trustee.

(d) SALE OF PROPERTY UNDER $2,500. Notwithstanding subdivision (a) of this rule, when all of the nonexempt property of the estate has an aggregate gross value less than $2,500, it shall be sufficient to give a general notice of intent to sell such

交后 21 日内不得签发裁定准予以下各项：

（a）第 2014 条中的申请；

（b）申请使用、出售、出租破产财产或其他致使以破产财产承担责任的行为的动议，包括申请清偿全部或部分破产申请被提交前成立的债权的动议，但不包括第 4001 条所述动议；或

（c）申请根据法典第 365 条确认或转让待履行合同或未完成租约的动议。

（经 Apr. 30, 2007, eff. Dec. 1, 2007; amended Mar. 26, 2009, eff. Dec. 1, 2009; Apr. 26, 2011, eff. Dec. 1, 2011. 增补）

第 6004 条　财产的使用、出售或出租

（a）**就财产的计划使用、出售或出租而发出的通知**。应根据第 2002 条（a）（2）、（c）（1）、（i）、（k）的规定，以及法典第 363 条（b）（2）的规定（如适用），就计划进行的除现金担保物外的财产在常规营业范围外的使用、出售或出租发出通知。

（b）**就该提议的异议**。除本条的附条（c）及（d）另有规定外，就财产的计划使用、出售或出租而提出的异议应在拟采取该行动前 7 日以前或法院规定的时间内而被提交并送达。就财产的计划使用、出售或出租提出异议应遵守第 9014 条的规定。

（c）**无负担出售并清除优先权及其他权益**。申请获准无负担出售财产并清除优先权及其他权益的动议应符合第 9014 条的规定并应被送达给其就拟售财产享有优先权或其他权益的主体。附条（a）所要求发出的通知应载明就该动议举行听证的日期以及异议可被提交并被送达给经管债务人或托管人的期间。

（d）**2500 美元以下的财产的出售**。即使存在附条（a）的规定，当所有非豁免破产财产的累计总价值少于 2500 美元时，仅需向全体债权人、契约受托人、根据法典而被指定或选任的委员会、联邦托管人以及法院可指定的其他人发出通

property other than in the ordinary course of business to all creditors, indenture trustees, committees appointed or elected pursuant to the Code, the United States trustee and other persons as the court may direct. An objection to any such sale may be filed and served by a party in interest within 14 days of the mailing of the notice, or within the time fixed by the court. An objection is governed by Rule 9014.

(e) HEARING. If a timely objection is made pursuant to subdivision (b) or (d) of this rule, the date of the hearing thereon may be set in the notice given pursuant to subdivision (a) of this rule.

(f) CONDUCT OF SALE NOT IN THE ORDINARY COURSE OF BUSINESS.

(1) *Public or Private Sale*. All sales not in the ordinary course of business may be by private sale or by public auction. Unless it is impracticable, an itemized statement of the property sold, the name of each purchaser, and the price received for each item or lot or for the property as a whole if sold in bulk shall be filed on completion of a sale. If the property is sold by an auctioneer, the auctioneer shall file the statement, transmit a copy thereof to the United States trustee, and furnish a copy to the trustee, debtor in possession, or chapter 13 debtor. If the property is not sold by an auctioneer, the trustee, debtor in possession, or chapter 13 debtor shall file the statement and transmit a copy thereof to the United States trustee.

(2) *Execution of Instruments*. After a sale in accordance with this rule the debtor, the trustee, or debtor in possession, as the case may be, shall execute any instrument necessary or ordered by the court to effectuate the transfer to the purchaser.

(g) SALE OF PERSONALLY IDENTIFIABLE INFORMATION.

(1) *Motion*. A motion for authority to sell or lease personally identifiable information under §363 (b) (1) (B) shall include a request for an order directing the United States trustee to appoint a consumer privacy ombudsman under §332. Rule 9014 governs the motion which shall be served on: any committee elected under §705 or appointed under §1102 of the Code, or if the case is a chapter 11 reorganization case and no committee of unsecured creditors has been appointed under §1102, on the creditors included on the list of creditors filed under Rule 1007 (d); and on such other entities as the court may direct. The motion shall be transmitted to the United States trustee.

美国联邦破产程序规则
（中英对照译本）

知以概括说明其在常规营业范围外出售前述财产的意图。就该出售所提出的异议可在该通知被邮寄后 14 日内或法院规定的期间内而由利益相关方提交并送达。该异议应符合第 9014 条的规定。

（e）**听证**。若有人根据本条的附条（b）或（d）及时提出异议，则根据本条的附条（a）而被发出的通知中可载明举行该听证的日期。

（f）**常规营业范围外的出售行为**。

（1）公开或私人出售。常规营业范围外的所有出售都可通过私人出售或公开发售进行。除非难以适用，否则在出售完成后应提交一份声明以逐项陈述所出售的财产、各买受人的姓名以及就每件或每批或者整体财产（若将其散装出售）所收取的价格。若该财产系由拍卖师出售，则拍卖师应提交该声明并将其副本移交给联邦托管人，并向托管人、经管债务人或第 13 章债务人提供该副本。若该财产并非由拍卖师所出售，则托管人、经管债务人或第 13 章债务人应提交该声明并将其副本移交给联邦托管人。

（2）文书的制作。根据本条规定完成出售后，债务人、托管人或经管债务人（视具体情形而定）应制作任何必要的文书或法院所裁定制作的文书从而使得向买受人所作的给付正式生效。

（g）**个人身份信息的出售**。

（1）动议。申请获准根据法典第 363 条（b）（1）（B）出售或出租个人身份信息的动议应载有申请裁定指定联邦托管人根据第 332 条任命消费者隐私监察员的请求。该动议应符合第 9014 条的规定并应被送达至：根据法典第 705 条被选任或第 1102 条被指定的任何委员会，或者若在第 11 章重整案件中并未根据第 1102 条而任命无担保债权人委员会，则应被送达至根据第 1007 条（d）而被提交的债权人名单上所列明的债权人；以及法院可指定的该类其他实体。该动议应被移交给联邦托管人。

U.S. Federal Rules of Bankruptcy Procedure
(Chinese-English bilingual version)

(2) *Appointment*. If a consumer privacy ombudsman is appointed under §332, no later than seven days before the hearing on the motion under §363 (b) (1) (B) , the United States trustee shall file a notice of the appointment, including the name and address of the person appointed. The United States trustee's notice shall be accompanied by a verified statement of the person appointed setting forth the person's connections with the debtor, creditors, any other party in interest, their respective attorneys and accountants, the United States trustee, or any person employed in the office of the United States trustee.

(h) STAY OF ORDER AUTHORIZING USE, SALE, OR LEASE OF PROPERTY. An order authorizing the use, sale, or lease of property other than cash collateral is stayed until the expiration of 14 days after entry of the order, unless the court orders otherwise.

(As amended Mar. 30, 1987, eff. Aug. 1, 1987; Apr. 30, 1991, eff. Aug. 1, 1991; Apr. 26, 1999, eff. Dec. 1, 1999; Apr. 23, 2008, eff. Dec. 1, 2008; Mar. 26, 2009, eff. Dec. 1, 2009.)

Rule 6005. Appraisers and Auctioneers

The order of the court approving the employment of an appraiser or auctioneer shall fix the amount or rate of compensation. No officer or employee of the Judicial Branch of the United States or the United States Department of Justice shall be eligible to act as appraiser or auctioneer. No residence or licensing requirement shall disqualify an appraiser or auctioneer from employment.

(As amended Apr. 30, 1991, eff. Aug. 1, 1991.)

Rule 6006. Assumption, Rejection or Assignment of an Executory Contract or Unexpired Lease

(a) PROCEEDING TO ASSUME, REJECT, OR ASSIGN. A proceeding to assume, reject, or assign an executory contract or unexpired lease, other than as part of a plan, is governed by Rule 9014.

(b) PROCEEDING TO REQUIRE TRUSTEE TO ACT. A proceeding by a party to an executory contract or unexpired lease in a chapter 9 municipality case, chapter

（2）任命。若已经根据第 332 条任命有消费者隐私监察员，则在就第 363 条（b）(1)(B) 中的动议举行听证前 7 日以前，联邦托管人应提交就该任命所应发出的通知，载明被任命的人的姓名和住址。联邦托管人的通知应附有被任命的人的宣誓声明以列明其与债务人、债权人、任何其他利益相关方、前述主体的律师及会计师、联邦托管人或在联邦托管人办公室任职的人之间的联系。

（h）**准予使用、出售或出租财产的裁定的冻结**。除非法院作出其他裁定，否则准予使用、出售或出租除现金担保物以外的财产的裁定将在该裁定被正式作出后 14 日内被冻结。

（经 Mar. 30, 1987, eff. Aug. 1, 1987; Apr. 30, 1991, eff. Aug. 1, 1991; Apr. 26, 1999, eff. Dec. 1, 1999; Apr. 23, 2008, eff. Dec. 1, 2008; Mar. 26, 2009, eff. Dec. 1, 2009. 修正）

第 6005 条　评估师和拍卖师

法院批准雇佣评估师或拍卖师的裁定应确定报酬的金额和费率。美国司法系统或美国司法部的官员或职员均不得担任评估师或拍卖师。任何人均不得仅因居住地或许可证的要求而丧失担任评估师或拍卖师的资格。

（经 Apr. 30, 1991, eff. Aug. 1, 1991. 修正）

第 6006 条　待履行合同或未完成租约的确认、拒绝确认或转让

（a）**确认、拒绝确认或转让的程序**。除作为计划的一部分外，确认、拒绝确认或转让待履行合同或未完成租约的程序应符合第 9014 条的规定。

（b）**要求托管人采取行动的程序**。在第 9 章市政机构破产案件、第 11 章重整案件、第 12 章家庭农场主债务调整案件或第 13 章个人债务调整案件中，待履

U.S. Federal Rules of Bankruptcy Procedure
(Chinese-English bilingual version)

11 reorganization case, chapter 12 family farmer's debt adjustment case, or chapter 13 individual's debt adjustment case, to require the trustee, debtor in possession, or debtor to determine whether to assume or reject the contract or lease is governed by Rule 9014.

(c) NOTICE. Notice of a motion made pursuant to subdivision (a) or (b) of this rule shall be given to the other party to the contract or lease, to other parties in interest as the court may direct, and, except in a chapter 9 municipality case, to the United States trustee.

(d) STAY OF ORDER AUTHORIZING ASSIGNMENT. An order authorizing the trustee to assign an executory contract or unexpired lease under §365 (f) is stayed until the expiration of 14 days after the entry of the order, unless the court orders otherwise.

(e) LIMITATIONS. The trustee shall not seek authority to assume or assign multiple executory contracts or unexpired leases in one motion unless: (1) all executory contracts or unexpired leases to be assumed or assigned are between the same parties or are to be assigned to the same assignee; (2) the trustee seeks to assume, but not assign to more than one assignee, unexpired leases of real property; or (3) the court otherwise authorizes the motion to be filed. Subject to subdivision (f), the trustee may join requests for authority to reject multiple executory contracts or unexpired leases in one motion.

(f) OMNIBUS MOTIONS. A motion to reject or, if permitted under subdivision (e), a motion to assume or assign multiple executory contracts or unexpired leases that are not between the same parties shall:

(1) state in a conspicuous place that parties receiving the omnibus motion should locate their names and their contracts or leases listed in the motion;

(2) list parties alphabetically and identify the corresponding contract or lease;

(3) specify the terms, including the curing of defaults, for each requested assumption or assignment;

(4) specify the terms, including the identity of each assignee and the adequate assurance of future performance by each assignee, for each requested assignment;

(5) be numbered consecutively with other omnibus motions to assume, assign, or reject executory contracts or unexpired leases; and

行合同或未完成租约的当事人要求托管人、经管债务人或债务人就是否确认或拒绝确认该合同或租约作出决定的程序应符合第 9014 条的规定。

（c）**通知**。应就根据本条的附条（a）或（b）所作出的动议而向该合同或租约的其他主体、法院可指定的其他利益相关方以及联邦托管人（但第 9 章市政机构破产案件中除外）发出通知。

（d）**准予转让的裁定的冻结**。除非法院作出其他裁定，否则准予托管人根据第 365 条（f）转让待履行合同或未完成租约的裁定在该裁定被正式作出后 14 日内将被冻结。

（e）**限制**。联邦托管人不得在一项动议中就多项待履行合同或未完成租约申请获准确认或转让，除非：（1）将被确认或转让的所有待履行合同或未完成租约均成立于相同主体间或将被转让给同一受让人；（2）托管人申请确认不动产的未完成租约，但并未申请将其转让给一名以上的受让人；或（3）法院出于其他原因而准予提交该类动议。在符合附条（f）规定的情况下，托管人可在一项动议中加入多项请求以申请获准拒绝确认多项待履行合同或未完成租约。

（f）**综合动议**。针对申请拒绝确认或在附条（e）允许的情况下申请确认或转让多项待履行合同或未完成租约的动议，若前述合同或租约的当事方并不相同，则该动议应符合以下条件：

（1）在显眼的位置注明收到该综合动议的当事方应在该动议中定位到其姓名以及所列的合同或租约；

（2）按字母顺序列明当事方，并注明其所对应的合同或租约；

（3）明确各项所请求的确认或转让的条款，包括纠正违约的有关事项；

（4）明确各项所请求的转让的条款，包括各受让人的身份以及确保各受让人在未来履行该合同或租约的充分保证；

（5）与其他申请确认、转让或拒绝确认待履行合同或未完成租约的综合动议连续编号；并且

U.S. Federal Rules of Bankruptcy Procedure
(Chinese-English bilingual version)

(6) be limited to no more than 100 executory contracts or unexpired leases.

(g) FINALITY OF DETERMINATION. The finality of any order respecting an executory contract or unexpired lease included in an omnibus motion shall be determined as though such contract or lease had been the subject of a separate motion.

(As amended Mar. 30, 1987, eff. Aug. 1, 1987; Apr. 30, 1991, eff. Aug. 1, 1991; Apr. 22, 1993, eff. Aug. 1, 1993; Apr. 26, 1999, eff. Dec. 1, 1999; Apr. 30 2007, eff. Dec. 1, 2007; Mar. 26, 2009, eff. Dec. 1, 2009.)

Rule 6007. Abandonment or Disposition of Property

(a) NOTICE OF PROPOSED ABANDONMENT OR DISPOSITION; OBJECTIONS; HEARING. Unless otherwise directed by the court, the trustee or debtor in possession shall give notice of a proposed abandonment or disposition of property to the United States trustee, all creditors, indenture trustees, and committees elected pursuant to §705 or appointed pursuant to §1102 of the Code. A party in interest may file and serve an objection within 14 days of the mailing of the notice, or within the time fixed by the court. If a timely objection is made, the court shall set a hearing on notice to the United States trustee and to other entities as the court may direct.

(b) MOTION BY PARTY IN INTEREST. A party in interest may file and serve a motion requiring the trustee or debtor in possession to abandon property of the estate. Unless otherwise directed by the court, the party filing the motion shall serve the motion and any notice of the motion on the trustee or debtor in possession, the United States trustee, all creditors, indenture trustees, and committees elected pursuant to §705 or appointed pursuant to §1102 of the Code. A party in interest may file and serve an objection within 14 days of service, or within the time fixed by the court. If a timely objection is made, the court shall set a hearing on notice to the United States trustee and to other entities as the court may direct. If the court grants the motion, the order effects the trustee's or debtor in possession's abandonment without further notice, unless otherwise directed by the court.

[(c) HEARING] (Abrogated Apr. 22, 1993, eff. Aug. 1, 1993)

(As amended Mar. 30, 1987, eff. Aug. 1, 1987; Apr. 30, 1991, eff. Aug. 1, 1991;

（6）该动议所针对的待履行合同或未完成租约不得超过 100 项。

（g）**终局性认定**。就综合动议中的某项待履行合同或未完成租约所作的裁定应被视为就该合同或租约而提交的单独动议从而就该裁定的终局性作出认定。

（经 Mar. 30, 1987, eff. Aug. 1, 1987; Apr. 30, 1991, eff. Aug. 1, 1991; Apr. 22, 1993, eff. Aug. 1, 1993; Apr. 26, 1999, eff. Dec. 1, 1999; Apr. 30 2007, eff. Dec. 1, 2007; Mar. 26, 2009, eff. Dec. 1, 2009. 修正）

第 6007 条　财产的放弃或处置

（a）**就计划放弃或处置财产而发出的通知；异议；听证**。除非法院作出其他指示，否则托管人或经管债务人应向联邦托管人、全体债权人、契约受托人以及根据法典第 705 条而被选任或根据第 1102 条而被指定的委员会发出通知以告知其计划放弃财产或如何处置财产。利益相关方可在该通知被邮寄后 14 日内或法院规定的时间内提交并送达异议。若有人及时提交异议，则法院应举行听证并就此向联邦托管人及法院可指定的其他实体发出通知。

（b）**利益相关方的动议**。利益相关方可提交并送达动议以请求托管人或经管债务人放弃破产财产。除非法院作出其他指示，否则提交动议的主体应向托管人或经管债务人、联邦托管人、全体债权人、契约受托人以及根据法典第 705 条被选任或根据第 1102 条被指定的委员会送达该动议以及就该动议而应发出的任何通知。利益相关方可在被送达后 14 日内或法院规定的时间内提交并送达异议。若有人及时提交异议，则法院应举行听证并就此向联邦托管人及法院可指定的其他实体发出通知。若法院准予该动议，则除非法院作出其他指示，否则该裁定将直接使托管人或经管债务人的抛弃行为生效，而无须其他额外通知。

[（c）听证]（经 Apr. 22, 1993, eff. Aug. 1, 1993 而废除）

（经 Mar. 30, 1987, eff. Aug. 1, 1987; Apr. 30, 1991, eff. Aug. 1, 1991; Apr. 22,

U.S. Federal Rules of Bankruptcy Procedure
(Chinese-English bilingual version)

Apr. 22, 1993, eff. Aug. 1, 1993; Mar. 26, 2009, eff. Dec. 1, 2009; Apr. 25, 2019, eff. Dec. 1, 2019.)

Rule 6008. Redemption of Property from Lien or Sale

On motion by the debtor, trustee, or debtor in possession and after hearing on notice as the court may direct, the court may authorize the redemption of property from a lien or from a sale to enforce a lien in accordance with applicable law.

Rule 6009. Prosecution and Defense of Proceedings by Trustee or Debtor in Possession

With or without court approval, the trustee or debtor in possession may prosecute or may enter an appearance and defend any pending action or proceeding by or against the debtor, or commence and prosecute any action or proceeding in behalf of the estate before any tribunal.

Rule 6010. Proceeding to Avoid Indemnifying Lien or Transfer to Surety

If a lien voidable under §547 of the Code has been dissolved by the furnishing of a bond or other obligation and the surety thereon has been indemnified by the transfer of, or the creation of a lien upon, nonexempt property of the debtor, the surety shall be joined as a defendant in any proceeding to avoid the indemnifying transfer or lien. Such proceeding is governed by the rules in Part VII.

(As amended Apr. 30, 1991, eff. Aug. 1, 1991.)

Rule 6011. Disposal of Patient Records in Health Care Business Case

(a) NOTICE BY PUBLICATION UNDER §351 (1)(A). A notice regarding the claiming or disposing of patient records under §351 (1)(A) shall not identify any patient by name or other identifying information, but shall:

(1) identify with particularity the health care facility whose patient records the trustee proposes to destroy;

1993, eff. Aug. 1, 1993; Mar. 26, 2009, eff. Dec. 1, 2009; Apr. 25, 2019, eff. Dec. 1, 2019. 修正）

第 6008 条　从财产上担保权或出售中赎回财产

应债务人、托管人或经管债务人的动议，按照法院可作出的指示发出通知并举行听证后，法院可准予从财产上担保权或为执行财产上担保权而根据相应法律进行的出售中赎回财产。

第 6009 条　托管人或经管债务人的起诉和抗辩

无论是否经过法院批准，托管人或经管债务人均可针对由债务人提起或向债务人提起的任何进行中的诉讼或程序而起诉或出庭以及抗辩，或者代表破产实体在任何法庭上提起任何诉讼和程序。

第 6010 条　撤销为补偿保证人而设的财产上担保权或所作转让的程序

若根据法典第 547 条可撤销的财产上担保权已经通过保证人提供保证金或履行其他义务而被解除，并且该保证人已经通过就债务人非豁免财产的给付或通过在其上设立优先权而得到补偿，则该保证人应作为被告而参与任何撤销该给付或财产上担保权的程序。该程序由第 VII 部分的规则所规定。

（经 Apr. 30, 1991, eff. Aug. 1, 1991. 修正）

第 6011 条　在医疗护理机构破产案件中就患者档案的处置

（a）第 351 条（1）（A）中通过公告而发出的通知。根据第 351 条（1）（A）就患者档案的认领或处置而发出的通知不得通过姓名或其他身份信息而标注各患者，但应：

（1）明确注明其患者档案将被托管人销毁的医疗护理机构；

(2) state the name, address, telephone number, email address, and website, if any, of a person from whom information about the patient records may be obtained;

(3) state how to claim the patient records; and

(4) state the date by which patient records must be claimed, and that if they are not so claimed the records will be destroyed.

(b) NOTICE BY MAIL UNDER §351 (1)(B). Subject to applicable nonbankruptcy law relating to patient privacy, a notice regarding the claiming or disposing of patient records under §351 (1)(B) shall, in addition to including the information in subdivision (a), direct that a patient's family member or other representative who receives the notice inform the patient of the notice. Any notice under this subdivision shall be mailed to the patient and any family member or other contact person whose name and address have been given to the trustee or the debtor for the purpose of providing information regarding the patient's health care, to the Attorney General of the State where the health care facility is located, and to any insurance company known to have provided health care insurance to the patient.

(c) PROOF OF COMPLIANCE WITH NOTICE REQUIREMENT. Unless the court orders the trustee to file proof of compliance with §351 (1)(B) under seal, the trustee shall not file, but shall maintain, the proof of compliance for a reasonable time.

(d) REPORT OF DESTRUCTION OF RECORDS. The trustee shall file, no later than 30 days after the destruction of patient records under §351 (3), a report certifying that the unclaimed records have been destroyed and explaining the method used to effect the destruction. The report shall not identify any patient by name or other identifying information.

(Added Apr. 23, 2008, eff. Dec. 1, 2008.)

（2）注明可向其获取有关患者档案的信息的人的姓名、住址、电话号码、电子邮件以及网址（如有）；

（3）注明认领患者档案的方式；以及

（4）注明患者档案可被认领的截止日期并说明若在此之前该档案仍未被认领则其将被销毁的后果。

（b）**第 351 条（1）（B）中通过邮寄而发出的通知**。在遵守有关患者隐私的相应非破产法规定的情况下，根据第 351 条（1）（B）就患者档案的认领或处置而发出的通知，除应载明附条（a）所述信息外，还应指示收到该通知的患者的家庭成员或其他代表人将该通知告知患者。根据本附条所作的任何通知均应被邮寄给患者以及任何家庭成员或其他因提供有关患者医疗护理的信息而已经向托管人或债务人提供姓名和住址的联系人、医疗护理机构所在州的总检察长以及任何已知的为患者提供医疗健康保险的保险公司。

（c）**符合通知要求的证明**。除非法院裁定托管人提交说明已符合第 351 条（1）（B）规定的密封证明，否则托管人不应提交，但应在合理期间内保存该合规证明。

（d）**销毁档案的报告**。托管人应在根据第 351 条（3）销毁患者档案后 30 日内提交证明无人认领的档案已被销毁并说明销毁手段的报告。该报告不得以姓名或其他个人信息标注各患者。

（经 Apr. 23, 2008, eff. Dec. 1, 2008. 增补）

PART VII
ADVERSARY PROCEEDINGS

Rule 7001. Scope of Rules of Part VII

An adversary proceeding is governed by the rules of this Part VII. The following are adversary proceedings:

(1) a proceeding to recover money or property, other than a proceeding to compel the debtor to deliver property to the trustee, or a proceeding under §554 (b) or §725 of the Code, Rule 2017, or Rule 6002;

(2) a proceeding to determine the validity, priority, or extent of a lien or other interest in property, but not a proceeding under Rule 3012 or Rule 4003 (d) ;

(3) a proceeding to obtain approval under §363 (h) for the sale of both the interest of the estate and of a co-owner in property;

(4) a proceeding to object to or revoke a discharge, other than an objection to discharge under §§727 (a) (8) , (a) (9) , or 1328 (f) ;

(5) a proceeding to revoke an order of confirmation of a chapter 11, chapter 12, or chapter 13 plan;

(6) a proceeding to determine the dischargeability of a debt;

(7) a proceeding to obtain an injunction or other equitable relief, except when a chapter 9, chapter 11, chapter 12, or chapter 13 plan provides for the relief;

(8) a proceeding to subordinate any allowed claim or interest, except when a chapter 9, chapter 11, chapter 12, or chapter 13 plan provides for subordination;

(9) a proceeding to obtain a declaratory judgment relating to any of the foregoing; or

(10) a proceeding to determine a claim or cause of action removed under 28 U.S.C. §1452.

第 VII 部分
对抗制诉讼程序

第 7001 条　第 VII 部分规则的适用范围

对抗制诉讼程序由第 VII 部分的规则所规制。下列各项均属于对抗制诉讼程序：

（1）除强制债务人将财产交付给托管人的程序外，追回金钱或财产的程序或法典第 554 条（b）或第 725 条或者本法第 2017 条或第 6002 条所述的程序；

（2）就财产上担保权或其他权益的有效性、优先性或范围进行认定的程序，但不包括本法第 3012 条或第 4003 条（d）所述的程序；

（3）申请获准根据第 363 条（h）一并出售破产实体以及共有人享有的财产权益的程序；

（4）对免责提出异议或撤销免责的程序，但不包括根据第 727 条（a）(8)、（a）(9) 或第 1328 条（f）而就免责提出的异议；

（5）撤销批准第 11 章、第 12 章或第 13 章计划的裁定的程序；

（6）就债务是否免责作出认定的程序；

（7）获得禁令或其他衡平救济的程序，但不包括第 9 章、第 11 章、第 12 章或第 13 章计划所规定的救济；

（8）将任何经确认的债权或权益居次的程序，但不包括第 9 章、第 11 章、第 12 章或第 13 章计划所规定的债权居次；

（9）取得与前述任意一项有关的宣告性判决的程序；或

（10）就根据《美国联邦法典》第 28 篇第 1452 条而被移送的诉讼请求或诉讼作出决定的程序。

U.S. Federal Rules of Bankruptcy Procedure
(Chinese-English bilingual version)

(As amended Mar. 30, 1987, eff. Aug. 1, 1987; Apr. 30, 1991, eff. Aug. 1, 1991; Apr. 26, 1999, eff.Dec. 1, 1999; Apr. 28, 2010, eff. Dec. 1, 2010; Apr. 27, 2017, eff. Dec. 1, 2017.)

Rule 7002. References to Federal Rules of Civil Procedure

Whenever a Federal Rule of Civil Procedure applicable to adversary proceedings makes reference to another Federal Rule of Civil Procedure, the reference shall be read as a reference to the Federal Rule of Civil Procedure as modified in this Part VII.

Rule 7003. Commencement of Adversary Proceeding

Rule 3 F.R.Civ.P. applies in adversary proceedings.

Rule 7004. Process; Service of Summons, Complaint

(a) SUMMONS; SERVICE; PROOF OF SERVICE.

(1) Except as provided in Rule 7004(a)(2), Rule 4(a),(b),(c)(1),(d)(5), (e)-(j), (1), and (m) F.R.Civ.P. applies in adversary proceedings. Personal service under Rule 4 (e) - (j) F.R.Civ.P. may be made by any person at least 18 years of age who is not a party, and the summons may be delivered by the clerk to any such person.

(2) The clerk may sign, seal, and issue a summons electronically by putting an "s/" before the clerk's name and including the court's seal on the summons.

(b) SERVICE BY FIRST CLASS MAIL. Except as provided in subdivision (h), in addition to the methods of service authorized by Rule 4 (e) - (j) F.R.Civ. P., service may be made within the United States by first class mail postage prepaid as follows:

(1) Upon an individual other than an infant or incompetent, by mailing a copy of the summons and complaint to the individual's dwelling house or usual place of abode or to the place where the individual regularly conducts a business or profession.

(2) Upon an infant or an incompetent person, by mailing a copy of the summons and complaint to the person upon whom process is prescribed to be served by the law of

（经 Mar. 30, 1987, eff. Aug. 1, 1987; Apr. 30, 1991, eff. Aug. 1, 1991; Apr. 26, 1999, eff. Dec. 1, 1999; Apr. 28, 2010, eff. Dec. 1, 2010; Apr. 27, 2017, eff. Dec. 1, 2017. 修正）

第 7002 条　《联邦民事诉讼规则》的引用

当适用于对抗制诉讼程序的《联邦民事诉讼规则》中的某一条引用了该法中的另一条文时，该引用应被理解为对经过第 VII 部分修改后的条文的引用。

第 7003 条　对抗制诉讼程序的启动

《联邦民事诉讼规则》第 3 条适用于对抗式诉讼程序。

第 7004 条　司法文书；传票、诉状的送达

（a）传票；送达；送达证明。

（1）除第 7004 条（a）（2）另有规定外，《联邦民事诉讼规则》第 4 条的（a）、（b）、（c）（1）、（d）（5）、（e）至（j）、（1）及（m）均适用于对抗式诉讼程序。《联邦民事诉讼规则》第 4 条的（e）至（j）中的直接送达可由任何年满 18 岁的当事人以外的主体进行，并且传票可由书记员交付给该类主体送达。

（2）书记员可以电子方式签署、盖章并签发传票，但须在书记员姓名前标注"s/"并在传票上盖法院章。

（b）以一级邮件送达。除附条（h）另有规定外，除《联邦民事诉讼规则》第 4 条的附条（e）至（j）所许可的送达方式外，还可在美国境内通过一级邮件进行送达，但须预付邮费并符合以下条件：

（1）若系向除婴儿或无行为能力人外的自然人送达，则应将该传票及诉状的副本邮寄到该自然人的住所或经常居住场所或者其日常经营或工作的场所。

（2）若系向婴儿或无行为能力人送达，则应将该传票及诉状的副本邮寄给根据送达地的州法的规定当有人在该州的一般管辖权法院就前述主体提起诉讼时应

the state in which service is made when an action is brought against such a defendant in the courts of general jurisdiction of that state. The summons and complaint in that case shall be addressed to the person required to be served at that person's dwelling house or usual place of abode or at the place where the person regularly conducts a business or profession.

(3) Upon a domestic or foreign corporation or upon a partnership or other unincorporated association, by mailing a copy of the summons and complaint to the attention of an officer, a managing or general agent, or to any other agent authorized by appointment or by law to receive service of process and, if the agent is one authorized by statute to receive service and the statute so requires, by also mailing a copy to the defendant.

(4) Upon the United States, by mailing a copy of the summons and complaint addressed to the civil process clerk at the office of the United States attorney for the district in which the action is brought and by mailing a copy of the summons and complaint to the Attorney General of the United States at Washington, District of Columbia, and in any action attacking the validity of an order of an officer or an agency of the United States not made a party, by also mailing a copy of the summons and complaint to that officer or agency. The court shall allow a reasonable time for service pursuant to this subdivision for the purpose of curing the failure to mail a copy of the summons and complaint to multiple officers, agencies, or corporations of the United States if the plaintiff has mailed a copy of the summons and complaint either to the civil process clerk at the office of the United States attorney or to the Attorney General of the United States.

(5) Upon any officer or agency of the United States, by mailing a copy of the summons and complaint to the United States as prescribed in paragraph (4) of this subdivision and also to the officer or agency. If the agency is a corporation, the mailing shall be as prescribed in paragraph (3) of this subdivision of this rule. The court shall allow a reasonable time for service pursuant to this subdivision for the purpose of curing the failure to mail a copy of the summons and complaint to multiple officers, agencies, or corporations of the United States if the plaintiff has mailed a copy of the summons and

向其送达司法文书的人。在这种情况下,该传票及诉状应被寄往被要求向其送达的人的住所或经常居住场所或者其日常经营或工作的场所。

(3)若系向国内或国外的公司或合伙或者其他非法人组织送达,则应将该传票及诉状的副本邮寄给根据任命或法院规定而被授权接受司法文书的送达的员工、管理人或总代理人或任何其他机构,并且若该代理人系由法律而授权接受送达并且该法作此要求,则也应向被告邮寄该副本。

(4)若系向美国送达,则应将该传票及诉状的副本寄给诉讼被提起的辖区内的美国联邦检察官办公室的民事诉讼书记员,并将传票及诉状的副本寄给美国华盛顿特区、哥伦比亚特区的美国司法部长,并且若该诉讼将影响未作为当事人的美国政府某官员或机构的裁定的有效性,则还应将该传票及诉状的副本寄给该官员或机构。若原告已经将传票及诉状的副本邮寄给美国检察官办公室的民事诉讼书记员或美国司法部长,则法院应准予其在合理期间内根据本款进行送达以纠正未能将该传票及诉状的副本邮寄给美国其他多名官员、代理机构或企业的行为。

(5)若系向美国政府官员或机构送达,则应按照本附条第(4)款的规定将该传票及诉状的副本邮寄给美国以及该官员或机构。若该机构为企业,则还应根据本附条第(3)款的规定进行邮寄。若原告已经将传票及诉状的副本邮寄给美国检察官办公室的民事诉讼书记员或美国司法部长,则法院应准予其在合理期间内根据本附条进行送达以纠正未能将该传票及诉状的副本邮寄给美国多名官员、代理机构或企业的行为。若联邦托管人为本案的托管人并且该送达系联邦托管人仅以托管人的身份所进行的,则该送达也可按照本附

complaint either to the civil process clerk at the office of the United States attorney or to the Attorney General of the United States. If the United States trustee is the trustee in the case and service is made upon the United States trustee solely as trustee, service may be made as prescribed in paragraph (10) of this subdivision of this rule.

(6) Upon a state or municipal corporation or other governmental organization thereof subject to suit, by mailing a copy of the summons and complaint to the person or office upon whom process is prescribed to be served by the law of the state in which service is made when an action is brought against such a defendant in the courts of general jurisdiction of that state, or in the absence of the designation of any such person or office by state law, then to the chief executive officer thereof.

(7) Upon a defendant of any class referred to in paragraph (1) or (3) of this subdivision of this rule, it is also sufficient if a copy of the summons and complaint is mailed to the entity upon whom service is prescribed to be served by any statute of the United States or by the law of the state in which service is made when an action is brought against such a defendant in the court of general jurisdiction of that state.

(8) Upon any defendant, it is also sufficient if a copy of the summons and complaint is mailed to an agent of such defendant authorized by appointment or by law to receive service of process, at the agent's dwelling house or usual place of abode or at the place where the agent regularly carries on a business or profession and, if the authorization so requires, by mailing also a copy of the summons and complaint to the defendant as provided in this subdivision.

(9) Upon the debtor, after a petition has been filed by or served upon the debtor and until the case is dismissed or closed, by mailing a copy of the summons and complaint to the debtor at the address shown in the petition or to such other address as the debtor may designate in a filed writing.

(10) Upon the United States trustee, when the United States trustee is the trustee in the case and service is made upon the United States trustee solely as trustee, by mailing a copy of the summons and complaint to an office of the United States trustee or another place designated by the United States trustee in the district where the case under the Code is pending.

条第（10）款的规定进行。

（6）若系向作为该诉讼当事人的州或市政机构或其他政府组织送达，则应将传票及诉状的副本邮寄给送达地所在州的州立法律规定当在该州的一般管辖权法院向该类被告提起诉讼时应向其送达的人或办公室，若州立法律并未指定该类人或办公室，则应送达其执行首长。

（7）若系向本附条第（1）款或第（3）款所述的任何被告送达，则也可将传票及诉状的副本邮寄给美国任何法律或送达地所在州的州法规定当在该州的一般管辖权法院向该类被告提起诉讼时应向其送达的实体。

（8）对于任何被告，如其代理人经任命或根据法律被授权收取送达的司法文书，则也可将传票及诉状的副本邮寄到代理人的住所或经常居住场所或日常经营或工作的场所，并且若该授权作此要求，则还应将传票及诉状的副本根据本附条的规定邮寄给该被告。

（9）若系在破产申请被提交或被送达给债务人后，但在案件被驳回或结案前向债务人送达，则应将传票及诉状的副本邮寄到破产申请上载明的地址或债务人在已被提交的书面文件中可指定的其他地址从而邮寄给债务人。

（10）若系向担任本案托管人的联邦托管人送达并且该送达仅基于其作为托管人的身份，则应将传票及诉状的副本邮寄到破产案件所在辖区内的联邦托管人办公室或联邦托管人所指定的其他地点。

(c) SERVICE BY PUBLICATION. If a party to an adversary proceeding to determine or protect rights in property in the custody of the court cannot be served as provided in Rule 4 (e) - (j) F.R.Civ.P. or subdivision (b) of this rule, the court may order the summons and complaint to be served by mailing copies thereof by first class mail, postage prepaid, to the party's last known address, and by at least one publication in such manner and form as the court may direct.

(d) NATIONWIDE SERVICE OF PROCESS. The summons and complaint and all other process except a subpoena may be served anywhere in the United States.

(e) SUMMONS: TIME LIMIT FOR SERVICE WITHIN THE UNITED STATES. Service made under Rule 4 (e), (g), (h)(1), (i), or (j)(2) F.R.Civ. P. shall be by delivery of the summons and complaint within 7 days after the summons is issued. If service is by any authorized form of mail, the summons and complaint shall be deposited in the mail within 7 days after the summons is issued. If a summons is not timely delivered or mailed, another summons will be issued for service. This subdivision does not apply to service in a foreign country.

(f) PERSONAL JURISDICTION. If the exercise of jurisdiction is consistent with the Constitution and laws of the United States, serving a summons or filing a waiver of service in accordance with this rule or the subdivisions of Rule 4 F.R.Civ.P. made applicable by these rules is effective to establish personal jurisdiction over the person of any defendant with respect to a case under the Code or a civil proceeding arising under the Code, or arising in or related to a case under the Code.

(g) SERVICE ON DEBTOR'S ATTORNEY. If the debtor is represented by an attorney, whenever service is made upon the debtor under this Rule, service shall also be made upon the debtor's attorney by any means authorized under Rule 5(b)F.R.Civ.P.

(h) SERVICE OF PROCESS ON AN INSURED DEPOSITORY INSTITUTION. Service on an insured depository institution (as defined in section 3 of the Federal Deposit Insurance Act) in a contested matter or adversary proceeding shall be made by certified mail addressed to an officer of the institution unless—

(1) the institution has appeared by its attorney, in which case the attorney shall be served by first class mail;

美国联邦破产程序规则
（中英对照译本）

（c）**公告送达**。若不能按照《联邦民事诉讼规则》第4条（e）至（j）或本附条第（b）款的规定向针对就法院所保管的财产所享有的权利作出认定或保护该权利的对抗制诉讼程序的当事人送达，则法院可裁定以一级邮件、预付邮件的方式将传票及诉状的副本邮寄到当事人最后为人所知的地址从而进行送达，并至少以该方式进行一次公告送达，也可以法院指定的方式进行送达。

（d）**全国范围内司法文书的送达**。传票、诉状以及除强制传唤令外的所有其他司法文书均可被送达至美国境内的任何地点。

（e）**传票：在美国境内进行送达的时间限制**。根据《联邦民事诉讼规则》第4条（e）、（g）、（h）（1）、（i）或（j）（2）所进行的送达应在该传票被签发后7日内通过交付该传票及诉状而实现。若该送达系通过任何经授权的邮寄方式而进行，则该传票及诉状应在该传票被签发后7日内被存入该邮件。若该传票未被及时交付或邮寄，则将签发其他传票并进行送达。本款不适用于在国外所进行的送达。

（f）**个人管辖权**。若管辖权的行使符合宪法及美国法律的规定，则根据本条或因本法而得以适用的《联邦民事诉讼规则》第4条各附条的规定而送达传票或提交放弃送达的声明，将成立对根据法典所提交的破产案件或根据法典所提起的民事诉讼或者因破产案件而产生或与破产案件有关的民事诉讼中的任何被告的个人管辖权。

（g）**向债务人的律师送达**。若债务人系由律师所代表，则当根据本条向债务人送达时，也应按照《联邦民事诉讼规则》第5条（b）所允许的任何方式向债务人的律师送达。

（h）**向受保存款机构送达司法文书**。除下列情形外，在争议事项或对抗制诉讼程序中向受保存款机构（定义见《联邦存款保险法》第3条）送达应通过挂号邮件的方式邮寄给该机构的工作人员：

（1）该机构系由其律师代表出席，在该情况下应以一级邮件的方式向该律师送达；

(2) the court orders otherwise after service upon the institution by certified mail of notice of an application to permit service on the institution by first class mail sent to an officer of the institution designated by the institution; or

(3) the institution has waived in writing its entitlement to service by certified mail by designating an officer to receive service.

(As amended Mar. 30, 1987, eff. Aug. 1, 1987; Apr. 30, 1991, eff. Aug. 1, 1991; Pub. L. 103-394, title I, §114, Oct. 22, 1994, 108 Stat. 4118; Apr. 23, 1996, eff. Dec. 1, 1996; Apr. 26, 1999, eff. Dec.1, 1999; Apr. 25, 2005, eff. Dec. 1, 2005; Apr. 12, 2006, eff. Dec. 1, 2006; Mar. 26, 2009, eff. Dec.1, 2009; Apr. 25, 2014, eff. Dec. 1, 2014; Apr. 26, 2018, eff. Dec. 1, 2018.)

Rule 7005. Service and Filing of Pleadings and Other Papers

Rule 5 F.R.Civ.P. applies in adversary proceedings.

Rule 7007. Pleadings Allowed

Rule 7 F.R.Civ.P. applies in adversary proceedings.

Rule 7007.1. Corporate Ownership Statement

(a) REQUIRED DISCLOSURE. Any nongovernmental corporation that is a party to an adversary proceeding, other than the debtor, shall file a statement that identifies any parent corporation and any publicly held corporation that owns 10% or more of its stock or states that there is no such corporation. The same requirement applies to a nongovernmental corporation that seeks to intervene.

(b) TIME FOR FILING; SUPPLEMENTAL FILING. The corporate ownership statement shall:

(1) be filed with the corporation's first appearance, pleading, motion, response, or other request addressed to the court; and

(2) be supplemented whenever the information required by this rule changes.

(Added Mar. 27, 2003, eff. Dec. 1, 2003; amended Apr. 30, 2007, eff. Dec. 1, 2007; Apr. 14, 2021,eff. Dec. 1, 2021.)

（2）在以挂号邮件的方式向该机构送达请求被准予通过向该机构所指定的内部工作人员邮寄一级邮件的方式进行送达的申请的通知后，法院作出其他裁定；或

（3）该机构通过指定接受送达的工作人员已经书面放弃其被以挂号邮件的方式送达的权利。

（经 Mar. 30, 1987, eff. Aug. 1, 1987; Apr. 30, 1991, eff. Aug. 1, 1991; Pub. L. 103-394, title I, §114, Oct. 22, 1994, 108 Stat. 4118; Apr. 23, 1996, eff. Dec. 1, 1996; Apr. 26, 1999, eff. Dec. 1, 1999; Apr. 25, 2005, eff. Dec. 1, 2005; Apr. 12, 2006, eff. Dec. 1, 2006; Mar. 26, 2009, eff. Dec. 1, 2009; Apr. 25, 2014, eff. Dec. 1, 2014; Apr. 26, 2018, eff. Dec. 1, 2018. 修正）

第 7005 条　诉状及其他文书的送达与提交

《联邦民事诉讼规则》第 5 条适用于对抗制诉讼程序。

第 7007 条　诉状的受理

《联邦民事诉讼规则》第 7 条适用于对抗制诉讼程序。

第 7007.1 条　公司所有权声明

（a）**披露要求**。对抗制诉讼程序中作为当事人（不包括债务人）的任何非政府企业均应提交一份声明以列明其任何母公司或持有该企业 10% 及以上股本证券的公众公司，或注明并不存在该类公司。该要求同样适用于寻求介入的非政府企业。

（b）**提交的时间；补充提交**。公司所有权声明应当：

（1）在公司首次出席法庭或向法庭提交诉状、动议或其他请求时一并被提交；并且

（2）当本条要求载明的信息发生变化时进行补充。

（经 Mar. 27, 2003, eff. Dec. 1, 2003; amended Apr. 30, 2007, eff. Dec. 1, 2007; Apr. 14, 2021, eff. Dec. 1, 2021. 增补）

U.S. Federal Rules of Bankruptcy Procedure
(Chinese-English bilingual version)

Rule 7008. General Rules of Pleading

Rule 8 F.R.Civ.P. applies in adversary proceedings. The allegation of jurisdiction required by Rule 8 (a) shall also contain a reference to the name, number, and chapter of the case under the Code to which the adversary proceeding relates and to the district and division where the case under the Code is pending. In an adversary proceeding before a bankruptcy court, the complaint, counterclaim, cross-claim, or third-party complaint shall contain a statement that the pleader does or does not consent to entry of final orders or judgment by the bankruptcy court.

(As amended Mar. 30, 1987, eff. Aug. 1, 1987; Apr. 25, 2014, eff. Dec. 1, 2014; Apr. 28, 2016, eff.Dec. 1, 2016.)

Rule 7009. Pleading Special Matters

Rule 9 F.R.Civ.P. applies in adversary proceedings.

Rule 7010. Form of Pleadings

Rule 10 F.R.Civ.P. applies in adversary proceedings, except that the caption of each pleading in such a proceeding shall conform substantially to the appropriate Official Form.

(As amended Apr. 30, 1991, eff. Aug. 1, 1991.)

Rule 7012. Defenses and Objections—When and How Presented—by Pleading or Motion—Motion for Judgment on the Pleadings

(a) WHEN PRESENTED. If a complaint is duly served, the defendant shall serve an answer within 30 days after the issuance of the summons, except when a different time is prescribed by the court. The court shall prescribe the time for service of the answer when service of a complaint is made by publication or upon a party in a foreign country. A party served with a pleading stating a cross-claim shall serve an answer thereto within 21 days after service. The plaintiff shall serve a reply to a counterclaim in the answer within 21 days after service of the answer or, if a reply is ordered by the court, within 21 days after service of the order, unless the order otherwise directs. The United States or an officer or agency thereof shall

美国联邦破产程序规则
（中英对照译本）

第 7008 条　诉状的一般规定

《联邦民事诉讼规则》第 8 条适用于对抗制诉讼程序。第 8 条（a）所要求的管辖权的主张也应说明与该对抗制诉讼程序有关的破产案件的名称、编号及所依章节以及破产案件所在的辖区及分区。在破产法院进行的对抗制诉讼程序中，控诉、反诉、交叉请求或第三人的诉讼请求均应说明请求人是否同意由破产法院作出最终裁定或判决。

（经 Mar. 30, 1987, eff. Aug. 1, 1987; Apr. 25, 2014, eff. Dec. 1, 2014; Apr. 28, 2016, eff. Dec. 1, 2016. 修正）

第 7009 条　有关诉状的特殊事项

《联邦民事诉讼程序》第 9 条适用于对抗制诉讼程序。

第 7010 条　诉状的形式

《联邦民事诉讼规则》第 10 条适用于对抗制诉讼程序，但在该类程序中的所有诉状的标题均应基本符合相应的官方模板的规定。

（经 Apr. 30, 1991, eff. Aug. 1, 1991. 修正）

第 7012 条　抗辩及异议—何时及如何提出—通过诉状或动议—申请就诉状作出判决的动议

（a）何时提出。若诉状已被通过适当方式而送达，则除非法院规定了其他期间，否则被告应在传票被签发后 30 日内送达答辩状。若诉状系通过公告方式而被送达或被送达至外国，则法院应规定送达答辩状的期间。被送达载有交叉请求的诉状的当事人应在被送达后 21 日内送达答辩状。原告应在被送达答辩状后 21 日内送达就答辩状中被提出的反诉所作的答复；若法院裁定作出答复，则除非法院作出其他指示，否则应在该裁定被送达后 21 日内送达答复。美国或美国政府的官员或机构应在传票被签发后 35 日内送达就诉状所作的答辩状，并且应在向美国联邦检察官送达主张有交叉请求或反诉的诉状后 35 日内送达就交叉请求所作的答辩状或就反诉所作的答复。除非法院裁定规定了其他期间，否则本条

serve an answer to a complaint within 35 days after the issuance of the summons, and shall serve an answer to a cross-claim, or a reply to a counterclaim, within 35 days after service upon the United States attorney of the pleading in which the claim is asserted. The service of a motion permitted under this rule alters these periods of time as follows, unless a different time is fixed by order of the court: (1)if the court denies the motion or postpones its disposition until the trial on the merits, the responsive pleading shall be served within 14 days after notice of the court's action; (2) if the court grants a motion for a more definite statement, the responsive pleading shall be served within 14 days after the service of a more definite statement.

(b) APPLICABILITY OF RULE 12 (b) - (i) F.R.CIV.P. Rule 12 (b) - (i) F.R.Civ.P. applies in adversary proceedings. A responsive pleading shall include a statement that the party does or does not consent to entry of final orders or judgment by the bankruptcy court.

(As amended Mar. 30, 1987, eff. Aug. 1, 1987; Apr. 23, 2008, eff. Dec. 1, 2008; Mar. 26, 2009, eff.Dec. 1, 2009; Apr. 28, 2016, eff. Dec. 1, 2016.)

Rule 7013. Counterclaim and Cross-Claim

Rule 13 F.R.Civ.P. applies in adversary proceedings, except that a party sued by a trustee or debtor in possession need not state as a counterclaim any claim that the party has against the debtor, the debtor's property, or the estate, unless the claim arose after the entry of an order for relief. A trustee or debtor in possession who fails to plead a counterclaim through oversight, inadvertence, or excusable neglect, or when justice so requires, may by leave of court amend the pleading, or commence a new adversary proceeding or separate action.

(As amended Mar. 30, 1987, eff. Aug. 1, 1987.)

Rule 7014. Third-Party Practice

Rule 14 F.R.Civ.P. applies in adversary proceedings.

Rule 7015. Amended and Supplemental Pleadings

Rule 15 F.R.Civ.P. applies in adversary proceedings.

中被准予的动议的送达将按以下方式调整以下期间：(1) 若法院否决该动议或将其推迟至实体审中进行处理，则应答文状应在就法院的前述行为发出通知后 14 日内而被送达；(2) 若法院准予了申请对方提供更具体的声明的动议，则应答文状应在更具体的声明被送达后 14 日内而被送达。

(b)《联邦民事诉讼规则》第 12 条 (b) 至 (i) 款的适用。《联邦民事诉讼规则》第 12 条的附条 (b) 至 (i) 适用于对抗制诉讼程序。应答诉状应载明当事人是否同意破产法院作出最终裁定或判决的声明。

（经 Mar. 30, 1987, eff. Aug. 1, 1987; Apr. 23, 2008, eff. Dec. 1, 2008; Mar. 26, 2009, eff. Dec. 1, 2009; Apr. 28, 2016, eff. Dec. 1, 2016. 修正）

第 7013 条　反诉及交叉请求

《联邦民事诉讼规则》第 13 条适用于对抗制诉讼程序，但托管人或经管债务人对其提起诉讼的当事人无须将任何其就债务人、债务人的财产或破产实体主张的任何权利请求认定为反诉，除非该权利请求系在破产救济令被正式作出后而成立。当托管人或经管债务人未能提起反诉系因疏忽、疏漏或可原谅的过失，或者出于司法公正的需要，则托管人或经管债务人可经法院许可修正其诉状或启动新的对抗制诉讼程序或提起单独的诉讼。

（经 Mar. 30, 1987, eff. Aug. 1, 1987. 修正）

第 7014 条　第三方当事人程序

《联邦民事诉讼规则》第 14 条适用于对抗制诉讼程序。

第 7015 条　修正及补充起诉状

《联邦民事诉讼规则》第 15 条适用于对抗制诉讼程序。

Rule 7016. Pretrial Procedures

(a) PRETRIAL CONFERENCES; SCHEDULING; MANAGEMENT. Rule 16 F.R.Civ.P. applies in adversary proceedings.

(b) DETERMINING PROCEDURE. The bankruptcy court shall decide, on its own motion or a party's timely motion, whether:

(1) to hear and determine the proceeding;

(2) to hear the proceeding and issue proposed findings of fact and conclusions of law; or

(3) to take some other action.

(As amended Apr. 28, 2016, eff. Dec. 1, 2016.)

Rule 7017. Parties Plaintiff and Defendant; Capacity

Rule 17 F.R.Civ.P. applies in adversary proceedings, except as provided in Rule 2010 (b).

(As amended Apr. 30, 1991, eff. Aug. 1, 1991.)

Rule 7018. Joinder of Claims and Remedies

Rule 18 F.R.Civ.P. applies in adversary proceedings.

Rule 7019. Joinder of Persons Needed for Just Determination

Rule 19 F.R.Civ.P. applies in adversary proceedings, except that (1) if an entity joined as a party raises the defense that the court lacks jurisdiction over the subject matter and the defense is sustained, the court shall dismiss such entity from the adversary proceedings and (2) if an entity joined as a party properly and timely raises the defense of improper venue, the court shall determine, as provided in 28 U.S.C. §1412, whether that part of the proceeding involving the joined party shall be transferred to another district, or whether the entire adversary proceeding shall be transferred to another district.

(As amended Mar. 30, 1987, eff. Aug. 1, 1987.)

美国联邦破产程序规则
（中英对照译本）

第 7016 条　审前程序

（a）**审前会议；日程安排裁定；管理**。《联邦民事诉讼规则》第 16 条适用于对抗制诉讼程序。

（b）**决定程序**。破产法院应在自身动议或当事人及时提出的动议下，就以下事项作出决定：

（1）是否举行听证并就该程序作出决定；

（2）是否举行听证并作出拟议的事实认定和法律结论；或

（3）采取其他措施。

（经 Apr. 28, 2016, eff. Dec. 1, 2016. 修正）

第 7017 条　原告及被告；诉讼能力

除第 2010 条（b）另有规定外，《联邦民事诉讼规则》第 17 条适用于对抗制诉讼程序。

（经 Apr. 30, 1991, eff. Aug. 1, 1991. 修正）

第 7018 条　权利主张和救济的合并

《联邦民事诉讼规则》第 18 条适用于对抗制诉讼程序。

第 7019 条　为获得公正裁决而有必要参加的人

《联邦民事诉讼规则》第 19 条适用于对抗制诉讼程序，除非：（1）作为当事人而参加的实体提出抗辩称法院就争议事项没有管辖权并且该抗辩得到支持，则法院应在该对抗制诉讼程序中将该实体驳回，并且（2）作为当事人而参加的实体适当并及时地提出审理不适当的抗辩，则法院应根据《美国联邦法典》第 28 篇第 1412 条的规定就程序中涉及被加入的当事人的部分是否应被移送至其他辖区或是否整个对抗制诉讼程序均应被移送至其他辖区作出决定。

（经 Mar. 30, 1987, eff. Aug. 1, 1987. 修正）

Rule 7020. Permissive Joinder of Parties

Rule 20 F.R.Civ.P. applies in adversary proceedings.

Rule 7021. Misjoinder and Non-Joinder of Parties

Rule 21 F.R.Civ.P. applies in adversary proceedings.

Rule 7022. Interpleader

Rule 22 (a) F.R.Civ.P. applies in adversary proceedings. This rule supplements—and does not limit—the joinder of parties allowed by Rule 7020.

(As amended Apr. 23, 2008, eff. Dec. 1, 2008.)

Rule 7023. Class Proceedings

Rule 23 F.R.Civ.P. applies in adversary proceedings.

Rule 7023.1. Derivative Actions

Rule 23.1 F.R.Civ.P. applies in adversary proceedings.

(As amended Apr. 23, 2008, eff. Dec. 1, 2008.)

Rule 7023.2. Adversary Proceedings Relating to Unincorporated Associations

Rule 23.2 F.R.Civ.P. applies in adversary proceedings.

Rule 7024. Intervention

Rule 24 F.R.Civ.P. applies in adversary proceedings.

Rule 7025. Substitution of Parties

Subject to the provisions of Rule 2012, Rule 25 F.R.Civ.P. applies in adversary proceedings.

第 7020 条　被准予参加的当事人

《联邦民事诉讼规则》第 20 条适用于对抗制诉讼程序。

第 7021 条　当事人的错误参加及不参加

《联邦民事诉讼规则》第 21 条适用于对抗制诉讼程序。

第 7022 条　竞合权利诉讼

《联邦民事诉讼规则》第 22 条（a）适用于对抗制诉讼程序。本条将补充（但不限制）根据第 7020 条被准予的当事人的参加。

（经 Apr. 23, 2008, eff. Dec. 1, 2008. 修正）

第 7023 条　集体诉讼

《联邦民事诉讼规则》第 23 条适用于对抗制诉讼程序。

第 7023.1 条　股东代表诉讼

《联邦民事诉讼规则》第 23.1 条适用于对抗制诉讼程序。

（经 Apr. 23, 2008, eff. Dec. 1, 2008. 修正）

第 7023.2 条　涉及非法人组织的对抗制诉讼程序

《联邦民事诉讼规则》第 23.2 条适用于对抗制诉讼程序。

第 7024 条　参加诉讼

《联邦民事诉讼规则》第 24 条适用于对抗制诉讼程序。

第 7025 条　当事人的更换

在符合第 2012 条规定的情况下,《联邦民事诉讼规则》第 25 条适用于对抗制诉讼程序。

U.S. Federal Rules of Bankruptcy Procedure
(Chinese-English bilingual version)

Rule 7026. General Provisions Governing Discovery

Rule 26 F.R.Civ.P. applies in adversary proceedings.

Rule 7027. Depositions Before Adversary Proceedings or Pending Appeal

Rule 27 F.R.Civ.P. applies to adversary proceedings.

Rule 7028. Persons Before Whom Depositions May Be Taken

Rule 28 F.R.Civ.P. applies in adversary proceedings.

Rule 7029. Stipulations Regarding Discovery Procedure

Rule 29 F.R.Civ.P. applies in adversary proceedings.

Rule 7030. Depositions Upon Oral Examination

Rule 30 F.R.Civ.P. applies in adversary proceedings.

Rule 7031. Deposition Upon Written Questions

Rule 31 F.R.Civ.P. applies in adversary proceedings.

Rule 7032. Use of Depositions in Adversary Proceedings

Rule 32 F.R.Civ.P. applies in adversary proceedings.

Rule 7033. Interrogatories to Parties

Rule 33 F.R.Civ.P. applies in adversary proceedings.

Rule 7034. Production of Documents and Things and Entry Upon Land for Inspection and Other Purposes

Rule 34 F.R.Civ.P. applies in adversary proceedings.

第 7026 条　有关证据开示的一般规定

《联邦民事诉讼规则》第 26 条适用于对抗制诉讼程序。

第 7027 条　对抗制诉讼程序前或上诉期间的书面证词

《联邦民事诉讼规则》第 27 条适用于对抗制诉讼程序。

第 7028 条　收集书面证词时的见证人

《联邦民事诉讼规则》第 28 条适用于对抗制诉讼程序。

第 7029 条　有关证据开示程序的约定

《联邦民事诉讼规则》第 29 条适用于对抗制诉讼程序。

第 7030 条　口头质询时的宣誓作证

《联邦民事诉讼规则》第 30 条适用于对抗制诉讼程序。

第 7031 条　书面质询时的宣誓作证

《联邦民事诉讼规则》第 31 条适用于对抗制诉讼程序。

第 7032 条　对抗制诉讼程序中书面证词的使用

《联邦民事诉讼规则》第 32 条适用于对抗制诉讼程序。

第 7033 条　向当事人所作的书面质询

《联邦民事诉讼规则》第 33 条适用于对抗制诉讼程序。

第 7034 条　材料和物品的制作以及出于调查及其他目的进入某地

《联邦民事诉讼规则》第 34 条适用于对抗制诉讼程序。

Rule 7035. Physical and Mental Examination of Persons

Rule 35 F.R.Civ.P. applies in adversary proceedings.

Rule 7036. Requests for Admission

Rule 36 F.R.Civ.P. applies in adversary proceedings.

Rule 7037. Failure to Make Discovery: Sanctions

Rule 37 F.R.Civ.P. applies in adversary proceedings.

Rule 7040. Assignment of Cases for Trial

Rule 40 F.R.Civ.P. applies in adversary proceedings.

Rule 7041. Dismissal of Adversary Proceedings

Rule 41 F.R.Civ.P. applies in adversary proceedings, except that a complaint objecting to the debtor's discharge shall not be dismissed at the plaintiff's instance without notice to the trustee, the United States trustee, and such other persons as the court may direct, and only on order of the court containing terms and conditions which the court deems proper.

(As amended Apr. 30, 1991, eff. Aug. 1, 1991.)

Rule 7042. Consolidation of Adversary Proceedings; Separate Trials

Rule 42 F.R.Civ.P. applies in adversary proceedings.

Rule 7052. Findings by the Court

Rule 52 F.R.Civ.P. applies in adversary proceedings, except that any motion under subdivision (b) of that rule for amended or additional findings shall be filed no later than 14 days after entry of judgment. In these proceedings, the reference in Rule 52 F.R.Civ.P. to the entry of judgment under Rule 58 F.R.Civ.P. shall be read as a reference to the entry of a judgment or order under Rule 5003 (a) .

第 7035 条　对人的身体及精神检查

《联邦民事诉讼规则》第 35 条适用于对抗制诉讼程序。

第 7036 条　申请采信

《联邦民事诉讼规则》第 36 条适用于对抗制诉讼程序。

第 7037 条　未能提供书面证词；处罚

《联邦民事诉讼规则》第 37 条适用于对抗制诉讼程序。

第 7040 条　案件审理的安排

《联邦民事诉讼规则》第 40 条适用于对抗制诉讼程序。

第 7041 条　对抗制诉讼程序的驳回

《联邦民事诉讼规则》第 41 条适用于对抗制诉讼程序，但就债务人的免责提出异议的控诉不得在未向托管人、联邦托管人以及法院可指定的该类其他主体发出通知的情况下而在原告的诉讼程序中被驳回，除非法院作出裁定且该裁定载有法院认为适当的条款及条件。

（经 Apr. 30, 1991, eff. Aug. 1, 1991. 修正）

第 7042 条　对抗制诉讼程序的合并；分别审理

《联邦民事诉讼规则》第 42 条适用于对抗制诉讼程序。

第 7052 条　法院的事实认定

《联邦民事诉讼规则》第 52 条适用于对抗制诉讼程序，但该条的附条（b）中申请修正或增加对其他事实的认定的动议应在判决被作出后 14 日内而被提交。在该类程序中，《联邦民事诉讼规则》第 52 条提到的该法第 58 条中判决的作出应被理解为本法第 5003 条（a）中判决或裁定的作出。

(As amended Mar. 26, 2009, eff. Dec. 1, 2009.)

Rule 7054. Judgments; Costs

(a) JUDGMENTS. Rule 54 (a) - (c) F.R.Civ.P. applies in adversary proceedings.

(b) COSTS; ATTORNEY'S FEES.

(1) *Costs Other Than Attorney's Fees*. The court may allow costs to the prevailing party except when a statute of the United States or these rules otherwise provides. Costs against the United States, its officers and agencies shall be imposed only to the extent permitted by law. Costs may be taxed by the clerk on 14 days' notice; on motion served within seven days thereafter, the action of the clerk may be reviewed by the court.

(2) *Attorney's Fees*.

(A) Rule 54 (d) (2) (A) - (C) and (E) F.R.Civ.P. applies in adversary proceedings except for the reference in Rule 54 (d) (2) (C) to Rule 78.

(B) By local rule, the court may establish special procedures to resolve fee-related issues without extensive evidentiary hearings.

(As amended Apr. 23, 2012, eff. Dec. 1, 2012; Apr. 25, 2014, eff. Dec. 1, 2014.)

Rule 7055. Default

Rule 55 F.R.Civ.P. applies in adversary proceedings.

Rule 7056. Summary Judgment

Rule 56 F.R.Civ.P. applies in adversary proceedings, except that any motion for summary judgment must be made at least 30 days before the initial date set for an evidentiary hearing on any issue for which summary judgment is sought, unless a different time is set by local rule or the court orders otherwise.

(As amended Apr. 23, 2012, eff. Dec. 1 2012.)

Rule 7058. Entering Judgment in Adversary Proceeding

Rule 58 F.R.Civ.P. applies in adversary proceedings. In these proceedings, the

美国联邦破产程序规则
（中英对照译本）

（经 Mar. 26, 2009, eff. Dec. 1, 2009. 修正）

第 7054 条　判决；诉讼费用

（a）**判决**。《联邦民事诉讼规则》第 54 条（a）至（c）适用于对抗制诉讼程序。

（b）**诉讼费用；律师费**。

（1）除律师费外的诉讼费用。除非美国法律或本法作出其他规定，否则法院可准予由胜诉方承担诉讼费用。由美国及其政府官员和机构所承担的诉讼费用仅能在法律所允许的范围内向其施加。书记员可在提前 14 日发出通知后确定诉讼费用的金额；若有人在其后 7 日内送达动议，则法院可对书记员的行为进行审议。

（2）律师费。

（A）《联邦民事诉讼规则》第 54 条（d）（2）（A）至（C）以及（E）适用于对抗制诉讼程序，但不包括第 54（d）（2）（C）中对第 78 条的引用。

（B）法院可通过地方规则设立特殊程序以在不进行大量证据听证的情况下解决与费用相关的事项。

（经 Apr. 23, 2012, eff. Dec. 1, 2012; Apr. 25, 2014, eff. Dec. 1, 2014. 修正）

第 7055 条　缺席

《联邦民事诉讼规则》第 55 条适用于对抗制诉讼程序。

第 7056 条　简易判决

《联邦民事诉讼规则》第 56 条适用于对抗制诉讼程序，但申请作出简易判决的任何动议必须在原本就该简易判决所涉事项举行证据听证而确定的日期前 30 日以前而被作出，除非地方法律或法院裁定规定了其他期间。

（经 Apr. 23, 2012, eff. Dec. 1 2012. 修正）

第 7058 条　在对抗制诉讼程序中作出判决

《联邦民事诉讼规则》第 58 条适用于对抗制诉讼程序。在该类程序中该条提

reference in Rule 58 F.R.Civ.P. to the civil docket shall be read as a reference to the docket maintained by the clerk under Rule 5003（a）.

（Added Mar. 26, 2009, eff. Dec. 1, 2009.）

Rule 7062. Stay of Proceedings to Enforce a Judgment

Rule 62 F.R.Civ.P. applies in adversary proceedings, except that proceedings to enforce a judgment are stayed for 14 days after its entry.

（As amended Apr. 30, 1991, eff. Aug. 1, 1991; Apr. 26, 1999, eff. Dec. 1, 1999; Apr. 26, 2018, eff.Dec. 1, 2018.）

Rule 7064. Seizure of Person or Property

Rule 64 F.R.Civ.P. applies in adversary proceedings.

Rule 7065. Injunctions

Rule 65 F.R.Civ.P. applies in adversary proceedings, except that a temporary restraining order or preliminary injunction may be issued on application of a debtor, trustee, or debtor in possession without compliance with Rule 65（c）.

Rule 7067. Deposit in Court

Rule 67 F.R.Civ.P. applies in adversary proceedings.

Rule 7068. Offer of Judgment

Rule 68 F.R.Civ.P. applies in adversary proceedings.

Rule 7069. Execution

Rule 69 F.R.Civ.P. applies in adversary proceedings.

Rule 7070. Judgment for Specific Acts; Vesting Title

Rule 70 F.R.Civ.P. applies in adversary proceedings and the court may enter a judgment divesting the title of any party and vesting title in others whenever the real or

到的民事案卷应被理解为根据本法第 5003 条（a）由书记员所保存的案卷。

（经 Mar. 26, 2009, eff. Dec. 1, 2009. 增补）

第 7062 条　执行判决的程序的冻结

《联邦民事诉讼规则》第 62 条适用于对抗制诉讼程序，但执行判决的程序在该裁定被作出后 14 日内将被冻结。

（经 Apr. 30, 1991, eff. Aug. 1, 1991; Apr. 26, 1999, eff. Dec. 1, 1999; Apr. 26, 2018, eff. Dec. 1, 2018. 修正）

第 7064 条　对人或财产的强制措施

《联邦民事诉讼规则》第 64 条适用于对抗制诉讼程序。

第 7065 条　禁令

《联邦民事诉讼规则》第 65 条适用于对抗制诉讼程序，但临时禁令或初步禁令可在当事人、托管人或经管债务人提出申请的情况下而被签发，并且无须遵守第 65 条（c）的规定。

第 7067 条　向法院缴纳的押金

《联邦民事诉讼规则》第 67 条适用于对抗制诉讼程序。

第 7068 条　判决要约

《联邦民事诉讼规则》第 68 条适用于对抗制诉讼程序。

第 7069 条　执行

《联邦民事诉讼规则》第 69 条适用于对抗制诉讼程序。

第 7070 条　就特定行为所作的判决；所有权的授予

《联邦民事诉讼规则》第 70 条适用于对抗制诉讼程序并且若所涉的不动产或动产在法院的管辖权范围内，则法院可作出判决以剥夺任何当事人的所有权并将

personal property involved is within the jurisdiction of the court.

(As amended Mar. 30, 1987, eff. Aug. 1, 1987.)

Rule 7071. Process in Behalf of and Against Persons Not Parties

Rule 71 F.R.Civ.P. applies in adversary proceedings.

Rule 7087. Transfer of Adversary Proceeding

On motion and after a hearing, the court may transfer an adversary proceeding or any part thereof to another district pursuant to 28 U.S.C. §1412, except as provided in Rule 7019 (2).

(As amended Mar. 30, 1987, eff. Aug. 1, 1987.)

该所有权赋予他人。

（经 Mar. 30, 1987, eff. Aug. 1, 1987. 修正）

第 7071 条　代表非当事人或对非当事人所进行的程序

《联邦民事诉讼规则》第 71 条适用于对抗制诉讼程序。

第 7087 条　对抗制诉讼程序的移送

除第 7019 条（2）另有规定外，在有人提出动议并举行听证后，法院可根据《美国联邦法典》第 28 篇第 1412 条将对抗制诉讼程序或该程序的任何部分移交给其他辖区。

（经 Mar. 30, 1987, eff. Aug. 1, 1987. 修正）

PART VIII

APPEALS TO DISTRICT COURT OR BANKRUPTCY APPELLATE PANEL

Rule 8001. Scope of Part VIII Rules; Definition of "BAP"; Method of Transmission

(a) GENERAL SCOPE. These Part VIII rules govern the procedure in a United States district court and a bankruptcy appellate panel on appeal from a judgment, order, or decree of a bankruptcy court. They also govern certain procedures on appeal to a United States court of appeals under 28U.S.C. §158 (d).

(b) DEFINITION OF "BAP." "BAP" means a bankruptcy appellate panel established by a circuit's judicial council and authorized to hear appeals from a bankruptcy court under 28 U.S.C. §158.

(c) METHOD OF TRANSMITTING DOCUMENTS. A document must be sent electronically under these Part VIII rules, unless it is being sent by or to an individual who is not represented by counsel or the court's governing rules permit or require mailing or other means of delivery.

(Added Apr. 25, 2014, eff. Dec. 1, 2014.)

Rule 8002. Time for Filing Notice of Appeal

(a) IN GENERAL.

(1) *Fourteen-Day Period.* Except as provided in subdivisions (b) and (c), a notice of appeal must be filed with the bankruptcy clerk within 14 days after entry of the judgment, order, or decree being appealed.

(2) *Filing Before the Entry of Judgment.* A notice of appeal filed after the

第 VIII 部分
向地区法院或破产上诉合议庭提起上诉

第 8001 条　第 VIII 部分规则的适用范围；"破产上诉合议庭"的定义；递交材料的方式

（a）一般适用范围。第 VIII 部分规则适用于美国地区法院以及破产上诉合议庭处理就破产法院的判决、裁定或法令提起的上诉的程序。其也适用于处理根据《美国联邦法典》第 28 篇第 158 条（d）向美国上诉法院提起的上诉的特定程序。

（b）"破产上诉合议庭"的定义。"破产上诉合议庭"指巡回司法理事会所建立的有权根据《美国联邦法典》第 28 篇第 158 条（d）审理就破产法院提起的上诉的破产上诉合议庭。

（c）递交材料的方式。根据第 VIII 部分的规则，必须以电子方式递交材料，除非该材料系由并未由律师所代表的自然人所递交或向其递交，或者法院所适用的规则允许或要求以邮寄或其他方式交付材料。

（经 Apr. 25, 2014, eff. Dec. 1, 2014. 增补）

第 8002 条　提交上诉通知书的时间

（a）一般规定。

（1）14 日期间。除附条（b）及附条（c）另有规定外，上诉通知书必须在被上诉的判决、裁定或法令被载入后 14 日内而被提交至破产法院书记员。

（2）判决被载入前提交。在破产法院宣告决定或裁定后，但在判决、裁定或

bankruptcy court announces a decision or order—but before entry of the judgment, order, or decree—is treated as filed on the date of and after the entry.

(3) *Multiple Appeals*. If one party files a timely notice of appeal, any other party may file a notice of appeal within 14 days after the date when the first notice was filed, or within the time otherwise allowed by this rule, whichever period ends later.

(4) *Mistaken Filing in Another Court*. If a notice of appeal is mistakenly filed in a district court, BAP, or court of appeals, the clerk of that court must state on the notice the date on which it was received and transmit it to the bankruptcy clerk. The notice of appeal is then considered filed in the bankruptcy court on the date so stated.

(5) *Entry Defined*.

(A) A judgment, order, or decree is entered for purposes of this Rule 8002 (a):

(i) when it is entered in the docket under Rule 5003 (a), or

(ii) if Rule 7058 applies and Rule 58 (a) F.R.Civ.P. requires a separate document, when the judgment, order, or decree is entered in the docket under Rule 5003 (a) and when the earlier of these events occurs:

- the judgment, order, or decree is set out in a separate document; or
- 150 days have run from entry of the judgment, order, or decree in the docket under Rule 5003 (a).

(B) A failure to set out a judgment, order, or decree in a separate document when required by Rule 58 (a) F.R.Civ.P. does not affect the validity of an appeal from that judgment, order, or decree.

(b) EFFECT OF A MOTION ON THE TIME TO APPEAL.

(1) *In General*. If a party files in the bankruptcy court any of the following motions and does so within the time allowed by these rules, the time to file an appeal runs for all parties from the entry of the order disposing of the last such remaining motion:

(A) to amend or make additional findings under Rule 7052, whether or not granting the motion would alter the judgment;

(B) to alter or amend the judgment under Rule 9023;

(C) for a new trial under Rule 9023; or

(D) for relief under Rule 9024 if the motion is filed within 14 days after the

美国联邦破产程序规则
（中英对照译本）

法令被载入前被提交的上诉通知书被视为其被载入后当日所被提交的通知。

（3）多项上诉。若某一当事人最先及时提交了上诉通知书，则任何其他当事人仍可在前述通知书被提交后 14 日内或本条所规定的其他时间内（以较晚结束者为准）提交上诉通知书。

（4）被错误提交至其他法院。若上诉通知书被错误提交至地区法院、破产上诉合议庭或上诉法院，则前述法院的书记员必须在通知书上注明其收到该通知的日期并将其移交给破产法院书记员。上诉通知书将被认定为系在注明的日期当日而被提交至破产法院。

（5）"载入"的定义。

（A）就第 8002 条（a）而言，某判决、裁定或法令被载入系指：

（i）其根据第 5003 条（a）被载入案卷；或

（ii）若适用第 7058 条并且《联邦民事诉讼规则》第 58 条（a）要求制作单独文件，则系指判决、裁定或法令根据第 5003 条（a）被载入案卷并且当以下事件发生时（以较早发生者为准）：

- 判决、裁定或法令被载入单独文件中；
- 判决、裁定或法令根据第 5003 条（a）被载入案卷后 150 日后。

（B）未能根据《联邦民事诉讼规则》第 58 条（a）的要求将判决、裁定或法令载入单独文件并不会影响就判决、裁定或法令所提起的上诉的有效性。

（b）**在上诉期间内提出的动议的效力。**

（1）一般规定。若某当事人在本法规定的相应时间内向破产法院提交有以下任意动议，则针对于所有当事人上诉期间均将从就最后一项剩余动议正式作出裁定时起算：

（A）根据第 7052 条申请修正或作出其他事实认定的动议，无论准予该动议是否将影响该判决；

（B）根据第 9023 条申请调整或修正判决的动议；

（C）根据第 9023 条申请举行新的庭审的动议；或

（D）在判决被正式作出后 14 日内根据第 9024 条被提交的申请获得救济的

U.S. Federal Rules of Bankruptcy Procedure
(Chinese-English bilingual version)

judgment is entered.

(2) *Filing an Appeal Before the Motion is Decided.* If a party files a notice of appeal after the court announces or enters a judgment, order, or decree—but before it disposes of any motion listed in subdivision (b)(1)—the notice becomes effective when the order disposing of the last such remaining motion is entered.

(3) *Appealing the Ruling on the Motion.* If a party intends to challenge an order disposing of any motion listed in subdivision (b)(1) —or the alteration or amendment of a judgment, order, or decree upon the motion—the party must file a notice of appeal or an amended notice of appeal. The notice or amended notice must comply with Rule 8003 or 8004 and be filed within the time prescribed by this rule, measured from the entry of the order disposing of the last such remaining motion.

(4) *No Additional Fee.* No additional fee is required to file an amended notice of appeal.

(c) APPEAL BY AN INMATE CONFINED IN AN INSTITUTION.

(1) *In General.* If an institution has a system designed for legal mail, an inmate confined there must use that system to receive the benefit of this Rule 8002 (c)(1). If an inmate files a notice of appeal from a judgment, order, or decree of a bankruptcy court, the notice is timely if it is deposited in the institution's internal mail system on or before the last day for filing and:

(A) it is accompanied by:

(i) a declaration in compliance with 28 U.S.C. §1746—or a notarized statement—setting out the date of deposit and stating that first-class postage is being prepaid; or

(ii) evidence (such as a postmark or date stamp) showing that the notice was so deposited and that postage was prepaid; or

(B) the appellate court exercises its discretion to permit the later filing of a declaration or notarized statement that satisfies Rule 8002 (c)(1)(A)(i).

(2) *Multiple Appeals.* If an inmate files under this subdivision the first notice of appeal, the 14-day period provided in subdivision (a)(3) for another party to file a notice of appeal runs from the date when the bankruptcy clerk dockets the first notice.

(d) EXTENDING THE TIME TO APPEAL.

动议。

（2）在就动议作出决定前提起上诉。若某当事人在法院宣告或载入判决、裁定或法令后，但在法院就附条（b）（1）所列的任何动议作出决定前，提交上诉通知书，则该通知书将在就最后一项剩余动议正式作出裁定后而生效。

（3）就动议的裁决所提起的上诉。若某当事人意图针对法院就附条（b）（1）所列的任何动议作出的裁定提出异议，或针对该动议所作的判决、裁定或法令作出调整或修正，则该当事人必须提交上诉通知书或经修正的上诉通知书。该通知书或修正通知书必须符合第8003条或第8004条的规定并在本条规定的期间内而被提交，该期间自就最后一项剩余动议正式作出裁定时起算。

（4）无额外费用。就提交经修正的上诉通知书而言，无须缴纳额外费用。

（c）**被拘役在某机构内的犯人所提起的上诉。**

（1）一般规定。若该机构有设计用于接收或邮寄合法邮件的系统，则被拘役在该机构内的犯人必须使用该系统从而得以适用第8002条（c）（1）并获益。若该犯人针对破产法院所作的判决、裁定或法令提交上诉通知书，则若该通知书在提交期间最后一日当日或之前被投递到该机构的内部邮寄系统并且符合以下条件，则该通知应被视为已被及时提交：

（A）其被附有以下材料：

（i）列有投递日期并注明该一级邮件的费用已被预付的根据《美国联邦法典》第28篇第1746条所作的说明，或者经公证的声明；或者

（ii）证明该通知已被以前述方式而被投递并且其费用已被预付的证据（如邮戳或日期戳）；或者

（B）上诉法院行使其自由裁量权并准予其迟延提交符合第8002条（c）（1）（A）（i）的条件的说明或经公证的声明。

（2）多项上诉。若该犯人根据本附条最先提交上诉通知书，则针对其他当事人而言，附条（a）（3）规定的用于提交上诉通知书的14日期间将自破产法院书记员将前述通知书载入案卷当日起算。

（d）**上诉期间的延长。**

(1) *When the Time May be Extended*. Except as provided in subdivision (d)(2), the bankruptcy court may extend the time to file a notice of appeal upon a party's motion that is filed:

(A) within the time prescribed by this rule; or

(B) within 21 days after that time, if the party shows excusable neglect.

(2) *When the Time May Not be Extended*. The bankruptcy court may not extend the time to file a notice of appeal if the judgment, order, or decree appealed from:

(A) grants relief from an automatic stay under §362, 922, 1201, or 1301 of the Code;

(B) authorizes the sale or lease of property or the use of cash collateral under §363 of the Code;

(C) authorizes the obtaining of credit under §364 of the Code;

(D) authorizes the assumption or assignment of an executory contract or unexpired lease under §365 of the Code;

(E) approves a disclosure statement under §1125 of the Code; or

(F) confirms a plan under §943, 1129, 1225, or 1325 of the Code.

(3) *Time Limits on an Extension*. No extension of time may exceed 21 days after the time prescribed by this rule, or 14 days after the order granting the motion to extend time is entered, whichever is later.

(Added Apr. 25, 2014, eff. Dec. 1, 2014; amended Apr. 26, 2018, eff. Dec. 1, 2018.)

Rule 8003. Appeal as of Right—How Taken; Docketing the Appeal

(a) FILING THE NOTICE OF APPEAL.

(1) *In General*. An appeal from a judgment, order, or decree of a bankruptcy court to a district court or BAP under 28 U.S.C. §158 (a)(1) or (a)(2) may be taken only by filing a notice of appeal with the bankruptcy clerk within the time allowed by Rule 8002.

(2) *Effect of Not Taking Other Steps*. An appellant's failure to take any step other than the timely filing of a notice of appeal does not affect the validity of the appeal, but

（1）可延长该期间的情形。除附条（d）（2）另有规定外，若当事人在以下期间内提交动议，则破产法院可延长提交上诉通知书的期间：

（A）在本条所规定的时间内；或

（B）若当事人证明其存在可以原谅的过失，则在前述期间届满后21日内。

（2）不得延长该期间的情形。针对就以下事项所作的判决、裁定或法令所提起的上诉，破产法院不得延长提交该上诉通知书的期间：

（A）准予解除法典第362条、第922条、第1201条或第1301条所规定的自动冻结；

（B）准予根据法典第363条出售或出租财产或者使用现金担保物；

（C）准予根据法典第364条获取信贷；

（D）准予根据法典第365条确认或转让待履行合同或未完成租约；

（E）批准根据法典第1125条所作的披露声明；或

（F）根据法典第943条、第1129条、第1225条或第1325条批准计划。

（3）延长期间的时间限制。该期间不得被延长至本法规定的期间届满后21日后或准予申请延长期间的动议的裁定被正式作出后14日后，以二者中较晚者为准。

（经 Apr. 25, 2014, eff. Dec. 1, 2014 增补；经 Apr. 26, 2018, eff. Dec. 1, 2018. 修正）

第 8003 条　作为权利的上诉——如何提起上诉；上诉案件的立案

（a）提交上诉通知书。

（1）一般规定。根据《美国联邦法典》第28篇第158条（a）（1）或（a）（2）就破产法院的判决、裁定或法令向地区法院或破产上诉合议庭提起上诉必须通过在第8002条规定的期间内向破产法院书记员提交上诉通知书来实现。

（2）未采取其他措施的效力。上诉人除及时提交上诉通知书外未采取其他任何措施并不会影响上诉的有效性，但系地区法院或破产上诉合议庭采取其认为适

is ground only for the district court or BAP to act as it considers appropriate, including dismissing the appeal.

(3) *Contents*. The notice of appeal must:

(A) conform substantially to the appropriate Official Form;

(B) be accompanied by the judgment, order, or decree, or the part of it, being appealed; and

(C) be accompanied by the prescribed fee.

(4) *Additional Copies*. If requested to do so, the appellant must furnish the bankruptcy clerk with enough copies of the notice to enable the clerk to comply with subdivision (c).

(b) JOINT OR CONSOLIDATED APPEALS.

(1) *Joint Notice of Appeal*. When two or more parties are entitled to appeal from a judgment, order, or decree of a bankruptcy court and their interests make joinder practicable, they may file a joint notice of appeal. They may then proceed on appeal as a single appellant.

(2) *Consolidating Appeals*. When parties have separately filed timely notices of appeal, the district court or BAP may join or consolidate the appeals.

(c) SERVING THE NOTICE OF APPEAL.

(1) *Serving Parties and Transmitting to the United States Trustee*. The bankruptcy clerk must serve the notice of appeal on counsel of record for each party to the appeal, excluding the appellant, and transmit it to the United States trustee. If a party is proceeding pro se, the clerk must send the notice of appeal to the party's last known address. The clerk must note, on each copy, the date when the notice of appeal was filed.

(2) *Effect of Failing to Serve or Transmit Notice*. The bankruptcy clerk's failure to serve notice on a party or transmit notice to the United States trustee does not affect the validity of the appeal.

(3) *Noting Service on the Docket*. The clerk must note on the docket the names of the parties served and the date and method of the service.

(d) TRANSMITTING THE NOTICE OF APPEAL TO THE DISTRICT COURT OR BAP; DOCKETING THE APPEAL.

当的措施的依据，包括驳回上诉。

（3）内容。上诉通知书必须符合以下条件：
（A）基本符合相应官方模板的要求；
（B）附有被上诉的判决、裁定或法令，或者其部分内容；并且

（C）附有所规定的费用。
（4）额外副本。若被作此要求，则上诉人必须向破产法院书记员提交该通知书的足够数量的副本以保证书记员能够履行附条（c）的要求。

（b）**联合上诉和上诉的合并**。
（1）联合上诉通知书。当有两名或两名以上的当事人有权就破产法院所作的判决、裁定或法令提起上诉并且其利害关系使得联合上诉具有可行性时，其可提交联合上诉通知书。其后前述当事人可作为一名上诉人而进行上诉。

（2）上诉的合并。当各当事人分别及时提交上诉通知书时，地区法院或破产上诉合议庭可将前述上诉进行合并。
（c）**上诉通知书的送达**。
（1）送达至当事人并移交给联邦托管人。破产法院书记员必须将上诉通知书送达给除上诉人外的各当事人的备案律师，并将其移交给联邦托管人。若有当事人自己出庭参与诉讼，则书记员必须将上诉通知书寄往该当事人最后为人所知的地址。书记员必须在每一份副本上注明上诉通知书被提交的日期。

（2）未能送达或移交通知书的效力。破产法院书记员未能将通知书送达至当事人或将其移交给联邦托管人并不会影响上诉的有效性。

（3）在案卷中注明送达信息。书记员必须在案卷中注明已被送达的当事人的姓名以及送达的日期及方式。

（d）**将上诉通知书移交给地区法院或破产上诉合议庭；上诉案件的立案**。

(1) *Transmitting the Notice*. The bankruptcy clerk must promptly transmit the notice of appeal to the BAP clerk if a BAP has been established for appeals from that district and the appellant has not elected to have the district court hear the appeal. Otherwise, the bankruptcy clerk must promptly transmit the notice to the district clerk.

(2) *Docketing in the District Court or BAP*. Upon receiving the notice of appeal, the district or BAP clerk must docket the appeal under the title of the bankruptcy case and the title of any adversary proceeding, and must identify the appellant, adding the appellant's name if necessary.

(Added Apr. 25, 2014, eff. Dec. 1, 2014.)

Rule 8004. Appeal by Leave—How Taken; Docketing the Appeal

(a) NOTICE OF APPEAL AND MOTION FOR LEAVE TO APPEAL. To appeal from an interlocutory order or decree of a bankruptcy court under 28 U.S.C. §158 (a) (3), a party must file with the bankruptcy clerk a notice of appeal as prescribed by Rule 8003 (a). The notice must:

(1) be filed within the time allowed by Rule 8002;

(2) be accompanied by a motion for leave to appeal prepared in accordance with subdivision (b); and

(3) unless served electronically using the court's transmission equipment, include proof of service in accordance with Rule 8011 (d).

(b) CONTENTS OF THE MOTION; RESPONSE.

(1) *Contents*. A motion for leave to appeal under 28 U.S.C. §158 (a) (3) must include the following:

(A) the facts necessary to understand the question presented;

(B) the question itself;

(C) the relief sought;

(D) the reasons why leave to appeal should be granted; and

(E) a copy of the interlocutory order or decree and any related opinion or memorandum.

(2) *Response*. A party may file with the district or BAP clerk a response in

（1）移交通知书。若针对就某辖区的破产法院所提起的上诉已经设立有破产上诉合议庭并且上诉人并未选择由地区法院来审理上诉案件，则破产法院书记员必须及时将上诉通知书移交给破产上诉合议庭的书记员。否则，破产法院书记员必须及时将通知书移交给地区法院书记员。

（2）地区法院或破产上诉合议庭的立案。在收到上诉通知书时，地区法院或破产上诉合议庭的书记员必须在破产案件以及任何对抗制诉讼程序的标题下记载该上诉，并且必须注明上诉人的身份并在必要的情况下载明其姓名。

（经 Apr. 25, 2014, eff. Dec. 1, 2014. 增补）

第 8004 条　须经许可的上诉——如何提起上诉；上诉案件的立案

（a）上诉通知书以及申请获准提起上诉的动议。为了根据《美国联邦法典》第 28 篇第 158 条（a）（3）针对破产法院在案件进行中所临时签发的裁定或法令提起上诉，当事人必须根据第 8003 条（a）向破产法院书记员提交上诉通知书。该通知书必须符合以下条件：

（1）在第 8002 条所规定的期间内而被提交；

（2）附有根据附条（b）所准备的申请获准提起上诉的动议；并且

（3）除非系使用法院的传输设备以电子方式送达，否则应附有第 8011 条（d）所述的送达证明。

（b）动议的内容；答复。

（1）内容。申请获准根据《美国联邦法典》第 28 篇第 158 条（a）（3）提起上诉的动议必须载有以下内容：

（A）助于理解被提出的问题的必要事实；

（B）问题本身；

（C）所寻求的救济；

（D）应被准予提起上诉的原因；以及

（E）临时裁定或法令以及任何相关观点或备忘录的副本。

（2）答复。当事人可在该动议被提交后 14 日内向地区法院或破产上诉合议

opposition or a cross-motion within 14 days after the motion is served.

(c) TRANSMITTING THE NOTICE OF APPEAL AND THE MOTION; DOCKETING THE APPEAL; DETERMINING THE MOTION.

(1) *Transmitting to the District Court or BAP*. The bankruptcy clerk must promptly transmit the notice of appeal and the motion for leave to the BAP clerk if a BAP has been established for appeals from that district and the appellant has not elected to have the district court hear the appeal. Otherwise, the bankruptcy clerk must promptly transmit the notice and motion to the district clerk.

(2) *Docketing in the District Court or BAP*. Upon receiving the notice and motion, the district or BAP clerk must docket the appeal under the title of the bankruptcy case and the title of any adversary proceeding, and must identify the appellant, adding the appellant's name if necessary.

(3) *Oral Argument Not Required*. The motion and any response or cross-motion are submitted without oral argument unless the district court or BAP orders otherwise.

(d) FAILURE TO FILE A MOTION WITH A NOTICE OF APPEAL. If an appellant timely files a notice of appeal under this rule but does not include a motion for leave, the district court or BAP may order the appellant to file a motion for leave, or treat the notice of appeal as a motion for leave and either grant or deny it. If the court orders that a motion for leave be filed, the appellant must do so within 14 days after the order is entered, unless the order provides otherwise.

(e) DIRECT APPEAL TO A COURT OF APPEALS. If leave to appeal an interlocutory order or decree is required under 28 U.S.C. §158 (a)(3), an authorization of a direct appeal by the court of appeals under 28 U.S.C. §158 (d)(2) satisfies the requirement.

(Added Apr. 25, 2014, eff. Dec. 1, 2014.)

Rule 8005. Election to Have an Appeal Heard by the District Court Instead of the BAP

(a) FILING OF A STATEMENT OF ELECTION. To elect to have an appeal heard by the district court, a party must:

庭提交反对答复或交叉动议。

（c）移交上诉通知书及动议；上诉案件的立案；就动议作出决定。

（1）移交给地区法院或破产上诉合议庭。若针对就某辖区的破产法院所提起的上诉已经设立有破产上诉合议庭并且上诉人并未选择由地区法院来审理上诉案件，则破产法院书记员必须及时将上诉通知书和申请获准提起上诉的动议移交给破产上诉合议庭。否则，破产法院书记员必须及时将通知书及动议移交给地区法院书记员。

（2）地区法院或破产上诉合议庭的立案。在收到上诉通知书及动议时，地区法院或破产上诉合议庭的书记员必须在破产案件以及任何对抗制诉讼程序的标题下记载该上诉，并且必须注明上诉人的身份并在必要的情况下载明其姓名。

（3）无须进行口头辩论。除非地区法院或破产上诉合议庭作出其他裁定，否则该动议以及任何答复或交叉动议均可被直接提交而无须口头辩论。

（d）在提交上诉通知书时未能提交动议。若上诉人根据本条及时提交上诉通知书，但并未附有申请获准提起上诉的动议，则地区法院或破产上诉合议庭可裁定上诉人提交申请获准提起上诉的动议或将上诉通知书视为该动议并准予或否决该动议。若法院裁定提交该动议，则除非法院作出其他裁定，否则上诉人必须在法院裁定被正式作出后 14 日内而提交该动议。

（e）向上诉法院直接上诉。若根据《美国联邦法典》第 28 篇第 158 条（a）(3)被要求通过提出申请从而就临时裁定或法令提起上诉，则上诉法院根据《美国联邦法典》第 28 篇第 158 条（d）(2)准许其直接提起上诉也符合该要求。

（经 Apr. 25, 2014, eff. Dec. 1, 2014. 增补）

第 8005 条　选择由地区法院代替破产上诉合议庭审理上诉案件

（a）选择声明的提交。为了选择由地区法院审理上诉案件，当事人必须履行以下各项：

(1) file a statement of election that conforms substantially to the appropriate Official Form; and

(2) do so within the time prescribed by 28 U.S.C. §158 (c) (1).

(b) TRANSMITTING THE DOCUMENTS RELATED TO THE APPEAL. Upon receiving an appellant's timely statement of election, the bankruptcy clerk must transmit to the district clerk all documents related to the appeal. Upon receiving a timely statement of election by a party other than the appellant, the BAP clerk must transmit to the district clerk all documents related to the appeal and notify the bankruptcy clerk of the transmission.

(c) DETERMINING THE VALIDITY OF AN ELECTION. A party seeking a determination of the validity of an election must file a motion in the court where the appeal is then pending. The motion must be filed within 14 days after the statement of election is filed.

(d) MOTION FOR LEAVE WITHOUT A NOTICE OF APPEAL—EFFECT ON THE TIMING OF AN ELECTION. If an appellant moves for leave to appeal under Rule 8004 but fails to file a separate notice of appeal with the motion, the motion must be treated as a notice of appeal for purposes of determining the timeliness of a statement of election.

(Added Apr. 25, 2014, eff. Dec. 1, 2014.)

Rule 8006. Certifying a Direct Appeal to the Court of Appeals

(a) EFFECTIVE DATE OF A CERTIFICATION. A certification of a judgment, order, or decree of a bankruptcy court for direct review in a court of appeals under 28 U.S.C. §158 (d) (2) is effective when:

(1) the certification has been filed;

(2) a timely appeal has been taken under Rule 8003 or 8004; and

(3) the notice of appeal has become effective under Rule 8002.

(b) FILING THE CERTIFICATION. The certification must be filed with the clerk of the court where the matter is pending. For purposes of this rule, a matter remains pending in the bankruptcy court for 30 days after the effective date under Rule

（1）提交基本符合相应官方模板要求的选择声明；并且

（2）在《美国联邦法典》第28篇第158条（c）（1）所规定的时间内提交。

（b）**移交与上诉有关的材料**。在收到上诉人及时提交的选择声明时，破产法院书记员必须将与上诉有关的所有材料移交给地区法院书记员。在收到由上诉人外的当事人及时提交的选择声明时，破产上诉合议庭的书记员必须将与上诉有关的所有材料移交给地区法院书记员并通知破产法院书记员其已经移交该材料。

（c）**就该选择的有效性作出认定**。申请就该选择的有效性作出认定的当事人必须向审理上诉案件的法院提交动议。该动议必须在该选择声明被提交后14日内而被提交。

（d）**在提交申请获准提起上诉的动议时未能提交上诉通知书——对选择时间的影响**。若上诉人根据第8004条提出动议以申请获准提起上诉，但其在提交该动议时未能提交单独的上诉通知书，则就认定选择声明被提交的时间线而言，该动议应被视为上诉通知书。

（经 Apr. 25, 2014, eff. Dec. 1, 2014. 增补）

第8006条　向上诉法院证明直接上诉

（a）**证明的生效日期**。为了由上诉法院根据《美国联邦法典》第28篇第158条（d）（2）进行直接审查而出具的破产法院所作的判决、裁定或法令的证明将在以下事件发生时而生效：

（1）该证明已经被提交；

（2）已经根据第8003条或第8004条而及时提起上诉；并且

（3）上诉通知书已经根据第8002条而生效。

（b）**提交证明**。该证明必须被提交给正在进行此案的法院的书记员。就本条而言，就直接审查所针对的判决、裁定或法令提起上诉的首份通知书根据第8002条生效后30日内该案仍系在破产法院进行。此后，该案则系在地区法院或

8002 of the first notice of appeal from the judgment, order, or decree for which direct review is sought. A matter is pending in the district court or BAP thereafter.

(c) JOINT CERTIFICATION BY ALL APPELLANTS AND APPELLEES.

(1) *How Accomplished*. A joint certification by all the appellants and appellees under 28 U.S.C.§158 (d)(2)(A) must be made by using the appropriate Official Form. The parties may supplement the certification with a short statement of the basis for the certification, which may include the information listed in subdivision (f)(2).

(2) *Supplemental Statement by the Court*. Within 14 days after the parties' certification, the bankruptcy court or the court in which the matter is then pending may file a short supplemental statement about the merits of the certification.

(d) THE COURT THAT MAY MAKE THE CERTIFICATION. Only the court where the matter is pending, as provided in subdivision (b), may certify a direct review on request of parties or on its own motion.

(e) CERTIFICATION ON THE COURT'S OWN MOTION.

(1) *How Accomplished*. A certification on the court's own motion must be set forth in a separate document. The clerk of the certifying court must serve it on the parties to the appeal in the manner required for service of a notice of appeal under Rule 8003 (c)(1). The certification must be accompanied by an opinion or memorandum that contains the information required by subdivision (f)(2)(A)-(D).

(2) *Supplemental Statement by a Party*. Within 14 days after the court's certification, a party may file with the clerk of the certifying court a short supplemental statement regarding the merits of certification.

(f) CERTIFICATION BY THE COURT ON REQUEST.

(1) *How Requested*. A request by a party for certification that a circumstance specified in 28U.S.C. §158 (d)(2)(A)(i)-(iii) applies—or a request by a majority of the appellants and a majority of the appellees—must be filed with the clerk of the court where the matter is pending within 60 days after the entry of the judgment, order, or decree.

(2) *Service and Contents*. The request must be served on all parties to the appeal in the manner required for service of a notice of appeal under Rule 8003 (c)(1), and it must include the following:

美国联邦破产程序规则
（中英对照译本）

破产上诉合议庭进行。

（c）**全体上诉人及被上诉人的合并证明。**

（1）如何完成。《美国联邦法典》第 28 篇第 158 条（d）（2）（A）中全体上诉人及被上诉人的合并证明必须根据相应的官方模板而制作。当事人可对该证明的依据进行简要说明以对该证明进行补充,该说明可载明附条（f）（2）所列的信息。

（2）由法院出具的补充声明。在当事人获得证明后的 14 日内,破产法院或此后进行此案的法院可提交就该证明的依据所作的简要补充声明。

（d）**可出具该证明的法院。**仅有附条（b）所述的正在进行此案的法院可应当事人的请求或在其自身动议下就直接审查出具证明。

（e）**在法院的自身动议下所出具的证明。**

（1）如何完成。法院在其自身动议下所作的证明必须被出具在单独的文件上。出具证明的法院的书记员必须以第 8003 条（c）（1）所规定的送达上诉通知书的方式将其送达给该上诉所涉及的各方当事人。该证明必须附有含有附条（f）（2）的（A）至（D）所要求的信息的观点或备忘录。

（2）当事人提交的补充声明。在法院出具证明后 14 日内,当事人可向出具证明的法院的书记员提交就该证明的依据所作的简要补充说明。

（f）**法院应请求出具证明。**

（1）如何提出请求。若当事人或者多数上诉人及多数被上诉人请求证明存在《美国联邦法典》第 28 篇第 158 条（d）（2）（A）（i）至（iii）所述的某种情形,则必须在判决、裁定或法令被载入后 60 日内提交至正在进行该案的法院的书记员。

（2）送达及内容。该请求必须被以第 8003 条（c）（1）规定的送达上诉通知书的方式而被送达至该上诉的所有当事人,并且其必须包含以下各项：

(A) the facts necessary to understand the question presented;

(B) the question itself;

(C) the relief sought;

(D) the reasons why the direct appeal should be allowed, including which circumstance specified in 28 U.S.C. §158 (d)(2)(A)(i) - (iii) applies; and

(E) a copy of the judgment, order, or decree and any related opinion or memorandum.

(3) *Time to File a Response or a Cross-Request*. A party may file a response to the request within 14 days after the request is served, or such other time as the court where the matter is pending allows. A party may file a cross-request for certification within 14 days after the request is served, or within 60 days after the entry of the judgment, order, or decree, whichever occurs first.

(4) *Oral Argument Not Required*. The request, cross-request, and any response are submitted without oral argument unless the court where the matter is pending orders otherwise.

(5) *Form and Service of the Certification*. If the court certifies a direct appeal in response to the request, it must do so in a separate document. The certification must be served on the parties to the appeal in the manner required for service of a notice of appeal under Rule 8003 (c)(1).

(g) PROCEEDING IN THE COURT OF APPEALS FOLLOWING A CERTIFICATION. Within 30 days after the date the certification becomes effective under subdivision (a), a request for permission to take a direct appeal to the court of appeals must be filed with the circuit clerk in accordance with F.R.App.P. 6 (c).

(Added Apr. 25, 2014, eff. Dec. 1, 2014; amended Apr. 26, 2018, eff. Dec. 1, 2018.)

Rule 8007. Stay Pending Appeal; Bonds; Suspension of Proceedings

(a) INITIAL MOTION IN THE BANKRUPTCY COURT.

(1) *In General*. Ordinarily, a party must move first in the bankruptcy court for the following relief:

（A）助于理解被提出的问题的必要事实；

（B）问题本身；

（C）所寻求的救济；

（D）应被准予直接上诉的原因，包括所适用的《美国联邦法典》第 28 篇第 158 条（d）（2）（A）（i）至（iii）中的具体哪种情形；以及

（E）判决、裁定或法令以及任何相关观点或备忘录的副本。

（3）提交答复或交叉请求的时间。当事人可在该请求被送达后 14 日内或者正在进行该案的法院所规定的其他时间内就该请求提交答复。当事人可在该请求被送达后 14 日内或该判决、裁定或法令被载入后 60 日内（以两者中较早者为准）提交交叉请求。

（4）无须进行口头辩论。除非正在进行该案的法院作出其他裁定，否则该请求、交叉请求以及任何答复均可被直接提交而无须口头辩论。

（5）证明的形式及送达。若法院要针对该请求就直接上诉作出证明，则其必须出具单独的文件。该证明必须以第 8003 条（c）（1）规定的送达上诉通知书的方式被送达给该上诉案件的各当事人。

（g）**提供证明后在上诉法院进行的程序**。在该证明根据附条（a）生效后 30 日内，必须根据《联邦上诉程序规则》第 6 条（c）向巡回法院书记员提交申请获准直接向上诉法院提起上诉的请求。

（经 Apr. 25, 2014, eff. Dec. 1, 2014 增补；经 Apr. 26, 2018, eff. Dec. 1, 2018. 修正）

第 8007 条　正在进行中的上诉的冻结；保证金；程序的中止

（a）首先在破产法院提起的动议。

（1）一般规定。通常情况下，当事人为申请以下救济必须首先在破产法院提起动议：

（A）a stay of a judgment, order, or decree of the bankruptcy court pending appeal;

（B）the approval of a bond or other security provided to obtain a stay of judgment;

（C）an order suspending, modifying, restoring, or granting an injunction while an appeal is pending; or

（D）the suspension or continuation of proceedings in a case or other relief permitted by subdivision（e）.

（2）*Time to File*. The motion may be made either before or after the notice of appeal is filed.

（b）MOTION IN THE DISTRICT COURT, THE BAP, OR THE COURT OF APPEALS ON DIRECT APPEAL.

（1）*Request for Relief*. A motion for the relief specified in subdivision（a）(1）— or to vacate or modify a bankruptcy court's order granting such relief—may be made in the court where the appeal is pending.

（2）*Showing or Statement Required*. The motion must:

（A）show that moving first in the bankruptcy court would be impracticable; or

（B）if a motion was made in the bankruptcy court, either state that the court has not yet ruled on the motion, or state that the court has ruled and set out any reasons given for the ruling.

（3）*Additional Content*. The motion must also include:

（A）the reasons for granting the relief requested and the facts relied upon;

（B）affidavits or other sworn statements supporting facts subject to dispute; and

（C）relevant parts of the record.

（4）*Serving Notice*. The movant must give reasonable notice of the motion to all parties.

（c）FILING A BOND OR OTHER SECURITY. The district court, BAP, or court of appeals may condition relief on filing a bond or other security with the bankruptcy court.

（d）BOND OR OTHER SECURITY FOR A TRUSTEE OR THE UNITED STATES. The court may require a trustee to file a bond or other security when the trustee appeals. A bond or other security is not required when an appeal is taken by the United States, its officer, or its agency or by direction of any department of the federal government.

美国联邦破产程序规则
（中英对照译本）

（A）上诉案件进行过程中对破产法院的判决、裁定或法令的冻结；

（B）准予通过提供押金或其他担保从而冻结判决；

（C）上诉案件进行过程中中止、变更、恢复或施加禁令的裁定；或

（D）本案程序的中止或继续或者附条（e）所准予的其他救济。

（2）提交时间。该动议在上诉通知书被提交之前或之后均可被提交。

（b）**在地区法院、破产上诉合议庭或上诉法院申请直接上诉的动议**。

（1）申请获得救济的请求。申请获得附条（a）（1）所述救济或者撤销或变更破产法院授予该种救济的裁定的动议可在正在进行上诉案件的法院作出。

（2）所要求的证明或声明。该动议必须符合以下条件：
（A）证明首先在破产法院提交该动议是不可行的；或
（B）若该动议曾被向破产法院提交，则须说明法院尚未就该动议作出裁决或法院已经就该动议作出裁决并列明作出该裁决的任何理由。

（3）其他内容。该动议也必须包含以下内容：
（A）授予所请求的救济的理由及所依据的事实；
（B）支持该争议所涉事实的宣誓书或其他宣誓声明；以及
（C）档案中的相关部分。
（4）送达通知。动议方必须向所有当事人就该动议发出合理的通知。

（c）**提交保证金或其他担保**。地区法院、破产上诉合议庭或上诉法院可以向破产法院提交保证金或其他担保为条件而授予救济。

（d）**托管人或美国提交保证金或其他担保**。当托管人提起上诉时，法院可要求托管人提交保证金或其他担保。当美国或其工作人员或其代理机关提起上诉，或者该上诉系在联邦政府的任何部门的指示下所提起时，无须提交保证金或其他担保。

(e) CONTINUATION OF PROCEEDINGS IN THE BANKRUPTCY COURT. Despite Rule 7062 and subject to the authority of the district court, BAP, or court of appeals, the bankruptcy court may:

(1) suspend or order the continuation of other proceedings in the case; or

(2) issue any other appropriate orders during the pendency of an appeal to protect the rights of all parties in interest.

(Added Apr. 25, 2014, eff. Dec. 1, 2014; amended Apr. 26, 2018, eff. Dec. 1, 2018.)

Rule 8008. Indicative Rulings

(a) RELIEF PENDING APPEAL. If a party files a timely motion in the bankruptcy court for relief that the court lacks authority to grant because of an appeal that has been docketed and is pending, the bankruptcy court may:

(1) defer considering the motion;

(2) deny the motion; or

(3) state that the court would grant the motion if the court where the appeal is pending remands for that purpose, or state that the motion raises a substantial issue.

(b) NOTICE TO THE COURT WHERE THE APPEAL IS PENDING. The movant must promptly notify the clerk of the court where the appeal is pending if the bankruptcy court states that it would grant the motion or that the motion raises a substantial issue.

(c) REMAND AFTER AN INDICATIVE RULING. If the bankruptcy court states that it would grant the motion or that the motion raises a substantial issue, the district court or BAP may remand for further proceedings, but it retains jurisdiction unless it expressly dismisses the appeal. If the district court or BAP remands but retains jurisdiction, the parties must promptly notify the clerk of that court when the bankruptcy court has decided the motion on remand.

(Added Apr. 25, 2014, eff. Dec. 1, 2014.)

Rule 8009. Record on Appeal; Sealed Documents

(a) DESIGNATING THE RECORD ON APPEAL; STATEMENT OF THE ISSUES.

(1) *Appellant.*

（e）**在破产法院的程序的继续**。尽管存在第 7062 条的规定，在地区法院、破产上诉合议庭或上诉法院的授权下，破产法院仍可实施以下各项：

（1）中止或裁定继续本案中的其他程序；或

（2）在上诉案件进行过程中签发任何其他适当的裁定以保护所有利害关系人的权利。

（经 Apr. 25, 2014, eff. Dec. 1, 2014 增补；经 Apr. 26, 2018, eff. Dec. 1, 2018. 修正）

第 8008 条　指示性裁决

（a）**上诉案件进行中的救济**。若当事人及时向破产法院提交动议申请获得某救济，但破产法院因某上诉案件已被立案并且正在进行中而无权授予该救济，则破产法院可实施以下各项：

（1）推迟审议该动议；

（2）否决该动议；或

（3）说明若正在进行上诉案件的法院为该动议得到处理而将该案发回，则法院将准予该动议，或者说明该动议引起了实质性争议。

（b）**向正在进行上诉案件的法院发出通知**。若破产法院说明其将准予该动议或该动议引起实质性争议，则动议方必须就此及时通知正在进行上诉案件的法院的书记员。

（c）**指示性裁决被作出后案件的发回**。若破产法院说明其将准予该动议或该动议引起实质性争议，则地区法院或破产上诉合议庭可出于推进程序的目的而将案件发回，但除非其明确驳回该上诉，否则其仍就上诉案件保留管辖权。若地区法院或破产上诉合议庭将案件发回但仍保留其管辖权，则当事人在破产法院就该动议作出决定时必须及时就此通知前述法院的书记员。

（经 Apr. 25, 2014, eff. Dec. 1, 2014. 增补）

第 8009 条　上诉档案；封存材料

（a）上诉档案的认定；问题说明。

（1）上诉人。

(A) The appellant must file with the bankruptcy clerk and serve on the appellee a designation of the items to be included in the record on appeal and a statement of the issues to be presented.

(B) The appellant must file and serve the designation and statement within 14 days after:

(i) the appellant's notice of appeal as of right becomes effective under Rule 8002; or

(ii) an order granting leave to appeal is entered.

A designation and statement served prematurely must be treated as served on the first day on which filing is timely.

(2) *Appellee and Cross-Appellant.* Within 14 days after being served, the appellee may file with the bankruptcy clerk and serve on the appellant a designation of additional items to be included in the record. An appellee who files a cross-appeal must file and serve a designation of additional items to be included in the record and a statement of the issues to be presented on the cross-appeal.

(3) *Cross-Appellee.* Within 14 days after service of the cross-appellant's designation and statement, a cross-appellee may file with the bankruptcy clerk and serve on the cross-appellant a designation of additional items to be included in the record.

(4) *Record on Appeal.* The record on appeal must include the following:

- docket entries kept by the bankruptcy clerk;
- items designated by the parties;
- the notice of appeal;
- the judgment, order, or decree being appealed;
- any order granting leave to appeal;
- any certification required for a direct appeal to the court of appeals;
- any opinion, findings of fact, and conclusions of law relating to the issues on appeal, including transcripts of all oral rulings;
- any transcript ordered under subdivision (b);
- any statement required by subdivision (c); and

美国联邦破产程序规则
（中英对照译本）

（A）上诉人必须向破产法院书记员提交并向被上诉人送达就各项材料将被列入上诉档案的认定以及对所要提出的问题的说明。

（B）上诉人必须在以下事件发生后 14 日内提交并送达该认定及说明：

（i）根据第 8002 条而生效的，上诉人就作为权利的上诉而发出的通知书；或

（ii）准予提起上诉的裁定被载入案卷时。
提前送达的认定和说明必须被视为在提交期间的首日即被及时提交。

（2）被上诉人及交叉上诉人。在被送达前述材料后 14 日内，被上诉人可向破产法院书记员提交并向上诉人送达将被列入上诉档案中的其他材料的认定。提交交叉上诉的被上诉人必须提交并送达将被列入上诉档案中的其他材料的认定以及在交叉上诉中所要提出的问题的说明。

（3）交叉被上诉人。在被送达交叉上诉人的指定及说明后 14 日内，交叉被上诉人可向破产法院书记员提交并向交叉上诉人送达将被列入上诉档案中的其他材料的认定。

（4）上诉档案。上诉档案必须包含以下各项：
- 破产法院书记员所保管的案件记录；
- 上诉通知书；
- 被上诉的判决、裁定或法令；
- 准予提起上诉的任何裁定；
- 为向上诉法院直接提起上诉所要求的任何证明；
- 与上诉所涉争议相关的任何观点、事实认定以及法律结论，包括对所有口头裁决的书面记录；
- 附条（b）所要求的任何书面记录；
- 附条（c）所要求的任何声明；以及

U.S. Federal Rules of Bankruptcy Procedure
(Chinese-English bilingual version)

- any additional items from the record that the court where the appeal is pending orders.

(5) *Copies for the Bankruptcy Clerk.* If paper copies are needed, a party filing a designation of items must provide a copy of any of those items that the bankruptcy clerk requests. If the party fails to do so, the bankruptcy clerk must prepare the copy at the party's expense.

(b) TRANSCRIPT OF PROCEEDINGS.

(1) *Appellant's Duty to Order.* Within the time period prescribed by subdivision (a) (1), the appellant must:

(A) order in writing from the reporter, as defined in Rule 8010 (a)(1), a transcript of such parts of the proceedings not already on file as the appellant considers necessary for the appeal, and file a copy of the order with the bankruptcy clerk; or

(B) file with the bankruptcy clerk a certificate stating that the appellant is not ordering a transcript.

(2) *Cross-Appellant's Duty to Order.* Within 14 days after the appellant files a copy of the transcript order or a certificate of not ordering a transcript, the appellee as cross-appellant must:

(A) order in writing from the reporter, as defined in Rule 8010 (a)(1), a transcript of such additional parts of the proceedings as the cross-appellant considers necessary for the appeal, and file a copy of the order with the bankruptcy clerk; or

(B) file with the bankruptcy clerk a certificate stating that the cross-appellant is not ordering a transcript.

(3) *Appellee's or Cross-Appellee's Right to Order.* Within 14 days after the appellant or cross-appellant files a copy of a transcript order or certificate of not ordering a transcript, the appellee or cross-appellee may order in writing from the reporter a transcript of such additional parts of the proceedings as the appellee or cross-appellee considers necessary for the appeal. A copy of the order must be filed with the bankruptcy clerk.

(4) *Payment.* At the time of ordering, a party must make satisfactory arrangements with the reporter for paying the cost of the transcript.

(5) *Unsupported Finding or Conclusion.* If the appellant intends to argue on

美国联邦破产程序规则
（中英对照译本）

- 正在进行上诉案件的法院所裁定载入该档案中的任何其他材料。
（5）向破产法院书记员提供的副本。若需要纸质副本，则提交材料认定的当事人必须向破产法院书记员提供其要求的其中任何材料的副本。若当事人未能提供该副本，则破产法院必须准备该副本，但由该当事人承担费用。

（b）**程序的书面记录**。
（1）上诉人裁定的义务。在附条（a）（1）规定的时间期间内，上诉人必须履行以下各项：

（A）书面裁定第8010条（a）（1）所述的记录人提供上诉人认为对上诉有必要但尚未存卷的程序的书面记录，并向破产法院的书记员提交该裁定的副本；或

（B）向破产法院的书记员提交说明上诉人并未裁定提供该书面记录的证明。

（2）交叉上诉人裁定的义务。在上诉人提交书面记录裁定的副本或并未裁定提供该书面记录的证明后14日内，被上诉人作为交叉上诉人必须履行以下各项：

（A）书面裁定第8010条（a）（1）所述的记录人提供交叉上诉人认为对上诉有必要的其他程序的书面记录，并向破产法院的书记员提交该裁定的副本；或

（B）向破产法院的书记员提交说明交叉上诉人并未裁定提供该书面记录的证明。

（3）被上诉人或交叉被上诉人裁定的权利。在上诉人或交叉上诉人提交书面记录裁定的副本或并未裁定提供该书面记录的证明后14日内，被上诉人或交叉被上诉人可书面裁定记录人提供被上诉人或交叉被上诉人认为对上诉有必要的其他程序的书面记录。该裁定的副本应被提交给破产法院书记员。

（4）支付。在作出裁定时，当事人必须与记录人间达成满意的安排以支付书面记录的费用。

（5）没有证据支持的认定或结论。若上诉人意图在上诉中辩称事实的认定或

U.S. Federal Rules of Bankruptcy Procedure
(Chinese-English bilingual version)

appeal that a finding or conclusion is unsupported by the evidence or is contrary to the evidence, the appellant must include in the record a transcript of all relevant testimony and copies of all relevant exhibits.

(c) STATEMENT OF THE EVIDENCE WHEN A TRANSCRIPT IS UNAVAILABLE. If a transcript of a hearing or trial is unavailable, the appellant may prepare a statement of the evidence or proceedings from the best available means, including the appellant's recollection. The statement must be filed within the time prescribed by subdivision (a)(1) and served on the appellee, who may serve objections or proposed amendments within 14 days after being served. The statement and any objections or proposed amendments must then be submitted to the bankruptcy court for settlement and approval. As settled and approved, the statement must be included by the bankruptcy clerk in the record on appeal.

(d) AGREED STATEMENT AS THE RECORD ON APPEAL. Instead of the record on appeal as defined in subdivision (a), the parties may prepare, sign, and submit to the bankruptcy court a statement of the case showing how the issues presented by the appeal arose and were decided in the bankruptcy court. The statement must set forth only those facts alleged and proved or sought to be proved that are essential to the court's resolution of the issues. If the statement is accurate, it—together with any additions that the bankruptcy court may consider necessary to a full presentation of the issues on appeal—must be approved by the bankruptcy court and must then be certified to the court where the appeal is pending as the record on appeal. The bankruptcy clerk must then transmit it to the clerk of that court within the time provided by Rule 8010. A copy of the agreed statement may be filed in place of the appendix required by Rule 8018(b) or, in the case of a direct appeal to the court of appeals, by F.R.App.P. 30.

(e) CORRECTING OR MODIFYING THE RECORD.

(1) *Submitting to the Bankruptcy Court*. If any difference arises about whether the record accurately discloses what occurred in the bankruptcy court, the difference must be submitted to and settled by the bankruptcy court and the record conformed accordingly. If an item has been improperly designated as part of the record on appeal, a party may move to strike that item.

法律结论并无证据支持或与证据相反，则上诉人必须在档案中载入所有相关证言的书面记录以及所有相关证物的副本。

（c）**无法提供书面记录时的证据声明**。若无法获得听证或庭审的书面记录，则上诉人可采取最佳可行手段以准备证据或程序的声明，包括上诉人的回忆。该声明必须在附条（a）(1)规定的时间内而被提交并被送达给被上诉人，而被上诉人可在被送达后14日内送达异议或其提出的修正。该声明以及任何异议或提出的修正其后必须被提交给破产法院以进行固定及批准。当进行固定及批准后，该声明必须由破产法院书记员载入上诉档案。

（d）**作为上诉档案的议定声明**。当事人也可准备、签署并向破产法院提交案件声明以说明上诉所涉争议是如何产生以及破产法院就此如何作出决定，以取代附条（a）所述的上诉档案。该声明仅能列明对法院解决该争议而言必不可少的所主张的事实以及被证明或试图证明的事实。若该声明准确无误，则其必须连同破产法院认为对于充分呈现上诉所涉争议所必需的任何补充事项一起被破产法院批准并经正在进行上诉案件的法院的认证从而作为上诉档案。破产法院书记员其后必须在第8010条规定的时间内将该声明移交给正在进行上诉案件的法院的书记员。该议定声明的副本可代替第8018条（b）所要求的附录而被提交，或者在直接提起上诉的情形中，代替《联邦上诉程序规则》第30条所要求的附录而被提交至上诉法院。

（e）**档案的修正或修改**。
（1）提交给破产法院。若就该档案是否准确地披露在破产法院所发生的事存在任何分歧，则该分歧应被提交至破产法院并由其解决，并且该档案也需进行相应的修改。若某材料被不当认定为上诉档案的一部分，则当事人可提出动议以撤回该材料。

(2) *Correcting in Other Ways.* If anything material to either party is omitted from or misstated in the record by error or accident, the omission or misstatement may be corrected, and a supplemental record may be certified and transmitted:

(A) on stipulation of the parties;

(B) by the bankruptcy court before or after the record has been forwarded; or

(C) by the court where the appeal is pending.

(3) *Remaining Questions.* All other questions as to the form and content of the record must be presented to the court where the appeal is pending.

(f) SEALED DOCUMENTS. A document placed under seal by the bankruptcy court may be designated as part of the record on appeal. In doing so, a party must identify it without revealing confidential or secret information, but the bankruptcy clerk must not transmit it to the clerk of the court where the appeal is pending as part of the record. Instead, a party must file a motion with the court where the appeal is pending to accept the document under seal. If the motion is granted, the movant must notify the bankruptcy court of the ruling, and the bankruptcy clerk must promptly transmit the sealed document to the clerk of the court where the appeal is pending.

(g) OTHER NECESSARY ACTIONS. All parties to an appeal must take any other action necessary to enable the bankruptcy clerk to assemble and transmit the record.

(Added Apr. 25, 2014, eff. Dec. 1, 2014.)

Rule 8010. Completing and Transmitting the Record

(a) REPORTER'S DUTIES.

(1) *Proceedings Recorded Without a Reporter Present.* If proceedings were recorded without a reporter being present, the person or service selected under bankruptcy court procedures to transcribe the recording is the reporter for purposes of this rule.

(2) *Preparing and Filing the Transcript.* The reporter must prepare and file a transcript as follows:

(A) Upon receiving an order for a transcript in accordance with Rule 8009 (b), the reportermust file in the bankruptcy court an acknowledgment of the request that shows when it was received, and when the reporter expects to have the transcript completed.

（2）以其他方式进行修正。若由于错误或意外而在档案中遗漏或错误陈述了对任意一方当事人而言重要的任何内容，则可修正该遗漏或错误陈述，并且补充档案可被通过以下方式而被证明并移交：

（A）应当事人的约定；

（B）在该档案已被转交前由破产法院进行证明并移交；或

（C）由正在进行上诉案件的法院进行证明并移交。

（3）剩余问题。有关档案的形式及内容的所有其他问题都必须被提交给正在进行上诉案件的法院。

（f）**封存材料**。由破产法院进行封闭式保存的材料也可被认定上诉档案的一部分。若作此认定，则当事人必须在不泄露机密或秘密信息的情况下对其进行确认，但破产法院书记员不得将其作为上诉档案的一部分而移交给正在进行上诉案件的法院的书记员。但是，当事人必须向正在进行上诉案件的法院提交动议以申请获得封存材料。若该动议得到准许，则动议方必须就该裁决通知破产法院，并且破产法院书记员必须及时将封存材料移交给正在进行上诉案件的法院的书记员。

（g）**其他必要措施**。上诉案件的所有当事人必须采取其他必要措施以使得破产法院书记员能够完成并移交该档案。

（经 Apr. 25, 2014, eff. Dec. 1, 2014. 增补）

第 8010 条　完成并移交档案

（a）**记录人的义务**。

（1）在没有记录人在场的情况下所记录的程序。若该程序系在没有记录人在场的情况下而被记录，则根据破产法院规则被选择书面制作该记录的人或公用事业机构就本条而言将被认定为记录人。

（2）准备并提交书面记录。记录人必须按照以下规定准备并提交书面记录：

（A）在收到第 8009 条（b）中的提供书面记录的裁定时，记录人必须向破产法院提交对该请求的知悉书，并载明其收到该裁定的时间以及记录人预计能够完成该书面记录的时间。

(B) After completing the transcript, the reporter must file it with the bankruptcy clerk, who will notify the district, BAP, or circuit clerk of its filing.

(C) If the transcript cannot be completed within 30 days after receiving the order, the reporter must request an extension of time from the bankruptcy clerk. The clerk must enter on the docket and notify the parties whether the extension is granted.

(D) If the reporter does not file the transcript on time, the bankruptcy clerk must notify the bankruptcy judge.

(b) CLERK'S DUTIES.

(1) *Transmitting the Record—In General*. Subject to Rule 8009 (f) and subdivision (b) (5) of this rule, when the record is complete, the bankruptcy clerk must transmit to the clerk of the court where the appeal is pending either the record or a notice that the record is available electronically.

(2) *Multiple Appeals*. If there are multiple appeals from a judgment, order, or decree, the bankruptcy clerk must transmit a single record.

(3) *Receiving the Record*. Upon receiving the record or notice that it is available electronically, the district, BAP, or circuit clerk must enter that information on the docket and promptly notify all parties to the appeal.

(4) *If Paper Copies Are Ordered*. If the court where the appeal is pending directs that paper copies of the record be provided, the clerk of that court must so notify the appellant. If the appellant fails to provide them, the bankruptcy clerk must prepare them at the appellant's expense.

(5) *When Leave to Appeal is Requested*. Subject to subdivision (c) , if a motion for leave to appeal has been filed under Rule 8004, the bankruptcy clerk must prepare and transmit the record only after the district court, BAP, or court of appeals grants leave.

(c) RECORD FOR A PRELIMINARY MOTION IN THE DISTRICT COURT, BAP, OR COURT OF APPEALS. This subdivision (c) applies if, before the record is transmitted, a party moves in the district court, BAP, or court of appeals for any of the following relief:

- leave to appeal;
- dismissal;

（B）在完成该书面记录后，记录人必须将其提交给破产法院书记员，而破产法院书记员将就此通知地区法院、破产上诉合议庭或巡回法院的书记员。

（C）若记录人无法在收到该裁定后30日内完成书面记录，则记录人必须向破产法院书记员申请延长该期间。书记员必须在案卷中载明并向当事人发出通知以说明是否准予延长该期间。

（D）若记录人未能按时提交书面记录，则破产法院书记员必须通知破产法官。

（b）**书记员的义务**。

（1）移交档案的一般规定。在符合第8009条（f）及本条的附条（b）(5)规定的情况下，当档案完成时，破产法院书记员必须将档案或档案可以通过电子方式提供的通知移交给正在进行上诉案件的法院的书记员。

（2）多项上诉。若就某判决、裁定或法令存在多项上诉，则破产法院必须移交一份档案。

（3）接收档案。在收到档案或通过电子方式提供档案的通知时，地区法院、破产上诉合议庭或巡回法院的书记员必须在案卷中载入该信息并及时通知上诉案件的所有当事人。

（4）若被裁定提供纸质副本。若正在进行上诉案件的法院裁定提供该档案的纸质副本，则该法院的书记员应就此通知上诉人。若上诉人未能提供该副本，则破产法院书记员必须准备该副本并由上诉人承担费用。

（5）当有人请求获准提起上诉时。在符合附条（c）规定的情况下，若有人根据第8004条提交申请获准提起上诉的动议，则破产法院书记员仅在地区法院、破产上诉合议庭或上诉法院准予该动议后才必须准备并移交该档案。

（c）**在向地区法院、破产上诉合议庭或上诉法院提起初步动议的情况下有关档案的规定**。若在档案被移交前，某当事人在地区法院、破产上诉合议庭或上诉法院就以下任意救济提起动议，则适用本款规定：

- 申请提起上诉；
- 驳回；

- a stay pending appeal;
- approval of a bond or other security provided to obtain a stay of judgment; or
- any other intermediate order.

The bankruptcy clerk must then transmit to the clerk of the court where the relief is sought any parts of the record designated by a party to the appeal or a notice that those parts are available electronically.

(Added Apr. 25, 2014, eff. Dec. 1, 2014; amended Apr. 26, 2018, eff. Dec. 1, 2018.)

Rule 8011. Filing and Service; Signature

(a) FILING.

(1) *With the Clerk*. A document required or permitted to be filed in a district court or BAP must be filed with the clerk of that court.

(2) *Method and Timeliness*.

(A) *Nonelectronic Filing*.

(i) *In General*. For a document not filed electronically, filing may be accomplished by mail addressed to the clerk of the district court or BAP. Except as provided in subdivision (a)(2)(A)(ii) and (iii), filing is timely only if the clerk receives the document within the time fixed for filing.

(ii) *Brief or Appendix*. A brief or appendix not filed electronically is also timely filed if, on or before the last day for filing, it is:

- mailed to the clerk by first-class mail—or other class of mail that is at least as expeditious—postage prepaid; or
- dispatched to a third-party commercial carrier for delivery within 3 days to the clerk.

(iii) *Inmate Filing*. If an institution has a system designed for legal mail, an inmate confined there must use that system to receive the benefit of this Rule 8011 (a)(2)(A)(iii). A document not filed electronically by an inmate confined in an institution is timely if it is deposited in the institution's internal mailing system on or before the last day for filing and:

- it is accompanied by a declaration in compliance with 28 U.S.C. §1746—or a

- 上诉案件进行过程中的冻结；
- 准予通过提供保证金或其他担保而获得判决的冻结；或
- 任何其他临时裁定。

破产法院书记员其后必须将上诉案件的当事人所指定的部分档案或通过电子方式提供该部分档案的通知移交给向其寻求救济的法院的书记员。

（经 Apr. 25, 2014, eff. Dec. 1, 2014 增补；经 Apr. 26, 2018, eff. Dec. 1, 2018. 修正）

第 8011 条　提交及送达；签名

（a）提交。

（1）向书记员提交。被要求或被准予向地区法院或破产上诉合议庭提交材料必须被提交给前述法院的书记员。

（2）方式及时间。

（A）以非电子方式提交。

（i）一般规定。若以非电子方式提交材料，则可通过邮寄给地区法院或破产上诉合议庭的书记员来完成。除附条（a）（2）（A）（ii）及（iii）另有规定外，仅当书记员在规定的提交期间内收到该材料时，才被视为及时提交该材料。

（ii）摘要或附录。针对以非电子方式提交的摘要或附录，若其在提交期间内最后一日当日或之前符合以下条件，则也应被视为已被及时提交：

- 已以一级邮件的方式或至少同样快捷的其他类别的邮件邮寄给书记员，并且已支付邮费；或
- 已交付给第三方商业承运人以在 3 日内交付给书记员。

（iii）由犯人提交材料。若某机构有设计用于接收或邮寄合法邮件的系统，则被拘役在该机构的犯人必须使用该系统从而得以适用第 8002 条（a）（2）（A）（iii）并获益。就被拘役在该机构的犯人以非电子方式所提交的材料而言，若该材料在提交期间最后一日当日或之前被投递到该机构的内部邮件系统并且符合以下条件，则该通知应被视为已被及时提交：

- 附有列有投递日期并注明该一级邮件的费用已被预付的根据《美国联邦法

notarized statement—setting out the date of deposit and stating that first-class postage is being prepaid; or evidence (such as a postmark or date stamp) showing that the notice was so deposited and that postage was prepaid; or

- the appellate court exercises its discretion to permit the later filing of a declaration or notarized statement that satisfies this Rule 8011 (a)(2)(A)(iii).

(B) *Electronic Filing.*

(i) By a Represented Person—Generally Required; Exceptions. An entity represented by an attorney must file electronically, unless nonelectronic filing is allowed by the court for good cause or is allowed or required by local rule.

(ii) By an Unrepresented Individual—When Allowed or Required. An individual not represented by an attorney:

- may file electronically only if allowed by court order or by local rule; and
- may be required to file electronically only by court order, or by a local rule that includes reasonable exceptions.

(iii) *Same as a Written Paper.* A document filed electronically is a written paper for purposes of these rules.

(C) *Copies. If* a document is filed electronically, no paper copy is required. If a document is filed by mail or delivery to the district court or BAP, no additional copies are required. But the district court or BAP may require by local rule or by order in a particular case the filing or furnishing of a specified number of paper copies.

(3) *Clerk's Refusal of Documents.* The court's clerk must not refuse to accept for filing any document transmitted for that purpose solely because it is not presented in proper form as required by these rules or by any local rule or practice.

(b) SERVICE OF ALL DOCUMENTS REQUIRED. Unless a rule requires service by the clerk, a party must, at or before the time of the filing of a document, serve it on the other parties to the appeal. Service on a party represented by counsel must be made on the party's counsel.

(c) MANNER OF SERVICE.

(1) *Nonelectronic Service.* Nonelectronic service may be by any of the following:

(A) personal delivery;

美国联邦破产程序规则
（中英对照译本）

典》第 28 篇第 1746 条所作的说明或者经公证的声明；或者证明该通知已被以前述方式而被投递并且其费用已被预付的证据（如邮戳或日期戳）；或者

- 上诉法院行使其自由裁量权并准予其迟延提交符合第 8011 条（a）(2)（A）(iii) 的条件的说明或经公证的声明。

（B）以电子方式提交。

（i）由被代表的人提交——般规定；例外。由律师所代表的实体必须以电子方式提交材料，除非法院出于正当事由准许或地方规则要求其以非电子方式提交。

（ii）由未被代表的自然人提交——当被准许或要求时。未由律师所代表的自然人：

- 仅当法院裁定或地方规则准许时才可以电子方式提交；并且
- 仅当法院裁定或地方规则作此要求并且载有合理的例外规定时，才可被要求以电子方式提交。

（iii）作为书面材料。就本法而言，以电子方式而被提交的材料即为书面材料。

（C）副本。若某材料被以电子方式提交，则无须提交纸质副本。若某材料系通过向地区法院或破产上诉合议庭邮寄或交付的方式而被提交，则无须提交其他纸质副本。但地区法院或破产上诉合议庭可通过地方规则或裁定而在具体案件中要求其提交或提供特定数量的纸质副本。

（3）书记员拒绝接受材料。法院书记员不得仅因被递交的材料未能按照本法或任何地方规则或实践所规定的适当方式而被提交因而拒绝接受前述材料。

（b）**所有被要求的材料的送达**。除非有规定要求由书记员进行送达，否则当事人必须在提交材料时或之前将其送达给上诉案件的其他当事人。向由律师所代表的当事人送达材料必须送达给该当事人的律师。

（c）**送达的方式**。

（1）以非电子方式送达。以非电子方式送达材料可通过以下任意方式实现：

（A）直接送达；

U.S. Federal Rules of Bankruptcy Procedure
(Chinese-English bilingual version)

(B) mail; or

(C) third-party commercial carrier for delivery within 3 days.

(2) *Electronic Service*. Electronic service may be made by sending a document to a registered user by filing it with the court's electronic-filing system or by using other electronic means that the person served consented to in writing.

(3) *When Service Is Complete*. Service by electronic means is complete on filing or sending, unless the person making service receives notice that the document was not received by the person served. Service by mail or by commercial carrier is complete on mailing or delivery to the carrier.

(d) PROOF OF SERVICE.

(1) *What Is Required*. A document presented for filing must contain either of the following if it was served other than through the court's electronic-filing system:

(A) an acknowledgment of service by the person served; or

(B) proof of service consisting of a statement by the person who made service certifying:

(i) the date and manner of service;

(ii) the names of the persons served; and

(iii) the mail or electronic address, the fax number, or the address of the place of delivery, as appropriate for the manner of service, for each person served.

(2) *Delayed Proof*. The district or BAP clerk may permit documents to be filed without acknowledgment or proof of service, but must require the acknowledgment or proof to be filed promptly thereafter.

(3) *Brief or Appendix*. When a brief or appendix is filed, the proof of service must also state the date and manner by which it was filed.

(e) SIGNATURE. Every document filed electronically must include the electronic signature of the person filing it or, if the person is represented, the electronic signature of counsel. A filing made through a person's electronic-filing account and authorized by that person, together with that person's name on a signature block, constitutes the person's signature. Every document filed in paper form must be signed by the person filing the document or, if the person is represented, by counsel.

（B）邮寄；或

（C）由第三方商业承运人在3日内交付。

（2）以电子方式送达。以电子方式送达可通过将材料提交至法院的电子提交系统从而将材料发送给注册用户来实现，或者使用被送达人书面同意的其他电子方式。

（3）送达完成的时间。就以电子方式送达而言，除非送达材料的人收到被送达人并未收到该材料的通知，否则当材料被提交或被发送时，该送达即已完成。就以邮寄方式或由商业承运人进行的送达而言，当材料被邮寄或被交付给承运人时，该送达即已完成。

（d）**送达证明**。

（1）所需要的信息。若某材料并非通过法院的电子提交系统而被提交，则将被提交的材料必须含有以下任一内容：

（A）被送达人出具的送达确认书；或

（B）送达证明，该证明应载有送达人证明以下各项的声明：

（i）送达的日期及方式；

（ii）被送达人的姓名；以及

（iii）所有被送达人的邮寄或电子地址、传真号码或交付地址（视送达方式而定）。

（2）证明的迟延提交。地区法院或破产上诉合议庭的书记员可在未被提供确认书或送达证明的情况下接收被提交的材料，但必须要求此后及时提交该确认书或证明。

（3）摘要或附录。当摘要或附录被提交时，送达证明也应注明被提交的日期及方式。

（e）**签名**。所有被以电子方式提交的材料均必须载有提交该材料的人的电子签名，若此人系由律师所代表，则应载有其律师的电子签名。通过此人的电子提交账户所制作的并经此人授权的文件，与此人在签名栏上的姓名一同构成此人的签名。所有被以纸质形式提交的材料必须经提交该材料的人的签署，若此人系由律师所代表，则应由该律师签署。

U.S. Federal Rules of Bankruptcy Procedure
(Chinese-English bilingual version)

(Added Apr. 25, 2014, eff. Dec. 1, 2014; amended Apr. 26, 2018, eff. Dec. 1, 2018.)

Rule 8012. Corporate Disclosure Statement

(a) NONGOVERNMENTAL CORPORATIONS. Any nongovernmental corporation that is a party to a proceeding in the district court or BAP must file a statement that identifies any parent corporation and any publicly held corporation that owns 10% or more of its stock or states that there is no such corporation. The same requirement applies to a nongovernmental corporation that seeks to intervene.

(b) DISCLOSURE ABOUT THE DEBTOR. The debtor, the trustee, or, if neither is a party, the appellant must file a statement that:

(1) identifies each debtor not named in the caption; and

(2) for each debtor that is a corporation, discloses the information required by Rule 8012 (a).

(c) TIME TO FILE; SUPPLEMENTAL FILING. A Rule 8012 statement must:

(1) be filed with the principal brief or upon filing a motion, response, petition, or answer in the district court or BAP, whichever occurs first, unless a local rule requires earlier filing;

(2) be included before the table of contents in the principal brief; and

(3) be supplemented whenever the information required by Rule 8012 changes.

(Added Apr. 25, 2014, eff. Dec. 1, 2014; amended Apr. 27, 2020, eff. Dec. 1, 2020.)

Rule 8013. Motions; Intervention

(a) CONTENTS OF A MOTION; RESPONSE; REPLY.

(1) *Request for Relief.* A request for an order or other relief is made by filing a motion with the district or BAP clerk.

(2) *Contents of a Motion.*

(A) *Grounds and the Relief Sought.* A motion must state with particularity the grounds for the motion, the relief sought, and the legal argument necessary to support it.

(B) *Motion to Expedite an Appeal.* A motion to expedite an appeal must explain what justifies considering the appeal ahead of other matters. If the district court or BAP

美国联邦破产程序规则
（中英对照译本）

（经 Apr. 25, 2014, eff. Dec. 1, 2014 增补；经 Apr. 26, 2018, eff. Dec. 1, 2018. 修正）

第 8012 条　公司披露声明

（a）**非政府性公司**。任何出席地区法院或破产上诉合议庭的非政府性公司当事人均必须提交声明以列明其任何母公司或持有其 10% 或 10% 以上的股份的公众公司，或者注明并不存在该类公司。该要求同样适用于寻求介入的非政府性公司。

（b）**关于债务人的披露**。债务人、托管人或上诉方（如债务人和托管人均非上诉方）须提交符合以下条件的声明：
（1）列明未在抬头提及的各债务人；并且
（2）针对各公司债务人，披露第 8012 条（a）要求的信息。

（c）**提交的时间；补充提交**。第 8012 条规定的声明应当：
（1）与主要辩护状一起提交或在向地区法院或破产上诉合议庭提交动议、答复、申请或答辩时提交（以先发生者为准），除非当地规则要求提前提交；
（2）列在主要辩护状的目录之前；并且
（3）当第 8012 条要求载明的信息发生变化时进行补充。

（经 Apr. 25, 2014, eff. Dec. 1, 2014; amended Apr. 27, 2020, eff. Dec. 1, 2020. 增补）

第 8013 条　动议；介入

（a）**动议的内容；答复；回复**。
（1）救济请求。若要申请裁定或提供其他救济，则应向地区法院或破产上诉合议庭的书记员提交动议。
（2）动议的内容。
（A）依据以及所寻求的救济。该动议必须具体说明该动议的依据、所寻求的救济以及支持该动议的必要法律论据。
（B）上诉案件加速进行的动议。申请加速进行上诉案件的动议必须解释在处理其他事项前首先审议上诉案件的正当性。若地区法院或破产上诉合议庭准予该

grants the motion, it may accelerate the time to transmit the record, the deadline for filing briefs and other documents, oral argument, and the resolution of the appeal. A motion to expedite an appeal may be filed as an emergency motion under subdivision (d).

(C) *Accompanying Documents.*

(i) Any affidavit or other document necessary to support a motion must be served and filed with the motion.

(ii) An affidavit must contain only factual information, not legal argument.

(iii) A motion seeking substantive relief must include a copy of the bankruptcy court's judgment, order, or decree, and any accompanying opinion as a separate exhibit.

(D) *Documents Barred or Not Required.*

(i) A separate brief supporting or responding to a motion must not be filed.

(ii) Unless the court orders otherwise, a notice of motion or a proposed order is not required.

(3) *Response and Reply; Time to File.* Unless the district court or BAP orders otherwise,

(A) any party to the appeal may file a response to the motion within 7 days after service of the motion; and

(B) the movant may file a reply to a response within 7 days after service of the response, but may only address matters raised in the response.

(b) DISPOSITION OF A MOTION FOR A PROCEDURAL ORDER. The district court or BAP may rule on a motion for a procedural order—including a motion under Rule 9006 (b) or (c)—at any time without awaiting a response. A party adversely affected by the ruling may move to reconsider, vacate, or modify it within 7 days after the procedural order is served.

(c) ORAL ARGUMENT. A motion will be decided without oral argument unless the district court or BAP orders otherwise.

(d) EMERGENCY MOTION.

(1) *Noting the Emergency.* When a movant requests expedited action on a motion because irreparable harm would occur during the time needed to consider a response, the movant must insert the word "Emergency" before the title of the motion.

动议，则将加速移交档案的时间并将提交摘要以及其他材料、进行口头辩论以及解决上诉案件的截止日期提前。申请加速进行上诉案件的动议可将其作为紧急动议而根据附条（d）提交。

（C）附随材料。

（i）支持该动议的任何必要的宣誓书或其他材料均应与该动议一同被送达并提交。

（ii）宣誓书仅能含有事实信息，而不得包含法律论据。

（iii）寻求实质性救济的动议必须含有破产法院的判决、裁定或法令的副本并将任何附随性观点作为单独证据。

（D）被禁止提交或无须提交的材料。

（i）不得提交支持或答复该动议的单独摘要。

（ii）除非法院作出其他裁定，否则无须提交就该动议或拟议裁定的通知。

（3）答复及回复；提交的时间。除非地区法院或破产上诉合议庭作出其他裁定，否则，

（A）上诉案件的任意当事人均可在该动议被送达后7日内提交就该动议所作的答复；并且

（B）动议方可在前述答复被送达后7日内就该答复提交回复，但仅能针对在答复中被提出的事项。

（b）**对申请作出程序性裁定的动议的处置**。地区法院或破产上诉合议庭可随时就申请作出程序性裁定的动议作出裁决［包括第9006条（b）或（c）所述的动议］，而无须等待当事人作出答复。受到该裁决不利影响的当事人可在该程序裁定被送达后7日内提出动议以申请重新审议、撤销或变更该裁决。

（c）**口头辩论**。除非地区法院或破产上诉合议庭作出其他裁定，否则法院将直接就该动议作出决定而无须进行口头辩论。

（d）**紧急动议**。

（1）标注紧急。当动议方申请加速处理该动议以避免在就审议答复所需的时间内发生不可弥补的损害时，动议方必须在该动议的标题前标明"紧急"一词。

(2) *Contents of the Motion.* The emergency motion must

(A) be accompanied by an affidavit setting out the nature of the emergency;

(B) state whether all grounds for it were submitted to the bankruptcy court and, if not, why the motion should not be remanded for the bankruptcy court to consider;

(C) include the e-mail addresses, office addresses, and telephone numbers of moving counsel and, when known, of opposing counsel and any unrepresented parties to the appeal; and

(D) be served as prescribed by Rule 8011.

(3) *Notifying Opposing Parties.* Before filing an emergency motion, the movant must make every practicable effort to notify opposing counsel and any unrepresented parties in time for them to respond. The affidavit accompanying the emergency motion must state when and how notice was given or state why giving it was impracticable.

(e) POWER OF A SINGLE BAP JUDGE TO ENTERTAIN A MOTION.

(1) *Single Judge's Authority.* A BAP judge may act alone on any motion, but may not dismiss or otherwise determine an appeal, deny a motion for leave to appeal, or deny a motion for a stay pending appeal if denial would make the appeal moot.

(2) *Reviewing a Single Judge's Action.* The BAP may review a single judge's action, either on its own motion or on a party's motion.

(f) FORM OF DOCUMENTS; LENGTH LIMITS; NUMBER OF COPIES.

(1) *Format of a Paper Document.* Rule 27 (d) (1) F.R.App.P. applies in the district court or BAP to a paper version of a motion, response, or reply.

(2) *Format of an Electronically Filed Document.* A motion, response, or reply filed electronically must comply with the requirements for a paper version regarding covers, line spacing, margins, typeface, and type style. It must also comply with the length limits under paragraph (3).

(3) *Length Limits.* Except by the district court's or BAP's permission, and excluding the accompanying documents authorized by subdivision (a) (2) (C):

(A) a motion or a response to a motion produced using a computer must include a certificate under Rule 8015 (h) and not exceed 5,200 words;

美国联邦破产程序规则
（中英对照译本）

（2）动议的内容。紧急动议必须符合以下条件：

（A）附有列明紧急情况的性质的宣誓书；

（B）说明该动议的所有依据是否已被提交至破产法院，以及在未提交的情况下，该动议不应被发回破产法院进行审议的原因；

（C）载明动议方律师的电子邮箱地址、办公室地址以及电话号码，以及在获知上诉案件的反对方律师以及未被代表的当事人的前述信息时，还应载明前述主体的前述信息；并且

（D）以第8011条规定的方式而送达。

（3）通知反对方。在提交紧急动议前，动议方必须尽一切可能的努力及时通知反对方律师以及未被代表的当事人以使其作出答复。紧急动议所附的宣誓书必须注明发出该通知的时间及方式或者说明难以发出该通知的原因。

（e）**破产上诉合议庭独任法官处理动议的权力**。

（1）独任法官的权力。破产上诉合议庭的法官可单独就任何动议采取措施，但不得驳回或以其他方式就上诉作出决定、否决申请获准提起上诉的动议或否决申请在上诉案件进行期间进行冻结的动议（若该否决将涉及对上诉案件的讨论）。

（2）审查独任法官的行为。破产上诉合议庭可自己提出动议或应当事人的动议审查独任法官的行为。

（f）**材料的形式；篇幅限制；副本数量**。

（1）纸质材料的格式。在地区法院或破产上诉合议庭，《联邦上诉程序规则》第27条（d）（1）适用于动议、答复或回复的纸质版本。

（2）以电子方式被提交的材料的格式。以电子方式被提交的动议、答复或回复在封面、行距、页边距、字体和字型方面也必须符合就纸质版本所规定的要求。其也必须符合第（3）款规定的篇幅限制。

（3）篇幅限制。除非地区法院或破产上诉合议庭作出其他许可，否则除附条（a）（2）（C）所述的附随材料外，其他材料必须符合以下条件：

（A）使用电脑而完成的动议或对动议所作的答复必须载有第8015条（h）中的证明并且不得超过5,200字；

(B) a handwritten or typewritten motion or a response to a motion must not exceed 20 pages;

(C) a reply produced using a computer must include a certificate under Rule 8015 (h) and not exceed 2,600 words; and

(D) a handwritten or typewritten reply must not exceed 10 pages.

(4) *Paper Copies.* Paper copies must be provided only if required by local rule or by an order in a particular case.

(g) INTERVENING IN AN APPEAL. Unless a statute provides otherwise, an entity that seeks to intervene in an appeal pending in the district court or BAP must move for leave to intervene and serve a copy of the motion on the parties to the appeal. The motion or other notice of intervention authorized by statute must be filed within 30 days after the appeal is docketed. It must concisely state the movant's interest, the grounds for intervention, whether intervention was sought in the bankruptcy court, why intervention is being sought at this stage of the proceeding, and why participating as an amicus curiae would not be adequate.

(Added Apr. 25, 2014, eff. Dec. 1, 2014; amended Apr. 26, 2018, eff. Dec. 1, 2018; Apr. 27, 2020,eff. Dec. 1, 2020.)

Rule 8014. Briefs

(a) APPELLANT'S BRIEF. The appellant's brief must contain the following under appropriate headings and in the order indicated:

(1) a corporate disclosure statement, if required by Rule 8012;

(2) a table of contents, with page references;

(3) a table of authorities—cases (alphabetically arranged), statutes, and other authorities—with references to the pages of the brief where they are cited;

(4) a jurisdictional statement, including:

(A) the basis for the bankruptcy court's subject-matter jurisdiction, with citations to applicable statutory provisions and stating relevant facts establishing jurisdiction;

(B) the basis for the district court's or BAP's jurisdiction, with citations to applicable statutory provisions and stating relevant facts establishing jurisdiction;

（B）手写或打印的动议或对动议所作的答复不得超过20页；

（C）使用电脑而完成的回复必须载有第8015条（h）中的证明并且不得超过2,600字；

（D）手写或打印的回复不得超过10页。

（4）纸质副本。仅当在具体案件中地方规则或裁定作此要求时，才必须提供纸质副本。

（g）**介入上诉案件**。除非法律作出其他规定，否则意图介入在地区法院或破产上诉合议庭进行的上诉案件的实体必须提出动议以申请获准介入此案并将该动议的副本送达给上诉案件的所有当事人。该动议或法律所准许的其他介入通知书必须在上诉案件被立案后30日内而被提交。其必须简要说明动议方的利害关系、介入的依据、是否曾在破产法院寻求介入该案、在该诉讼阶段寻求介入的原因以及作为法庭之友参加案件并不适当的原因。

（经 Apr. 25, 2014, eff. Dec. 1, 2014 增补；经 Apr. 26, 2018, eff. Dec. 1, 2018; Apr. 27, 2020,eff. Dec. 1, 2020. 修正）

第8014条　摘要

（a）**上诉人的摘要**。上诉人的摘要必须在相应的标题下按指定的顺序载有以下内容：

（1）公司披露声明，若第8012条对此作出要求；

（2）带有页码的目录；

（3）参考资料［案件（按字母顺序排列）、法律以及其他资料］，标明在该摘要中其被引用的页面；

（4）管辖权声明，包括以下各项：

（A）破产法院具有标的物管辖权的依据，并引用相应的法律规定及说明成立管辖权的相关事实；

（B）地区法院或破产上诉合议庭具有管辖权的依据，并引用相应的法律规定及说明成立管辖权的相关事实；

(C) the filing dates establishing the timeliness of the appeal; and

(D) an assertion that the appeal is from a final judgment, order, or decree, or information establishing the district court's or BAP's jurisdiction on another basis;

(5) a statement of the issues presented and, for each one, a concise statement of the applicable standard of appellate review;

(6) a concise statement of the case setting out the facts relevant to the issues submitted for review, describing the relevant procedural history, and identifying the rulings presented for review, with appropriate references to the record;

(7) a summary of the argument, which must contain a succinct, clear, and accurate statement of the arguments made in the body of the brief, and which must not merely repeat the argument headings;

(8) the argument, which must contain the appellant's contentions and the reasons for them, with citations to the authorities and parts of the record on which the appellant relies;

(9) a short conclusion stating the precise relief sought; and

(10) the certificate of compliance, if required by Rule 8015 (a) (7) or (b).

(b) APPELLEE'S BRIEF. The appellee's brief must conform to the requirements of subdivision (a) (1) - (8) and (10), except that none of the following need appear unless the appellee is dissatisfied with the appellant's statement:

(1) the jurisdictional statement;

(2) the statement of the issues and the applicable standard of appellate review; and

(3) the statement of the case.

(c) REPLY BRIEF. The appellant may file a brief in reply to the appellee's brief. A reply brief must comply with the requirements of subdivision (a) (2) - (3).

(d) STATUTES, RULES, REGULATIONS, OR SIMILAR AUTHORITY. If the court's determination of the issues presented requires the study of the Code or other statutes, rules, regulations, or similar authority, the relevant parts must be set out in the brief or in an addendum.

(e) BRIEFS IN A CASE INVOLVING MULTIPLE APPELLANTS OR APPELLEES. In a case involving more than one appellant or appellee, including

（C）确定上诉时间线的提交日期；以及

（D）认定该上诉系针对最终判决、裁定或法令的主张或者地区法院或破产上诉合议庭具有管辖权的其他依据的有关信息；

（5）对所提出的问题的陈述，并就每项问题，简要说明适用的上诉审查标准；

（6）对案件的简要陈述，该陈述应在对档案进行相应引用的情况下列明与被提交审查的问题有关的事实、描述相关程序的历史并确定提交审查的裁决；

（7）论点摘要，该摘要必须简短、清楚且准确地陈述在摘要的正文所提出的论点，而不得仅仅是重复论点标题；

（8）论点，其必须在对上诉人所依据的参考资料以及部分档案进行引用的情况下说明上诉人的观点及其理由；

（9）说明所寻求的确切救济的简短结论；以及

（10）合规证明，若第8015条（a）（7）或（b）对此作出要求。

（b）**被上诉人的摘要**。被上诉人的摘要必须符合附条（a）（1）至（8）以及（10）的要求，但除非被上诉人对上诉人的陈述并不满意，否则无须提供以下各项：

（1）管辖权声明；

（2）对问题以及适用的上诉审查标准的陈述；以及

（3）对案件的陈述。

（c）**回复摘要**。上诉人可针对被上诉人摘要作出回复摘要。该回复摘要必须符合附条（a）（2）至（3）的要求。

（d）**法律、规则、法规或类似规范性文件**。若法院就所提出的问题作出裁定需要对法典或其他法律、规则或类似规范性文件进行研究，则相关部分必须被列入摘要或附录。

（e）**在涉及多名上诉人或被上诉人的案件中的摘要**。在涉及多名上诉人或被上诉人的案件中，包括在合并审理的案件中，任何数量的上诉人或被上诉人均可

consolidated cases, any number of appellants or appellees may join in a brief, and any party may adopt by reference a part of another's brief. Parties may also join in reply briefs.

(f) CITATION OF SUPPLEMENTAL AUTHORITIES. If pertinent and significant authorities come to a party's attention after the party's brief has been filed—or after oral argument but before a decision—a party may promptly advise the district or BAP clerk by a signed submission setting forth the citations. The submission, which must be served on the other parties to the appeal, must state the reasons for the supplemental citations, referring either to the pertinent page of a brief or to a point argued orally. The body of the submission must not exceed 350 words. Any response must be made within 7 days after the party is served, unless the court orders otherwise, and must be similarly limited.

(Added Apr. 25, 2014, eff. Dec. 1, 2014.)

Rule 8015. Form and Length of Briefs; Form of Appendices and Other Papers

(a) PAPER COPIES OF A BRIEF. If a paper copy of a brief may or must be filed, the following provisions apply:

(1) *Reproduction.*

(A) A brief may be reproduced by any process that yields a clear black image on light paper. The paper must be opaque and unglazed. Only one side of the paper may be used.

(B) Text must be reproduced with a clarity that equals or exceeds the output of a laser printer.

(C) Photographs, illustrations, and tables may be reproduced by any method that results in a good copy of the original. A glossy finish is acceptable if the original is glossy.

(2) *Cover.* The front cover of a brief must contain:

(A) the number of the case centered at the top;

(B) the name of the court;

(C) the title of the case as prescribed by Rule 8003 (d)(2) or 8004 (c)(2);

(D) the nature of the proceeding and the name of the court below;

合并其摘要，并且任意当事人均可通过引用而采用他人摘要的一部分。各方当事人也可合并其回复摘要。

（f）**对补充参考资料的引用**。若当事人在提交摘要或进行口头辩论后，但在决定被作出前注意到其他相关且重要的参考资料，则当事人可通过提交引用该资料的签署文件从而及时对地区法院或破产上诉合议庭的书记员提出建议。该文件应被送达给该上诉案件的其他当事人，且必须说明进行补充引用的原因并注明引用该资料的摘要的页面或口头辩论的论点。该文件的正文不得超过350字。除非法院作出其他裁定（该裁定也必须规定有类似的限制），否则当事人必须在被送达后7日内作出答复。

（经 Apr. 25, 2014, eff. Dec. 1, 2014. 增补）

第8015条　摘要的格式及篇幅；附录及其他文件的格式

（a）**摘要的纸质副本**。若可提交或必须提交纸质副本，则适用以下规定：

（1）复制。
（A）可以通过能够在轻型纸上产生清晰黑色图像的任何过程来复制摘要。该纸张必须是不透明且无光的。该纸张只能被单面使用。

（B）文本的复制清晰度必须等于或超过激光打印机的输出清晰度。

（C）照片、插图及目录可通过任何能产生原件的优质副本的方式进行复制。若原件是光面的，则光面副本也可被接受。

（2）封面。摘要的封面必须包括以下内容：
（A）在最上方中部注明案件编号；
（B）法院名称；
（C）第8003条（d）（2）或第8004条（c）（2）所规定的案件的标题；
（D）程序的性质并在下面载明法院名称；

(E) the title of the brief, identifying the party or parties for whom the brief is filed; and

(F) the name, office address, telephone number, and e-mail address of counsel representing the party for whom the brief is filed.

(3) *Binding*. The brief must be bound in any manner that is secure, does not obscure the text, and permits the brief to lie reasonably flat when open.

(4) *Paper Size, Line Spacing, and Margins*. The brief must be on 8½-by-11 inch paper. The text must be double-spaced, but quotations more than two lines long may be indented and single-spaced. Headings and footnotes may be single-spaced. Margins must be at least one inch on all four sides. Page numbers may be placed in the margins, but no text may appear there.

(5) *Typeface*. Either a proportionally spaced or monospaced face may be used.

(A) A proportionally spaced face must include serifs, but sans-serif type may be used in headings and captions. A proportionally spaced face must be 14-point or larger.

(B) A monospaced face may not contain more than 10½ characters per inch.

(6) *Type Styles*. A brief must be set in plain, roman style, although italics or boldface may be used for emphasis. Case names must be italicized or underlined.

(7) *Length*.

(A) *Page Limitation*. A principal brief must not exceed 30 pages, or a reply brief 15 pages, unless it complies with subparagraph (B).

(B) *Type-volume Limitation*.

(i) A principal brief is acceptable if it contains a certificate under Rule 8015 (h) and:

- contains no more than 13,000 words; or
- uses a monospaced face and contains no more than 1,300 lines of text.

(ii) A reply brief is acceptable if it includes a certificate under Rule 8015 (h) and contains no more than half of the type volume specified in item (i).

(b) ELECTRONICALLY FILED BRIEFS. A brief filed electronically must comply with subdivision (a), except for (a)(1), (a)(3), and the paper requirement of (a)(4).

美国联邦破产程序规则
（中英对照译本）

（E）摘要的标题，并列明为其提交摘要的当事人；以及

（F）代表为其提交摘要的律师的姓名、办公室地址、电话号码以及电子邮件地址。

（3）装订。该摘要必须以安全的方式进行装订，不得遮挡文本，并能使得该摘要被打开时能被合理平放。

（4）纸张尺寸、行距以及页边距。摘要必须使用 8½×11 英寸的纸。文本必须使用双倍行距，但超过两行的引用可以缩进并使用单倍行距。标题和脚注可以使用单倍行距。所有页边距均至少为 1 英寸。可将页码放在页边中，但此处不得显示任何文本。

（5）字体。可使用比例间隔字体或等宽字体。

（A）比例间隔字体必须包含衬线，但标题和题注可以使用无衬线字体。比例间隔字体必须至少达到 14 点。

（B）等宽字体每英寸不得超过 10½ 个字符。

（6）字型。摘要必须采用简单的罗马字型，但也可使用斜体或加粗以用于强调。案件名称必须为斜体或加下画线。

（7）篇幅。

（A）篇幅限制。除附款（B）另有规定外，主要摘要不得超过 30 页，回复摘要不得超过 15 页。

（B）字数限制。

（i）若主要摘要载有第 8015 条（h）所规定的证明并且符合以下条件，则也可接受该摘要：

- 不超过 13,000 字；或
- 使用等宽字体并且不超过 1,300 行文本。

（ii）若回复摘要载有第 8015 条（h）所规定的证明并且其字数不超过（i）项所规定的字数的一半，则也可接受该摘要。

（b）**以电子方式提交的摘要**。以电子方式提交的摘要必须符合附条（a）中除（a）(1)、（a）(3)以及（a）(4)对纸张的要求外的其他规定。

(c) PAPER COPIES OF APPENDICES. A paper copy of an appendix must comply with subdivision (a)(1), (2), (3), and (4), with the following exceptions:

(1) An appendix may include a legible photocopy of any document found in the record or of a printed decision.

(2) When necessary to facilitate inclusion of odd-sized documents such as technical drawings, an appendix may be a size other than 8½-by-11 inches, and need not lie reasonably flat when opened.

(d) ELECTRONICALLY FILED APPENDICES. An appendix filed electronically must comply with subdivision (a)(2) and (4), except for the paper requirement of (a)(4).

(e) OTHER DOCUMENTS.

(1) *Motion*. Rule 8013 (f) governs the form of a motion, response, or reply.

(2) *Paper Copies of Other Documents*. A paper copy of any other document, other than a submission under Rule 8014 (f), must comply with subdivision (a), with the following exceptions:

(A) A cover is not necessary if the caption and signature page together contain the information required by subdivision (a)(2).

(B) Subdivision (a)(7) does not apply.

(3) *Other Documents Filed Electronically*. Any other document filed electronically, other than a submission under Rule 8014 (f), must comply with the appearance requirements of paragraph (2).

(f) LOCAL VARIATION. A district court or BAP must accept documents that comply with the form requirements of this rule and the length limits set by Part VIII of these rules. By local rule or order in a particular case, a district court or BAP may accept documents that do not meet all the form requirements of this rule or the length limits set by Part VIII of these rules.

(g) ITEMS EXCLUDED FROM LENGTH. In computing any length limit, headings, footnotes, and quotations count toward the limit, but the following items do not:

- cover page;
- disclosure statement under Rule 8012;
- table of contents;

（c）**附录的纸质副本**。附录的纸质副本必须符合附条（a）的（1）、（2）、（3）及（4）的规定，但存在以下例外：

（1）附录可包含档案中的任何材料或书面决定的清晰的影印本。

（2）在必要情形下，为便于载入技术图纸类的不常见尺寸的文件，附录的尺寸可以不是 8½×11 英寸，并且无须保证在打开时能被合理平放。

（d）**以电子方式提交的附录**。被以电子方式提交的附录必须符合附条（a）(2) 和（4）的规定，但不包括附条（a）(4) 中的纸质要求。

（e）**其他材料**。

（1）动议。第 8013 条（f）适用于动议、答复或回复的格式。

（2）其他材料的纸质副本。除第 8014 条（f）所述的文件外，任何其他材料的纸质副本均必须符合附条（a）的规定，但存在以下例外：

（A）若题注连同签名页含有附条（a）(2) 所要求的信息，则无须封面。

（B）不适用附条（a）(7) 的规定。

（3）以电子方式提交的其他材料。除第 8014 条（f）所规定的文件外被以电子方式提交的任何其他材料均必须符合第（2）款中的形式要求。

（f）**地区差异**。地区法院或破产上诉合议庭必须接受符合本条的格式要求以及本法第 VIII 部分所规定的篇幅限制的材料，但地区法院或破产上诉合议庭也可基于特定案件中的地方规则或裁定而接受未能完全符合本条的格式要求或本法第 VIII 部分所规定的篇幅限制的材料。

（g）**不被计入篇幅的项目**。在计算任何篇幅限制时，标题、脚注以及引用均将被计入该篇幅限制内，但以下各项不包括在内：

- 封面；
- 第 8012 条规定的披露声明；
- 目录；

- table of citations;
- statement regarding oral argument;
- addendum containing statutes, rules, or regulations;
- certificates of counsel;
- signature block;
- proof of service; and
- any item specifically excluded by these rules or by local rule.

(h) CERTIFICATE OF COMPLIANCE.

(1) *Briefs and Documents That Require a Certificate.* A brief submitted under Rule 8015 (a) (7) (B), 8016 (d) (2), or 8017 (b) (4) —and a document submitted under Rule 8013 (f) (3) (A), 8013 (f) (3) (C), or 8022 (b) (1)— must include a certificate by the attorney, or an unrepresented party, that the document complies with the type-volume limitation. The individual preparing the certificate may rely on the word or line count of the word-processing system used to prepare the document. The certificate must state the number of words—or the number of lines of monospaced type—in the document.

(2) Acceptable Form. The certificate requirement is satisfied by a certificate of compliance that conforms substantially to the appropriate Official Form.

(Added Apr. 25, 2014, eff. Dec. 1, 2014; amended Apr. 26, 2018, eff. Dec. 1, 2018; Apr. 27, 2020,eff. Dec. 1, 2020.)

Rule 8016. Cross-Appeals

(a) APPLICABILITY. This rule applies to a case in which a cross-appeal is filed. Rules 8014 (a) - (c), 8015 (a) (7) (A) - (B), and 8018 (a) (1) - (3) do not apply to such a case, except as otherwise provided in this rule.

(b) DESIGNATION OF APPELLANT. The party who files a notice of appeal first is the appellant for purposes of this rule and Rule 8018 (a) (4) and (b) and Rule 8019. If notices are filed on the same day, the plaintiff, petitioner, applicant, or movant in the proceeding below is the appellant. These designations may be modified by the parties' agreement or by court order.

- 引用目录；
- 关于口头辩论的陈述；
- 包含法律、规则或法规的附录；
- 律师证书；
- 签名区；
- 送达证明；以及
- 由本法或地方规则所明确排除的任何项目。

（h）**合规证明**。

（1）需要证明的摘要及材料。根据第 8015（a）（7）（B）、8016（d）（2）或 8017（b）（4）条所提交的摘要以及根据第 8013（f）（3）（A）、8013（f）（3）（C）或 8022（b）（1）所提交的材料必须载有由律师或未被律师代表的当事人所出具的证明前述材料符合字数限制的证明。准备该证明的自然人可使用用于准备该材料的文字处理系统所统计的字数或行数。该证明必须注明该材料的字数或等距行数。

（2）可接受的格式。基本符合相应官方模板的合规证明即满足本条中对证明的要求。

（经 Apr. 25, 2014, eff. Dec. 1, 2014 增补；经 Apr. 26, 2018, eff. Dec. 1, 2018; Apr. 27, 2020, eff. Dec. 1, 2020. 修正）

第 8016 条　交叉上诉

（a）**适用范围**。本条适用于已被提交交叉上诉的案件。除本条另有规定外，第 8014 条（a）至（c）、第 8015 条（a）（7）（A）至（B）以及第 8018 条（a）（1）至（3）不适用于该类案件。

（b）**上诉人的认定**。就本条、第 8018 条（a）（4）和（b）以及第 8019 条而言，最先提交上诉通知书的当事人为上诉人。若通知书系在同日而被提交，则原告、申请人、上诉人或动议方在其后程序中均为上诉人。前述认定可由当事人的协议或法院裁定而被予以修改。

(c) BRIEFS. In a case involving a cross-appeal:

(1) Appellant's Principal Brief. The appellant must file a principal brief in the appeal. That brief must comply with Rule 8014 (a).

(2) Appellee's Principal and Response Brief. The appellee must file a principal brief in the cross-appeal and must, in the same brief, respond to the principal brief in the appeal. That brief must comply with Rule 8014 (a), except that the brief need not include a statement of the case unless the appellee is dissatisfied with the appellant's statement.

(3) Appellant's Response and Reply Brief. The appellant must file a brief that responds to the principal brief in the cross-appeal and may, in the same brief, reply to the response in the appeal. That brief must comply with Rule 8014 (a) (2) - (8) and (10), except that none of the following need appear unless the appellant is dissatisfied with the appellee's statement in the cross-appeal:

(A) the jurisdictional statement;

(B) the statement of the issues and the applicable standard of appellate review; and

(C) the statement of the case.

(4) Appellee's Reply Brief. The appellee may file a brief in reply to the response in thecross-appeal. That brief must comply with Rule 8014 (a) (2) - (3) and (10) and must be limited to the issues presented by the cross-appeal.

(d) LENGTH.

(1) Page Limitation. Unless it complies with paragraph (2), the appellant's principal brief must not exceed 30 pages; the appellee's principal and response brief, 35 pages; the appellant's response and reply brief, 30 pages; and the appellee's reply brief, 15 pages.

(2) Type-volume Limitation.

(A) The appellant's principal brief or the appellant's response and reply brief is acceptable if it includes a certificate under Rule 8015 (h) and:

(i) contains no more than 13,000 words; or

(ii) uses a monospaced face and contains no more than 1,300 lines of text.

(B) The appellee's principal and response brief is acceptable if it includes a

（c）**摘要**。在涉及交叉上诉的案件中：

（1）上诉人的主要摘要。上诉人必须在上诉中提交主要摘要。该摘要必须符合第8014条（a）的规定。

（2）被上诉人的主要诉讼及答复摘要。被上诉人必须在交叉上诉中提交主要摘要，并且必须在同一摘要中就上诉中的主要摘要作出答复。前述摘要必须符合第8014条（a）的规定，但除非被上诉人对上诉人就本案的陈述并不满意，否则该摘要中无须载明该陈述。

（3）上诉人的答复及回复摘要。上诉人必须就交叉上诉的主要摘要提交答复摘要，并且可在同一摘要中就交叉上诉人对上诉的答复作出回复。前述摘要必须符合第8014条（a）（2）至（8）以及（10）的规定，但除非上诉人对被上诉人在交叉上诉中的陈述并不满意，否则该摘要无须载明以下各项：

（A）管辖权声明；

（B）对问题的陈述以及所适用的上诉审查标准；以及

（C）对案件的陈述。

（4）被上诉人的回复摘要。被上诉人可针对上诉人就交叉上诉的答复提交回复摘要。该摘要必须符合第8014条（a）（2）至（3）以及（10）的规定，并且其范围仅限于交叉上诉所提出的问题。

（d）**篇幅**。

（1）篇幅限制。除第（2）款另有规定外，上诉人的主要摘要不得超过30页；被上诉人的主要摘要及答复摘要不得超过35页；上诉人的答复摘要及回复摘要不得超过30页；并且被上诉人的回复摘要不得超过15页。

（2）字数限制。

（A）若上诉人的主要摘要或上诉人的答复及回复摘要载有第8015条（h）所规定的证明并符合以下条件，则也可接受前述摘要：

（i）不超过13000字；或

（ii）使用等宽字体并且不超过1300行文本。

（B）若被上诉人的主要及答复摘要载有第8015条（h）所规定的证明并符合

certificate under Rule 8015 (h) and:

(i) contains no more than 15,300 words; or

(ii) uses a monospaced face and contains no more than 1,500 lines of text.

(C) The appellee's reply brief is acceptable if it includes a certificate under Rule 8015 (h) and contains no more than half of the type volume specified in subparagraph (A).

(e) TIME TO SERVE AND FILE A BRIEF. Briefs must be served and filed as follows, unless the district court or BAP by order in a particular case excuses the filing of briefs or specifies different time limits:

(1) the appellant's principal brief, within 30 days after the docketing of notice that the record has been transmitted or is available electronically;

(2) the appellee's principal and response brief, within 30 days after the appellant's principal brief is served;

(3) the appellant's response and reply brief, within 30 days after the appellee's principal and response brief is served; and

(4) the appellee's reply brief, within 14 days after the appellant's response and reply brief is served, but at least 7 days before scheduled argument unless the district court or BAP, for good cause, allows a later filing.

(Added Apr. 25, 2014, eff. Dec. 1, 2014; amended Apr. 26, 2018, eff. Dec. 1, 2018.)

Rule 8017. Brief of an Amicus Curiae

(a) DURING INITIAL CONSIDERATION OF A CASE ON THE MERITS.

(1) *Applicability*. This Rule 8017 (a) governs amicus filings during a court's initial consideration of a case on the merits.

(2) *When Permitted*. The United States or its officer or agency or a state may file an amicus brief without the consent of the parties or leave of court. Any other amicus curiae may file a brief only by leave of court or if the brief states that all parties have consented to its filing, but a district court or BAP may prohibit the filing of or may strike an amicus brief that would result in a judge's disqualification. On its own motion, and with notice to all parties to an appeal, the district court or BAP may request a brief by an amicus curiae.

以下条件，则也可接受前述摘要：

（ⅰ）不超过 15300 字；或

（ⅱ）使用等宽字体并且不超过 1500 行文本。

（C）若被上诉人的回复摘要载有第 8015 条（h）所规定的证明并且其字数不超过（A）分段所规定的字数的一半，则也可接受该摘要。

（e）**送达并提交摘要的时间**。前述摘要必须被按照以下方式送达并提交，除非地区法院或破产上诉合议庭在具体案件裁定豁免提交摘要或规定了其他时间限制：

（1）上诉人的主要摘要，将说明上诉档案已被移送或可通过电子方式提供的通知载入案卷后 30 日内；

（2）被上诉人的主要摘要及答复摘要，在上诉人的主要摘要被送达后 30 日内；

（3）上诉人的答复及回复摘要，在被上诉人的主要摘要及答复摘要送达后 30 日内；以及

（4）被上诉人的回复摘要，在上诉人的答复及回复摘要被送达后 14 日内，以及安排的辩论日前至少 7 日以前，除非地区法院或破产上诉合议庭出于正当事由准予迟延提交。

（经 Apr. 25, 2014, eff. Dec. 1, 2014 增补；经 Apr. 26, 2018, eff. Dec. 1, 2018. 修正）

第 8017 条　法庭之友的摘要

（a）**在初步审议案情期间**。

（1）适用范围。第 8017 条（a）适用于法院初步审议案情时的法庭之友申请。

（2）得到许可时。美国或其官员、机构或州均可在未经当事人同意或法院许可的情况下提交法庭之友摘要。任何其他法庭之友仅可在法院作出许可或在摘要中注明所有当事人均已同意其提交法庭之友摘要的情况下才可提交该摘要，但地区法院或破产上诉合议庭仍可禁止其提交或驳回可能造成法官丧失审判资格的法庭之友摘要。应其自身动议并在向上诉案件的所有当事人发出通知后，地区法院或破产上诉合议庭可要求某位法庭之友提交摘要。

(3) *Motion for Leave to File*. The motion must be accompanied by the proposed brief and state:

(A) the movant's interest; and

(B) the reason why an amicus brief is desirable and why the matters asserted are relevant to the disposition of the appeal.

(4) *Contents and Form*. An amicus brief must comply with Rule 8015. In addition to the requirements of Rule 8015, the cover must identify the party or parties supported and indicate whether the brief supports affirmance or reversal. If an amicus curiae is a corporation, the brief must include a disclosure statement like that required of parties by Rule 8012. An amicus brief need not comply with Rule 8014, but must include the following:

(A) a table of contents, with page references;

(B) a table of authorities—cases (alphabetically arranged), statutes, and other authorities—with references to the pages of the brief where they are cited;

(C) a concise statement of the identity of the amicus curiae, its interest in the case, and the source of its authority to file;

(D) unless the amicus curiae is one listed in the first sentence of subdivision (a) (2), a statement that indicates whether:

(i) a party's counsel authored the brief in whole or in part;

(ii) a party or a party's counsel contributed money that was intended to fund preparing or submitting the brief; and

(iii) a person—other than the amicus curiae, its members, or its counsel—contributed money that was intended to fund preparing or submitting the brief and, if so, identifies each such person;

(E) an argument, which may be preceded by a summary and need not include a statement of the applicable standard of review; and

(F) a certificate of compliance, if required by Rule 8015 (h).

(5) *Length*. Except by the district court's or BAP's permission, an amicus brief must be no more than one-half the maximum length authorized by these rules for a party's principal brief. If the court grants a party permission to file a longer brief, that extension does not affect the length of an amicus brief.

（3）申请获准提交的动议。该动议必须附有拟议的摘要并注明以下内容：

（A）动议方的利害关系；以及

（B）需要法庭之友摘要以及所主张的事项与上诉案件的审理有关的原因。

（4）内容及形式。法庭之友摘要必须符合第 8015 条的规定。除第 8015 条的要求外，封面还必须标明其支持的当事人并说明该摘要系肯定原审裁决或反对原审裁决。若法庭之友为公司，则该摘要还必须载有第 8012 条就当事人所要求的披露声明。法庭之友摘要无须符合第 8014 条的规定，但仍必须含有以下内容：

（A）带有页码的目录；

（B）参考资料［案件（按字母顺序排列）、法律以及其他资料］，标明在该摘要中其被引用的页面；

（C）对法庭之友的身份、其在案件中的利害关系以及提交摘要的权利来源的简要陈述；

（D）除附条（a）（2）的首句所述的法庭之友外，还须含有说明是否存在以下情况的陈述：

（i）当事人的律师撰写全部或部分摘要；

（ii）当事人或当事人的律师提供了准备或提交该摘要的资金；并且

（iii）除法庭之友、其成员或其律师外，有其他人提供了准备或提交该摘要的资金，若存在这种情况，标明该类人的身份；

（E）论点，其可被放在总结之前并且无须包含对上诉审查标准的陈述；以及

（F）合规证明，若第 8015 条（h）对此提出要求。

（5）篇幅。除非地区法院或破产上诉合议庭作出其他许可，否则法庭之友摘要不得超过本法就当事人的主要摘要所规定的最长篇幅的一半。若法院准许当事人提交更长篇幅的摘要，该篇幅的增长并不影响法庭之友摘要的篇幅。

(6) *Time for Filing*. An amicus curiae must file its brief, accompanied by a motion for filing when necessary, no later than 7 days after the principal brief of the party being supported is filed. An amicus curiae that does not support either party must file its brief no later than 7 days after the appellant's principal brief is filed. The district court or BAP may grant leave for later filing, specifying the time within which an opposing party may answer.

(7) *Reply Brief*. Except by the district court's or BAP's permission, an amicus curiae may not file a reply brief.

(8) *Oral Argument*. An amicus curiae may participate in oral argument only with the district court's or BAP's permission.

(b) DURING CONSIDERATION OF WHETHER TO GRANT REHEARING.

(1) *Applicability*. This Rule 8017 (b) governs amicus filings during a district court's or BAP's consideration of whether to grant rehearing, unless a local rule or order in a case provides otherwise.

(2) *When Permitted*. The United States or its officer or agency or a state may file an amicus brief without the consent of the parties or leave of court. Any other amicus curiae may file a brief only by leave of court.

(3) *Motion for Leave to File*. Rule 8017 (a) (3) applies to a motion for leave.

(4) Contents, Form, and Length. Rule 8017 (a) (4) applies to the amicus brief. The brief must include a certificate under Rule 8015 (h) and not exceed 2,600 words.

(5) *Time for Filing*. An amicus curiae supporting the motion for rehearing or supporting neither party must file its brief, accompanied by a motion for filing when necessary, no later than 7 days after the motion is filed. An amicus curiae opposing the motion for rehearing must file its brief, accompanied by a motion for filing when necessary, no later than the date set by the court for the response.

(Added Apr. 25, 2014, eff. Dec. 1, 2014; amended Apr. 26, 2018, eff. Dec. 1, 2018.)

Rule 8018. Serving and Filing Briefs; Appendices

(a) TIME TO SERVE AND FILE A BRIEF. The following rules apply unless the district court or BAP by order in a particular case excuses the filing of briefs or specifies different time limits:

（6）提交的时间。法庭之友必须在其所支持的当事人提交主要摘要后 7 日内提交法庭之友摘要，并在需要的情况下附有申请提交的动议。并不支持任意一方当事人的法庭之友必须在上诉人提交主要摘要后 7 日内提交其摘要。地区法院或破产上诉合议庭可准予其迟延提交的申请，但须明确反对方可进行答辩的时间。

（7）回复摘要。除非地区法院或破产上诉合议庭作出其他许可，否则法庭之友不得提交回复摘要。

（8）口头辩论。法庭之友仅可在地区法院或破产上诉合议庭的许可下参与口头辩论。

（b）**在审议是否准予重审期间。**

（1）适用范围。除非地方规则或案件中所作的裁定另有规定，否则第 8017 条（b）适用于地区法院或破产上诉合议庭审议是否准予重审时的法庭之友申请。

（2）得到许可时。美国或其官员、机构或州可在未经当事人或法庭许可的情况下提交法庭之友摘要。任何其他法庭之友仅可在法院作出许可时提交摘要。

（3）申请获准提交的动议。第 8017 条（a）（3）适用于该动议。

（4）内容、形式及篇幅。第 8017 条（a）（4）适用于法庭之友摘要。该摘要必须含有第 8015 条（h）所述的证明并且不得超过 2600 字。

（5）提交的时间。支持申请举行重审的动议或不支持任意一方当事人的法庭之友必须在该动议被提交后 7 日内提交其摘要，并在需要的情况下附有申请提交该摘要的动议。反对申请举行重审的动议必须在法院确定作出答复之日前提交其摘要，并在需要的情况下附有申请提交该摘要的动议。

（经 Apr. 25, 2014, eff. Dec. 1, 2014 增补；经 Apr. 26, 2018, eff. Dec. 1, 2018. 修正）

第 8018 条　送达并提交摘要；附录

（a）**送达并提交摘要的时间。** 除非地区法院或破产上诉合议庭在具体案件中裁定豁免提交摘要或规定了其他时间限制，否则将适用以下规则：

U.S. Federal Rules of Bankruptcy Procedure
(Chinese-English bilingual version)

(1) The appellant must serve and file a brief within 30 days after the docketing of notice that the record has been transmitted or is available electronically.

(2) The appellee must serve and file a brief within 30 days after service of the appellant's brief.

(3) The appellant may serve and file a reply brief within 14 days after service of the appellee's brief, but a reply brief must be filed at least 7 days before scheduled argument unless the district court or BAP, for good cause, allows a later filing.

(4) If an appellant fails to file a brief on time or within an extended time authorized by the district court or BAP, an appellee may move to dismiss the appeal—or the district court or BAP, after notice, may dismiss the appeal on its own motion. An appellee who fails to file a brief will not be heard at oral argument unless the district court or BAP grants permission.

(b) DUTY TO SERVE AND FILE AN APPENDIX TO THE BRIEF.

(1) *Appellant*. Subject to subdivision (e) and Rule 8009 (d), the appellant must serve and file with its principal brief excerpts of the record as an appendix. It must contain the following:

(A) the relevant entries in the bankruptcy docket;

(B) the complaint and answer, or other equivalent filings;

(C) the judgment, order, or decree from which the appeal is taken;

(D) any other orders, pleadings, jury instructions, findings, conclusions, or opinions relevant to the appeal;

(E) the notice of appeal; and

(F) any relevant transcript or portion of it.

(2) *Appellee*. The appellee may also serve and file with its brief an appendix that contains material required to be included by the appellant or relevant to the appeal or cross-appeal, but omitted by the appellant.

(3) *Cross-Appellee*. The appellant as cross-appellee may also serve and file with its response an appendix that contains material relevant to matters raised initially by the principal brief in the cross-appeal, but omitted by the cross-appellant.

(c) FORMAT OF THE APPENDIX. The appendix must begin with a table

美国联邦破产程序规则
（中英对照译本）

（1）上诉人必须在说明上诉档案已被移送或可通过电子方式提供的通知载入案卷后 30 日内送达并提交摘要。

（2）被上诉人必须在上诉人的摘要被送达后 30 日内送达并提交摘要。

（3）上诉人可在被上诉人的摘要被送达后 14 日内送达并提交回复摘要，但回复摘要必须在安排的辩论日前至少 7 日以前而被提交，除非地区法院或破产上诉合议庭出于正当事由准予迟延提交。

（4）若上诉人未能及时提交或在地区法院或破产上诉合议庭所准予的延长期间内提交摘要，则被上诉人可提出动议申请驳回上诉，或者地区法院或破产上诉合议庭在通知后也可在其自身动议下驳回上诉。除非地区法院或破产上诉合议庭作出许可，否则未能提交摘要的被上诉人在口头辩论环节不得发表意见。

（b）送达并提交摘要附录的义务。

（1）上诉人。在符合附条（e）及第 8009 条（d）规定的情况下，上诉人必须在送达并提交其主要摘要时一并送达并提交上诉档案的摘要并将其作为附录。摘要必须包含以下内容：

（A）破产案卷中的相关记录；

（B）诉状及答辩，或者其他类似文件；

（C）上诉所针对的判决、裁定或法令；

（D）与上诉案件有关的任何其他裁定、诉状、陪审团指示、事实、结论或意见；

（E）上诉通知书；以及

（F）任何相关书面记录或书面记录的一部分。

（2）被上诉人。被上诉人也可在送达并提交其摘要时一并送达并提交附录，该附录含有本要求上诉人提供或者与上诉或交叉上诉有关的，但上诉人遗漏的材料。

（3）交叉被上诉人。上诉人作为交叉被上诉人也可在送达并提交其答复时一并送达并提交附录，该附录含有与在交叉上诉中的主要摘要所首先提出的事项相关的，但交叉上诉人遗漏的材料。

（c）附录的格式。 附录必须以目录为开头，并且该目录要标明每部分开始的

of contents identifying the page at which each part begins. The relevant docket entries must follow the table of contents. Other parts of the record must follow chronologically. When pages from the transcript of proceedings are placed in the appendix, the transcript page numbers must be shown in brackets immediately before the included pages. Omissions in the text of documents or of the transcript must be indicated by asterisks. Immaterial formal matters (captions, subscriptions, acknowledgments, and the like) should be omitted.

(d) EXHIBITS. Exhibits designated for inclusion in the appendix may be reproduced in a separate volume or volumes, suitably indexed.

(e) APPEAL ON THE ORIGINAL RECORD WITHOUT AN APPENDIX. The district court or BAP may, either by rule for all cases or classes of cases or by order in a particular case, dispense with the appendix and permit an appeal to proceed on the original record, with the submission of any relevant parts of the record that the district court or BAP orders the parties to file.

(Added Apr. 25, 2014, eff. Dec. 1, 2014.)

Rule 8018.1. District-Court Review of a Judgment that the Bankruptcy Court Lacked the Constitutional Authority to Enter

If, on appeal, a district court determines that the bankruptcy court did not have the power under Article III of the Constitution to enter the judgment, order, or decree appealed from, the district court may treat it as proposed findings of fact and conclusions of law.

(Added Apr. 26, 2018, eff. Dec. 1, 2018.)

Rule 8019. Oral Argument

(a) PARTY'S STATEMENT. Any party may file, or a district court or BAP may require, a statement explaining why oral argument should, or need not, be permitted.

(b) PRESUMPTION OF ORAL ARGUMENT AND EXCEPTIONS. Oral argument must be allowed in every case unless the district judge—or all the BAP judges assigned to hear the appeal—examine the briefs and record and determine that oral argument is unnecessary because

页码。在目录后应载明相关的案卷记录。上诉档案的其他部分必须按时间顺序排列。当程序的书面记录中某些部分被载入附录时，必须在被载入的页面前的括号中注明该书面记录的原页码。对文件或书面记录中的文本的省略必须用星号进行表示。无关紧要的形式事项（题注、签署、致谢以及类似事项）均应被予以省略。

（d）**证据**。被认定应被载入附录中的证据可在进行相应的索引的情况下在单独的部分再次呈现。

（e）**就无附录的原始档案处理上诉案件**。地区法院或破产上诉合议庭可通过就所有案件或某类案件的规则或在具体案件中作出裁定，从而免除提交附录的义务并准予就原始档案处理上诉案件，但仍需提交地区法院或破产上诉合议庭裁定当事人提交的档案中的任何相关部分。

（经 Apr. 25, 2014, eff. Dec. 1, 2014. 增补）

第 8018.1 条　地区法院对破产法院未经宪法授权而作出的判决的审查

若在上诉案件审理中，地区法院认为破产法院根据《宪法》第 III 条无权作出被上诉的判决、裁定或法令，则地区法院可将其视为被提出的事实认定及法律结论。

（经 Apr. 26, 2018, eff. Dec. 1, 2018. 增补）

第 8019 条　口头辩论

（a）**当事人的陈述**。任何当事人均可提交说明应该或无须被准予举行口头辩论的原因的陈述，地区法院或破产上诉合议庭也可要求其提供该陈述。

（b）**口头辩论的推定及例外**。除非地区法院的法官或破产上诉合议庭内被指派审理上诉的所有法官在审查摘要及档案后认为出于以下原因无须举行口头辩论，否则在所有案件中均应准予举行口头辩论：

U.S. Federal Rules of Bankruptcy Procedure
(Chinese-English bilingual version)

(1) the appeal is frivolous;

(2) the dispositive issue or issues have been authoritatively decided; or

(3) the facts and legal arguments are adequately presented in the briefs and record, and the decisional process would not be significantly aided by oral argument.

(c) NOTICE OF ARGUMENT; POSTPONEMENT. The district court or BAP must advise all parties of the date, time, and place for oral argument, and the time allowed for each side. A motion to postpone the argument or to allow longer argument must be filed reasonably in advance of the hearing date.

(d) ORDER AND CONTENTS OF ARGUMENT. The appellant opens and concludes the argument. Counsel must not read at length from briefs, the record, or authorities.

(e) CROSS-APPEALS AND SEPARATE APPEALS. If there is a cross-appeal, Rule 8016(b) determines which party is the appellant and which is the appellee for the purposes of oral argument. Unless the district court or BAP directs otherwise, a cross-appeal or separate appeal must be argued when the initial appeal is argued. Separate parties should avoid duplicative argument.

(f) NONAPPEARANCE OF A PARTY. If the appellee fails to appear for argument, the district court or BAP may hear the appellant's argument. If the appellant fails to appear for argument, the district court or BAP may hear the appellee's argument. If neither party appears, the case will be decided on the briefs unless the district court or BAP orders otherwise.

(g) SUBMISSION ON BRIEFS. The parties may agree to submit a case for decision on the briefs, but the district court or BAP may direct that the case be argued.

(h) USE OF PHYSICAL EXHIBITS AT ARGUMENT; REMOVAL. Counsel intending to use physical exhibits other than documents at the argument must arrange to place them in the courtroom on the day of the argument before the court convenes. After the argument, counsel must remove the exhibits from the courtroom unless the district court or BAP directs otherwise. The clerk may destroy or dispose of the exhibits if counsel does not reclaim them within a reasonable time after the clerk gives notice to remove them.

美国联邦破产程序规则
（中英对照译本）

（1）该上诉并无正当依据；

（2）决定性事项已被作出权威性决定；或

（3）在摘要及档案中已经充分陈述有事实及法律论据，并且口头辩论并不会显著有助于决议过程。

（c）**辩论通知；推迟**。地区法院或破产上诉合议庭必须将口头辩论的日期、时间及地点以及允许各方发言的时间告知所有当事人。若要申请推迟辩论或延长辩论时间，则必须在听证日前以合理方式提交动议。

（d）**辩论的顺序及内容**。上诉人首先发言并作最后陈述。律师不得长篇朗读摘要、档案或参考资料中的内容。

（e）**交叉上诉及单独上诉**。若存在交叉上诉，则就口头辩论而言，应根据第8016条（b）决定上诉人及被上诉人。除非地区法院或破产上诉合议庭作出其他指示，否则在就初始上诉展开辩论时也必须就交叉上诉或单独上诉展开辩论。不同当事人应避免进行重复性的论述。

（f）**当事人的缺席**。若被上诉人未能出庭辩论，则地区法院或破产上诉合议庭仍可听取上诉人的陈述。若上诉人未能出庭辩论，则地区法院或破产上诉合议庭仍可听取被上诉人的陈述。除非地区法院或破产上诉合议庭作出其他裁定，否则当双方均未出席时，法院将就摘要对此案作出决定。

（g）**摘要的提交**。当事人可同意基于摘要对此案作出决定，但地区法院或破产上诉合议庭仍可要求就此案展开辩论。

（h）**在辩论中使用证物；移除**。计划在辩论中使用除文件以外的证物的律师必须在辩论当日开庭前将其放置在法庭上。在辩论后，除非地区法院或破产上诉合议庭作出其他指示，否则律师必须将其从法庭上移除。若在书记员发出移除该证物的通知后，该律师在合理时间内仍未认领该证物，则书记员可销毁或处置该类证物。

U.S. Federal Rules of Bankruptcy Procedure
(Chinese-English bilingual version)

(Added Apr. 25, 2014, eff. Dec. 1, 2014.)

Rule 8020. Frivolous Appeal and Other Misconduct

(a) FRIVOLOUS APPEAL—DAMAGES AND COSTS. If the district court or BAP determines that an appeal is frivolous, it may, after a separately filed motion or notice from the court and reasonable opportunity to respond, award just damages and single or double costs to the appellee.

(b) OTHER MISCONDUCT. The district court or BAP may discipline or sanction an attorney or party appearing before it for other misconduct, including failure to comply with any court order. First, however, the court must afford the attorney or party reasonable notice, an opportunity to show cause to the contrary, and, if requested, a hearing.

(Added Apr. 25, 2014, eff. Dec. 1, 2014.)

Rule 8021. Costs

(a) AGAINST WHOM ASSESSED. The following rules apply unless the law provides or the district court or BAP orders otherwise:

(1) if an appeal is dismissed, costs are taxed against the appellant, unless the parties agree otherwise;

(2) if a judgment, order, or decree is affirmed, costs are taxed against the appellant;

(3) if a judgment, order, or decree is reversed, costs are taxed against the appellee;

(4) if a judgment, order, or decree is affirmed or reversed in part, modified, or vacated, costs are taxed only as the district court or BAP orders.

(b) COSTS FOR AND AGAINST THE UNITED STATES. Costs for or against the United States, its agency, or its officer may be assessed under subdivision (a) only if authorized by law.

(c) COSTS ON APPEAL TAXABLE IN THE BANKRUPTCY COURT. The following costs on appeal are taxable in the bankruptcy court for the benefit of the party entitled to costs under this rule:

（经 Apr. 25, 2014, eff. Dec. 1, 2014. 增补）

第 8020 条 无正当依据的上诉以及其他错误行为

（a）**无正当依据的上诉：损害及成本费用**。若地区法院或破产上诉法庭认为某上诉并无正当依据，则在有人单独提交动议或法院发出通知并提供他人答复的合理机会后，可裁决被上诉人获得损害赔偿以及一倍或两倍的成本费用。

（b）**其他错误行为**。地区法院或破产上诉合议庭可因其他行为（包括未能遵守任何法院裁定）而对出席法庭的律师或当事人施加纪律处分或处罚。但首先法院必须向律师或当事人发出合理的通知，提供其证明相反事由的机会并在其作出请求的情况下，举行听证。

（经 Apr. 25, 2014, eff. Dec. 1, 2014. 增补）

第 8021 条 成本费用

（a）**确定承担成本费用的主体**。除非法律另有规定或者地区法院或破产上诉合议庭作出其他裁定，否则适用以下规则：

（1）若上诉被驳回，则除非当事人间另有协议，否则应由上诉人承担成本费用；

（2）若原判决、裁定或法令被予以维持，则由上诉人承担成本费用；

（3）若作出与原判决、裁定或法令相反的判决、裁定或法令，则由被上诉人承担成本费用；

（4）若判决、裁定或法令部分被予以维持，或部分被作出相反裁决，或被改判或被撤销，则应根据地区法院或破产上诉合议庭的裁定来收取成本费用。

（b）**支持美国获得或判决其承担成本费用**。在法律许可的情况下，可根据附条（a）决定美国、其机构或其官员是否可获得或被判决承担成本费用。

（c）**在破产法院可被裁决的上诉中的成本费用**。在上诉中发生的以下各项属于在破产法院可被判决给根据本条有权获得该费用的当事人的成本费用：

(1) the production of any required copies of a brief, appendix, exhibit, or the record;

(2) the preparation and transmission of the record;

(3) the reporter's transcript, if needed to determine the appeal;

(4) premiums paid for a bond or other security to preserve rights pending appeal; and

(5) the fee for filing the notice of appeal.

(d) BILL OF COSTS; OBJECTIONS. A party who wants costs taxed must, within 14 days after entry of judgment on appeal, file with the bankruptcy clerk and serve an itemized and verified bill of costs. Objections must be filed within 14 days after service of the bill of costs, unless the bankruptcy court extends the time.

(Added Apr. 25, 2014, eff. Dec. 1, 2014; amended Apr. 26, 2018, eff. Dec. 1, 2018;Apr. 27, 2020,eff. Dec. 1, 2020.)

Rule 8022. Motion for Rehearing

(a) TIME TO FILE; CONTENTS; RESPONSE; ACTION BY THE DISTRICT COURT OR BAP IF GRANTED.

(1) *Time.* Unless the time is shortened or extended by order or local rule, any motion for rehearing by the district court or BAP must be filed within 14 days after entry of judgment on appeal.

(2) *Contents.* The motion must state with particularity each point of law or fact that the movant believes the district court or BAP has overlooked or misapprehended and must argue in support of the motion. Oral argument is not permitted.

(3) *Response.* Unless the district court or BAP requests, no response to a motion for rehearing is permitted. But ordinarily, rehearing will not be granted in the absence of such a request.

(4) *Action by the District Court or BAP.* If a motion for rehearing is granted, the district court or BAP may do any of the following:

(A) make a final disposition of the appeal without reargument;

(B) restore the case to the calendar for reargument or resubmission; or

(C) issue any other appropriate order.

(b) FORM OF THE MOTION; LENGTH. The motion must comply in form with

（1）制作任何所要求的摘要、附录、证物或档案的副本而产生的费用；

（2）准备或移交档案所产生的费用；

（3）记录人制作书面记录的费用（若就上诉案件作出决定需要该书面记录）；

（4）为在上诉案件进行期间保有权利支付保证金或其他担保而产生的费用；

（5）提交上诉通知书的费用。

（d）**成本费用清单；异议**。希望收取该成本费用的当事人必须在上诉判决被正式作出后14日内向破产法院书记员提交经核实且逐项列明的成本费用清单。若有人对此表示异议，则必须在成本费用清单被送达后14日内提交该异议，除非法院对该期间予以延长。

（经 Apr. 25, 2014, eff. Dec. 1, 2014 增补；经 Apr. 26, 2018, eff. Dec. 1, 2018 和 Apr. 27, 2020, eff. Dec. 1, 2020 修正）

第8022条 申请重审的动议

（a）**提交时间；内容；答复；被准予后地区法院或破产上诉合议庭所采取的措施**。

（1）时间。除非该期间被裁定或地方规则予以缩短或延长，否则任何申请由地区法院或破产上诉合议庭举行重审的动议均应在上诉判决被正式作出后14日内被提交。

（2）内容。该动议必须具体说明动议方认为地区法院或破产上诉合议庭忽略或误解的各个法律或事实要点，并且就支持该动议展开论述。不得就该动议举行口头辩论。

（3）答复。除非地区法院破产上诉合议庭作此要求，否则不得就申请重审的动议作出答复。但通常情况下，若并未作此要求，则重审也不会得到准许。

（4）地区法院或破产上诉合议庭所采取的措施。若申请重审的动议得到准许，则地区法院或破产上诉合议庭可采取以下任意措施：

（A）在不再此举行辩论的情况下就上诉作出最终处理；

（B）将案件载入日历中以进行重新辩论或重新提交；或

（C）签发任何其他适当裁定。

（b）**动议的格式；篇幅**。该动议必须符合第8013条（f）（1）及（2）的格式要求。

Rule 8013 (f) (1) and (2). Copies must be served and filed as provided by Rule 8011. Except by the district court's or BAP's permission:

(1) a motion for rehearing produced using a computer must include a certificate under Rule 8015 (h) and not exceed 3,900 words; and

(2) a handwritten or typewritten motion must not exceed 15 pages.

(Added Apr. 25, 2014, eff. Dec. 1, 2014; amended Apr. 26, 2018, eff. Dec. 1, 2018.)

Rule 8023. Voluntary Dismissal

The clerk of the district court or BAP must dismiss an appeal if the parties file a signed dismissal agreement specifying how costs are to be paid and pay any fees that are due. An appeal may be dismissed on the appellant's motion on terms agreed to by the parties or fixed by the district court or BAP.

(Added Apr. 25, 2014, eff. Dec. 1, 2014.)

Rule 8024. Clerk's Duties on Disposition of the Appeal

(a) JUDGMENT ON APPEAL. The district or BAP clerk must prepare, sign, and enter the judgment after receiving the court's opinion or, if there is no opinion, as the court instructs. Noting the judgment on the docket constitutes entry of judgment.

(b) NOTICE OF A JUDGMENT. Immediately upon the entry of a judgment, the district or BAP clerk must:

(1) transmit a notice of the entry to each party to the appeal, to the United States trustee, and to the bankruptcy clerk, together with a copy of any opinion; and

(2) note the date of the transmission on the docket.

(c) RETURNING PHYSICAL ITEMS. If any physical items were transmitted as the record on appeal, they must be returned to the bankruptcy clerk on disposition of the appeal.

(Added Apr. 25, 2014, eff. Dec. 1, 2014.)

副本必须根据第 8011 条的规定而被送达及提交。除非地区法院或破产上诉合议庭作出其他许可，否则该动议须符合以下条件：

（1）使用电脑制作的申请重审的动议必须载有第 8015 条（h）中的证明并不得超过 3900 字；并且

（2）手写或打印的动议不得超过 15 页。

（经 Apr. 25, 2014, eff. Dec. 1, 2014 增补；经 Apr. 26, 2018, eff. Dec. 1, 2018 修正）

第 8023 条　自愿撤诉

若当事人提交了经签署的撤诉协议，且该协议规定了如何支付将支付的成本费用以及任何到期的费用，则地区法院或破产上诉合议庭的书记员必须驳回上诉。上诉可根据当事人达成的合意或者地区法院或破产上诉合议庭所确定的条款而在上诉人的动议下被驳回。

（经 Apr. 25, 2014, eff. Dec. 1, 2014. 增补）

第 8024 条　书记员就上诉案件的处理所承担的义务

（a）**就上诉案件所作的判决**。地区法院或破产上诉合议庭的书记员必须在收到法院的观点后准备、签署并作出判决；若不存在法院观点，则应按法院的指示履行以上各项。应注明案卷中的判决即意味着判决被正式作出。

（b）**判决通知**。在将判决载入案卷时，地区法院或破产上诉合议庭的书记员必须履行以下内容：

（1）将判决被载入的通知以及法院任何观点的副本移交给上诉案件的各当事人、联邦托管人以及破产法院书记员；并且

（2）在案卷中注明移交的日期。

（c）**归还实物**。若有任何实物曾被作为上诉档案而被移交，则书记员必须将其归还给处理上诉案件的破产法院书记员。

（经 Apr. 25, 2014, eff. Dec. 1, 2014. 增补）

U.S. Federal Rules of Bankruptcy Procedure
(Chinese-English bilingual version)

Rule 8025. Stay of a District Court or BAP Judgment

(a) AUTOMATIC STAY OF JUDGMENT ON APPEAL. Unless the district court or BAP orders otherwise, its judgment is stayed for 14 days after entry.

(b) STAY PENDING APPEAL TO THE COURT OF APPEALS.

(1) *In General*. On a party's motion and notice to all other parties to the appeal, the district court or BAP may stay its judgment pending an appeal to the court of appeals.

(2) *Time Limit*. The stay must not exceed 30 days after the judgment is entered, except for cause shown.

(3) *Stay Continued*. If, before a stay expires, the party who obtained the stay appeals to the court of appeals, the stay continues until final disposition by the court of appeals.

(4) *Bond or Other Security*. A bond or other security may be required as a condition for granting or continuing a stay of the judgment. A bond or other security may be required if a trustee obtains a stay, but not if a stay is obtained by the United States or its officer or agency or at the direction of any department of the United States government.

(c) AUTOMATIC STAY OF AN ORDER, JUDGMENT, OR DECREE OF A BANKRUPTCY COURT. If the district court or BAP enters a judgment affirming an order, judgment, or decree of the bankruptcy court, a stay of the district court's or BAP's judgment automatically stays the bankruptcy court's order, judgment, or decree for the duration of the appellate stay.

(d) POWER OF A COURT OF APPEALS NOT LIMITED. This rule does not limit the power of a court of appeals or any of its judges to do the following:

(1) stay a judgment pending appeal;

(2) stay proceedings while an appeal is pending;

(3) suspend, modify, restore, vacate, or grant a stay or an injunction while an appeal is pending; or

(4) issue any order appropriate to preserve the status quo or the effectiveness of any judgment to be entered.

第 8025 条　地区法院或破产上诉合议庭的判决的冻结

（a）上诉判决的自动冻结。除非地区法院或破产上诉合议庭作出其他裁定，否则其判决将在被正式作出后 14 日内被冻结。

（b）向上诉法院上诉期间内的冻结。

（1）一般规定。应当事人的动议并向上诉案件的所有其他当事人发出通知后，地区法院或破产上诉合议庭可在向上诉法院上诉期间内冻结其判决。

（2）时间限制。除非主张存在特定事由，否则该冻结自判决被正式作出时起算不得超过 30 日。

（3）冻结的继续。若在冻结到期前，获得该冻结的当事人向上诉法院提起上诉，则在冻结在上诉法院作出最终处理前均将继续。

（4）保证金或其他担保。保证金或其他担保可被要求作为准予或继续冻结判决的条件。若托管人获得冻结，则可要求其提供保证金或其他担保；但若系美国、其官员或机构获得冻结，或者系在美国政府的任何部门的指示下而获得冻结，则不得要求其提供保证金或其他担保。

（c）破产法院的裁定、判决或法令的自动冻结。若地区法院或破产上诉合议庭正式裁决维持破产法院的裁定、判决或法令，则对地区法院或破产上诉合议庭的判决的冻结将在上诉期间内自动冻结破产法院的裁定、判决或法令。

（d）上诉法院的权力并不受限制。本条并不限制上诉法院或其任何法官采取以下措施的权力：

（1）在上诉案件进行期间冻结判决；

（2）在上诉案件进行期间冻结程序；

（3）在上诉案件进行期间中止、变更、恢复、撤销或提供冻结或禁令；或

（4）签发任何适当的裁定以保持现状或将被作出的任何判决的效力。

U.S. Federal Rules of Bankruptcy Procedure
(Chinese-English bilingual version)

(Added Apr. 25, 2014, eff. Dec. 1, 2014.)

Rule 8026. Rules by Circuit Councils and District Courts; Procedure When There is No Controlling Law

(a) LOCAL RULES BY CIRCUIT COUNCILS AND DISTRICT COURTS.

(1) *Adopting Local Rules.* A circuit council that has authorized a BAP under 28 U.S.C. §158 (b) may make and amend rules governing the practice and procedure on appeal from a judgment, order, or decree of a bankruptcy court to the BAP. A district court may make and amend rules governing the practice and procedure on appeal from a judgment, order, or decree of a bankruptcy court to the district court. Local rules must be consistent with, but not duplicative of, Acts of Congress and these Part VIII rules. Rule 83 F.R.Civ.P. governs the procedure for making and amending rules to govern appeals.

(2) *Numbering.* Local rules must conform to any uniform numbering system prescribed by the Judicial Conference of the United States.

(3) *Limitation on Imposing Requirements of Form.* A local rule imposing a requirement of form must not be enforced in a way that causes a party to lose any right because of a nonwillful failure to comply.

(b) PROCEDURE WHEN THERE IS NO CONTROLLING LAW.

(1) *In General.* A district court or BAP may regulate practice in any manner consistent with federal law, applicable federal rules, the Official Forms, and local rules.

(2) *Limitation on Sanctions.* No sanction or other disadvantage may be imposed for noncompliance with any requirement not in federal law, applicable federal rules, the Official Forms, or local rules unless the alleged violator has been furnished in the particular case with actual notice of the requirement.

(Added Apr. 25, 2014, eff. Dec. 1, 2014.)

Rule 8027. Notice of a Mediation Procedure

If the district court or BAP has a mediation procedure applicable to bankruptcy appeals, the clerk must notify the parties promptly after docketing the appeal of:

美国联邦破产程序规则
（中英对照译本）

（经 Apr. 25, 2014, eff. Dec. 1, 2014. 增补）

第 8026 条　巡回理事会及地区法院的规则；没有约束法时采用的程序

（a）**由巡回理事会及地区法院制定的地方规则。**

（1）适用地方规则。根据《美国联邦法典》第 28 篇第 158 条（b）建立破产上诉合议庭的巡回理事会可制定并修订规制就破产法院的判决、裁定或法令向破产上诉合议庭提起的上诉案件的实践及程序的规则。地区法院可制定并修订规制就破产法院的判决、裁定或法令向地区法院提起的上诉案件的实践及程序的规则。地方规则不得违反《国会法案》以及本部分的规则，但也不得重复于前述规定。制定或修订规制上诉案件的规则应符合《联邦民事诉讼规则》第 83 条的规定。

（2）编号。地方规则必须符合美国司法会议所规定的统一编号系统。

（3）规定格式要求的限制。就规定格式要求的地方规则而言，其实施方式不得使当事人因非出于故意而未能遵守的行为丧失任何权利。

（b）**没有约束法时采用的程序。**

（1）一般规定。地区法院或破产上诉合议庭可以任何符合联邦法律、相应联邦规则、官方模板以及地方规则的方式就法律实践作出规定。

（2）处罚限制。不得因未能遵守联邦法律、相应联邦规则、官方模板或地方规则未有规定的要求而施加处罚或任何其他不利条件，除非在具体案件中已经实际向涉嫌违反者就该要求发出了通知。

（经 Apr. 25, 2014, eff. Dec. 1, 2014. 增补）

第 8027 条　调解程序的通知

若地区法院或破产上诉合议庭就可提供适用于破产上诉的调解程序，则书记员必须在上诉案件立案后及时就以下各项向当事人发出通知：

(a) the requirements of the mediation procedure; and

(b) any effect the mediation procedure has on the time to file briefs.

(Added Apr. 25, 2014, eff. Dec. 1, 2014.)

Rule 8028. Suspension of Rules in Part VIII

In the interest of expediting decision or for other cause in a particular case, the district court or BAP, or where appropriate the court of appeals, may suspend the requirements or provisions of the rules in Part VIII, except Rules 8001, 8002, 8003, 8004, 8005, 8006, 8007, 8012, 8020, 8024, 8025,8026, and 8028.

(Added Apr. 25, 2014, eff. Dec. 1, 2014.)

（a）调解程序的要求；以及

（b）调解程序对提交摘要的时间的任何效力。

（经 Apr. 25, 2014, eff. Dec. 1, 2014. 增补）

第 8028 条　第 VIII 部分中规则的中止

为了加快裁决的速度或在特定案件中出于其他事由，地区法院或破产上诉合议庭或者相应的上诉法院可中止第 VIII 部分规则中的要求或规定的适用，但不包括第 8001 条、8002 条、8003 条、8004 条、8005 条、8006 条、8007 条、8012 条、8020 条、8024 条、8025 条、8026 条及 8028 条。

（经 Apr. 25, 2014, eff. Dec. 1, 2014 增补）

PART IX
GENERAL PROVISIONS

Rule 9001. General Definitions

The definitions of words and phrases in §§101, 902, 1101, and 1502 of the Code, and the rules of construction in §102, govern their use in these rules. In addition, the following words and phrases used in these rules have the meanings indicated:

(1) "Bankruptcy clerk" means a clerk appointed pursuant to 28 U.S.C. §156 (b).

(2) "Bankruptcy Code" or "Code" means title 11 of the United States Code.

(3) "Clerk" means bankruptcy clerk, if one has been appointed, otherwise clerk of the district court.

(4) "Court" or "judge" means the judicial officer before whom a case or proceeding is pending.

(5) "Debtor." When any act is required by these rules to be performed by a debtor or when it is necessary to compel attendance of a debtor for examination and the debtor is not a natural person: (A) if the debtor is a corporation, "debtor" includes, if designated by the court, any or all of its officers, members of its board of directors or trustees or of a similar controlling body, acontrolling stockholder or member, or any other person in control; (B) if the debtor is a partnership, "debtor" includes any or all of its general partners or, if designated by the court, any other person in control.

(6) "Firm" includes a partnership or professional corporation of attorneys or accountants.

(7) "Judgment" means any appealable order.

第 IX 部分
一般规定

第 9001 条　通用定义

法典第 101、902、1101 及 1502 条中的词汇及词组的定义以及第 102 条的解释规则仍适用于本法中前述各项的使用。除此之外，本法中使用的以下词汇及词组具有以下含义：

（1）"破产法院书记员"指根据《美国联邦法典》第 28 篇第 156 条（b）所任命的书记员。

（2）"破产法典"或"法典"指《美国联邦法典》第 11 篇。

（3）"书记员"，若任命有破产法院书记员，则指破产法院书记员，否则指地区法院的书记员。

（4）"法院"或"法官"指正在处理案件或程序的司法官员。

（5）"债务人"当本法要求债务人履行任何行为或当有必要强制债务人出席接受质询时，若债务人并非自然人，则（A）若债务人为公司，则"债务人"包括法院所指定的全部或部分高管、董事会或委员会或者类似主管机构的成员，控股股东或控股成员或者任何其他控制人；（B）若债务人为合伙，则"债务人"包括其全部或部分普通合伙人，或者法院指定的任何其他控制人。

（6）"事务所"包括律师或会计师的合伙组织或专业公司。

（7）"判决"指任何可上诉的裁定。

(8) "Mail" means first class, postage prepaid.

(9) "Notice provider" means any entity approved by the Administrative Office of the United States Courts to give notice to creditors under Rule 2002 (g)(4).

(10) "Regular associate" means any attorney regularly employed by, associated with, or counsel to an individual or firm.

(11) "Trustee" includes a debtor in possession in a chapter 11 case.

(12) "United States trustee" includes an assistant United States trustee and any designee of the United States trustee.

(As amended Mar. 30, 1987, eff. Aug. 1, 1987; Apr. 30, 1991, eff. Aug. 1, 1991; Apr. 25, 2005, eff.Dec. 1, 2005; Apr. 28, 2010, eff. Dec. 1, 2010.)

Rule 9002. Meanings of Words in the Federal Rules of Civil Procedure When Applicable to Cases Under the Code

The following words and phrases used in the Federal Rules of Civil Procedure made applicable to cases under the Code by these rules have the meanings indicated unless they are inconsistent with the context:

(1) "Action" or "civil action" means an adversary proceeding or, when appropriate, a contested petition, or proceedings to vacate an order for relief or to determine any other contested matter.

(2) "Appeal" means an appeal as provided by 28 U.S.C. §158.

(3) "Clerk" or "clerk of the district court" means the court officer responsible for the bankruptcy records in the district.

(4) "District Court," "trial court," "court," "district judge," or "judge" means bankruptcy judge if the case or proceeding is pending before a bankruptcy judge.

(5) "Judgment" includes any order appealable to an appellate court.

(As amended Mar. 30, 1987, eff. Aug. 1, 1987; Apr. 22, 1993, eff. Aug. 1, 1993.)

Rule 9003. Prohibition of Ex Parte Contacts

(a) GENERAL PROHIBITION. Except as otherwise permitted by applicable

（8）"邮件"指预付邮费的一级邮件。

（9）"送达人"指经美国法院行政办公室批准，根据第2002条（g）（4）向债权人发出通知的任何实体。

（10）"长期员工"指个人或事务所长期雇佣、建立合伙或向其征求法律意见的律师。

（11）"托管人"包括第11章案件中的经管债务人。

（12）"联邦托管人"包括联邦托管人的助理以及联邦托管人所指定的人。

（经 Mar. 30, 1987, eff. Aug. 1, 1987; Apr. 30, 1991, eff. Aug. 1, 1991; Apr. 25, 2005, eff.Dec. 1, 2005; Apr. 28, 2010, eff. Dec. 1, 2010. 修正）

第9002条 《联邦民事诉讼规则》中的词汇适用于根据法典所提起的案件中的含义

当《联邦民事诉讼规则》中的词汇及词组因本法规定而适用于根据法典所提起的案件时，除非与上下文相抵触，否则具有以下含义：

（1）"诉讼"或"民事诉讼"指对抗制诉讼程序，或在相应的情况下，也指争议申请或者撤销救济令或就任何其他争议事项作出决定的程序。

（2）"上诉"指《美国联邦法典》第28篇第158条所规定的上诉。

（3）"书记员"或"地区法院的书记员"指负责该辖区内破产档案的法院官员。

（4）若案件或程序正由破产法官处理，则"地区法院"、"审判法院"、"法院"、"地区法官"或"法官"均指破产法官。

（5）"判决"包括可就其向上诉法院提起上诉的任何裁定。

（经 Mar. 30, 1987, eff. Aug. 1, 1987; Apr. 22, 1993, eff. Aug. 1, 1993. 修正）

第9003条 禁止单方接触

（a）一般禁止。除非相应法律作出其他许可，否则任何检查人、任何利益相

law, any examiner, any party in interest, and any attorney, accountant, or employee of a party in interest shall refrain from ex parte meetings and communications with the court concerning matters affecting a particular case or proceeding.

(b) UNITED STATES TRUSTEE. Except as otherwise permitted by applicable law, the United States trustee and assistants to and employees or agents of the United States trustee shall refrain from ex parte meetings and communications with the court concerning matters affecting a particular case or proceeding. This rule does not preclude communications with the court to discuss general problems of administration and improvement of bankruptcy administration, including the operation of the United States trustee system.

(As amended Mar. 30, 1987, eff. Aug. 1, 1987; Apr. 30, 1991, eff. Aug. 1, 1991.)

Rule 9004. General Requirements of Form

(a) LEGIBILITY; ABBREVIATIONS. All petitions, pleadings, schedules and other papers shall be clearly legible. Abbreviations in common use in the English language may be used.

(b) CAPTION. Each paper filed shall contain a caption setting forth the name of the court, the title of the case, the bankruptcy docket number, and a brief designation of the character of the paper.

Rule 9005. Harmless Error

Rule 61 F.R.Civ.P. applies in cases under the Code. When appropriate, the court may order the correction of any error or defect or the cure of any omission which does not affect substantial rights.

Rule 9005.1. Constitutional Challenge to a Statute—Notice, Certification, and Intervention

Rule 5.1 F.R.Civ.P. applies in cases under the Code.

(Added Apr. 30, 2007, eff. Dec. 1, 2007.)

关方以及任何律师、会计师或利益相关方的员工应避免就影响特定案件或程序的事项与法院进行单方会面和交流。

（b）**联邦托管人**。除非相应法律作出其他许可，否则联邦托管人或其助理以及联邦托管人的员工或机构均应避免就影响特定案件或程序的事项与法院进行单方会面和交流。本条并未禁止与法院进行交流以讨论行政管理以及改进破产管理的一般性问题，包括联邦托管人制度的运行。

（经 Mar. 30, 1987, eff. Aug. 1, 1987; Apr. 30, 1991, eff. Aug. 1, 1991. 修正）

第 9004 条　对格式的一般性要求

（a）**易读性；缩写**。所有申请、诉状、报表以及其他文件均应明了易读。可以使用英语中常用的缩写。

（b）**标题**。所有被提交的文件均应包含标题以列明法院的名称、案件的名称、破产案卷编号以及文件性质的简要说明。

第 9005 条　无害的错误

《联邦民事诉讼规则》第 61 条适用于根据法典所提起的案件。在适当情形下，法院可裁定纠正并不影响实质权利的任何错误或缺陷或者纠正任何遗漏。

第 9005.1 条　对法律的宪法挑战——通知、证明以及介入

《联邦民事诉讼规则》第 5.1 条适用于根据法典所提起的案件。

（经 Apr. 30, 2007, eff. Dec. 1, 2007. 增补）

U.S. Federal Rules of Bankruptcy Procedure
(Chinese-English bilingual version)

Rule 9006. Computing and Extending Time; Time for Motion Papers

(a) COMPUTING TIME. The following rules apply in computing any time period specified in these rules, in the Federal Rules of Civil Procedure, in any local rule or court order, or in any statute that does not specify a method of computing time.

(1) *Period Stated in Days or a Longer Unit.* When the period is stated in days or a longer unit of time:

(A) exclude the day of the event that triggers the period;

(B) count every day, including intermediate Saturdays, Sundays, and legal holidays; and

(C) include the last day of the period, but if the last day is a Saturday, Sunday, or legal holiday, the period continues to run until the end of the next day that is not a Saturday, Sunday, or legal holiday.

(2) *Period Stated in Hours.* When the period is stated in hours:

(A) begin counting immediately on the occurrence of the event that triggers the period;

(B) count every hour, including hours during intermediate Saturdays, Sundays, and legal holidays; and

(C) if the period would end on a Saturday, Sunday, or legal holiday, then continue the period until the same time on the next day that is not a Saturday, Sunday, or legal holiday.

(3) *Inaccessibility of Clerk's Office.* Unless the court orders otherwise, if the clerk's office is inaccessible:

(A) on the last day for filing under Rule 9006 (a) (1), then the time for filing is extended to the first accessible day that is not a Saturday, Sunday, or legal holiday; or

(B) during the last hour for filing under Rule 9006 (a) (2), then the time for filing is extended to the same time on the first accessible day that is not a Saturday, Sunday, or legal holiday.

(4) *"Last Day" Defined.* Unless a different time is set by a statute, local rule, or order in the case, the last day ends:

(A) for electronic filing, at midnight in the court's time zone; and

第 9006 条　期间的计算与延长；与动议书相关的期间规定

（a）**期间的计算**。以下规则适用于本法、《联邦民事诉讼规则》、任何地方规则或法院裁定或者任何并未明确说明期间计算方法的法律中所述的任何期间的计算。

（1）采用日或更长时间单位的期间。当期间采用日或更长的时间单位时：

（A）排除触发该期间的事件所发生的当日；
（B）将每日均计入期间，包括期间内的星期六、星期日及法定节假日；并且
（C）将最后一日计入期间，但若最后一日为星期六、星期日或法定节假日，则将其顺延至非星期六、星期日或法定节假日的次日。

（2）以时计算的期间。当期间以时计算时：
（A）在触发该期间的事件发生时立刻起算；

（B）将每小时均计入期间，包括星期六、星期日及法定节假日内的小时；并且
（C）若该期间的最后一日为星期六、星期日或法定节假日，则将其顺延至非星期六、星期日或法定节假日的次日的同一时刻。

（3）无法访问书记员办公室。除非法院作出其他裁定，否则若在以下时间内无法访问书记员办公室，则将适用以下规定：
（A）第 9006 条（a）（1）所规定的提交期间的最后一日，则提交期间应被顺延至非星期六、星期日或法定节假日的可访问该办公室的第一日；或
（B）第 9006 条（a）（2）所规定的提交期间的最后一小时，则提交期间应被顺延至非星期六、星期日或法定节假日的可访问办公室的第一日的同一时刻。

（4）"最后一日"的定义。除非法律、地方规则或案件中的裁定规定有其他时间，否则最后一日将结束于：
（A）就以电子方式提交而言，法院所在时区的午夜；并且

U.S. Federal Rules of Bankruptcy Procedure
(Chinese-English bilingual version)

(B) for filing by other means, when the clerk's office is scheduled to close.

(5) *"Next Day" Defined*. The "next day" is determined by continuing to count forward when the period is measured after an event and backward when measured before an event.

(6) *"Legal Holiday" Defined*. "Legal holiday" means:

(A) the day set aside by statute for observing New Year's Day, Martin Luther King Jr.'s Birthday, Washington's Birthday, Memorial Day, Independence Day, Labor Day, Columbus Day, Veterans' Day, Thanksgiving Day, or Christmas Day;

(B) any day declared a holiday by the President or Congress; and

(C) for periods that are measured after an event, any other day declared a holiday by the state where the district court is located. (In this rule, "state" includes the District of Columbia and any United States commonwealth or territory.)

(b) ENLARGEMENT.

(1) *In General*. Except as provided in paragraphs (2) and (3) of this subdivision, when an act is required or allowed to be done at or within a specified period by these rules or by a notice given thereunder or by order of court, the court for cause shown may at any time in its discretion (1) with or without motion or notice order the period enlarged if the request therefor is made before the expiration of the period originally prescribed or as extended by a previous order or (2) on motion made after the expiration of the specified period permit the act to be done where the failure to act was the result of excusable neglect.

(2) *Enlargement Not Permitted*. The court may not enlarge the time for taking action under Rules 1007 (d), 2003 (a) and (d), 7052, 9023, and 9024.

(3) *Enlargement Governed By Other Rules*. The court may enlarge the time for taking action under Rules 1006 (b) (2), 1017 (e), 3002 (c), 4003 (b), 4004 (a), 4007 (c), 4008 (a), 8002, and 9033, only to the extent and under the conditions stated in those rules. In addition, the court may enlarge the time to file the statement required under Rule 1007 (b) (7), and to file schedules and statements in a small business case under §1116 (3) of the Code, only to the extent and under the conditions stated in Rule 1007 (c).

(B) 就以其他方式提交而言，书记员办公室安排关门的时间。

(5)"次日"的定义。"次日"的确定方法是在事件发生后计算时间时继续向前计算以及在事件发生前计算时间时向后计算。

(6)"法定节假日"的定义。"法定节假日"的含义如下：

(A) 经立法而确定的用于庆祝新年、马丁·路德·金的诞辰、华盛顿的诞辰、阵亡将士纪念日、独立日、劳动节、哥伦比亚纪念日、退伍军人节、感恩节或圣诞节的日子；

(B) 由总统或国会宣布为节日的日子；以及

(C) 就在事件发生后所计算的期间而言，指地区法院所在州所宣布的任何其他节日。（在本条中，"州"包括哥伦比亚特区以及任何美国自由邦或领地。）

(b) 延长。

(1) 一般规定。除本附条第(2)款及第(3)款另有规定外，当某行为被要求或被准予在本法或根据本法而发出的通知或者法院的裁定所规定的某时间或某期间内完成，则法院出于所主张的特定事由可随时行使其自由裁量权（1)若申请延长期间的请求系在所规定的原期间或经先前裁定予以延长的期间届满前而被作出，则无论是否有人提出动议或是否发出通知，法院均可裁定延长该期间；或者（2)在规定的准予完成该行为的期间届满前无人提交动议，在该期间届满后有人提交动议且未能及时提交动议系因可以原谅的过失，则应该动议法院可裁定延长该期间。

(2) 不得延长的期间。法院不得延长根据第1007(d)、2003(a)与(d)、7052、9023及9024条采取相应措施的期间。

(3) 由其他规则所规制的期间的延长。法院在本法规定的条件下可在规定的范围内延长根据第1006(b)(2)条、1017(e)条、3002(c)条、4003(b)条、4004(a)条、4007(c)条、4008(a)条、8002条及9033条采取措施的期间。除此之外，法院在第1007条(c)规定的条件下也可在规定的范围内延长根据第1007条(b)(7)提交所要求的声明的期间以及根据法典第1116条(3)在小企业破产案件中提交报表及声明的期间。

U.S. Federal Rules of Bankruptcy Procedure
(Chinese-English bilingual version)

(c) REDUCTION.

(1) *In General*. Except as provided in paragraph (2) of this subdivision, when an act is required or allowed to be done at or within a specified time by these rules or by a notice given thereunder or by order of court, the court for cause shown may in its discretion with or without motion or notice order the period reduced.

(2) *Reduction Not Permitted*. The court may not reduce the time for taking action under Rules 2002(a)(7), 2003(a), 3002(c), 3014, 3015, 4001(b)(2),(c)(2), 4003(a), 4004(a), 4007(c), 4008(a), 8002, and 9033(b). In addition, the court may not reduce the time under Rule 1007(c) to file the statement required by Rule 1007(b)(7).

(d) MOTION PAPERS. A written motion, other than one which may be heard ex parte, and notice of any hearing shall be served not later than seven days before the time specified for such hearing, unless a different period is fixed by these rules or by order of the court. Such an order may for cause shown be made on ex parte application. When a motion is supported by affidavit, the affidavit shall be served with the motion. Except as otherwise provided in Rule 9023, any written response shall be served not later than one day before the hearing, unless the court permits otherwise.

(e) TIME OF SERVICE. Service of process and service of any paper other than process or of notice by mail is complete on mailing.

(f) ADDITIONAL TIME AFTER SERVICE BY MAIL OR UNDER RULE 5(b)(2)(D) OR (F) F.R.CIV.P. When there is a right or requirement to act or undertake some proceedings within a prescribed period after being served and that service is by mail or under Rule 5(b)(2)(D)(leaving with the clerk) or (F)(other means consented to) F.R.Civ.P., three days are added after the prescribed period would otherwise expire under Rule 9006(a).

(g) GRAIN STORAGE FACILITY CASES. This rule shall not limit the court's authority under §557 of the Code to enter orders governing procedures in cases in which the debtor is an owner or operator of a grain storage facility.

(As amended Mar. 30, 1987, eff. Aug. 1, 1987; Apr. 25, 1989, eff. Aug. 1, 1989; Apr. 30, 1991, eff. Aug. 1, 1991; Apr. 23, 1996, eff. Dec. 1, 1996; Apr. 26, 1999, eff.

美国联邦破产程序规则
（中英对照译本）

（c）缩短。

（1）一般规定。除本附条第（2）款另有规定外，当某行为被要求或被准予在本法或根据本法而发出的通知或者法院的裁定所规定的某时间或某期间内完成，则无论是否有人提交动议或是否发出通知，法院均可出于所主张的特定事由行使其自由裁量权裁定缩短期间。

（2）不得缩短的期间。法院不得缩短根据第2002（a）(7)条、2003（a）条、3002（c）条、3014条、3015条、4001（b）(2)条或（c）(2)条、4003（a）条、4004（a）条、4007（c）条、4008（a）条、8002条以及9033（b）条采取措施的期间。除此之外，法院也不得缩短根据第1007条（c）提交第1007条（b）(7)所要求的声明的期间。

（d）动议书。除可就其举行单方听证的书面动议外，除非本法或法院裁定规定了不同的期间，否则其他书面动议以及任何听证的通知必须在举行听证日前7日以前被送达。出于所主张的特定事由，法院也可基于单方申请作出该裁定。当有宣誓书支持该动议，则该宣誓书应与该动议一同被送达。除第9023条另有规定外，除非法院作出其他许可，否则任何书面答复均应在听证被举行前一日以前而被送达。

（e）送达的时间。若邮寄方式送达司法文书以及除司法文书外的任何文件或通知，则当邮寄时即已完成送达。

（f）邮寄送达或根据《联邦民事诉讼规则》第5（b）(2)(D)或(F)送达后的额外时间。针对邮寄送达或根据《联邦民事诉讼规则》第5（b）(2)(D)（交付给书记员）或(F)（其他所同意的方式）所完成的送达，若有人有权或被要求在被送达后的规定时间内采取或实施某些程序，则该时间将在第9006条（a）所规定的期间届满后额外延长三日。

（g）谷物贮藏设施的有关案件。本条并未限制法院根据法典第557条裁定规制谷物贮藏设施的所有人或经营者的破产案件中的程序。

（经 Mar. 30, 1987, eff. Aug. 1, 1987; Apr. 25, 1989, eff. Aug. 1, 1989; Apr. 30, 1991, eff.Aug. 1, 1991; Apr. 23, 1996, eff. Dec. 1, 1996; Apr. 26, 1999, eff. Dec. 1,

Dec. 1, 1999; Apr. 23, 2001, eff.Dec. 1, 2001; Apr. 25, 2005, eff. Dec. 1, 2005; Apr. 23, 2008, eff. Dec. 1, 2008; Mar. 26, 2009, eff.Dec. 1, 2009; Apr. 16, 2013, eff. Dec. 1, 2013; Apr. 28, 2016, eff. Dec. 1, 2016.)

Rule 9007. General Authority to Regulate Notices

When notice is to be given under these rules, the court shall designate, if not otherwise specified herein, the time within which, the entities to whom, and the form and manner in which the notice shall be given. When feasible, the court may order any notices under these rules to be combined.

(As amended Mar. 30, 1987, eff. Aug. 1, 1987.)

Rule 9008. Service or Notice by Publication

Whenever these rules require or authorize service or notice by publication, the court shall, to the extent not otherwise specified in these rules, determine the form and manner thereof, including the newspaper or other medium to be used and the number of publications.

Rule 9009. Forms

(a) OFFICIAL FORMS. The Official Forms prescribed by the Judicial Conference of the United States shall be used without alteration, except as otherwise provided in these rules, in a particular Official Form, or in the national instructions for a particular Official Form. Official Forms may be modified to permit minor changes not affecting wording or the order of presenting information, including changes that:

(1) expand the prescribed areas for responses in order to permit complete responses;

(2) delete space not needed for responses; or

(3) delete items requiring detail in a question or category if the filer indicates—either by checking "no" or "none" or by stating in words—that there is nothing to report on that question or category.

(b) DIRECTOR'S FORMS. The Director of the Administrative Office of the

1999; Apr. 23, 2001, eff.Dec. 1, 2001; Apr. 25, 2005, eff. Dec. 1, 2005; Apr. 23, 2008, eff. Dec. 1, 2008; Mar. 26, 2009, eff.Dec. 1, 2009; Apr. 16, 2013, eff. Dec. 1, 2013; Apr. 28, 2016, eff. Dec. 1, 2016. 修正）

第 9007 条　规制通知的一般权力

当有人将根据本法发出通知时，若本法未有明确规定，则法院应规定发出通知的期间、向其发出通知的实体以及发出通知的形式及方式。在可行的情况下，法院可裁定合并本法中的任何通知。

（经 Mar. 30, 1987, eff. Aug. 1, 1987. 修正）

第 9008 条　以公告方式送达或通知

当本条要求或准予以公告方式送达或发出通知时，在本法未有明确规定的情况下，法院应决定公告的形式及方式，包括将使用的报纸或其他媒介以及公告的数量。

第 9009 条　模板

（a）**官方模板**。除非本法、某特定官方模板或某特定官方模板的国家指示说明中另有规定，否则美国司法会议所规定的官方模板应被不加改动地使用。但也可在不影响措辞或信息提供顺序的情况下作出微小改动，包括以下各项：

（1）扩大用于提供答复的规定区域以提供完整的答复；

（2）删除提供答复所不需要的空间；或

（3）若填写者通过勾"否"或"无"或者用注明并无就该问题或类别的说明，则可删除要求其就该问题或类别进行详细说明的部分。

（b）**主任的模板**。美国法院行政办公室主任可规定额外其他模板从而根据法

U.S. Federal Rules of Bankruptcy Procedure
(Chinese-English bilingual version)

United States Courts may issue additional forms for use under the Code.

(c) CONSTRUCTION. The forms shall be construed to be consistent with these rules and the Code.

(As amended Apr. 30, 1991, eff. Aug. 1, 1991; Apr. 23, 2008, eff. Dec. 1, 2008; Apr. 27, 2017, eff.Dec. 1, 2017.)

Rule 9010. Representation and Appearances; Powers of Attorney

(a) AUTHORITY TO ACT PERSONALLY OR BY ATTORNEY. A debtor, creditor, equity security holder, indenture trustee, committee or other party may (1) appear in a case under the Code and act either in the entity's own behalf or by an attorney authorized to practice in the court, and (2) perform any act not constituting the practice of law, by an authorized agent, attorney in fact, or proxy.

(b) NOTICE OF APPEARANCE. An attorney appearing for a party in a case under the Code shall file a notice of appearance with the attorney's name, office address and telephone number, unless the attorney's appearance is otherwise noted in the record.

(c) POWER OF ATTORNEY. The authority of any agent, attorney in fact, or proxy to represent a creditor for any purpose other than the execution and filing of a proof of claim or the acceptance or rejection of a plan shall be evidenced by a power of attorney conforming substantially to the appropriate Official Form. The execution of any such power of attorney shall be acknowledged before one of the officers enumerated in 28 U.S.C. §459, §953, Rule 9012, or a person authorized to administer oaths under the laws of the state where the oath is administered.

(As amended Mar. 30, 1987, eff. Aug. 1, 1987; Apr. 30, 1991, eff. Aug. 1, 1991.)

Rule 9011. Signing of Papers; Representations to the Court; Sanctions; Verification and Copies of Papers

(a) SIGNATURE. Every petition, pleading, written motion, and other paper, except a list, schedule, or statement, or amendments thereto, shall be signed by at least one attorney of record in the attorney's individual name. A party who is not represented by an attorney shall sign all papers. Each paper shall state the signer's address and telephone

典予以使用。

（c）**解释**。前述模板应根据与本法及法典规定相符合的方式进行解释。

（经 Apr. 30, 1991, eff. Aug. 1, 1991; Apr. 23, 2008, eff. Dec. 1, 2008; Apr. 27, 2017, eff.Dec. 1, 2017. 增补）

第 9010 条　代表及出席；律师的权力

（a）**亲自行动或由律师代表的权利**。债务人、债权人、股本证券持有人、契约受托人、委员会或其他当事人可（1）出席根据法典所提交的案件并亲自行动或由被准予在法院执业的律师代表其行动，以及（2）由授权代理人、事实代理人或表决代理人实施除法律实务外的行为。

（b）**出席通知书**。在根据法典而提交的破产案件中，除非律师的出席被以其他方式载于档案中，否则代表当事人出席的律师应提交出席通知书以告知其姓名、办公地址及电话号码。

（c）**授权书**。任何代理人、事实代理人或表决代理人出于除制作及提交债权证明或者接受或拒绝计划外的任何目的而代表债权人时，均应由基本符合相应官方模板的授权书来予以证明。该类授权书的制作应经《美国联邦法典》第 28 篇第 459 条、第 953 条或本法第 9012 条所列明的官员中的一员或被授权根据主持宣誓所在地的州法主持宣誓的人的认证。

（经 Mar. 30, 1987, eff. Aug. 1, 1987; Apr. 30, 1991, eff. Aug. 1, 1991. 确认）

第 9011 条　文件的签署；向法院证明；处罚；文件的核证与副本

（a）**签署**。除清单、报表或声明外的所有申请、诉状、书面动议以及其他文件或者前述各项的修正文本均必须由至少一名备案律师在其上签署其个人姓名。未由律师所代表的当事人应在所有文件上签署其姓名。所有文件均应被注明签署人的住址及电话号码（如有）。未经签署的文件不得采用，除非签名的遗漏在引

number, if any. An unsigned paper shall be stricken unless omission of the signature is corrected promptly after being called to the attention of the attorney or party.

(b) REPRESENTATIONS TO THE COURT. By presenting to the court (whether by signing, filing, submitting, or later advocating) a petition, pleading, written motion, or other paper, an attorney or unrepresented party is certifying that to the best of the person's knowledge, information, and belief, formed after an inquiry reasonable under the circumstances,—

(1) it is not being presented for any improper purpose, such as to harass or to cause unnecessary delay or needless increase in the cost of litigation;

(2) the claims, defenses, and other legal contentions therein are warranted by existing law or by a nonfrivolous argument for the extension, modification, or reversal of existing law or the establishment of new law;

(3) the allegations and other factual contentions have evidentiary support or, if specifically so identified, are likely to have evidentiary support after a reasonable opportunity for further investigation or discovery; and

(4) the denials of factual contentions are warranted on the evidence or, if specifically so identified, are reasonably based on a lack of information or belief.

(c) SANCTIONS. If, after notice and a reasonable opportunity to respond, the court determines that subdivision (b) has been violated, the court may, subject to the conditions stated below, impose an appropriate sanction upon the attorneys, law firms, or parties that have violated subdivision (b) or are responsible for the violation.

(1) *How Initiated.*

(A) *By Motion.* A motion for sanctions under this rule shall be made separately from other motions or requests and shall describe the specific conduct alleged to violate subdivision (b). It shall be served as provided in Rule 7004. The motion for sanctions may not be filed with or presented to the court unless, within 21 days after service of the motion (or such other period as the court may prescribe), the challenged paper, claim, defense, contention, allegation, or denial is not withdrawn or appropriately corrected, except that this limitation shall not apply if the conduct alleged is the filing of a petition in violation of subdivision (b). If warranted, the court may award to the party

美国联邦破产程序规则
（中英对照译本）

起律师或当事人的注意后已被及时补正。

（b）**向法院证明**。通过向法院出示（无论是通过签署、提交、交付或其后提起诉讼）申请、诉状、书面动议或其他文件，律师或无律师代表的当事人须证明经过合理的调查后根据其掌握的内容和信息以及所相信的情况：

（1）前述文件并非出于任何不正当的目的而被提交，如干扰诉讼或造成不必要的迟延或者增加诉讼成本；

（2）其中的权利主张、抗辩以及其他法律主张存在现行法律或者扩张、修改或推翻现行法律或制定新的法律的重要论据的支持；

（3）其主张及其他事实观点存在证据支持，或者具体说明在有合理机会进行进一步的调查后有可能找到该证据；以及

（4）对某事实观点的否认存在证据支持或者具体说明由于信息或确信的缺乏有合理理由否认该事实观点。

（c）**处罚**。若在发出通知并提供作出答复的合理机会后法院认定律师、律师事务所或当事人已经违反了附条（b）的规定，则法院可在下列条件下向前述主体或就该违法行为负责的主体施加相应的处罚。

（1）如何提起。

（A）通过提交动议。根据本条申请施加处罚的动议应有别于其他动议或请求而被单独作出，并且应当说明被主张违反附条（b）规定的具体行为。该动议应根据第 7004 条而被送达。若在动议被送达后 21 日内（或法官可规定的其他期间内），被提出异议的文件、权利主张、抗辩、争议、主张或否认被撤回或得到相应的修正，则不得向法院提交或出示申请处罚的动议，但若该动议所针对的行为系违反（b）款规定而提交破产申请的行为，则不适用前述限制。若有充分证据支持，则法院可准予该动议中的胜诉方获得在提出或反对该动议的过程中所承担的合理的支出以及律师费。如无特殊情况，律师事务所应就其合伙人、成员以

prevailing on the motion the reasonable expenses and attorney's fees incurred in presenting or opposing the motion. Absent exceptional circumstances, a law firm shall be held jointly responsible for violations committed by its partners, associates, and employees.

（B） *On Court's Initiative*. On its own initiative, the court may enter an order describing the specific conduct that appears to violate subdivision （b） and directing an attorney, law firm, or party to show cause why it has not violated subdivision （b） with respect thereto.

（2） *Nature of Sanction; Limitations*. A sanction imposed for violation of this rule shall be limited to what is sufficient to deter repetition of such conduct or comparable conduct by others similarly situated. Subject to the limitations in subparagraphs（A）and（B）, the sanction may consist of, or include, directives of a nonmonetary nature, an order to pay a penalty into court, or, if imposed on motion and warranted for effective deterrence, an order directing payment to the movant of some or all of the reasonable attorneys' fees and other expenses incurred as a direct result of the violation.

（A） Monetary sanctions may not be awarded against a represented party for a violation of subdivision （b）（2）.

（B） Monetary sanctions may not be awarded on the court's initiative unless the court issues its order to show cause before a voluntary dismissal or settlement of the claims made by or against the party which is, or whose attorneys are, to be sanctioned.

（3） *Order*. When imposing sanctions, the court shall describe the conduct determined to constitute a violation of this rule and explain the basis for the sanction imposed.

（d） INAPPLICABILITY TO DISCOVERY. Subdivisions （a） through （c） of this rule do not apply to disclosures and discovery requests, responses, objections, and motions that are subject to the provisions of Rules 7026 through 7037.

（e） VERIFICATION. Except as otherwise specifically provided by these rules, papers filed in a case under the Code need not be verified. Whenever verification is required by these rules, an unsworn declaration as provided in 28 U.S.C. §1746 satisfies the requirement of verification.

（f） COPIES OF SIGNED OR VERIFIED PAPERS. When these rules require

及员工的违法行为与其共同承担责任。

（B）法院主动提起。法院可主动签发裁定以指出可能违反附条（b）规定的具体行为并裁定律师、律师事务所或当事人说明其未违反附条（b）相应规定的事由。

（2）处罚的性质；限制。对违反本条规定而施加的处罚应被限于足以防止处于类似情形中的他人重复该行为或类似行为的范围。在遵守附款（A）及附款（B）限制的情况下，该处罚可由后述各项组成或包含后述各项：非金钱性质的指令、向法院支付罚金的裁定或者基于动议并且出于实现有效威慑的目的，也可包括裁定向动议人支付部分或全部合理的律师费用以及因该违法行为而直接导致的其他支出的裁定。

（A）不得因对附条（b）（2）规定的违反而对由律师所代表的当事人处以金钱处罚。
（B）除非在将被处罚的当事人或其律师自愿撤回案件或就对其享有的权利主张达成和解前法院签发裁定以说明特定事由，否则法院不得主动施加金钱处罚。

（3）裁定。当施加处罚时，法院应指出被认定为违反本条规定的行为并说明施加该处罚的依据。

（d）**不适用于披露**。本条附条（a）至附条（c）不适用于第7026条至第7037条所规定的披露以及披露请求、答复、异议以及动议。

（e）**核证**。除本法另有规定外，在根据法典所提交的案件中被提交的文件无须核证。当本法要求就某材料进行核证时，《美国联邦法典》第28篇第1746条所规定的未经宣誓程序的声明即符合核证要求。

（f）**已签署或经核证的文件的副本**。当本法要求提供已签署或经核证的文件

copies of a signed or verified paper, it shall suffice if the original is signed or verified and the copies are conformed to the original.

(As amended Mar. 30, 1987, eff. Aug. 1, 1987; Apr. 30, 1991, eff. Aug. 1, 1991; Apr. 11, 1997, eff.Dec. 1, 1997.)

Rule 9012. Oaths and Affirmations

(a) PERSONS AUTHORIZED TO ADMINISTER OATHS. The following persons may administer oaths and affirmations and take acknowledgments: a bankruptcy judge, clerk, deputy clerk, United States trustee, officer authorized to administer oaths in proceedings before the courts of the United States or under the laws of the state where the oath is to be taken, or a diplomatic or consular officer of the United States in any foreign country.

(b) AFFIRMATION IN LIEU OF OATH. When in a case under the Code an oath is required to be taken a solemn affirmation may be accepted in lieu thereof.

(As amended Mar. 30, 1987, eff. Aug. 1, 1987; Apr. 30, 1991, eff. Aug. 1, 1991.)

Rule 9013. Motions: Form and Service

A request for an order, except when an application is authorized by the rules, shall be by written motion, unless made during a hearing. The motion shall state with particularity the grounds therefor, and shall set forth the relief or order sought. Every written motion, other than one which may be considered ex parte, shall be served by the moving party within the time determined under Rule 9006 (d). The moving party shall serve the motion on:

(a) the trustee or debtor in possession and on those entities specified by these rules; or

(b) the entities the court directs if these rules do not require service or specify the entities to be served.

(As amended Mar. 30, 1987, eff. Aug. 1, 1987; Apr. 16, 2013, eff. Dec. 1, 2013.)

Rule 9014. Contested Matters

(a) MOTION. In a contested matter not otherwise governed by these rules, relief

的副本时，只要原件已经签署或核证并且副本与原件相符即可。

（经 Mar. 30, 1987, eff. Aug. 1, 1987; Apr. 30, 1991, eff. Aug. 1, 1991; Apr. 11, 1997, eff.Dec. 1, 1997. 修正）

第9012条 宣誓及发誓

（a）**经授权主持宣誓的人**。后述主体可主持宣誓及作证并对其予以认证：破产法官、书记员、副书记员、联邦托管人、被授权在美国法院所处理的程序中或根据宣誓地所在州的法律在主持宣誓的官员或者美国在任何境外国家的外交或领事官员。

（b）**代替宣誓的发誓**。当在根据法典所提交的案件中被要求宣誓，则可由庄严的发誓代替宣誓。

（经 Mar. 30, 1987, eff. Aug. 1, 1987; Apr. 30, 1991, eff. Aug. 1, 1991. 增补）

第9013条 动议：格式及送达

除非系在听证中作出请求，否则除本法准予的申请外，均应通过提交书面动议从而申请法院作出裁定。该动议应具体说明其理由，并应注明所寻求的救济或裁定。除可被认定为单方动议外的所有书面动议均应由动议方在根据第9006条（d）而确定的时间内被送达。动议方应将该动议送达给：

（a）托管人或经管债务人以及本法所规定的实体；或
（b）本法并未要求送达或规定向其送达的实体时，法院所指定的实体。

（经 Mar. 30, 1987, eff. Aug. 1, 1987; Apr. 16, 2013, eff. Dec. 1, 2013. 修正）

第9014条 争议事项

（a）**动议**。在本法未有其他规定的争议事项中，应通过提交动议而寻求救济，

shall be requested by motion, and reasonable notice and opportunity for hearing shall be afforded the party against whom relief is sought. No response is required under this rule unless the court directs otherwise.

(b) SERVICE. The motion shall be served in the manner provided for service of a summons and complaint by Rule 7004 and within the time determined under Rule 9006 (d). Any written response to the motion shall be served within the time determined under Rule 9006 (d). Any paper served after the motion shall be served in the manner provided by Rule 5 (b) F.R.Civ.P.

(c) APPLICATION OF PART VII RULES. Except as otherwise provided in this rule, and unless the court directs otherwise, the following rules shall apply: 7009, 7017, 7021, 7025, 7026, 7028-7037, 7041, 7042, 7052, 7054-7056, 7064, 7069, and 7071. The following subdivisions of Fed. R. Civ. P. 26, as incorporated by Rule 7026, shall not apply in a contested matter unless the court directs otherwise: 26 (a) (1) (mandatory disclosure), 26 (a) (2) (disclosures regarding expert testimony) and 26 (a) (3) (additional pre-trial disclosure), and 26 (f) (mandatory meeting before scheduling conference/discovery plan). An entity that desires to perpetuate testimony may proceed in the same manner as provided in Rule 7027 for the taking of a deposition before an adversary proceeding. The court may at any stage in a particular matter direct that one or more of the other rules in Part VII shall apply. The court shall give the parties notice of any order issued under this paragraph to afford them a reasonable opportunity to comply with the procedures prescribed by the order.

(d) TESTIMONY OF WITNESSES. Testimony of witnesses with respect to disputed material factual issues shall be taken in the same manner as testimony in an adversary proceeding.

(e) ATTENDANCE OF WITNESSES. The court shall provide procedures that enable parties to ascertain at a reasonable time before any scheduled hearing whether the hearing will be an evidentiary hearing at which witnesses may testify.

(As amended Mar. 30, 1987, eff. Aug. 1, 1987; Apr. 26, 1999, eff. Dec. 1, 1999; Apr. 29, 2002, eff.Dec. 1, 2002; Apr. 26, 2004, eff. Dec. 1, 2004; Apr. 16, 2013, eff. Dec. 1, 2013.)

美国联邦破产程序规则
（中英对照译本）

并且应向该救济所针对的当事人发出合理的通知并提供发表意见的机会。除非法院作出其他指示，否则本条并不要求作出答复。

（b）**送达**。该动议应被以第7004条规定的用以送达传票及诉状的方式而在根据第9006条（d）所确定的时间内送达。就该动议所作的任何书面答复均应在根据第9006条（d）所确定的时间内被送达。在该动议后所要送达的任何文件均应以《联邦民事诉讼规则》第5条（b）所规定的方式送达。

（c）**第VII部分规则的适用**。除本条另有规定外，除非法院作出其他指示，否则以下条文均应得以适用：第7009条、7017条、7021条、7025条、7026条、7028条至7037条、7041条、7042条、7052条、7054条至7056条、7064条、7069条以及7071条。除非法院作出其他指示，否则第7026条所引用的《联邦民事诉讼规则》第26条中的下列各款均不得适用于争议事项中：26（a）（1）（强制披露）、26（a）（2）（就专家证词所作的披露）、26（a）（3）（额外的审前披露）以及26（f）（预定会议/调查计划前的强制会见）。希望保全证言的实体可以第7027条规定的方式在对抗制诉讼程序前进行宣誓。法院可在某一事项的任何阶段指示适用第VII部分中的一项或多项其他规则。法院应就根据本段所签发的任何裁定向当事人发出通知从而提供其合理机会以履行该裁定所规定的程序。

（d）**证人证言**。针对有争议的重大事实问题，应以对抗制诉讼程序中收集证言的方式收集证人证言。

（e）**证人的出席**。法院应对程序予以规定从而使得当事人能够在任何预定听证前的合理时间内确定该听证是否为证人可以作证的证据听证。

（经 Mar. 30, 1987, eff. Aug. 1, 1987; Apr. 26, 1999, eff. Dec. 1, 1999; Apr. 29, 2002, eff. Dec. 1, 2002; Apr. 26, 2004, eff. Dec. 1, 2004; Apr. 16, 2013, eff. Dec. 1, 2013. 修正）

U.S. Federal Rules of Bankruptcy Procedure
(Chinese-English bilingual version)

Rule 9015. Jury Trials

(a) APPLICABILITY OF CERTAIN FEDERAL RULES OF CIVIL PROCEDURE. Rules 38, 39, 47-49, and 51, F.R.Civ.P., and Rule 81 (c) F.R.Civ.P. in so far as it applies to jury trials, apply in cases and proceedings, except that a demand made under Rule 38 (b) F.R.Civ.P. shall be filed in accordance with Rule 5005.

(b) CONSENT TO HAVE TRIAL CONDUCTED BY BANKRUPTCY JUDGE. If the right to a jury trial applies, a timely demand has been filed pursuant to Rule 38(b) F.R.Civ.P., and the bankruptcy judge has been specially designated to conduct the jury trial, the parties may consent to have a jury trial conducted by a bankruptcy judge under 28 U.S.C. §157 (e) by jointly or separately filing a statement of consent within any applicable time limits specified by local rule.

(c) APPLICABILITY OF RULE 50 F.R.CIV.P. Rule 50 F.R.Civ.P. applies in cases and proceedings, except that any renewed motion for judgment or request for a new trial shall be filed no later than 14 days after the entry of judgment.

(Added Apr. 11, 1997, eff. Dec. 1, 1997; amended Mar. 26, 2009, eff. Dec. 1, 2009.)

Rule 9016. Subpoena

Rule 45 F.R.Civ.P. applies in cases under the Code.

(As amended Mar. 30, 1987, eff. Aug. 1, 1987.)

Rule 9017. Evidence

The Federal Rules of Evidence and Rules 43, 44 and 44.1 F.R.Civ.P. apply in cases under the Code.

Rule 9018. Secret, Confidential, Scandalous, or Defamatory Matter

On motion or on its own initiative, with or without notice, the court may make any order which justice requires (1) to protect the estate or any entity in respect of a trade secret or other confidential research, development, or commercial information, (2) to protect any entity against scandalous or defamatory matter contained in any paper filed in a case under the Code, or (3) to protect governmental matters that are

美国联邦破产程序规则
（中英对照译本）

第 9015 条　陪审团庭审

（a）《联邦民事诉讼规则》的适用。《联邦民事诉讼规则》第 38 条、39 条、47 条至 49 条以及第 51 条，与《联邦民事诉讼规则》第 81 条（c）中适用于陪审团庭审的部分仍将适用于相应案件及程序，但根据《联邦民事诉讼规则》第 38 条（b）所提出的诉讼请求应被根据第 5005 条而提交。

（b）同意由破产法官举行庭审。若有权由陪审团进行审理，并且已经及时根据《联邦民事诉讼规则》第 38 条（b）提交诉讼请求，而且破产法官已经被明确指示举行陪审团庭审，则当事人可通过在地方规则所规定的相应时限内联合或单独提交同意声明从而同意由破产法官根据《美国联邦法典》第 28 篇第 157 条（e）举行陪审团庭审。

（c）《联邦民事诉讼规则》第 50 条的适用。《联邦民事诉讼规则》第 50 条仍适用于相应案件及程序，但再次申请获得裁决的任何动议或申请重新举行庭审的任何请求均应在判决被载入案卷后 14 日内被提交。

（经 Apr. 11, 1997, eff. Dec. 1, 1997 增补；经 Mar. 26, 2009, eff. Dec. 1, 2009. 修正）

第 9016 条　传票

《联邦民事诉讼规则》第 45 条适用于根据法典所提交的破产案件。

（经 Mar. 30, 1987, eff. Aug. 1, 1987. 修正）

第 9017 条　证据

《联邦证据规则》以及《联邦民事诉讼规则》第 43 条、44 条以及 44.1 条适用于根据法典所提交的破产案件。

第 9018 条　秘密、机密、绯闻或诽谤事项

法院可应动议或主动在发出通知或不发出通知的情况下出于正义而作出任何裁定从而（1）就商业秘密或其他机密研究、研发或商业信息，保护破产财团或任何实体，（2）保护任何实体使其在根据法典所提交的案件中免受在被提交的任何文件中涉及的绯闻或诽谤性事件的影响，或（3）保护因法律法规而应保密的政府事项。若根据本条作出裁定并且并未发出通知，则受此影响的任何实体均可

made confidential by statute or regulation. If an order is entered under this rule without notice, any entity affected thereby may move to vacate or modify the order, and after a hearing on notice the court shall determine the motion.

(As amended Mar. 30, 1987, eff. Aug. 1, 1987.)

Rule 9019. Compromise and Arbitration

(a) COMPROMISE. On motion by the trustee and after notice and a hearing, the court may approve a compromise or settlement. Notice shall be given to creditors, the United States trustee, thedebtor, and indenture trustees as provided in Rule 2002 and to any other entity as the court may direct.

(b) AUTHORITY TO COMPROMISE OR SETTLE CONTROVERSIES WITHIN CLASSES. After a hearing on such notice as the court may direct, the court may fix a class or classes of controversies and authorize the trustee to compromise or settle controversies within such class or classes without further hearing or notice.

(c) ARBITRATION. On stipulation of the parties to any controversy affecting the estate the court may authorize the matter to be submitted to final and binding arbitration.

(As amended Mar. 30, 1987, eff. Aug. 1, 1987; Apr. 30, 1991, eff. Aug. 1, 1991; Apr. 22, 1993, eff.Aug. 1, 1993.)

Rule 9020. Contempt Proceedings

Rule 9014 governs a motion for an order of contempt made by the United States trustee or a party in interest.

(As amended Mar. 30, 1987, eff. Aug. 1, 1987; Apr. 30, 1991, eff. Aug. 1, 1991; Apr. 23, 2001, eff.Dec. 1, 2001.)

Rule 9021. Entry of Judgment

A judgment or order is effective when entered under Rule 5003.

(As amended Mar. 30, 1987, eff. Aug. 1, 1987; Mar. 26, 2009, eff. Dec. 1, 2009.)

提交动议以申请撤销或变更该裁定，并且在发出通知并举行听证后，法院应就该动议作出决定。

（经 Mar. 30, 1987, eff. Aug. 1, 1987. 修正）

第 9019 条　和解及仲裁

（a）和解。应托管人的动议，经过通知和听证后，法院可批准和解协议。应根据第 2002 条的规定向债权人、联邦托管人、债务人以及契约受托人和法院可指定的任何其他实体发出通知。

（b）就某类争议达成和解的许可。在发出通知（法院可对此作出指示）和举行听证后，法院可对争议事项进行分类，并准予托管人在不进行其他听证或通知的情况下就某类或多类内的争议达成和解。

（c）仲裁。根据影响破产财团的任何争议事项而由当事人达成的协议，法院可准予将该争议移交仲裁，并且该仲裁结果具有约束力且为终局裁决。

（经 Mar. 30, 1987, eff. Aug. 1, 1987; Apr. 30, 1991, eff. Aug. 1, 1991; Apr. 22, 1993, eff.Aug. 1, 1993. 修正）

第 9020 条　藐视法庭程序

联邦托管人或利益相关方申请藐视法庭裁定的动议将由第 9014 条所规制。

（经 Mar. 30, 1987, eff. Aug. 1, 1987; Apr. 30, 1991, eff. Aug. 1, 1991; Apr. 23, 2001, eff.Dec. 1, 2001. 修正）

第 9021 条　判决的载入

根据第 5003 条将判决或裁定载入案卷时，判决或裁定生效。

（经 Mar. 30, 1987, eff. Aug. 1, 1987; Mar. 26, 2009, eff. Dec. 1, 2009. 修正）

U.S. Federal Rules of Bankruptcy Procedure
(Chinese-English bilingual version)

Rule 9022. Notice of Judgment or Order

(a) JUDGMENT OR ORDER OF BANKRUPTCY JUDGE. Immediately on the entry of a judgment or order the clerk shall serve a notice of entry in the manner provided in Rule 5 (b) F.R.Civ.P. on the contesting parties and on other entities as the court directs. Unless the case is a chapter 9 municipality case, the clerk shall forthwith transmit to the United States trustee a copy of the judgment or order. Service of the notice shall be noted in the docket. Lack of notice of the entry does not affect the time to appeal or relieve or authorize the court to relieve a party for failure to appeal within the time allowed, except as permitted in Rule 8002.

(b) JUDGMENT OR ORDER OF DISTRICT JUDGE. Notice of a judgment or order entered by a district judge is governed by Rule 77 (d) F.R.Civ.P. Unless the case is a chapter 9 municipality case, the clerk shall forthwith transmit to the United States trustee a copy of a judgment or order entered by a district judge.

(As amended Mar. 30, 1987, eff. Aug. 1, 1987; Apr. 30, 1991, eff. Aug. 1, 1991; Apr. 23, 2001, eff.Dec. 1, 2001.)

Rule 9023. New Trials; Amendment of Judgments

Except as provided in this rule and Rule 3008, Rule 59 F.R.Civ.P. applies in cases under the Code.A motion for a new trial or to alter or amend a judgment shall be filed, and a court may on its own order a new trial, no later than 14 days after entry of judgment. In some circumstances, Rule 8008 governs post-judgment motion practice after an appeal has been docketed and is pending.

(As amended Mar. 26, 2009, eff. Dec. 1, 2009; Apr. 25, 2014, eff. Dec. 1, 2014.)

Rule 9024. Relief from Judgment or Order

Rule 60 F.R.Civ.P. applies in cases under the Code except that (1) a motion to reopen a case under the Code or for the reconsideration of an order allowing or disallowing a claim against the estate entered without a contest is not subject to the one year limitation prescribed in Rule 60 (c), (2) a complaint to revoke a discharge in a chapter 7 liquidation case may be filed only within the time allowed by §727 (e) of the

美国联邦破产程序规则
(中英对照译本)

第 9022 条　判决或裁定的通知

（a）**破产法官的判决或裁定**。在载入判决或裁定后，书记员应立刻以《联邦民事诉讼规则》第 5 条（b）所规定的方式将载入通知送达给争议事项的各方当事人以及法院可指定的其他实体。除第 9 章市政机构破产案件外，书记员应立刻将判决或裁定的副本移交给联邦托管人。应在案卷中注明通知已被送达。未发出载入通知并不影响提起上诉的期间或者为未能在规定的时间内（除第 8002 条另有许可外）提起上诉的当事人提供救济或授权法院向其提供救济。

（b）**地区法官的判决或裁定**。就地区法官所作的判决或裁定的通知应符合《联邦民事诉讼规则》第 77 条（d）的规定。除第 9 章市政机构破产案件外，书记员应立刻将地区法官所作出的判决或裁定的副本移交给联邦托管人。

（经 Mar. 30, 1987, eff. Aug. 1, 1987; Apr. 30, 1991, eff. Aug. 1, 1991; Apr. 23, 2001, eff.Dec. 1, 2001. 修正）

第 9023 条　新的庭审；判决的修正

除本条及第 3008 条另有规定外，《联邦民事诉讼规则》第 59 条适用于根据法典所提交的破产案件。若要申请举行新的庭审或者变更或修正判决，则应在判决被载入后 14 日内提交动议，并且法院也可在该期间内主动裁定举行新的庭审。在某些情形下，在上诉已被载入案卷并就其进行审理期间内所提交的判决后动议由第 8008 条所规制。

（经 Mar. 26, 2009, eff. Dec. 1, 2009; Apr. 25, 2014, eff. Dec. 1, 2014. 修正）

第 9024 条　就判决或裁定获得救济

《联邦民事诉讼规则》第 60 条适用于根据法典所提交的破产案件，但是（1）申请重启根据法典所提交的破产案件的动议，或申请重新审议未有异议的情况下所作的确认或否认就破产财团享有的债权的裁定的动议并不适用于第 60 条（c）所规定的一年的时间限制；（2）申请撤销第 7 章清算案件中的免责的诉状仅能在法典第 727 条（e）所规定的时间内被提交；并且（3）申请撤销批准计划的裁定

Code, and (3) a complaint to revoke an order confirming a plan may be filed only within the time allowed by §1144, §1230, or §1330. In some circumstances, Rule 8008 governs post-judgment motion practice after an appeal has been docketed and is pending.

(As amended Apr. 30, 1991, eff. Aug. 1, 1991; Apr. 23, 2008, eff. Dec. 1, 2008; Apr. 25, 2014, eff.Dec. 1, 2014.)

Rule 9025. Security: Proceedings Against Security Providers

Whenever the Code or these rules require or permit a party to give security, and security is given with one or more security providers, each provider submits to the jurisdiction of the court, and liability may be determined in an adversary proceeding governed by the rules in Part VII.

(As amended Apr. 26, 2018, eff. Dec. 1, 2018)

Rule 9026. Exceptions Unnecessary

Rule 46 F.R.Civ.P. applies in cases under the Code.

Rule 9027. Removal

(a) NOTICE OF REMOVAL.

(1) *Where Filed; Form and Content.* A notice of removal shall be filed with the clerk for the district and division within which is located the state or federal court where the civil action is pending. The notice shall be signed pursuant to Rule 9011 and contain a short and plain statement of the facts which entitle the party filing the notice to remove, contain a statement that upon removal of the claim or cause of action, the party filing the notice does or does not consent to entry of final orders or judgment by the bankruptcy court, and be accompanied by a copy of all process and pleadings.

(2) *Time for Filing; Civil Action Initiated Before Commencement of the Case Under the Code.* If the claim or cause of action in a civil action is pending when a case under the Code is commenced, a notice of removal may be filed only within the longest of (A) 90 days after the order for relief in the case under the Code, (B) 30 days after entry of an order terminating a stay, if the claim or cause of action in a civil action

的诉状仅能在第 1144 条、第 1230 条或第 1330 条所规定的时间内被提交。在某些情况下，在上诉已被载入案卷并就其进行审理期间内所提交的判决后动议由第 8008 条所规制。

（经 Apr. 30, 1991, eff. Aug. 1, 1991; Apr. 23, 2008, eff. Dec. 1, 2008; Apr. 25, 2014, eff.Dec. 1, 2014. 修正）

第 9025 条　担保：针对担保人所提起的程序

当法典或本法要求或准予当事人提供担保，并且该担保系由一位或多位担保人所提供时，法院对各位担保人均具有管辖权，并且可通过由第 VII 部分的规则所规制的对抗制诉讼程序判决其承担责任。

（经 Apr. 26, 2018, eff. Dec. 1, 2018 修正）

第 9026 条　没有必要的例外

《联邦民事诉讼规则》第 46 条适用于根据法典所提交的案件。

第 9027 条　移案

（a）移案通知书。

（1）提交的地点；格式及内容。应向正在审理该民事诉讼的州或联邦法院所在区域及辖区内的书记员提交移案通知书。该通知应根据第 9011 条被签署并载有当事人提交移案通知书所依据的事实的简要陈述，载有权利主张或诉因被移送后提交该通知的当事人是否同意由破产法院作出最后裁定或判决的陈述，并附有所有司法文书及诉状的副本。

（2）提交时间；根据法典所提交的破产案件启动前提起的民事诉讼。若在根据法典提交的破产案件启动时某权利主张或诉因在民事诉讼中即已在审理中，则仅可在后述期间内（以较长者为准）提交移案通知书（A）根据法典所提交的破产案件中破产救济令被作出后 90 日内，（B）若在民事诉讼中该权利主张或诉因曾被根据法典第 362 条冻结，则自终止冻结的裁定被正式作出后 30 日内，或（C）

has been stayed under §362 of the Code, or (C) 30 days after a trustee qualifies in a chapter 11 reorganization case but not later than 180 days after the order for relief.

(3) *Time for filing; civil action initiated after commencement of the case under the Code.* If a claim or cause of action is asserted in another court after the commencement of a case under the Code, a notice of removal may be filed with the clerk only within the shorter of (A) 30 days after receipt, through service or otherwise, of a copy of the initial pleading setting forth the claim or cause of action sought to be removed, or (B) 30 days after receipt of the summons if the initial pleading has been filed with the court but not served with the summons.

(b) NOTICE. Promptly after filing the notice of removal, the party filing the notice shall serve a copy of it on all parties to the removed claim or cause of action.

(c) FILING IN NON-BANKRUPTCY COURT. Promptly after filing the notice of removal, the party filing the notice shall file a copy of it with the clerk of the court from which the claim or cause of action is removed. Removal of the claim or cause of action is effected on such filing of a copy of the notice of removal. The parties shall proceed no further in that court unless and until the claim or cause of action is remanded.

(d) REMAND. A motion for remand of the removed claim or cause of action shall be governed by Rule 9014 and served on the parties to the removed claim or cause of action.

(e) PROCEDURE AFTER REMOVAL.

(1) After removal of a claim or cause of action to a district court the district court or, if the case under the Code has been referred to a bankruptcy judge of the district, the bankruptcy judge, may issue all necessary orders and process to bring before it all proper parties whether served by process issued by the court from which the claim or cause of action was removed or otherwise.

(2) The district court or, if the case under the Code has been referred to a bankruptcy judge of the district, the bankruptcy judge, may require the party filing the notice of removal to file with the clerk copies of all records and proceedings relating to the claim or cause of action in the court from which the claim or cause of action was removed.

(3) Any party who has filed a pleading in connection with the removed claim or cause of action, other than the party filing the notice of removal, shall file a statement

在第 11 章重整案件中存在合格的托管人后 30 日内，但不得超过破产救济令被作出后 180 日。

（3）提交时间；根据法典所提交的破产案件启动后提起的民事诉讼。若在根据法典提交的破产案件启动后有人在其他法院提出其权利主张或诉因，则仅能在后述期间内（以较短者为准）提交移案通知书（A）因送达或其他方式而收到载有被寻求移送的权利主张或诉因的原始诉状的副本后 30 日内，或（B）若原始诉状已被提交法院，但仅送达了传票而未送达原始诉状，则在收到传票后 30 日内。

（b）**通知**。在提交移案通知书后，提交该通知书的当事人应及时将其副本送达给所要移送的权利主张或诉因所涉的所有当事人。

（c）**在非破产法院提交**。在提交移案通知书后，提交该通知书的当事人应及时向移出该权利主张或诉因的法院的书记员提交其副本。权利主张或诉因的移送将在向其提交该移案通知书的副本时生效。除非且直至该权利主张或诉因被发回，否则当事人不得在该法院继续进行诉讼。

（d）**发回**。申请发回被移送的权利主张或诉因的动议由第 9014 条所规制并应被送达给所移送的权利主张或诉因所涉的所有当事人。

（e）**移案后的程序**。
（1）在向地区法院移送权利主张或诉因后，地区法院或破产法官（若根据法典所提交的案件被移送给辖区内的破产法官）可签发所有必要的裁定及司法文书以传见所有适格当事人，无论其是否因送达而收到移出权利主张或诉因的法院所签发的司法文书。

（2）地区法院或破产法官（若根据法典所提交的案件被移送给辖区内的破产法官）可要求提交移案通知书的当事人向书记员提交移出权利主张或诉因的法院内与该权利主张或诉因相关的所有档案及记录的副本。

（3）除提交移案通知书的当事人外，任何提交与所移送权利主张或诉因相关的诉状的当事人均应提交声明以说明其是否同意由破产法院作出最终裁定或判

U.S. Federal Rules of Bankruptcy Procedure
(Chinese-English bilingual version)

that the party does or does not consent to entry of final orders or judgment by the bankruptcy court. A statement required by this paragraph shall be signed pursuant to Rule 9011 and shall be filed not later than 14 days after the filing of the notice of removal. Any party who files a statement pursuant to this paragraph shall mail a copy to every other party to the removed claim or cause of action.

(f) PROCESS AFTER REMOVAL. If one or more of the defendants has not been served with process, the service has not been perfected prior to removal, or the process served proves to be defective, such process or service may be completed or new process issued pursuant to Part VII of these rules. This subdivision shall not deprive any defendant on whom process is served after removal of the defendant's right to move to remand the case.

(g) APPLICABILITY OF PART VII. The rules of Part VII apply to a claim or cause of action removed to a district court from a federal or state court and govern procedure after removal. Repleading is not necessary unless the court so orders. In a removed action in which the defendant has not answered, the defendant shall answer or present the other defenses or objections available under the rules of Part VII within 21 days following the receipt through service or otherwise of a copy of the initial pleading setting forth the claim for relief on which the action or proceeding is based, or within 21 days following the service of summons on such initial pleading, or within seven days following the filing of the notice of removal, whichever period is longest.

(h) RECORD SUPPLIED. When a party is entitled to copies of the records and proceedings in any civil action or proceeding in a federal or a state court, to be used in the removed civil action or proceeding, and the clerk of the federal or state court, on demand accompanied by payment or tender of the lawful fees, fails to deliver certified copies, the court may, on affidavit reciting the facts, direct such record to be supplied by affidavit or otherwise. Thereupon the proceedings, trial and judgment may be had in the court, and all process awarded, as if certified copies had been filed.

(i) ATTACHMENT OR SEQUESTRATION; SECURITIES. When a claim or cause of action is removed to a district court, any attachment or sequestration of property in the court from which the claim or cause of action was removed shall hold

决。本段所要求的声明应根据第 9011 条而被签署并应在移案通知书被提交后 14 日内而被提交。任何根据本段提交声明的当事人均应向所移送的权利主张或诉因所涉的所有其他当事人邮寄该声明的副本。

（f）**移案后的司法文书**。若有一名或多名被告人并未收到司法文书，移案前的送达存在瑕疵或者所送达的司法文书被证明存在问题，则可根据本法第 VII 部分完成该司法文书或送达或者签发新的司法文书。本款并未剥夺在移案后被送达司法文书的被告人提出动议以申请将案件发回的权利。

（g）**第 VII 部分的适用**。第 VII 部分的规则适用于被从联邦或州法院移送到地区法院的权利主张或诉因并且移案后的程序也由其规制。除非法院作出其他裁定，否则无须重新提交诉状。若在被移送的诉讼中被告人尚未作出答辩，则被告人应在因送达或其他方式而收到列有该诉讼或程序所依据的寻求救济的权利主张的原始诉状的副本后 21 日内，就该原始诉状而发出的传票被送达后 21 日内，或者移案通知书被提交后 7 日内，以前述较长期间为准，根据第 VII 部分的规则答辩或提出其他抗辩或异议。

（h）**所提供的档案**。若当事人有权获得在联邦或州法院所进行的任何民事诉讼或程序中获得档案或记录的副本，且该副本将被用于被移送的民事诉讼或程序中，但是联邦或州法院的书记员在有人提出请求并支付或收取了合法费用后未能交付核证副本，则该法院可在宣誓时引用该事实，指示以宣誓书或其他方式提供该档案。在前述程序完成后，可视为已经提交有核证副本从而在法院进行审理、判决并发出所有司法文书。

（i）**查封或扣押；担保**。当权利主张或诉因被移送到地区法院时，针对移出该权利主张或诉因的法院所进行的财产的查封或扣押，应以该财产在该权利主张或诉因被移出的法院等待最终判决或裁决被作出时本会被采取的措施而被继续查

the property to answer the final judgment or decree in the same manner as the property would have been held to answer final judgment or decree had it been rendered by the court from which the claim or cause of action was removed. All bonds, undertakings, or security given by either party to the claim or cause of action prior to its removal shall remain valid and effectual notwithstanding such removal. All injunctions issued, orders entered and other proceedings had prior to removal shall remain in full force and effect until dissolved or modified by the court.

(As amended Mar. 30, 1987, eff. Aug. 1, 1987; Apr. 30, 1991, eff. Aug. 1, 1991; Apr. 29, 2002, eff.Dec. 1, 2002; Mar. 26, 2009, eff. Dec. 1, 2009; Apr. 28, 2016, eff. Dec. 1, 2016.)

Rule 9028. Disability of a Judge

Rule 63 F.R.Civ.P. applies in cases under the Code.

(As amended Mar. 30, 1987, eff. Aug. 1, 1987.)

Rule 9029. Local Bankruptcy Rules; Procedure When There Is No Controlling Law

(a) LOCAL BANKRUPTCY RULES.

(1) Each district court acting by a majority of its district judges may make and amend rules governing practice and procedure in all cases and proceedings within the district court's bankruptcy jurisdiction which are consistent with—but not duplicative of—Acts of Congress and these rules and which do not prohibit or limit the use of the Official Forms. Rule 83 F.R.Civ.P. governs the procedure for making local rules. A district court may authorize the bankruptcy judges of the district, subject to any limitation or condition it may prescribe and the requirements of 83 F.R.Civ.P., to make and amend rules of practice and procedure which are consistent with—but not duplicative of—Acts of Congress and these rules and which do not prohibit or limit the use of the Official Forms. Local rules shall conform to any uniform numbering system prescribed by the Judicial Conference of the United States.

(2) A local rule imposing a requirement of form shall not be enforced in a manner

封或扣押。尽管权利主张或诉因已被移送，移送前由任一当事人提供的担保、承诺或抵押仍将有效。移送前所签发的所有禁令、裁定及其他程序在被法院解除或变更前也仍将完全有效。

（经 Mar. 30, 1987, eff. Aug. 1, 1987; Apr. 30, 1991, eff. Aug. 1, 1991; Apr. 29, 2002, eff.Dec. 1, 2002; Mar. 26, 2009, eff. Dec. 1, 2009; Apr. 28, 2016, eff. Dec. 1, 2016. 修正）

第 9028 条　法官无法履职

《联邦民事诉讼规则》第 63 条适用于根据法典所提交的案件。

（经 Mar. 30, 1987, eff. Aug. 1, 1987. 修正）

第 9029 条　地方破产规则；没有约束法时采用的程序

（a）地方破产规则。

（1）各地区法院经其多数地区法官同意后均可制定并修改规制其在就破产案件的管辖权范围内所管辖的所有案件及诉讼的实践及程序的规则，但其不得违反《国会法案》以及本法的规定，也不得重复于前述规定，同时其不得禁止或限制官方模板的使用。制定地方规则的程序应符合《联邦民事诉讼规则》第 83 条的规定。地区法院可授权该辖区内的破产法官在遵守地区法院可规定的任何限制或条件以及《联邦民事诉讼规则》第 83 条的要求的情况下制定并修改前述实践及程序的规则，但其不得违反《国会法案》以及本法的规定，但也不得重复于前述规定，同时其不得禁止或限制官方模板的使用。地方规则必须符合美国司法会议所规定的统一编号系统。

（2）就规定格式要求的地方规则而言，其实施方式不得使当事人因非出于故

that causes a party to lose rights because of a nonwillful failure to comply with the requirement.

(b) PROCEDURE WHEN THERE IS NO CONTROLLING LAW. A judge may regulate practice in any manner consistent with federal law, these rules, Official Forms, and local rules of the district. No sanction or other disadvantage may be imposed for noncompliance with any requirement not in federal law, federal rules, Official Forms, or the local rules of the district unless the alleged violator has been furnished in the particular case with actual notice of the requirement.

(As amended Mar. 30, 1987, eff. Aug. 1, 1987; Apr. 30, 1991, eff. Aug. 1, 1991; Apr. 27, 1995, eff.Dec. 1, 1995.)

Rule 9030. Jurisdiction and Venue Unaffected

These rules shall not be construed to extend or limit the jurisdiction of the courts or the venue of any matters therein.

(As amended Mar. 30, 1987, eff. Aug. 1, 1987.)

Rule 9031. Masters Not Authorized

Rule 53 F.R.Civ.P. does not apply in cases under the Code.

Rule 9032. Effect of Amendment of Federal Rules of Civil Procedure

The Federal Rules of Civil Procedure which are incorporated by reference and made applicable by these rules shall be the Federal Rules of Civil Procedure in effect on the effective date of these rules and as thereafter amended, unless otherwise provided by such amendment or by these rules.

(As amended Apr. 30, 1991, eff. Aug. 1, 1991.)

Rule 9033. Proposed Findings of Fact and Conclusions of Law

(a) SERVICE. In a proceeding in which the bankruptcy court has issued proposed findings of fact and conclusions of law, the clerk shall serve forthwith copies on all parties by mail and note the date of mailing on the docket.

意而未能遵守其要求的行为而丧失权利。

（b）**没有约束法时采用的程序**。法官可以任何符合联邦法律、本法、官方模板以及该辖区的地方规则的方式就法律实践作出规定。不得仅因未能遵守联邦法律、相应联邦规则、官方模板或该辖区的地方规则未有规定的要求而施加处罚或其他不利条件，除非在具体案件中已经实际向涉嫌违反者就该要求发出了通知。

（经 Mar. 30, 1987, eff. Aug. 1, 1987; Apr. 30, 1991, eff. Aug. 1, 1991; Apr. 27, 1995, eff.Dec. 1, 1995. 修正）

第 9030 条　管辖权及管辖区域不受影响

本法不得被解释为扩大或限制法院的管辖权或其中任何事项的管辖区域。

（经 Mar. 30, 1987, eff. Aug. 1, 1987. 修正）

第 9031 条　未被准予的事项

《联邦民事诉讼规则》第 53 条不适用于根据法典所提交的案件。

第 9032 条　《联邦民事诉讼规则》的修正案的影响

通过引用而并入且因本法而得以适用的《联邦民事诉讼规则》中的规则应被理解为本法生效之日有效且随后经修正的《联邦民事诉讼规则》中的相应规则，除非该修正案或本法另有规定。

（经 Apr. 30, 1991, eff. Aug. 1, 1991. 修正）

第 9033 条　拟定的事实认定及法律结论

（a）**送达**。若针对于某程序，破产法院已经签发了拟定的事实认定及法律结论，则书记员应立刻将其副本以邮寄的方式送达给所有当事人并在案卷中注明邮寄的日期。

(b) OBJECTIONS: TIME FOR FILING. Within 14 days after being served with a copy of the proposed findings of fact and conclusions of law a party may serve and file with the clerk written objections which identify the specific proposed findings or conclusions objected to and state the grounds for such objection. A party may respond to another party's objections within 14 days after being served with a copy thereof. A party objecting to the bankruptcy judge's proposed findings or conclusions shall arrange promptly for the transcription of the record, or such portions of it as all parties may agree upon or the bankruptcy judge deems sufficient, unless the district judge otherwise directs.

(c) EXTENSION OF TIME. The bankruptcy judge may for cause extend the time for filing objections by any party for a period not to exceed 21 days from the expiration of the time otherwise prescribed by this rule. A request to extend the time for filing objections must be made before the time for filing objections has expired, except that a request made no more than 21 days after the expiration of the time for filing objections may be granted upon a showing of excusable neglect.

(d) STANDARD OF REVIEW. The district judge shall make a de novo review upon the record or, after additional evidence, of any portion of the bankruptcy judge's findings of fact or conclusions of law to which specific written objection has been made in accordance with this rule. The district judge may accept, reject, or modify the proposed findings of fact or conclusions of law, receive further evidence, or recommit the matter to the bankruptcy judge with instructions.

(Added Mar. 30, 1987, eff. Aug. 1, 1987; amended Mar. 26, 2009, eff. Dec. 1, 2009; Apr. 28, 2016,eff. Dec. 1, 2016.)

Rule 9034. Transmittal of Pleadings, Motion Papers, Objections, and Other Papers to the United States Trustee

Unless the United States trustee requests otherwise or the case is a chapter 9 municipality case, any entity that files a pleading, motion, objection, or similar paper relating to any of the following matters shall transmit a copy thereof to the United States trustee within the time required by these rules for service of the paper:

（b）**异议：提交的时间**。在被送达拟定的事实认定及法律结论的副本后14日内，当事人可送达并向书记员提交书面异议以注明其所反对的具体的认定或结论并说明该异议的依据。当事人可在被送达该异议的副本后14日内就其异议作出答复。除非地区法官作出其他指示，否则就破产法官拟定的认定或结论提出异议的当事人应及时安排取得档案的书面记录或者可由全体当事人就此达成合意或破产法官认为已经足够的书面记录的一部分。

（c）**期间的延长**。破产法官可出于正当事由延长任何当事人提交异议的期间但不得延至本条所规定的期间届满后21日后。申请延长提交异议的期间的请求必须在提交异议的期间届满前而被作出，但若能证明其系存在可以原谅的过失，则也可在提交异议的期间届满后21日内作出该请求。

（d）**审查标准**。地区法官应基于档案或在收到补充证据后，就根据本条所作的书面异议所针对的破产法官所作的事实认定或法律结论的部分进行完全审查。地区法官可接受、拒绝或修改拟定的事实认定或法律结论，接受新的证据或将该事项重新移交给破产法官并作出指示。

（经 Mar. 30, 1987, eff. Aug. 1, 1987 增补；经 Mar. 26, 2009, eff. Dec. 1, 2009; Apr. 28, 2016,eff. Dec. 1, 2016. 修正）

第9034条　将诉状、动议书、异议以及其他文件移交给联邦托管人

除非联邦托管人作出其他请求，除第9章市政机构破产案件外，任何提交有与以下任何事项相关的诉状、动议、异议或类似文件的实体均应在本法就文件的送达所要求的期间内将其副本移交给联邦托管人：

(a) a proposed use, sale, or lease of property of the estate other than in the ordinary course of business;

(b) the approval of a compromise or settlement of a controversy;

(c) the dismissal or conversion of a case to another chapter;

(d) the employment of professional persons;

(e) an application for compensation or reimbursement of expenses;

(f) a motion for, or approval of an agreement relating to, the use of cash collateral or authority to obtain credit;

(g) the appointment of a trustee or examiner in a chapter 11 reorganization case;

(h) the approval of a disclosure statement;

(i) the confirmation of a plan;

(j) an objection to, or waiver or revocation of, the debtor's discharge;

(k) any other matter in which the United States trustee requests copies of filed papers or the court orders copies transmitted to the United States trustee.

(Added Apr. 30, 1991, eff. Aug. 1, 1991.)

Rule 9035. Applicability of Rules in Judicial Districts in Alabama and North Carolina

In any case under the Code that is filed in or transferred to a district in the State of Alabama or the State of North Carolina and in which a United States trustee is not authorized to act, these rules apply to the extent that they are not inconsistent with any federal statute effective in the case.

(Added Apr. 30, 1991, eff. Aug. 1, 1991; amended Apr. 11, 1997, eff. Dec. 1, 1997.)

Rule 9036. Notice and Service by Electronic Transmission

(a) IN GENERAL. This rule applies whenever these rules require or permit sending a notice or serving a paper by mail or other means.

(b) NOTICES FROM AND SERVICE BY THE COURT.

(1) Registered Users. The clerk may send notice to or serve a registered user by filing the notice or paper with the court's electronic-filing system.

（a）在常规营业范围外对破产财产的计划使用、出售或出租；

（b）就争议事项的和解或调解的批准；

（c）破产案件的驳回或被转换至其他章节；

（d）专业人员的雇佣；

（e）申请支付报酬或报销费用；

（f）申请使用现金担保物或获准借贷的动议或与前述事项相关的协议的批准；

（g）第 11 章重整案件中托管人或监督人的任命；

（h）披露声明的批准；

（i）计划的批准；

（j）就债务人的免责的异议或者放弃或撤销免责；

（k）联邦托管人要求就其取得被提交文件的副本或法院裁定将其副本移交给联邦托管人的任何其他事项。

（经 Apr. 30, 1991, eff. Aug. 1, 1991. 增补）

第 9035 条　本法在阿拉巴马州和北卡罗来纳州内的司法辖区内的适用

在根据法典而向联邦托管人未被授权行事的阿拉巴马州或北卡罗来纳州内的辖区提交或移送的任何案件中，本法将在不违反适用于该案有效的任何联邦法律规定情况下得以适用。

（经 Apr. 30, 1991, eff. Aug. 1, 1991 增补；经 Apr. 11, 1997, eff. Dec. 1, 1997. 修正）

第 9036 条　电子通知与送达

（a）**一般规定**。本条适用于法律要求或允许通过邮件或其他方式进行通知或送达文件的情形。

（b）**法院的通知及送达**。

（1）已注册用户。书记员可以通过在法院电子提交系统提交通知或文件从而向已注册用户发送通知或送达文件。

(2) All Recipients. For any recipient, the clerk may send notice or serve a paper by electronic means that the recipient consented to in writing, including by designating an electronic address for receipt of notices. But these exceptions apply:

(A) if the recipient has registered an electronic address with the Administrative Office of the United States Courts' bankruptcy-noticing program, the clerk shall send the notice to or serve the paper at that address; and

(B) if an entity has been designated by the Director of the Administrative Office of the United States Courts as a high-volume paper-notice recipient, the clerk may send the notice to or serve the paper electronically at an address designated by the Director, unless the entity has designated an address under §342 (e) or (f) of the Code.

(c) NOTICES FROM AND SERVICE BY AN ENTITY. An entity may send notice or serve a paper in the same manner that the clerk does under (b), excluding (b)(2)(A) and (B).

(d) COMPLETING NOTICE OR SERVICE. Electronic notice or service is complete upon filing or sending but is not effective if the filer or sender receives notice that it did not reach the person to be served. It is the recipient's responsibility to keep its electronic address current with the clerk.

(e) INAPPLICABILITY. This rule does not apply to any paper required to be served in accordance with Rule 7004.

(Added Apr. 22, 1993, eff. Aug. 1, 1993; amended Apr. 25, 2005, eff. Dec. 1, 2005; Apr. 25, 2019,eff. Dec. 1, 2019; Apr. 14, 2021, eff. Dec. 1, 2021.)

Rule 9037. Privacy Protection for Filings Made with the Court

(a) REDACTED FILINGS. Unless the court orders otherwise, in an electronic or paper filing made with the court that contains an individual's social-security number, taxpayer-identification number, or birth date, the name of an individual, other than the debtor, known to be and identified as a minor, or a financial-account number, a party or nonparty making the filing may include only:

(1) the last four digits of the social-security number and taxpayer-identification number;

（2）所有收件人。除下列情形外，对于任何收件人，书记员可以通过收件人书面同意的电子方式发送通知或送达文件，包括指定用于接收通知的电子地址：

（A）若收件人已在美国法院行政办公室的破产通知系统中登记有电子地址，则书记员应将通知发送或将文件送达该地址；并且

（B）如果某实体被美国法院行政办公室主任指定为大量纸质通知的收件人，则书记员可将通知发送或将文件送达至主任指定的电子地址，除非该实体根据法典第342条（e）或（f）指定了地址。

（c）**各实体发出及送达的通知**。各实体可按（b）附条中除（b）(2)(A)及(B)外的规定的书记员采用的相同方式发出及送达文件。

（d）**完成通知与送达**。电子通知或送达在提交或发送时即已完成，但若提交者或发送者收到其并未被送达给应被送达的人的通知，则并未生效。收件人有义务向书记员实时更新其电子地址。

（e）**不适用**。本条不适用于根据第7004条被要求送达的任何文件。

（经 Apr. 22, 1993, eff. Aug. 1, 1993 增补；经 Apr. 25, 2005, eff. Dec. 1, 2005; Apr. 25, 2019,eff. Dec. 1, 2019; Apr. 14, 2021, eff. Dec. 1, 2021. 修正）

第 9037 条　向法院提交材料的情形下的隐私保护

（a）**提交材料的匿名化处理**。除非法院作出其他裁定，否则在以电子或纸质形式提交给法院的含有个人社保账号、纳税人识别号码、出生日期、除债务人外已知或被认定为未成年人的自然人姓名或者财务账号的材料中，制作该材料的当事人或非当事人仅可以下列形式载明各项：

（1）社保账号以及纳税人识别号码的后四位数字；

U.S. Federal Rules of Bankruptcy Procedure
(Chinese-English bilingual version)

(2) the year of the individual's birth;

(3) the minor's initials; and

(4) the last four digits of the financial-account number.

(b) EXEMPTIONS FROM THE REDACTION REQUIREMENT. The redaction requirement does not apply to the following:

(1) a financial-account number that identifies the property allegedly subject to forfeiture in a forfeiture proceeding;

(2) the record of an administrative or agency proceeding unless filed with a proof of claim;

(3) the official record of a state-court proceeding;

(4) the record of a court or tribunal, if that record was not subject to the redaction requirement when originally filed;

(5) a filing covered by subdivision (c) of this rule; and

(6) a filing that is subject to §110 of the Code.

(c) FILINGS MADE UNDER SEAL. The court may order that a filing be made under seal without redaction. The court may later unseal the filing or order the entity that made the filing to file a redacted version for the public record.

(d) PROTECTIVE ORDERS. For cause, the court may by order in a case under the Code:

(1) require redaction of additional information; or

(2) limit or prohibit a nonparty's remote electronic access to a document filed with the court.

(e) OPTION FOR ADDITIONAL UNREDACTED FILING UNDER SEAL. An entity making a redacted filing may also file an unredacted copy under seal. The court must retain the unredacted copy as part of the record.

(f) OPTION FOR FILING A REFERENCE LIST. A filing that contains redacted information may be filed together with a reference list that identifies each item of redacted information and specifies an appropriate identifier that uniquely corresponds to each item listed. The list must be filed under seal and may be amended as of right. Any reference in the case to a listed identifier will be construed to refer to the

（2）自然人出生日期的年份；

（3）未成年人姓名的首字母；以及

（4）财务账号的后四位数字。

（b）匿名化处理要求的豁免。 匿名化处理要求并不适用于以下各项：

（1）与被主张在没收程序中被没收的财产相关的财务账号；

（2）管理或代理程序的记录（除非一并提交有债权证明）；

（3）州法院程序的官方档案；

（4）在先前被提交时即未适用匿名化处理要求的法院或法庭档案；

（5）本条的附条（c）所涉的材料；以及

（6）法典第110条所述的材料。

（c）密封材料。 法院可裁定被密封的材料无须对其进行匿名化处理。法院其后可开封该材料或裁定制作该材料的实体提交匿名化处理后的版本用作公共档案。

（d）保护令。 出于特定事由，法院可在根据法典所提交的案件中签发裁定以采取以下措施：

（1）要求对其他信息进行匿名化处理；或

（2）限制或禁止非当事人对被提交至法院的文件进行远程电子访问。

（e）选择额外提交未经匿名化处理的密封材料。 制作匿名化处理材料的实体也可提交密封的未经匿名化处理的材料。法院必须保留未经匿名化处理的副本以作为档案的一部分。

（f）选择提交引用清单。 在提交载有匿名化处理信息的材料时，可一并提交一份引用清单以列明各项被处理的信息并注明与所列各项相对应的被匿名化对象。该清单必须被以密封方式提交并且提交人享有对其进行修正的权利。该案中对所列的被匿名化对象的任何引用均将被理解为对其所对应的信息的引用。

corresponding item of information.

(g) WAIVER OF PROTECTION OF IDENTIFIERS. An entity waives the protection of subdivision (a) as to the entity's own information by filing it without redaction and not under seal.

(h) MOTION TO REDACT A PREVIOUSLY FILED DOCUMENT.

(1) *Content of the Motion; Service.* Unless the court orders otherwise, if an entity seeks to redact from a previously filed document information that is protected under subdivision (a), the entity must:

(A) file a motion to redact identifying the proposed redactions;

(B) attach to the motion the proposed redacted document;

(C) include in the motion the docket or proof-of-claim number of the previously filed document; and

(D) serve the motion and attachment on the debtor, debtor's attorney, trustee (if any), United States trustee, filer of the unredacted document, and any individual whose personal identifying information is to be redacted.

(2) *Restricting Public Access to the Unredacted Document; Docketing the Redacted Document.* The court must promptly restrict public access to the motion and the unredacted document pending its ruling on the motion. If the court grants it, the court must docket the redacted document. The restrictions on public access to the motion and unredacted document remain in effect until a further court order. If the court denies it, the restrictions must be lifted, unless the court orders otherwise.

(Added Apr. 30, 2007, eff. Dec. 1, 2007; amended Apr. 25, 2019, eff. Dec. 1, 2019.)

（g）**被匿名化对象的保护的放弃**。某实体可通过在提交其未经匿名化处理且并未密封的信息从而放弃附条（a）所提供的保护。

（h）**申请对私下提交的文件进行匿名化处理的动议**。
（1）动议的内容；送达。除非法院作出其他裁定，否则若有实体意图在私下提交的文件中对附条（a）所保护的信息进行匿名化处理，则该实体必须履行以下各项：
（A）提交申请匿名化处理并注明拟定处理方案的动议；
（B）提交该动议时一并提交拟定进行匿名化处理的文件；
（C）在该动议中载明先前被提交的文件的案卷编号或债权证明编号；以及

（D）将该动议以及所附的文件送达给债务人、债务人的律师、托管人（如有）、联邦托管人、未匿名化处理的文件的提交人以及其个人身份信息将被匿名化处理的任何自然人。
（2）限制对未匿名化处理的文件的公众访问；将经匿名化处理的文件存入案卷。法院在其就该动议进行审理期间必须及时限制对该动议以及尚未匿名化处理的文件的公众访问。若法院准予该动议，则法院必须将经匿名化处理的文件存入案卷。对该动议以及尚未匿名化处理的文件的公众访问的限制在法院作出裁定前均将有效。若法院否决该动议，则除非法院作出其他裁定，否则必须解除该限制。

（经 Apr. 30, 2007, eff. Dec. 1, 2007 增补；经 Apr. 25, 2019, eff. Dec. 1, 2019. 修正）

PART X

UNITED STATES TRUSTEES (Abrogated Apr. 30, 1991, eff. Aug. 1, 1991)

OFFICIAL FORMS

[The Official Forms prescribed pursuant to Rule 9009 may be found on the United States Courts website.]

APPENDIX

(As added Apr. 26, 2018, eff. Dec. 1, 2018.)

LENGTH LIMITS STATED IN PART VIII OF THE FEDERAL RULES OF BANKRUPTCY PROCEDURE

Appendix: Length Limits Stated in Part VIII of the Federal Rules of Bankruptcy Procedure is set out in the order of the Supreme Court amending the Federal Rules of Bankruptcy Procedure, April 26, 2018, available at the Supreme Court website.

第 X 部分
联邦托管人（经 Apr. 30, 1991, eff. Aug. 1, 1991 而被废除）

官方模板

［第 9009 条所规定的官方模板见于美国法院官网。①］

附录

（经 Apr. 26, 2018, eff. Dec. 1, 2018. 增补）

《联邦破产程序规则》第 VIII 部分所述的篇幅限制

附录：《联邦破产程序规则》第 VIII 部分所规定的篇幅限制系来源于美国最高法院于 2018 年 4 月 26 日修订《联邦破产程序规则》的裁定，并可见于美国最高法院官网。②

---

① 即 https://www.uscourts.gov/。
② 即 https://www.supremecourt.gov/。

PROPOSED AMENDMENTS TO THE FEDERAL RULES OF BANKRUPTCY PROCEDURE

Court Order

April 11, 2022

SUPREME COURT OF THE UNITED STATES

ORDERED:

1. The Federal Rules of Bankruptcy Procedure are amended to include amendments to Rules 1007, 1020, 2009, 2012, 2015, 3002, 3010, 3011, 3014, 3016, 3017.1, 3018, 3019, 5005, 7004, and 8023, and to add new Rule 3017.2.

2. The foregoing amendments to the Federal Rules of Bankruptcy Procedure shall take effect on December 1, 2022, and shall govern in all proceedings in bankruptcy cases thereafter commenced and, in so far as just and practicable, all proceedings then pending.

3. THE CHIEF JUSTICE is authorized to transmit to the Congress the foregoing amendments to the Federal Rules of Bankruptcy Procedure in accordance with the provisions of Section 2075 of Title 28, United States Code.

对《联邦破产程序规则》的拟议修正案

法院裁定

2022 年 4 月 11 日

美国最高法院

裁定：

1. 对《联邦破产程序规则》予以修订，包括对第 1007、1020、2009、2012、2015、3002、3010、3011、3014、3016、3017.1、3018、3019、5005、7004 及 8023 条的修正以及新增第 3017.2 条。

2. 对《联邦破产程序规则》的以下修订将于 2022 年 12 月 1 日生效，并将适用于其后启动的破产案件的所有程序以及在公正可行的情况下适用于所有当时正在进行的程序。

3. 首席大法官被授权根据《美国联邦法典》第 28 篇第 2075 条将《联邦破产程序规则》的以下修正案递交国会。

U.S. Federal Rules of Bankruptcy Procedure
(Chinese-English bilingual version)

Rule 1007.Lists, Schedules, Statements, and Other Documents; Time Limits

* * * * *

(b) SCHEDULES, STATEMENTS, AND OTHER DOCUMENTS REQUIRED.

* * * * *

(5) An individual debtor in a chapter 11 case (unless under subchapter V) shall file a statement of current monthly income, prepared as prescribed by the appropriate Official Form.

* * * * *

(h) INTERESTS ACQUIRED OR ARISING AFTER PETITION. If, as provided by § 541 (a) (5) of the Code, the debtor acquires or becomes entitled to acquire any interest in property, the debtor shall within 14 days after the information comes to the debtor's knowledge or within such further time the court may allow, file a supplemental schedule in the chapter 7 liquidation case, chapter 11 reorganization case, chapter 12 family farmer's debt adjustment case, or chapter 13 individual debt adjustment case. If any of the property required to be reported under this subdivision is claimed by the debtor as exempt, the debtor shall claim the exemptions in the supplemental schedule. This duty to file a supplemental schedule continues even after the case is closed, except for property acquired after an order is entered:

(1) confirming a chapter 11 plan [other than one confirmed under § 1191 (b)] ; or

(2) discharging the debtor in a chapter 12 case, a chapter 13 case, or a case under subchapter V of chapter 11 in which the plan is confirmed under §1191 (b) .

* * * * *

第1007条 清单、报表、声明和其他文件；时间限制

* * * * *

（b）报表、声明和其他被要求的文件。

* * * * *

（5）第11章案件（不包括第五附章）中的个人债务人应提交按照相应官方模板的规定准备的当前月收入的说明。

* * * * *

（h）**申请后取得或产生的权益。**若按照法典第541条（a）（5）的规定，债务人取得或有权取得任何财产权益，则债务人应在其获知该信息后的14日内或法院可准予的更长的期间内，在第7章清算案件、第11章重整案件、第12章家庭农场主债务调整案件或第13章个人债务调整案件中提交补充清单。若债务人主张豁免本附条中被要求进行报告的财产，则债务人应在该补充清单中主张进行豁免。即使本案结案，债务人仍然承担根据本附条提交补充报表的责任，除非该些财产系（债务人）在下列裁定被正式作出后取得：

（1）批准第11章计划［不包括根据第1191条（b）批准的计划］的裁定；或

（2）在第12章、第13章案件或第11章第五附章案件［计划已根据第1191条（b）获得批准］中对债务人免责的裁定。

* * * * *

U.S. Federal Rules of Bankruptcy Procedure
(Chinese-English bilingual version)

Rule 1020.Chapter 11 Reorganization Case for Small Business Debtors

(a) SMALL BUSINESS DEBTOR DESIGNATION. In a voluntary chapter 11 case, the debtor shall state in the petition whether the debtor is a small business debtor and, if so, whether the debtor elects to have subchapter V of chapter 11 apply. In an involuntary chapter 11 case, the debtor shall file within 14 days after entry of the order for relief a statement as to whether the debtor is a small business debtor and, if so, whether the debtor elects to have subchapter V of chapter 11 apply. The status of the case as a small business case or a case under subchapter V of chapter 11 shall be in accordance with the debtor's statement under this subdivision, unless and until the court enters an order finding that the debtor's statement is incorrect.

(b) OBJECTING TO DESIGNATION. The United States trustee or a party in interest may file an objection to the debtor's statement under subdivision (a) no later than 30 days after the conclusion of the meeting of creditors held under § 341 (a) of the Code, or within 30 days after any amendment to the statement, whichever is later.

(c) PROCEDURE FOR OBJECTION OR DETERMINATION. Any objection or request for a determination under this rule shall be governed by Rule 9014 and served on: the debtor; the debtor's attorney; the United States trustee; the trustee; the creditors included on the list filed under Rule 1007 (d) or, if a committee has been appointed under § 1102 (a) (3), the committee or its authorized agent; and any other entity as the court directs.

Rule 2009. Trustees for Estates When Joint Administration Ordered

(a) ELECTION OF SINGLE TRUSTEE FOR ESTATES BEING JOINTLY ADMINISTERED. If the court orders a joint administration of two or more estates under Rule 1015 (b), creditors may elect a single trustee for the estates being jointly

第 1020 条　第 11 章小企业重整案件

（a）**小企业债务人的认定**。在第 11 章中的自愿破产案件里，债务人应在破产申请中注明其是否为小企业债务人，如是，债务人是否选择适用第 11 章第五附章的规定。在第 11 章中的强制破产案件里，在破产救济令被正式作出后 14 日内，债务人应提交一份声明以表明其是否为小企业债务人，如是，债务人是否选择适用第 11 章第五附章的规定。应按照债务人根据本附条所作的声明确定案件是否为小企业破产案件或第 11 章第五附章适用的案件，除非并且直至法院正式作出裁定认定债务人的声明有误。

（b）**对该认定的异议**。联邦托管人或利益相关方可在根据法典第 341 条（a）举行的债权人会议结束后 30 日内或在就（a）附条中债务人的声明作出任何修改后 30 日内，以二者中较晚者为准，就该声明提交异议。

（c）**异议或认定的程序**。本条中就该认定的任何异议或请求均应按照第 9014 条的规定进行并送达给：债务人、债务人的律师、联邦托管人、托管人。根据第 1007 条（d）被提交的清单所载的债权人或者根据第 1102 条（a）（3）被任命的委员会（如有）或其授权的代理机构；以及法院指定的任何其他实体。

第 2009 条　被裁定合并管理时多个破产实体的托管人

（a）**选任一位托管人合并管理多个破产实体**。除法典第 7 章第五附章或第 11 章第五附章的案件外，若法院根据第 1015 条（b）裁定合并管理两个或两个以上的破产实体，则债权人可仅选任一位托管人以管理被合并的多个破产实体。

administered, unless the case is under subchapter V of chapter 7 or subchapter V of chapter 11 of the Code.

(b) RIGHT OF CREDITORS TO ELECT SEPARATE TRUSTEE. Notwithstanding entry of an order for joint administration under Rule 1015 (b), the creditors of any debtor may elect a separate trustee for the estate of the debtor as provided in § 702 of the Code, unless the case is under subchapter V of chapter 7 or subchapter V of chapter 11 of the Code.

(c) APPOINTMENT OF TRUSTEES FOR ESTATES BEING JOINTLY ADMINISTERED.

* * * * *

(2) *Chapter 11 Reorganization Cases*. If the appointment of a trustee is ordered or is required by the Code, the United States trustee may appoint one or more trustees for estates being jointly administered in chapter 11 cases.

* * * * *

Rule 2012.Substitution of Trustee or Successor Trustee; Accounting

(a) TRUSTEE. If a trustee is appointed in a chapter 11 case (other than under subchapter V), or the debtor is removed as debtor in possession in a chapter 12 case or in a case under subchapter V of chapter 11, the trustee is substituted automatically for the debtor in possession as a party in any pending action, proceeding, or matter.

* * * * *

Rule 2015.Duty to Keep Records, Make Reports, and Give Notice of Case or Change of Status

(a) TRUSTEE OR DEBTOR IN POSSESSION. A trustee or debtor in possession shall:

(1) in a chapter 7 liquidation case and, if the court directs, in a chapter 11 reorganization case (other than under subchapter V), file and transmit to the United

（b）债权人选任单独托管人的权利。除法典第7章第五附章或第11章第五附章的案件外，即使法院根据第1015条（b）正式作出合并管理的裁定，各位债务人的债权人仍可根据法典第702条为其债务人的破产实体选任单独的托管人。

（c）任命被合并管理的多个破产实体的托管人。

* * * * *

（2）第11章重整案件。在案件均为第11章案件的情况下，若法院裁定任命或法典要求任命托管人，则联邦托管人可为被合并管理的多个破产实体任命一位或多位托管人。

* * * * *

第2012条　托管人的取代或继任托管人；账目

（a）**托管人**。若在第11章（不包括第五附章）案件中被任命有托管人，或在第12章案件或第11章第五附章案件中债务人不再作为经管债务人，则在任何进行中的诉讼、程序或事项中，托管人都将自动取代经管债务人而作为当事人。

* * * * *

第2015条　保存档案、制作档案以及就案件或状态的变化发出通知的义务

（a）**托管人或经管债务人**。托管人或经管债务人应履行以下各项：

（1）在第7章清算案件中，以及在法院作此指示的情况下在第11章（不包括第五附章）重整案件中，应在成为合格的托管人或经管债务人后30日内向法

U.S. Federal Rules of Bankruptcy Procedure
(Chinese-English bilingual version)

States trustee a complete inventory of the property of the debtor within 30 days after qualifying as a trustee or debtor in possession, unless such an inventory has already been filed;

(2) keep a record of receipts and the disposition of money and property received;

(3) file the reports and summaries required by § 704 (a) (8) of the Code, which shall include a statement, if payments are made to employees, of the amounts of deductions for all taxes required to be withheld or paid for and in behalf of employees and the place where these amounts are deposited;

(4) as soon as possible after the commencement of the case, give notice of the case to every entity known to be holding money or property subject to withdrawal or order of the debtor, including every bank, savings or building and loan association, public utility company, and landlord with whom the debtor has a deposit, and to every insurance company which has issued a policy having a cash surrender value payable to the debtor, except that notice need not be given to any entity who has knowledge or has previously been notified of the case;

(5) in a chapter 11 reorganization case (other than under subchapter V), on or before the last day of the month after each calendar quarter during which there is a duty to pay fees under 28 U.S.C. §1930 (a) (6), file and transmit to the United States trustee a statement of any disbursements made during that quarter and of any fees payable under 28U.S.C. § 1930 (a) (6) for that quarter; and

(6) in a chapter 11 small business case, unless the court, for cause, sets another reporting interval, file and transmit to the United States trustee for each calendar month after the order for relief, on the appropriate Official Form, the report required by §308. If the order for relief is within the first 15 days of a calendar month, a report shall be filed for the portion of the month that follows the order for relief. If the order for relief is after the 15th day of a calendar month, the period for the remainder of the month shall be included in the report for the next calendar month. Each report shall be filed no later than 21 days after the last day of the calendar month following the month covered by the report. The obligation to file reports under this subparagraph terminates on the effective date of the plan, or conversion or dismissal of the case.

院提交并向联邦托管人移交债务人财产的完整清单，除非该清单已被提交；

（2）保存有关收取的金钱和财产的收据和处置的记录；

（3）提交法典第704条（a）（8）要求的报告和摘要，并且若向员工付款，则应包含一份声明，以说明就所有被要求代缴或已经为雇员或代表雇员支付的所有税款而扣除的款项以及存有这些款项的地点；

（4）在案件被启动后，应尽快就该案向已知的所有因代缴或债务人的裁定而持有相应金钱或财产的各位实体发出通知，包括各银行、储蓄或房屋贷款协会、公用事业公司和债务人向其支付押金的房东，以及签发应向债务人支付退保金的保单的各家保险公司，但该通知无须向任何已经知道或先前已经就该案接到通知的任何实体发出；

（5）在第11章（不包括第五附章）重整案件中，应在有义务根据《美国联邦法典》第28篇第1930条（a）（6）支付费用的每个日历季度后的下一个月的最后一日或之前，向法院提交并向联邦托管人移交一份声明，载明在该季度内根据《美国联邦法典》第28篇第1930条（a）（6）所支出的任何该季度内应付的费用；以及

（6）在第11章小企业案件中，除非法院出于特定事由确定了其他的报告频率，否则应在破产救济令被作出后的每个日历月向法院提交并向联邦托管人移交以相应的官方模板所制作的法典第308条所要求的报告。若破产救济令系在日历月的前15日内作出，则被提交的报告应针对日历月在破产救济令被作出后的剩余期间。若破产救济令系在日历月的第15日后作出，则该月剩余的期间也应被计入就下一日历月所作的报告中。所有报告均应在该报告所针对的月份后的下一日历月的最后一天后的21日内被提交。根据本款提交报告的义务将在计划生效当日或案件被转换或被驳回时被终止。

(b) TRUSTEE, DEBTOR IN POSSESSION, AND DEBTOR IN A CASE UNDER SUBCHAPTER V OF CHAPTER 11. In a case under subchapter V of chapter 11, the debtor in possession shall perform the duties prescribed in (a)(2)-(4) and, if the court directs, shall file and transmit to the United States trustee a complete inventory of the debtor's property within the time fixed by the court. If the debtor is removed as debtor in possession, the trustee shall perform the duties of the debtor in possession prescribed in this subdivision (b). The debtor shall perform the duties prescribed in (a)(6).

(c) CHAPTER 12 TRUSTEE AND DEBTOR IN POSSESSION. In a chapter 12 family farmer's debt adjustment case, the debtor in possession shall perform the duties prescribed in clauses (2)-(4) of subdivision (a) of this rule and, if the court directs, shall file and transmit to the United States trustee a complete inventory of the property of the debtor within the time fixed by the court. If the debtor is removed as debtor in possession, the trustee shall perform the duties of the debtor in possession prescribed in this subdivision (c).

(d) CHAPTER 13 TRUSTEE AND DEBTOR.

(1) Business Cases. In a chapter 13 individual's debt adjustment case, when the debtor is engaged in business, the debtor shall perform the duties prescribed by clauses (2)-(4) of subdivision (a) of this rule and, if the court directs, shall file and transmit to the United States trustee a complete inventory of the property of the debtor within the time fixed by the court.

(2) Nonbusiness Cases. In a chapter 13 individual's debt adjustment case, when the debtor is not engaged in business, the trustee shall perform the duties prescribed by clause (2) of subdivision (a) of this rule.

(e) FOREIGN REPRESENTATIVE. In a case in which the court has granted recognition of a foreign proceeding under chapter 15, the foreign representative shall file any notice required under § 1518 of the Code within 14 days after the date when the representative becomes aware of the subsequent information.

(f) TRANSMISSION OF REPORTS. In a chapter 11 case the court may direct that copies or summaries of annual reports and copies or summaries of other reports shall be mailed to the creditors, equity security holders, and indenture trustees. The

美国联邦破产程序规则
(中英对照译本)

（b）**第 11 章第五附章案件中的托管人、经管债务人以及债务人**。在第 11 章第五附章案件中，经管债务人应当履行（a）附条的（2）至（4）条规定的义务，并且若法院作出指示，则应当在法院规定的时间内向法院提交并向联邦托管人移交债务人财产的完整清单。若债务人不再担任经管债务人，则联邦托管人应履行（a）(6) 规定的义务。

（c）**第 12 章托管人和经管债务人**。在第 12 章家庭农场主的债务调整案件中，经管债务人应履行本条（a）附条的（2）至（4）规定的义务，并且若法院作出指示，则应在法院规定的时间内向法院提交并向联邦托管人移交完整的债务人的财产清单。若债务人不再担任经管债务人，则联邦托管人应履行附条（c）规定的经管债务人的义务。

（d）**第 13 章托管人和债务人**。
（1）商业破产案件。在第 13 章个人债务调整案件中，若债务人从事商事业务，则债务人应履行本条（a）附条的第（2）至（4）款所规定的义务，并且若法院作出指示，则应在法院规定的时间内向法院提交并向联邦托管人移交完整的债务人的财产清单。

（2）非商业破产案件。在第 13 章个人债务调整案件中，若债务人不从事商事业务，则联邦托管人应履行本条（a）附条的第（2）款所规定的义务。

（e）**外国代表**。当法院已经根据第 15 章准予承认外国程序时，外国代表应在获知任何后续信息后 14 日内提交法典第 1518 条所要求的通知。

（f）**报告的移交**。在第 11 章案件中，法院可指示应将年度报告的副本或摘要以及其他报告的副本或摘要邮寄给债权人、股本证券持有人以及契约受托人。法院也可指示将任何该类报告的摘要进行公告。根据本附条而被邮寄或公告的各

U.S. Federal Rules of Bankruptcy Procedure
(Chinese-English bilingual version)

court may also direct the publication of summaries of any such reports. A copy of every report or summary mailed or published pursuant to this subdivision shall be transmitted to the United States trustee.

Rule 3002.Filing Proof of Claim or Interest

* * * * *

(c) TIME FOR FILING. In a voluntary chapter 7 case, chapter 12 case, or chapter 13 case, a proof of claim is timely filed if it is filed not later than 70 days after the order for relief under that chapter or the date of the order of conversion to a case under chapter 12 or chapter 13. In an involuntary chapter 7 case, a proof of claim is timely filed if it is filed not later than 90 days after the order for relief under that chapter is entered. But in all these cases, the following exceptions apply:

* * * * *

(6) On motion filed by a creditor before or after the expiration of the time to file a proof of claim, the court may extend the time by not more than 60 days from the date of the order granting the motion. The motion may be granted if the court finds that the notice was insufficient under the circumstances to give the creditor a reasonable time to file a proof of claim.

* * * * *

Rule 3010.Small Dividends and Payments in Cases Under Chapter 7, Subchapter V of Chapter 11, Chapter 12, and Chapter 13

* * * * *

(b) CASES UNDER SUBCHAPTER V OF CHAPTER 11, CHAPTER 12, AND CHAPTER 13. In a case under subchapter V of chapter 11, chapter 12, or chapter 13, no payment in an amount less than $15 shall be distributed by the trustee to any creditor unless authorized by local rule or order of the court. Funds not distributed because of this subdivision shall accumulate and shall be paid whenever the accumulation aggregates $15. Any funds remaining shall be distributed with the final payment.

报告的副本或摘要均应被移交给联邦托管人。

第 3002 条 提交债权或权益证明

* * * * *

（c）提交时间。在第 7 章、第 12 章或第 13 章自愿破产案件中，若债权证明系在根据该章作出破产救济令或将案件转换至第 12 章或第 13 章案件的裁定后 70 日内即被提交，则该债权证明应被视为已被及时提交。在第 7 章强制破产案件中，若债权证明系在根据该章正式作出破产救济令后 90 日内即被提交，则该债权证明应被视为已被及时提交。但在所有该类案件中，仍适用以下例外：

* * * * *

（6）若债权人在提交债权证明的期间届满前或届满后提交动议，则法院可延长该期间，但不得超过自准予该动议的裁定被作出之日起 60 日。若法院认为该情形下该通知不足以为债权人提供合理时间以用于提交债权证明，则法院可准予该动议。

* * * * *

第 3010 条 在第 7 章、第 11 章第五附章、第 12 章、第 13 章案件中的小额还款

* * * * *

（b）第 11 章第五附章、第 12 章以及第 13 章案件。在第 11 章第五附章、第 12 章或第 13 章案件中，除非当地法律或法院裁定作此授权，否则托管人不得向任何债权人分配金额少于 15 美元的还款。因本附条规定而未能得以分配的资金应进行累计并且每当累计达到 15 美元时即应进行支付。剩余资金应在最终还款时进行分配。

U.S. Federal Rules of Bankruptcy Procedure
(Chinese-English bilingual version)

Rule 3011.Unclaimed Funds in Cases Under Chapter 7, Subchapter V of Chapter 11, Chapter 12, and Chapter 13

The trustee shall file a list of all known names and addresses of the entities and the amounts which they are entitled to be paid from remaining property of the estate that is paid into court pursuant to § 347 (a) of the Code.

Rule 3014.Election Under § 1111 (b) by Secured Creditor in Chapter 9 Municipality or Chapter 11 Reorganization Case

An election of application of § 1111 (b) (2) of the Code by a class of secured creditors in a chapter 9 or 11 case may be made at any time prior to the conclusion of the hearing on the disclosure statement or within such later time as the court may fix. If the disclosure statement is conditionally approved pursuant to Rule 3017.1, and a final hearing on the disclosure statement is not held, the election of application of § 1111 (b) (2) may be made not later than the date fixed pursuant to Rule 3017.1 (a) (2) or another date the court may fix. In a case under subchapter V of chapter 11 in which § 1125 of the Code does not apply, the election may be made not later than a date the court may fix. The election shall be in writing and signed unless made at the hearing on the disclosure statement. The election, if made by the majorities required by § 1111 (b) (1) (A) (i), shall be binding on all members of the class with respect to the plan.

Rule 3016.Filing of Plan and Disclosure Statement in a Chapter 9 Municipality or Chapter 11 Reorganization Case

(a) IDENTIFICATION OF PLAN. Every proposed plan and any modification thereof shall be dated and, in a chapter 11 case, identified with the name of the entity or entities submitting or filing it.

(b) DISCLOSURE STATEMENT. In a chapter 9 or 11 case, a disclosure statement, if required under § 1125 of the Code, or evidence showing compliance with § 1126 (b) shall be filed with the plan or within a time fixed by the court, unless the plan is intended to provide adequate information under § 1125 (f) (1). If the plan

第 3011 条 第 7 章、第 11 章第五附章、第 12 章和第 13 章案件中无人主张的资金

托管人应提交一份清单以列明所有已知的各实体的姓名和住址以及其有权就根据法典第 347 条（a）交予法院的剩余破产财产得以分配的金额。

第 3014 条 在第 9 章市政机构破产案件或第 11 章重整案件中担保债权人根据第 1111 条（b）所作的选择

在就披露声明举行的听证结束前或在法院可确定的更长期间内的任意时间，在第 9 章或第 11 章案件中，担保债权人小组可随时选择适用法典第 1111 条（b）（2）的规定。若披露声明被根据本法第 3017.1 条有条件批准通过，并且并未就披露声明举行最终听证，则可在根据第 3017.1 条（a）（2）确定的日期或法院可确定的其他日期前选择适用法典第 1111 条（b）（2）的规定。除非系在就披露声明举行的听证上而作出该选择，否则该选择应以书面形式作出并签署。在第 11 章第五附章案件（不包括法典第 1125 条适用的案件）中，可在不晚于法院确定的日期作出该选择。若该选择系根据第 1111 条（b）（1）（A）（i）的要求而经多数作出，则其就该计划而言应约束该小组内的所有成员。

第 3016 条 在第 9 章市政机构破产案件或第 11 章重整案件中计划和披露声明的提交

（a）**计划的标注**。所有被提出的计划和任何修改都应注明日期，并且在第 11 章案件中，还应注明提交该计划的实体（们）的姓名。

（b）**披露声明**。在第 9 章或第 11 章案件中，披露声明（如法典第 1125 条要求）或用于说明符合第 1126 条（b）的规定的证明应在计划被提交时或法院规定的时间内而被提交，除非提出者意图通过计划本身而根据第 1125 条（f）（1）提供充分信息。若提出者意图通过计划本身而根据第 1125 条（f）（1）提供充分信息，

is intended to provide adequate information under § 1125 (f)(1), it shall be so designated, and Rule 3017.1 shall apply as if the plan is a disclosure statement.

* * * * *

(d) STANDARD FORM SMALL BUSINESS DISCLOSURE STATEMENT AND PLAN. In a small business case or a case under subchapter V of chapter 11, the court may approve a disclosure statement and may confirm a plan that conform substantially to the appropriate Official Forms or other standard forms approved by the court.

Rule 3017.1. Court Consideration of Disclosure Statement in a Small Business Case or in a Case Under Subchapter V of Chapter 11

(a) CONDITIONAL APPROVAL OF DISCLOSURE STATEMENT. In a small business case or in a case under subchapter V of chapter 11 in which the court has ordered that § 1125 applies, the court may, on application of the plan proponent or on its own initiative, conditionally approve a disclosure statement filed in accordance with Rule 3016. On or before conditional approval of the disclosure statement, the court shall:

(1) fix a time within which the holders of claims and interests may accept or reject the plan;

(2) fix a time for filing objections to the disclosure statement;

(3) fix a date for the hearing on final approval of the disclosure statement to be held if a timely objection is filed; and

(4) fix a date for the hearing on confirmation.

* * * * *

Rule 3017.2. Fixing of Dates by the Court in Subchapter V Cases in Which There Is No Disclosure Statement

In a case under subchapter V of chapter 11 in which §1125 does not apply, the court shall:

(a) fix a time within which the holders of claims and interests may accept or reject the plan;

则该计划应被认定为披露声明并适用第 3017.1 条的规定。

* * * * *

（d）**小企业披露声明和计划的标准模板**。在小企业破产案件或第 11 章第五附章案件中，法院可批准基本符合相应官方模板或法院所批准的其他标准格式的披露声明和计划。

第 3017.1 条　在小企业案件或第 11 章第五附章案件中法院就披露声明的审议

（a）**披露声明的有条件批准**。在小企业案件或第 11 章第五附章案件（法院已裁定适用第 1125 条）中，法院可在计划的提出者提出申请的情况下或主动有条件地批准根据第 3016 条被提交的披露声明。在有条件地批准披露声明时或之前，法院应履行以下各项：

（1）确定享有债权和权益的主体可接受或拒绝计划的时间；

（2）确定就披露声明提交异议的期间；

（3）在有人及时提出异议的情况下，确定就披露声明的最终批准举行听证的日期；以及

（4）确定就计划的批准举行听证的日期。

* * * * *

第 3017.2 条　法院在不涉及披露声明的第五附章案件中对时间的确定

在不适用第 1125 条的第 11 章第五附章案件中，法院应：

（a）确定债权或权益持有人可接受或拒绝计划的时间；

(b) fix a date on which an equity security holder or creditor whose claim is based on a security must be the holder of record of the security in order to be eligible to accept or reject the plan;

(c) fix a date for the hearing on confirmation; and

(d) fix a date for transmitting the plan, notice of the time within which the holders of claims and interests may accept or reject it, and notice of the date for the hearing on confirmation.

Rule 3018. Acceptance or Rejection of Plan in a Chapter 9 Municipality or a Chapter 11 Reorganization Case

(a) ENTITIES ENTITLED TO ACCEPT OR REJECT PLAN; TIME FOR ACCEPTANCE OR REJECTION. A plan may be accepted or rejected in accordance with § 1126 of the Code within the time fixed by the court pursuant to Rule 3017, 3017.1, or 3017.2. Subject to subdivision (b) of this rule, an equity security holder or creditor whose claim is based on a security of record shall not be entitled to accept or reject a plan unless the equity security holder or creditor is the holder of record of the security on the date the order approving the disclosure statement is entered or on another date fixed by the court under Rule 3017.2, or fixed for cause after notice and a hearing. For cause shown, the court after notice and hearing may permit a creditor or equity security holder to change or withdraw an acceptance or rejection. Notwithstanding objection to a claim or interest, the court after notice and hearing may temporarily allow the claim or interest in an amount which the court deems proper for the purpose of accepting or rejecting a plan.

* * * * *

Rule 3019. Modification of Accepted Plan in a Chapter 9 Municipality or a Chapter 11 Reorganization Case

* * * * *

(b) MODIFICATION OF PLAN AFTER CONFIRMATION IN INDIVIDUAL DEBTOR CASE. If the debtor is an individual, a request to modify the plan under

（b）确定股本证券持有人或债权系基于证券的债务人必须被登记为证券持有人以有权接受或拒绝计划的日期；

（c）确定就（计划的）批准而举行听证会的日期；以及

（d）确定发出以下文件的日期：计划、就债权或权益持有人可接受或拒绝计划的时间的通知以及就（计划的）批准而举行听证会的日期的通知。

第3018条　第9章市政机构破产案件或第11章重整案件中对计划的接受或拒绝

（a）**有权接受或拒绝计划的实体；接受或拒绝的时间。**该计划可在法院根据第3017条、第3017.1条、第3017.2条确定的时间内由实体根据法典第1126条予以接受或拒绝。在符合本条（b）附条规定的情况下，股本证券持有人或其债权基于已登记的证券的债权人无权就计划发表接受或拒绝意见，除非该股本证券持有人或债权人在批准披露声明的裁定被正式作出之日或法院根据第3017.2条确定的或出于特定事由经过通知和听证后确定的其他日期是已登记的证券的持有人。出于被主张的特定事由，经过通知和听证后，法院可准予债权人或股本证券持有人变更或撤销其接受或拒绝意见。即使有人就债权或权益提出异议，法院出于征集计划的接受或拒绝意见的目的，经过通知和听证后可暂时在其认为适当的金额内对债权或权益予以确认。

* * * * *

第3019条　第9章市政机构破产案件或第11章重整案件中已被接受的计划的修改

* * * * *

（b）**个人债务人案件中批准后对计划的修改。**若债务人为自然人，则根据法典第1127条（e）申请修改计划的请求应符合第9014条的规定。该请求应注明

§ 1127 (e) of the Code is governed by Rule 9014. The request shall identify the proponent and shall be filed together with the proposed modification. The clerk, or some other person as the court may direct, shall give the debtor, the trustee, and all creditors not less than 21 days' notice by mail of the time fixed to file objections and, if an objection is filed, the hearing to consider the proposed modification, unless the court orders otherwise with respect to creditors who are not affected by the proposed modification. A copy of the notice shall be transmitted to the United States trustee, together with a copy of the proposed modification. Any objection to the proposed modification shall be filed and served on the debtor, the proponent of the modification, the trustee, and any other entity designated by the court, and shall be transmitted to the United States trustee.

(c) MODIFICATION OF PLAN AFTER CONFIRMATION IN A SUBCHAPTER V CASE. In a case under subchapter V of chapter 11, a request to modify the plan under § 1193 (b) or (c) of the Code is governed by Rule 9014, and the provisions of this Rule 3019 (b) apply.

Rule 5005. Filing and Transmittal of Papers

*****

(b) TRANSMITTAL TO THE UNITED STATES TRUSTEE.

(1) The complaints, notices, motions, applications, objections and other papers required to be transmitted to the United States trustee may be sent by filing with the court's electronic-filing system in accordance with Rule 9036, unless a court order or local rule provides otherwise.

(2) The entity, other than the clerk, transmitting a paper to the United States trustee other than through the court's electronic-filing system shall promptly file as proof of such transmittal a statement identifying the paper and stating the manner by which and the date on which it was transmitted to the United States trustee.

(3) Nothing in these rules shall require the clerk to transmit any paper to the United States trustee if the United States trustee requests in writing that the paper not be transmitted.

提出者的身份并应与拟议的修改方案被一同提交。除非法院针对未受拟议修改方案影响的债权人作出其他裁定，否则书记员或法院可指定的其他人，应以邮寄的方式至少提前 21 日向债务人、托管人以及全体债权人发出通知以告知其确定的用于提交异议的期间以及在有人提交异议的情况下，告知其确定的用于举行听证以审议拟议修改方案的时间。该通知的副本应与拟议修改方案的副本被一同移交给联邦托管人。对拟议修改方案的任何异议均应被提交至法院并送达给债务人、修改方案的提出者、托管人以及法院所指定的任何其他实体，并且应被移交给联邦托管人。

（c）**第五附章案件中经批准的计划的修改**。在第 11 章第五附章案件中，法典第 1193 条（b）或（c）要求修改计划应符合第 9014 条的规定且适用于第 3019 条（b）的规定。

第 5005 条　材料的提交和移送

* * * * *

（b）**向联邦托管人移送**。

（1）除非法院作出其他裁定或地方规则另有规定，否则被要求向联邦托管人移送的申诉、通知、动议、申请、异议以及其他材料可以根据第 9036 条通过法院的电子提交系统来提交。

（2）除通过法院的电子提交系统外，除书记员外其他向联邦托管人移交材料的实体应及时提交宣誓声明以作为移交的证据，并注明该材料的信息以及被移交给联邦托管人的方式及日期。

（3）本条并未要求书记员在联邦托管人书面请求获得未经移送的材料的情况下向其移送任何材料。

U.S. Federal Rules of Bankruptcy Procedure
(Chinese-English bilingual version)

Rule 7004.Process; Service of Summons, Complaint
* * * * *

(i) SERVICE OF PROCESS BY TITLE. This subdivision (i) applies to service on a domestic or foreign corporation or partnership or other unincorporated association under Rule 7004 (b)(3) or on an officer of an insured depository institution under Rule 7004 (h). The defendant's officer or agent need not be correctly named in the address - or even be named - if the envelope is addressed to the defendant's proper address and directed to the attention of the officer's or agent's position or title.

Rule 8023.Voluntary Dismissal

(a) STIPULATED DISMISSAL. The clerk of the district court or BAP must dismiss an appeal if the parties file a signed dismissal agreement specifying how costs are to be paid and pay any court fees that are due.

(b) APPELLANT'S MOTION TO DISMISS. An appeal may be dismissed on the appellant's motion on terms agreed to by the parties or fixed by the district court or BAP.

(c) OTHER RELIEF. A court order is required for any relief under Rule 8023 (a) or (b) beyond the dismissal of an appeal—including approving a settlement, vacating an action of the bankruptcy court, or remanding the case to it.

(d) COURT APPROVAL. This rule does not alter the legal requirements governing court approval of a settlement, payment, or other consideration.

第7004条　司法文书；传票、诉状的送达

* * * * *

（i）**通过职位送达司法文书**。附条（i）适用于根据第7004条（b）(3)向国内或国外的该公司或合伙或者其他非法人组织送达或者根据第7004条（h）向受保存款机构送达。只要信封是被寄到被告人的适当地址并指向被告人的员工或代理人的职位或头衔，则被告人的员工或代理人的姓名无须在地址栏中被正确书写。

第8023条　自愿撤诉

（a）**按规定驳回**。若当事人提交了经签署的撤诉协议且该协议规定了如何支付将支付的成本费用以及任何到期的费用，则地区法院或破产上诉合议庭的书记员必须驳回上诉。

（b）**在上诉人的动议下撤回**。上诉可根据当事人达成的合意或破产上诉合议庭所确定的条款而在上诉人的动议下被驳回。

（c）**其他救济**。除驳回上诉外，法院须就根据第8023条（a）或（b）条所作出任何救济包括批准和解、撤回破产法庭的诉讼或发回重审作出裁定。

（d）**法院的批准**。本条并未调整法院批准和解、付款或其他对价的法律要求。